Jacob R. Freese

The Old World

Palestine, Syria, and Asia Minor: travel, incident, description and history

Jacob R. Freese

The Old World
Palestine, Syria, and Asia Minor: travel, incident, description and history

ISBN/EAN: 9783337245269

Printed in Europe, USA, Canada, Australia, Japan

Cover: Foto ©ninafisch / pixelio.de

More available books at **www.hansebooks.com**

The Old World.

PALESTINE

SYRIA AND ASIA MINOR

TRAVEL, INCIDENT, DESCRIPTION
AND HISTORY.

By JACOB R. FREESE, M.D.,
U. S. Commissioner to Paris Exposition, 1867.

POOL OF SILOAM.

PHILADELPHIA
J. B. LIPPINCOTT & CO.
1869.

Entered according to Act of Congress, in the year 1869, by

J. B. LIPPINCOTT & CO.,

In the Clerk's Office of the District Court of the United States, for the Eastern District of Pennsylvania.

LIPPINCOTT'S PRESS,
PHILADELPHIA.

TO MY OWN DEAR

LILY WIFE,

WHO ACCOMPANIED ME IN MY TOUR THROUGH

EGYPT, PALESTINE, SYRIA, ASIA MINOR,

AND DURING ALL OF MY WANDERINGS IN THE OLD WORLD—
ENJOYING WHERE I ENJOYED, AND SUFFERING WHERE
I SUFFERED, ALWAYS CHEERFUL, HAPPY,
AND SYMPATHIZING—

This Volume is Respectfully Inscribed,

AS A SOUVENIR

OF THOSE MANY HAPPY AND NEVER-TO-BE-FORGOTTEN
DAYS, BY

THE AUTHOR.

CONTENTS.

	PAGE
AUTHOR'S PREFACE...................................	15

CHAPTER I.

ENTRANCE INTO PALESTINE.

Our last View of Alexandria—Steamers—First Glimpse of Palestine—Landing at Jaffa—Reflections—Town of Jaffa—Marriage Incident—Maronite Wedding—American Colony—Plain of Sharon—Arrival at Ramlah—Ancient Lydda—Latrone—Emmouse—Terrible Roads—Valley of Ajalon—Valley of Elah—First Glimpse of the Walls of Jerusalem—Views of Other Travelers over the Same Route........................... 19

CHAPTER II.

'CITY OF THE GREAT KING.'

Disappointment in First View of Jerusalem—First Impressions—Tradition, how Estimated—Church of the Holy Sepulchre—Fanaticism of the Monks—Ceremony of the Crucifixion—Pilgrims to the Tomb—The Holy Fire—Easter, or Palm Sunday—Chapels and Altars—Thoughts on the Identity of the Tomb and Holy Places.. 42

CHAPTER III.

IN AND ABOUT JERUSALEM.

Incidents of Travel—Garden of Gethsemane—The Mount of Olives —View from the Minaret—Tomb and Chapel of the Virgin— The Greek Grotto—Place of St. Stephen's Martyrdom—Via Doloroso—Pilate's House—Church of Flagellation—Ecce Homo—Lazarus and Dives—House of Veronica—The Virgin Mary's Residence—House of Caiaphas—Door of Sepulchre and Stone on which the Cock Crew—Old Coptic Books—Armenian Convent—English Hospital................................ 67

CHAPTER IV.

PAST AND PRESENT OF THE HOLY CITY.

Difficulties of Sight-seeing in Jerusalem—The Walls of the City— Valley of Jehoshaphat—Room of the Last Supper—Tomb of David—The Jews' Wailing Place—Robinson's Arch—The Lepers' Quarters—Pool of Bethesda—Fountain of the Virgin— Pool of Siloam—Pool of Hezekiah—Upper and Lower Pool of Gihon—The Tombs of Absalom, Jehoshaphat, St. James, and other Open Tombs on the Hillsides—The Tombs of the Kings, the Judges, and the Prophets—The Mosque of Omar......... 78

CHAPTER V.

OFF FOR THE JORDAN AND DEAD SEA.

Off for the Jordan and Dead Sea—A Difficulty with our Dragoman —Village of Bethany—Tomb of Lazarus—Road from Bethany to Jericho—The Wilderness—The Fountain of Elisha—Jericho —An Arab Funeral—Falling Among Thieves—The River Jordan—Easter Baptismals—Greek and Russian Pilgrims— Baptism of Jesus—The Bedouins of the Jordan—Their Wonderful Horses—Anecdotes Thereof—Oriental Tradition of the Building of Solomon's Temple—Bedouin Customs—Attack and Defence—The Dead Sea—Bath Therein—Peculiarity of the Waters—Ancient Accounts—Apples of Sodom—General Description... 93

CHAPTER VI.

OVER THE HILLS TO BETHLEHEM.

Laughable Situation—Bathing under Difficulties—Off for Mar Saba—Examination of the Convent—General Description—Views of Other Travelers—From Mar Saba to Bethlehem—The Town and its Surroundings—The Convent, Within and Without—Burial-ground—Milk Grotto—Pools of Solomon—The Fountain—Abraham's Oak—Hebron, its People and Surroundings—Valley of Eshcol—Rachel's Tomb—The English Church at Jerusalem—Something of its History and Workings.......... 123

CHAPTER VII.

NORTHWARD THROUGH SAMARIA.

Reflections on Leaving Jerusalem—El-Bir and the Gibeonites—Mr. Skinner's Experience Among Them—" Hewers of Wood "—The Fuel of Palestine—Bethel, Past and Present—Mosque of Settein—Ancient Shiloh—Mount Hermon—Jacob's Well—Tomb of Joseph—Valley of Nablous—Mount Gerizim and Mount Ebal—Nablous—Ascent of Mount Gerizim—Ruins of Ancient Samaritan Temple—Ancient Samaritans, and Something of their History—Present Synagogue—Why they Never Quit Nablous..................................... 143

CHAPTER VIII.

DESOLATION AND BEAUTY.

Copy of Old Law—Ancient Samaria and Present Sebustieh—Church of St. John—Other Ruins—Sanur—First View of Esdraelon and Mountains of Nazareth—Jenin—A Sabbath in the Holy Land—A New Experience—The Plain of Jezreel—Valley of Esdraelon—Past and Present of the Country—Ancient Shunem—Nain—Endor—First View of Nazareth—Mr. Skinner's Narrative... 167

1 *

CHAPTER IX.

ONWARD THROUGH GALILEE.

Nazareth—Latin Convent—Place of Annunciation—The Synagogue in which Jesus Taught—The Place to which they led Him out—The Stone on which He ate—Fountain of the Virgin—Lamartine's View of Convents in Palestine—The Present Town—Peculiar Features of its Inhabitants—View from the Hill-top back of Nazareth—From Nazareth to Mount Tabor—Ascent—Ruins Thereon—View Therefrom—Descent—Deborah—Onward to the Sea of Galilee—First View—Reflections—Mount of Beatitude—Dr. Robinson's Reflections on the same Route—Lord Egerton's Experience—Our first Bath in the Sea—Unexpected Bath in the Jordan—Hot Springs and Bathing-Houses—Six Days on the Sea-shore—Wanderings and Reflections... 183

CHAPTER X.

THE SEA OF GALILEE.

Its Size and Situation—Calm and Storm—Its Different Names—Views of Ancient Writers—Past and Present Appearance—Magdala—Gennesaret—Fountain of the Fig—Capernaum—Bethsaida—Of other Ancient Cities—Tiberias—Walls and Citadel—Convent of St. Peter—Illustrations of Moslem Respect for Power and Position—Call from the Commandant—Call from the Governor—Return Call by Ourselves—Manners and Customs of Turkish Officials........................ 201

CHAPTER XI.

DESOLATE PLACES.

On leaving Tiberias—Where Joseph was cast into the Pit—Stephens' Views as to its Identity—The City of Safed—Description—The Ruins throughout Palestine—Cause and Effect—Measurement of Distances in Palestine—Lake of El Huleh—

Syrian Cultivation—The Mill of Malaha—Hasbeiyah River—
Banias, the Ancient Cæsarea Philippi—Castle of Banias—
View from the Ruins—The Great Fountain—Historical and
Biblical Associations—Leaving the Footsteps of Jesus........ 220

CHAPTER XII.

AMONG THE DRUSES.

The Cold Winds of Hermon—Arrival at Beit-Jin—Among the
Druses—Their History and Religion—Domestic Virtues and
Vices—But One Wife—Marriage Ceremony—Origin of the
Druses—Strange Incidents and Superstitions—Arrival at Kafr-
Howaran—Tent-life in Palestine.......................... 234

CHAPTER XIII.

"THE GARDEN OF EDEN."

Valley of Damascus—"Garden of Eden"—Getting within the
Walls of the City—Dr. Robinson's Experience—Also that of
Maj. Skinner—Our Tents Pitched on the Banks of the Abana
—The Surroundings of the City—Sights without the Walls—
Something of its History—Population and General Appearance
—Interior Decorations—The English Lady—Truth Stranger
than Fiction—Coffee-shops—The Recitation of Fables........ 254

CHAPTER XIV.

SIGHTS OF DAMASCUS.

A Man Hanging at the Street Corner—The Moslem's Theory of
Punishment—Mosque of St. John—The Old Castle—Govern-
ment Mill—Convents and Monkish Tales—The Bazaars—Lost
Arts—The Saddlers of Damascus—The Barbers—Style of
Shops—Restaurants—Gold and Silversmiths—The Street called
"Straight"—The City Wall—Where Paul was let down—Ori-
entalism of Damascus—Life and Adventures of Assaad and
Abdallah-el-Satadgi.. 273

CHAPTER XV.

ANTI-LEBANON.

Leaving Damascus—Last View from the Dome of Victory—Mohammed's Paradise—Fountain of the Barada—Ancient Temples—Robinson's and Prime's Comments—Cliffs of Abila—Grave of Abel—Tents Pitched in Wrong Place—Remedy—Ravine and River—Old Tombs—Remarkable Road—Zebdani—Home-like Appearance of Valley—Village of Bludin—Mountains of Anti-Lebanon—Valley of Baalbec—Fountains of Baalbec.. 294

CHAPTER XVI.

BAALBEC.

The Ruins at Baalbec—Theories as to their Origin—The Platform on which Built—The Temple of the Sun—Quadrangular Court—Hexagonal Court—Temple of Jupiter—The Great Stones—Queries and Answers—Inscriptions....................... 306

CHAPTER XVII.

AMONG THE MARONITES.

Faces Westward—Thoughts of Home—The Circular Temple—Mosque of Salah-e'deen—Modern Baalbec—Moslem Temple and Convents—Tomb of Noah—Village of Maalakha—The Maronites and their Peculiarities—Latin Convent—The Great French Road from Damascus to Beyrout—Turkish Governor and Suite—Beautiful Views from the Mountains of Lebanon—Arrival at Beyrout... 319

CHAPTER XVIII.

BEYROUT.

Suggestions as to Change of Route—Reasons therefor—Opinions of another Tourist—Syria as a whole—Beyrout and its Surroundings—Coffee-houses—Turkish Baths—Our Consul—Excellent Treaty Stipulation—Missionary Station—Departure from Holy Land—Reflections.............................. 345

CHAPTER XIX.

COAST-TOWNS OF SYRIA.

Once more on the Sea—Russian Pilgrims—Tea-drinking—Praying—Singing—Dress—Spirit of the Crusaders—Tripoli—Latakiah—On Minaret—Latakiah Tobacco—Ancient Laodicea—Alexandretta—Bath—Consequences—Warning.................... 368

CHAPTER XX.

THE CEDARS OF LEBANON.

Syrian Dwelling-houses—The Simplest and Best Forms—Flat Roofs and Incidents—Heights and Cedars of Lebanon—Beautiful Views—"Trees of Eden"—The Metualis—Their Peculiarities—Legends and Incidents............................. 387

CHAPTER XXI.

ASIA MINOR.

From Alexandretta to Mersyn—Rhodes—Islands of the Archipelago—Accident to our Steamer—Smyrna—American Mission—Tomb of Polycarp—The Old Castle—View Therefrom—The City and its Suburbs—Ephesus—Ancient Lesbos—Ancient Troy—Dardanelles—Metropolitan Bishop—Abydos—Hero and Leander—Byron—Sea of Marmora—First View of Constantinople—Its Situation—Style of Architecture—Real Condition.. 406

CHAPTER XXII.

CONSTANTINOPLE.

Constantinople: its Situation and Commerce—American Consul—American Minister Resident—Mosque of St. Sophia—Mosque of Sultan Achmed—The Hippodrome—The Janizaries—The Thousand-and-one Columns—Mosque of Mohammed II.—The Seraglio—Burnt Pillar—Pigeon Mosque—Mosque of Suleiman the Magnificent—The Bazaars.......................... 417

CHAPTER XXIII.

CLOSING SIGHTS.

Constantinople continued—English Chapel—Lord Lyons—The Whirling Dervishes—Sultan's Palace, Mosque, and Barracks—Public Gardens—Scutari—View Therefrom—Palace of Sweet Waters—The Sultan Himself—View of the "Houris"—Street Amusements—Bazaar Shopping—Departure............... 431

CHAPTER XXIV.

GENERAL DIRECTIONS FOR, AND PECULIARITIES OF, EASTERN TRAVEL.

General Directions for Visiting Syria—A Christian Dragoman Preferable—None needed from Cairo to Jerusalem—Landing at Jaffa or Beyrout—Thence to Jerusalem—Plans of Future Travel—Contract with Dragomen—A Third Plan Possible—Dragomen at Jerusalem and Beyrout—Arms—Clothing—Customs of the Country—Horseback and Muleback—Urquhart's Experiences—Baking Bread—Modes of Salutation—Saddles, where and how best Procured—Lines of Steamers........... 441

ILLUSTRATIONS.

BETHLEHEM	Frontispiece.
POOL OF SILOAM	Vignette Title.
	PAGE
HOLY SEPULCHRE	45
GARDEN OF GETHSEMANE	68
VALLEY OF JEHOSAPHAT	78
MOSQUE OF OMAR	90
CHURCH OF THE NATIVITY	129
PLOUGHING IN SYRIA	225
DRUSE MARRIAGE PROCESSION	240
RUINS OF BAALBEC	306
FLAT HOUSE-TOPS OF SYRIA	390
CEDARS OF LEBANON	394

PREFACE.

HE who would write understandingly of Palestine must know of it, see it and feel it:—must know of it from a careful perusal of the Book of books; must see it for himself with all its beauties and deformities, and must feel within himself the hallowed associations which cluster around its mountains and valleys, lakes and rivers, towns and cities.

Thus knowing, seeing, and feeling, no one can make the tour of the Holy Land without pleasure and profit. He may, and indeed must, suffer more or less of personal discomfort while traveling day after day and week after week over paths the most rugged, mountains the most desolate, and plains the most sterile of all the world beside; but with every step new scenes and associations will open before him, making more vivid the mental pictures his readings have produced of the days of the ancient patriarchs, prophets and kings of Israel; the birth, the life, the death and the resurrection of a once crucified, but now glorified, Redeemer; the trials and triumphs of the apostles, whom Christ "chose as his own;" the weary days and watchful nights of the early Christians, who suffered rebukes, buffetings and even death in maintaining the faith "once delivered to the saints;" and the oft-repeated struggles of the Crusaders, who, to rescue the cross from the hands of infidels, poured out their life-blood on the plain of Esdraelon, around the walls of Jerusalem, and wherever else they could meet the Moslem face to face and hand to hand.

On leaving the borders of Dan, and entering upon what is more properly called Syria (as the Palestine of the Bible only extended "from Dan to Beersheba"), one meets with scenes of a somewhat different character, though scarcely less interesting. It is here that the descendants of Noah "built great cities" immediately after the flood, and whose reputed tombs remain even until this day.

Thence northward, through Asia Minor, some of the sites of the "seven churches of Asia," of which St. John wrote in the Revelation, are reached; and not far from these are the island of Patmos, the site of ancient Troy, and Stamboul the wonderful!

It was my privilege, during the months of March and April, 1867, to spend forty-one days traveling through Palestine and Syria—the days on horseback and the nights in tents—and during all this time I spared no pains to see what was to be seen and learn what was to be learned. How well or ill I improved my opportunities the following pages will best determine.

On the first of May following I left Syria, and for some two weeks thereafter was engaged in traveling upon the sea, and in examining the towns and cities of Asia Minor, and finally reached Constantinople; and here, too, I must refer my readers to the chapters following as proof of my industry in sight-seeing.

Next to seeing the country for oneself is to read a faithful account given by one who has seen it; and I think it no egotism to say that in faithfulness of description the following pages will bear comparison with others heretofore written by travelers.

Most of the chapters (originally in the form of letters for a public journal) were written at the time, and upon or near the spots described, while everything connected with them was fresh in our mind's eye. And while nothing, knowingly, has been "set down in malice," neither has any fact, deemed of importance or interest, been omitted.

The engravings are copied from views and sketches purchased

by myself in the Old World, and have in every case been selected with special reference to their faithfulness of representation.

In the preparation of this volume I have endeavored to make it instructive as well as entertaining, and to this end I have not hesitated to draw from any and all sources within my reach. It will be observed that I have quoted from the ably-written works of Robinson, Stephens, Prime, Burckhardt, Lords Lindsay and Egerton, Kelly, Olin, Russell, Skinner, Elliot, Addison, Lamartine, Perrier, Volney and others; and if, in any instance, I have failed to give the proper credit, this general acknowledgment will suffice for all. I have no pride of authorship to subserve, and have only aimed to give the greatest amount of practical information in the least possible space.

I would also acknowledge my indebtedness to Prof. Ellis A. Apgar, the State School Superintendent of New Jersey, for carefully revising these pages before placing them in the hands of my publishers.

J. R. F.

TRENTON, N. J., 1868.

THE OLD WORLD.

PALESTINE.

CHAPTER I.

ENTRANCE INTO PALESTINE.

IT is near noon of the 19th of March, when our good ship Illysus starts from the harbor of Alexandria for the port of Jaffa. The day is bright and beautiful; scores of vessels are in the harbor, and the loading and unloading of merchandise presents a busy and cheerful scene; the waters of the bay reflect back the sunlight like a great mirror of polished glass; the Pasha's palace and other public buildings of the city have enchantment added by "distance to the view;" Cleopatra's Needle and Pompey's Pillar loom up in the distance like great sentinels of the mighty and far-gone past; and thus it is that we have our last, long, lingering view of the once famous city of Philip.

Our ship is one of the French line of steamers which ply regularly between Alexandria and Smyrna, and, though not large, its appointments are unexceptionable in every particular. The officers are attentive, the staterooms clean and spacious, the tables are good, the decks are clean, and everything presents a comfortable appearance. These steamers leave Alexandria for ports north on the 8th, 18th and 28th of each month, and usually reach Jaffa about noon of the day following. The fare, first-class, is 72 francs, equaling about $14.

There are two other lines of steamers which ply between Alexandria and Jaffa and parts farther north, viz., the Austrian and Russian ; but, from the best information we can obtain, neither of these is as good as the French line.

Our boat, on this trip, has an unusually large number of first-class passengers—more, indeed, than the staterooms will accommodate, but by improvising sleeping-places in the cabin and in the officers' quarters, all are very comfortably accommodated. Among the passengers are no less than sixteen Americans, bound for the Holy Land, and all, like ourselves, making the tour of Europe and the East. It is pleasant to meet with friends and countrymen at home, but doubly so in a far-distant land, where everything is new, and strange, and untried ; and it gives us pleasure to add that now, more than ever before, the American, traveling in foreign lands, is proud to own himself a citizen of the Great Republic! If in ancient days the name of Roman citizen was talismanic, that of American is doubly so in this our day! Thanks to Victory!

Before nightfall we are out of sight of land, and not until near noon of the day following do we get our first glimpse of Syria ; and not until four o'clock of the afternoon of the same day do we reach Jaffa. A delay of some four hours from the usual time in leaving Alexandria, causes, of course, a corresponding delay in reaching

Jaffa. Still, the time is ample for getting ourselves and baggage on shore and our tents pitched before the night comes on.

The harbor of Jaffa—if it can be called a harbor at all—is so shallow that vessels of any considerable size cannot approach within a half mile of the shore, and, as a consequence, passengers and luggage have to be taken off in row-boats. The noise and confusion of this procedure is easier imagined than described; and a like remark is applicable to the passing of baggage through the Jaffa custom-house. Patience and bucksheesh, however, will bring both to an end ere long. Finally we reach a high hill, just outside of the town, and here our tents are pitched in company with about a dozen others.

How we unfurl the " stars and stripes" to the kisses of the soft sea breeze, and how an English flag near by flaunts jauntingly at ours; how dragomen, and servants, and horsemen, and muleteers chatter and splutter and frisk about; how the natives gather on the outskirts of our camp and look on in amazement at this inordinate influx of "howadjis;" how the dinner, steaming hot and luscious, comes ere long from off the "Egyptian cook stove," which said stove is nothing more than a piece of sheet iron, about ten inches wide by twenty-four in length, perforated with holes and standing upon four iron legs, upon which charcoal is thrown, and by the ignition of which an Egyptian cook boils and fries and roasts every sort of eatable; and how, after dinner is over, we walk out upon the sea-shore, and, while the stars look down as in days of old, think of the time when, just here, Noah built the ark in obedience to the command of the Most High —how, just here, Hiram, king of Tyre, brought the cedars of Lebanon for the building of Solomon's Temple

—how, just here, Jonah embarked to flee from the command of God, but found himself, ere long, in the belly of a whale—how, just here, Peter saw the vision from the house-top of " Simon the Tanner," which taught him the lesson that God is no respecter of persons—how, just here, Peter recalled Tabitha to life—and how, just here, the first Napoleon carried on a most desperate siege, and, after the capitulation of the city, ordered four thousand Turkish soldiers to be inhumanly butchered,—are not all these things written upon our own brain and on the pages of sacred and profane history, and would a more minute description thereof add anything to the interest of the reader!

A French writer, who visited Palestine many years ago, thus describes the town and its surroundings:

"The town of Jaffa stands on a hill that rises abruptly from the sea, from which, at some distance, it has a very picturesque appearance; though, on closer inspection, it appears a miserable place; but it has a fine climate and a fine country round it, and the orange-gardens are the most luxuriant on the shores of the Mediterranean. It is popularly believed to have existed before the Deluge, and to have been the city where Noah dwelt and built his ark. It was the port whence Jonah embarked for Tarshish when he was thrown overboard and swallowed by a whale; and St. Jerome himself does not disdain to record the heathen tradition which made the rocks of Jaffa the scene of Andromeda's exposure to the monster, and of her rescue by Perseus. But a more recent and a gloomier association attached to the name of this town belongs to Napoleon's history—the poisoning of the French invalids and the massacre of four thousand prisoners.

"The ancient harbor of this sole seaport of Judea is still traceable, and the rocks that formed the pier rise high out of the sea which breaks upon them with tremendous violence. This pier was, evidently, an artificial construction, and, although no mortar was used in the building of it, yet the joinings have become filled up and the whole forms a continuous mass resembling that at Rhodes and Tyre, though it is much smaller than the latter. The ships of Solomon, at least those trading on the Mediterranean, could not therefore have been very large or numerous, or they could not have found accommodation in this harbor. In common with all the cothons of that period, it is now so filled up with sand as only to allow an entrance to the small coasting craft. Trade was rather brisk at the time of our visit, and the place seemed thriving. The imports were mostly pilgrims and corn for the Pasha's army; and the exports chiefly fruits from the neighboring gardens. There is a good bazaar, and the gate, on the land side, is remarkably handsome; and beside it stands a noble Turkish fountain, formed of various colored marbles, pouring forth jets of the purest water. It furnishes a good specimen of the gate of an Eastern town, having within it the seat of judgment, as well as the receipt of custom, and was guarded by a strong military force, that formed a pleasing group as they surrounded its marble deewan."

There is one incident of the evening of which we must speak more in detail, since it illustrates the manners and customs of the people, and the striking similarity of the present with the past. We refer to a Syrian marriage ceremony, or, rather, the taking home of the bride after the marriage. While standing on our camp-ground in the early evening, we hear, at a distance, a loud sound of voices and rude instruments, and pretty soon observe lights approaching on the road which passes our tents. We wait with some anxiety to see what it is, and, when the procession comes near, we are informed by our dragoman that it is a newly-married husband taking home his bride. The first part of the procession consists of men, old and young, bearing lighted torches, and in their midst two or three are playing upon pipes and drums. Next follow some half dozen men and boys carrying large glass lighted lanterns, and immediately behind, or, as it were, in the midst of these, walks the bridegroom. The bride, with her face closely covered and with one hand resting upon the shoulder of the bridegroom, walks closely behind him, while, immediately behind her, fifty or more women and young girls follow, singing and shouting continually. Close to the bridegroom is a man carrying a chair, and whenever the procession halts, as it does frequently, the bridegroom sits down upon this chair, while the men shout and dance around him. When the husband sits the bride still stands with her hand resting on his shoulder. She utters no sound, and, by her pensive, silent tread, seems more like a lamb going to the slaughter than a new-made bride going to the home of her liege lord.

We follow them some distance as the procession wends its way to a small village just outside of the city, but observe nothing in addition to the above. One of the natives says that the husband gave " twenty French pounds" (Napoleons) for the bride, and thinks he has paid a high price for her. He says she is " mush-tieb," which means not good, but it may be that he is a rejected suitor or has some other reason for speaking thus slightingly of the bride.

While upon the subject of marriage ceremonies as observed throughout Palestine and Syria, it may prove of interest to our readers to quote Russell's account of the ceremony of fetching a bride on the eve of a nuptial-day, together with a general description of a Maronite wedding:

"The priests," he says, "from their easy access to families, have a principal share in matrimonial negotiations; and, having opportunities of being acquainted with the tempers of the children, they are supposed to be sincere in their reports. The female relations of the youth, too (as among the Moslems), are employed in the search of a bride. When the choice is determined, flowers and other small presents are, from time to time, sent from the family of the bridegroom to that of the bride, and the relations interchange visits; but the girl, before company, will not so much as touch a flower that has come from the other house; and, if the bridegroom happens to be named in her presence, she suddenly assumes a reserved air, becomes silent, or retires. The women know this so well, that, when the young lady happens to be rather pert, they threaten to make her soon change her tone, and the hint is sufficient to silence her.

"After the bride has been demanded in form, and other matters have been adjusted, a certain number of the male relations are invited to an entertainment by her father, in order to settle the wedding-day, which is usually fixed at the distance of a fortnight.

"In the afternoon of the day preceding that of the nuptials the same company again repair to the bride's house, and proceeding thence, after supper, to the house of the bridegroom, they find most of the persons assembled who have been invited to the wedding. The bridegroom and *shebeen*, or brideman, do not, at first, make their appearance, but, after a short search, are discovered lurking, as it were, on purpose, in a dishabille not suited to the approaching ceremony. From their refuge they are led in triumph round the court-yard, amid the shouts of the assembly, and then conducted into a chamber to dress, where the wedding garments are ready displayed; but, before these are put on, a priest pronounces a long benediction over them. When the bridegroom is dressed, he is again obliged to make several turns in procession, in the same manner as before. The women all this time remain in a separate apartment.

"About midnight all the men and most of the women, each carrying a wax taper, set out in procession, preceded by a band of music, in order to fetch the bride. Upon their arrival at her house they are refused admission, a party of the bride's kindred standing ready to dispute the entrance; and, in consequence of this, a mock skirmish usually ensues, in which the bridegroom's party is always victorious. The women, now advancing to the inner apartments, soon return in triumph with the bride, who is entirely covered with a large veil, and attended only by her *shebeeny*, or bridesmaid, and one or two female relations, for the mother and nearest kindred are not, by custom, allowed to accompany her. The paternal house is in deep affliction at her departure, but she is received by the expecting crowds with repeated shouts of joy, and in that manner conducted to the bridegroom's house. Their course, however, is extremely slow, for decorum imperatively requires that every step of the bashful bride toward the abode of her destined spouse should be made with the utmost seeming reluctance. A very bad opinion, indeed, would be conceived of the girl who, on such an occasion, did not consume an hour, at least, in walking a distance of ten minutes. Just in the inverse ratio of her speed is the honor due to her virtuous breeding and maiden modesty.

"On her passing the threshold she is saluted with a general *zilarett*, a shrill, vibrating cry uttered by the

Arab women on joyful occasions, made by a quick and somewhat tremulous application of the tongue to the palate, producing the sound treli li li li li li li, repeated as often as can be done with one breath (the same as we have ourselves just heard from the women and young girls forming the marriage procession, witnessed by us this evening) ; and, after the long veil has been exchanged for one of red gauze, she is led into a long apartment, and seated in state at the upper end upon the deewan.

" In this situation it would be an offence to decency to utter a syllable or to smile, she being by etiquette obliged to remain all the time with her eyelids shut, but she is prepared to rise up and kiss the hand of every female who enters the room to congratulate her, each being announced by a person placed near her on purpose. The women pass the remainder of the night in loud rejoicings, while the men, on their part, are not less noisy. There is abundance of arrack, wine, coffee and other refreshments, and only a few of the elderly guests retire to rest. When it happens that the house is not sufficiently large to afford separate apartments for the men and women, an adjoining house is borrowed for the reception of the men.

" About nine in the morning, the bishop, or, in the lower ranks, a priest, comes to perform the nuptial ceremony. The music ceases the moment he enters, and a respectful silence reigns through the house. The women all veil for his reception, and, as soon as he is robed in his canonicals, he enters the harem, followed by the bridegroom and the men in select procession. The bride appears, standing in front of the deewan, supported by two women besides the shebeeny ; the rest of the women fill up the space behind. The bridegroom, dressed in a kind of splendid robe, and attended by the shebeen, is placed on the bride's left hand. The bishop then proceeds, and, in the course of the nuptial service, puts a crown, first on the head of the bridegroom and next upon the bride's; he afterward crowns both the shebeen and the shebeeny. The man answers audibly to the usual matrimonial question, but the consent of the woman is denoted by a gentle inclination of the head. The bishop immediately joins their hands, and, after several prayers and benedictions, puts a ring upon the bridegroom's finger, delivering another to the shebeeny, to be put on the finger of the bride. Toward the conclusion of the service, the bishop ties a piece of ribbon round the bridegroom's neck, which remains till a priest in the afternoon comes to take it off.

" The ceremony thus finished, the men return to the outer apartments, where, it being too early for the whole company to dine, a dinner is served up to the bishop and his suite with a few select persons. The pause occasioned by the bishop's presence is at an end the moment he quits the house; the music then strikes up in full chorus, and, as if to make up for time lost, the noise on all hands is redoubled. The Christians, on these occasions, are more noisy than the Mohammedans, for, besides the musical band, which performs almost incessantly, many of the men join with the professed singers in the chorus. Some of them also show their skill in dancing, which they seldom do on any other occasion. Interludes of buffoons and jugglers are, from time to time, introduced by way of variety. The company pass the whole day in this manner; arrack and wine circulate briskly; the table at dinner and supper is covered with profusion; and fruits, sweetmeats, coffee and tobacco are served at intervals.

" Between eleven and twelve at night, the bridegroom, accompanied by a few of the near relations, is introduced into the women's apartment, where a collation of fruit and wine is prepared. The bride receives him standing up, and is, with difficulty, prevailed on at his entreaty to resume her place. This interview is soon over, for, after the young couple have drunk a glass to each other, the bridegroom drinks a bumper to the female guests, and then returns to the company, who are waiting without to receive him with loud acclamations.

" The remainder of the night is spent in the same way as the preceding one. Next morning, the bridegroom presents jewels and other ornaments to his wife; her kindred, at the same time, making her presents in money. It is not till after some days that others, who have been invited to the wedding, send presents of various kinds, and that she receives congratulatory messages and flowers from her acquaintance.

" The nuptial feast concludes with a collation on the afternoon of the third day, after which the whole company take leave, except a few intimate friends, who stay to sup with the bridegroom, and consign him, at midnight, in a condition most heartily fatigued, to the arms of his bride.

" The succeeding week is filled up in receiving complimentary messages; and, on the seventh day, the bride entertains her mother and near relations, who come then to pay their first visit.

" However the other women may be amused, the bride herself enjoys but a small share in the pleasures of the wedding-festivities. The ceremonies she is obliged to go through for three days are fatiguing to the last degree, and the incessant din, joined to the natural timidity of the sex, keeps her in a state of perpetual anxiety. As she knows herself exposed to the captious observation of her own sex, she dreads to move a limb, lest it should be censured as an offence against the decorum of her situation ; and, if those whose office it is to take care of her refreshments should happen to neglect their duty, she dares hardly venture to open her lips to ask for a glass of water. I have heard several married ladies describe the distress of their situation with much pleasantry. Some have assured me, that they were not only half frightened out of their wits by the incessant bustle and sudden shouts, but in risk, also, of perishing from thirst, being neglected by the servants in the hurry of their attention to the company. Besides these restrictions, which terminate with the three ceremonial days, the newly-married woman is enjoined strict silence for the space of a month, and must consider it an indulgence if allowed to utter a few words to her husband. Among the Armenians, this term is said to be protracted to a twelve-month. It is sometimes jocosely remarked by the husbands that when their wives are particularly observant of the precepts they receive on this head from the old women, they seldom fail to make up for it by their loquacity after the expiration of the term."

Next morning, before starting for Jerusalem, we ride through Jaffa, and make a special point of visiting the house of "Simon the Tanner, by the sea-side." The town is located on a high mound, and the streets, which are paved with rough stones, are very difficult of ascent and descent. Not only are they steep and rough, but so filthy that it is anything but pleasant to go through them. The houses are built mostly of stone, but without a single convenience or comfort about them. They look picturesque, at a distance, but, when you see them closely, they present little more than bare walls. The present population of the town is said to be about six thousand. The house of "Simon the Tanner," so called, is a rough stone, two-story building, situated near the sea. The tradition which marks this as the site of the house is of long standing, and we see no reason to doubt its correctness.

We also ride out to the "American Colony"—about half a mile from Jaffa—about which so much has been said and written of late. The buildings and improvements, thereabouts, look more like enterprise than anything in Syria, and it only takes half an eye to observe that Yankees are about. The houses are of frame, the lumber of which was brought from America in the same ship that brought over the colonists. As the affairs of this so-called "colony" have excited a good deal of angry discussion, a few words of its history may prove of interest.

Some two years ago a Mr. Adams (Eld. G. J.) came to Syria, as a tourist. On his return to the United States he traveled through some of the Eastern States, delivering lectures, the burden of which was that "Messiah was soon to return and re-establish Israel." He organized what he called the "Church of the Messiah," of which he himself became the "President," and then proposed that such of his followers as felt disposed should join him in establishing a colony in Palestine, as one of the appointed means of God whereby Israel was to be restored. He represented to his hearers that Jaffa was the natural sea-port of Syria; that, "in the restoration of Israel, it must soon become a large and beautiful city;" and that land, or town lots, purchased near there, must so increase in value that the possessors would speedily become rich. The enterprise, as he represented it, was to possess the double character of religion and speculation—the first, to help the coming of the Messiah, the second, to help themselves.

Thirty families, including one hundred and fifty-six

souls, agreed to unite with him in the enterprise, and such of them as had funds made advance payments to him on the town lots, the plot for which, about seven acres, he had made partial arrangements to purchase while in Syria, some twelve months before, at a cost of seven hundred and fifty pounds sterling. They chartered a ship, loaded it partly with lumber and provisions, and in September, 1866, landed at Jaffa. Long before they reached their destination, serious difficulties arose among this motley crew of religious speculators, and from that time until the present, criminations and recriminations have been constantly going on among them. Soon after their arrival eleven of the number died, and many others were sick. Those opposed to Mr. Adams say that all these deaths are attributable to his negligence in failing to procure them such accommodations as he had promised on their arrival. Mr. Adams and his friends say that he did all, and more than he had promised. Notwithstanding all these difficulties and discouragements, they immediately proceeded to erect houses on the town lots they had purchased, and now have several very respectable Yankee houses put up or in the course of erection. They also rented a considerable tract of land near Jaffa, and now have growing some three hundred acres of wheat, one hundred and fifty acres of barley, fifty acres of beans, and a large field of potatoes.

The dissenters, who number about one-third of the original colonists, have appealed to the United States Minister at Constantinople, and to the United States Consul at Jerusalem, for redress against Mr. Adams and his associates, and the matter, for some time past, has been undergoing investigation.

We very much regret that any difficulty should have

arisen among these colonists; for, viewed simply as an enterprise, apart from the religious idea connected therewith, the example which they could and would have set the Syrians of American ingenuity, thrift, and go-a-headativeness, could not have failed to work a wholesome influence.

It is noon of March 21st when we finally turn our backs upon Jaffa, with our faces toward Jerusalem. Our tents and baggage have preceded us to Ramlah, where we ordered them pitched for the night. Our course is over the plain of Sharon, one of the most beautiful in the world—constantly reminding us of our Western prairies. Wild flowers bloom everywhere, and every now and then Lily and Lu stop to gather some of the choicest, but of the far-famed rose of Sharon few, if any, are now to be found. It is nearly five o'clock when we reach Ramlah, but, before dismounting, we ride to the old square tower, on the outer edge of the town, from which to have another view of the plain of Sharon and the surrounding country.

This tower is of Saracenic architecture, and rises to a height of probably eighty feet. The top is reached from a winding staircase within, which is, by no means, easy to climb. Once up, however, the view amply repays the labor. On the east the hills of Ephraim and Judah rise in majestic grandeur, while, to the west, the blue sky, and no less blue waters of the Mediterranean, bound the vision; to the northward the plain of Sharon stretches out far toward the land of the Philistines, while to the southward the same beautiful plain extends as far as the eye can reach. At our feet lies the village of Ramlah, with its convents, and mosques, and ruins of ancient date; while only a little way off the ancient Joppa (Jaffa) of biblical history lifts its head over the waters of the sea.

It is dusk of evening before we descend from the tower, and nearly dark before we reach our tents on the plain near Ramlah.

Another traveler, who passed over this same route, and saw the plain at a season when Nature had put on her loveliest garb, thus describes it:

" For nearly two miles after leaving the town our road lay through the richest and most beautiful garden of orange and lemon trees, then covered with fruit and flowers, and tall, waving cypresses, corals, and fragrant mimosas; intersected with enormous nopals, or prickly pears, with the scammony in flowers twining through their invulnerable armor. We saw extensive water-melon beds, the fruit of which, having just come to maturity, were guarded by men sitting under temporary sheds erected for the purpose; the sight immediately brought to our recollection Isaiah's striking image of loneliness, ' The daughter of Zion is left as a lodge in a garden of cucumbers (c. i., v. 5). The water-melons, or *pasteques*, grown here are peculiar to the district of Jaffa, and are said to degenerate if transplanted elsewhere. They are justly celebrated throughout the Levant for their exquisite flavor and their refreshing coolness.

" From hence to Ramlah, our way lay again through the plain of Sharon, one of the most fertile and beautiful in the East. Although not a sixth part of it is cultivated, yet where it was tilled the crops looked most luxuriant. Upon a space of ten or twelve acres, I observed fourteen ploughs at work; and so simple and light is the construction of these implements that the husbandman, when returning from his labor in the evening, takes his plough home upon his shoulder. The share is of wood, and armed only at the end with a tooth or point of iron, which, of course, does little more than scratch the ground.

The beam is very slender, as well as the rude handle by which it is directed. I do not think we passed a dozen head of cattle of any kind; but the monotony of the plain is occasionally relieved by groves and clumps of aged and magnificent olives, which give it quite the appearance of a well laid-out English park or demesne. Most of these olives must be centuries old, from their great size and proverbial slowness of growth; and are probably the lineal descendants of those we read of in David's time, which were so plentiful in the low plains that Baal Hanan, the Gadite, was placed as overseer over them. Numbers of tall white storks paced about through the groves, like so many spectres, enjoying their solitary grandeur amid the scenes of other days. The day was delightful; a light breeze refreshing the traveler and the weary pilgrim as they journeyed to the holy city; the fields were decked with thousands of gay flowers—the scarlet anemone, and a beautiful specimen of small red tulip, intermingled with the white cistus, the pink phlox, and the blue iris, and with crimson and white asters, asphodels, and lilies, forming an enameled carpet that perfumed the air, and offered a scene replete with everything that could gratify the eye or charm the imagination. This plain of Sharon is about fifteen miles broad, and nearly twice as many long, bordered on the one side by the blue waters of the Mediterranean, and the rugged hill-country of Judea on the other. Writers, who have described the 'goodly land' of Palestine as so unfertile as to warrant the assertion of Voltaire, that he would not receive a present of it from the sultan, can never have beheld the plain of Sharon when arrayed in the lovely garb of spring. After harvest, indeed, the scene changes, when the sun scorches up every trace of herbage, leaving the red soil exposed, with nothing to break the melancholy monotony of its aspect except the pale foliage of an olive or the motionless shade of a mastic.

"Ramlah, the ancient Arimathea, the city of 'Joseph the counselor, the good man and just,' is a wretched, dilapidated place, but exhibits marks of having once been a more extensive and flourishing town than it is at present. The only monument of importance belonging to it is the Martyr's Tower, situated about a quarter of a mile from the town. It is attached to a building of great extent, consisting of rows of Gothic arches, like cloisters, and has itself much the appearance of one of our old cathedral towers. The view, from the top, is very splendid."

We had nearly forgotten to mention our visit to ancient Lydda, now called Ludd, while on our way from Jaffa to Ramlah. A detour of some three miles from the main road carries us to this village, at which we dismount to examine the ruins of the once magnificent church of St. George, so often spoken of in the history of the Crusaders. Only a small portion of the structure now remains, but quite enough to show its former grandeur. A Moslem minaret near by has been built from the stones of the ancient church, and no better evidence is needed of the difference between the class of men who lived in Syria then and those now residing here than a glance at the architecture of these two edifices. We cannot but exclaim, in the words of another, "How has the mighty fallen!"

Next morning, bright and early, we are on our horses and away for Jerusalem. Our eyes long to look upon the city of the great king—upon the city where Jesus lived, and died, and rose again—and we hasten onward.

About three hours from Ramlah, we pass a small village called Latrone, the birth-place, as it is believed, of the penitent thief, who said to Jesus, in the hour of his extremity, "Lord, remember me when thou comest into thy kingdom," and to whom the Saviour replied, "To-day shalt thou be with me in Paradise."

A little further on, we reach a small village called Emmouse, which is generally conceded to be the Emmaus to which two of the apostles were journeying when Jesus, after his resurrection, joined them on the way, and "expounded unto them in all the Scriptures the things concerning himself;" and to which village he accompanied them, and, after tarrying and breaking bread with them, "vanished out of their sight."

From this point, and up the mountains of Ephraim, the road, or path (for all the roads of Syria are only paths), becomes more difficult, and, at times, almost impassable, because of roughness and steepness. Indeed, with all our experience and reading, we had never conceived the possibility of such roads as these, and, but for the wonderful agility and sure-footedness of our horses, we should never have got over them alive. No American horse, unused to such steep, rocky paths, could travel over them for a single mile without breaking his neck or his legs, and nothing short of actual seeing could have convinced us that any horse could do so. To ride over and on the top of stone fences, ascending and descending at an angle of, at least, forty-five degrees, would be considered quite a feat in an American horse, and yet this would be nothing in comparison with riding over some of the mountain-paths between the plains of Sharon and Jerusalem. We tremble for Lily and Lu as our horses pass over some of these terrible ascents and descents of broken rock; but, thanks to a good Providence, our horses never once miss their foothold from the plain of Sharon to the gates of Jerusalem.

After leaving Emmouse, the next point of interest is

the valley of Ajalon, near Yalo. Here it was that the armies of Israel fought with the Amorites, and where, at the command of Joshua, "the sun stood still, and the moon stayed, until the people had avenged themselves upon their enemies."

We pass several wells and cisterns on the road of more or less celebrity, at one of which we stop for luncheon; also several Arab villages, here and there, on the mountain slopes, but nothing more of biblical interest attracts our attention until we reach the dry bed of the brook, in the valley of Elah, from whence David gathered the pebbles with which to slay Goliath. We, too, gather some pebbles from the bed of the brook as mementoes of the place, and then hurry on, and on, to Jerusalem.

The road, it seems to us, grows rougher and longer the nearer we approach the Holy City, and again and again we wonder how it could come to pass that God would permit the placing of his most holy temple in the midst of a country so rugged and desolate. Was it that the toilsomeness of the journey thither, and the utter desolation which meets the eye at every step, should create a more lively appreciation of Jerusalem when once reached? We hope so, and still press our jaded horses onward, that we may have a glimpse, at least, of the Holy City before the sun goes down. At length we reach the summit of a rocky path, and, rising in our stirrups, catch the first faint glimpse of the Mount of Olives and the walls of Jerusalem!

To show that we are not alone, or singular, in our description of the desolation of the country, and the terrible condition of the road between Ramlah and Jerusalem, we will again quote from the author from whom we quoted that glowing description of the plain of Sharon.

He says: "When we reached the hill-country of

Judea, a complete change came over the scene. The eye was no longer refreshed with verdant sward, and the beauty of the plain we had traversed after leaving Joppa; and the hum of bees, the low of cattle, and even the music of the goat's bell was no longer heard. A solemn wildness reigns in these elevated regions, the hills of which rise in concentric circles, one above another, the naked strata of gray limestone protruding at regular intervals, like so many seats in a stadium. The road was a mere horse-track, rough and stony as if it had been the bed of a river; but the dreariness and monotony of the view were occasionally relieved by valleys and ravines clothed with low woods of dwarf oak, which was then putting forth its young leaves and long green catkins. Every place seemed admirably adapted for robbery; but we passed all the defiles without meeting with a human being.

"While musing upon the great events of which this country has been the seat, I was struck by the announcement of mid-day from a little mosque on a peak in the midst of the wildest part of the hills. Although it came from a Mohammedan minaret, there was something deeply impressive in the exclamation, 'God is great!' the only sound that broke the almost death-like stillness of the grand solitudes through which we were filing.

"About midway to Jerusalem, we passed through a deep, narrow gorge, wooded to an extent that we could scarcely have imagined, from the rocky and barren desert in which it was situated. The ascent out of this valley is fearfully precipitous, and has long been noticed in modern history as the hiding-place or fastness of the lawless Bedouin. A large band of Ibrahim Pasha's cavalry was here completely destroyed. The huge rocks, the close wood on either side, and the overhanging crags form a complete cover for the enemy, who might attack the largest body of men passing through it, while they would remain secure from harm, especially from horsemen. This valley is probably the Bethhoron of Scripture ; ascending from it the traveler again enters upon the rugged Apennine country, from whose heights he has a last glimpse of the blue waters of the Mediterranean.

"We next arrived at the Valley of Jeremiah—on all hands a melancholy solitude ! Here, it has been conjectured, stood the village in which the prophet was born. At one end of it is a castle, singularly situated on a rock ; it is still called Modin—is still a place of great strength, and is known as occupying the site of the city and tombs of the illustrious and patriotic Maccabees.

"From the long and sterile valley of Jeremiah the road passes through a narrow gullet into a smaller tract, wherein are a few villages and patches of vineyards. At the end of the defile runs a brook into the valley of Elah, or the Terebinthine Valley, whence it is said David picked up the stones with which he slew Goliath ; on the left hand rose the hills toward Samaria, bleak and desolate. The road now becomes more rocky, the scene more wild and cheerless, and no object presents itself to arrest the traveler's attention, or to beguile, for a moment, his impatience for the first sight of the Holy City. At length it opens upon him at the issue from a defile. The view of it from this approach is sudden and near, and for that reason, perhaps, more impressive than if the mind had been prepared for it by a more distant vision. The first involuntary exclamation that bursts forth is that which prophecy has said shall be in the mouth of 'all that pass'—' Is this the city that men call the perfection of beauty, the joy of the whole earth ?' It is impossible that any delineation can be more just or any image more vivid than is contained in these few words: 'How doth the city sit solitary!' The sight carried across a tract of gray, desolate, and barren rock, and the ruins of the Moslem burial-ground, with crumbling tombs on every hand, rests upon a bare dead wall, above which little is seen but the graceless domes of houses, and the tops and minarets of a few mosques, and the wild hills in the distance beyond Jordan, at the foot of which lies the Dead Sea. Scarcely a sign of vegetation can be traced, with the exception of the leaden green of a few ragged olives; and the city, placed on the brow of the hill, as if an object for observation, looks as if a portion of it had fallen down the steep, and presents one of the most gloomy and melancholy spectacles that imagination can conceive."

CHAPTER II.

"CITY OF THE GREAT KING."

NO one should ever have his first view of Jerusalem from the Jaffa road. Better go five, yes, fifty miles, around and approach the Holy City from the Damascus road, or, still better, from the Mount of Olives, than have your heart sink within you from disappointment in first viewing the city from the rough, barren hill-top of the road from Jaffa.

In our mind the city of Jerusalem has always been associated with beauty and loveliness. Notwithstanding its frequent destructions and oft-repeated desolations, and notwithstanding the curse of heaven, which we know has rested upon it from the hour of its rejection and crucifixion of the Divine Redeemer until the present, still, in our imagination, it has ever remained "the city of the great King," "the joy of the whole earth," "a thing of beauty and a joy for ever!"

Judge, then, of our disappointment when, after hours of tedious travel over roads the worst we have ever seen, and over a country so dreary and desolate that the eye tires with the hideous deformity of nature everywhere present, we find Jerusalem to seem like a confused mass of rough stone walls, with here and there a Moslem minaret pointing derisively toward heaven. We say "seemed," for subsequent views from more favorable points change our first impressions somewhat, though at no time, during all our stay in Jerusalem, can we rid our mind of the unfavorable impression which our first view made upon it.

The Russian convent, which stands upon a commanding eminence just outside the Jaffa gate, is, by far, the best building, or collection of buildings, in or about Jerusalem. It first meets the eye as we reach the summit of the Jaffa road, and beyond the walls we have a fine view of the Mount of Olives, but the greater portion of the city looks dark, dreary, and unsatisfactory; and the utter desolation of the country around, which has but one exception in a small valley south of the city, adds much to the dreariness of the scene, and makes one feel from the very first that the curse of God rests upon this once favored city, and upon everything connected with it. Nor is this feeling at all changed by a closer inspection of it. The houses, generally, are mere stone walls, without a single comfort of civilization about them; the streets are narrow, roughly paved, dirty, and in some places almost impassable either for horses or footmen; the people, with but few exceptions, are hard-featured, miserably clad, and seem the very impersonation of squalid wretchedness; while even the holy places about the city lose much of their solemnity and interest because of their miserable surroundings, and the class of persons with which one is constantly brought in contact in visiting them.

Cursed of God, and cursed *with* men; cursed within, and cursed without; cursed in the rulers, and cursed in the ruled; cursed in the past, and doubly cursed in the present, Jerusalem sits like a widow in her weeds, with none so poor as to do her reverence. Again and again, as we walk through its streets and view it from distant points, do the words of Jesus ring in our ears:

"O Jerusalem, Jerusalem, which killest the prophets, and stonest them that are sent unto thee; how often would I have gathered thy children together, as a hen doth gather her brood under her wings, and ye would not! Behold, your house is left unto you desolate!"

During our stay in Jerusalem we visit every place of biblical interest, and some of them again, and again, and again. We read what is written, and hear what is said, concerning each; and endeavor, so far as is possible, to get a proper appreciation of all. To points that are merely traditionary we only give such credit as circumstances and surroundings would seem to justify; while to the eternal hills and valleys, about which there never has been, nor can be, any dispute, we give such attention and reverence as their importance demands. In our description of the Holy Places in Jerusalem and throughout Syria we shall represent them exactly as they are at present, giving such impressions of identity as force themselves on our own mind while viewing them.

And here we may say that our rule of identification is this: Where history and tradition both agree as to the spot, of course there can be no doubt; where history and tradition point to different places, we always give preference to the former; where history is silent and tradition of long standing fixes a locality, we credit it, unless natural obstacles, or other well-settled facts relative to corroborative subjects, contradict it; where traditions conflict, we always give credit to the older; and, as a good surveyor will never destroy even a poor landmark until he is able to establish a better one, so would we never wholly set aside even a tradition until we were able to substitute a fact therefor.

HOLY SEPULCHRE.

It should be borne in mind that in the early ages of the world tradition was their only history; and, this being so, great pains were taken to transmit from father to son, and from son to son, every material fact bearing upon the history of nations, families, and localities; and this habit being once established would naturally continue in strong force, even after written history came into general use. To such as are disposed to cavil at everything except where proof positive can be given, tradition is of little or no value, while at least two-thirds of their pleasure as travelers is irretrievably lost. We prefer to be occasionally mistaken than eternally doubting. If, in all this, our readers should think us over-credulous, they have only to throw in their doubts wherever it pleases them to do so, as we freely accord to others what we claim for ourself—the right to think and judge of each and every subject, independent of the thoughts and judgment of others.

The first place of biblical interest which we visit in Jerusalem is the Church of the Holy Sepulchre. This we visit on the first morning of our arrival, and twice subsequently. The building is large, very irregular in form, and in bad repair. The principal dome, which has remained quite open ever since it was destroyed by fire (because of the dispute between the Greeks and Latins as to who should have the privilege of repairing it), is now undergoing repair, and will probably be completed within the coming year. We ascend to the dome, where the repairs are being made, and in descending we stop a while on the top of the edifice, from which we have an interesting view of the contiguous portions of the city and the distant hills.

This church, it is said, covers not only the site of the Holy Sepulchre, but also the rock of Calvary; the Stone of Unction; the places where Jesus appeared to Mary his mother after the resurrection, and also to Mary Magdalen; the tombs of Adam, Joseph, Melchisedeck, Nicodemus, Godfrey, and Baldwin; a part of the pillar of flagellation, which visitors have the privilege of touching with a stick through a hole in the wall; the place of Christ's bonds; the spot where the Empress Helena discovered what she thought to be the True Cross; and some twenty other places designated as of more or less interest.

The church is situated in a hollow, or what seems to have been a sort of amphitheatre. Before it is an open square court, one side of which is bounded by the church itself and the other three sides by buildings. Along the front of this court runs a narrow street or passage-way, with steps running down to and up from it. Around the court sit venders of beads, shells, crosses, and other Catholic emblems.

"The approach to it from every direction," to use the graphic description of another, "lies through narrow, filthy lanes, and small bazaars generally filled with ragged Arab women, the venders of vegetables and snails, the latter of which are much eaten here, especially during Lent. After many crooked turnings we arrive in the large square court in front of the church. Here the scene exhibited, in the height of the pilgrim season, is of the most motley and extraordinary appearance. On the upper raised steps are tables spread with coffee, sherbet, sweetmeats and refreshments; throughout the court are seated pedlers and the Bethlehemite venders of holy merchandise, such as crosses, beads, rosaries and amulets, and mother-o'-pearl shells, which are brought generally from the Red Sea, and engraved with religious subjects chiseled in relief; models of the Holy Sepulchre in wood inlaid with mother-o'-pearl, and drinking-cups from the deposits of the Jordan, with verses from the Bible engraved on them; they are nearly as black as ebony and take a fine polish. Through these wares hundreds of persons pass and repass; pilgrims of many nations in their different costumes; Latin, Armenian, Russian, Greek, and Coptish friars, with Turkish, Arnaout, and Arab soldiers—all forming the most extraordinary scene that could be found in any spot upon the globe; and a polyglot language is heard such as few other places in the world could exhibit."

We enter the church by a low door, on the left of which sits a number of Turkish guards, and just beyond where they sit, and within the walls of the church, we can see their kitchen and cooking utensils. These guards are kept here day and night by the government, to keep the peace among the Latins, Greeks, Armenians, and other professing Christians, who claim jurisdiction over different parts of this edifice. It is a standing disgrace to the Christian world that the professed followers of Christ cannot live in peace and unity even within the walls which enclose the Holy Sepulchre! Shame upon such Christianity!

The first object which strikes the eye as we enter, is the " Stone of Unction." This is a large flat marble slab, raised several inches above the floor, and over which numerous lamps are suspended. At almost any hour of the day, pilgrims from different parts of the world may be seen kneeling beside this stone and kissing it. Upon this stone, it is said, our Saviour's body was washed, anointed, and prepared for the tomb.

Turning to the right from the Stone of Unction, we ascend a stairway to a neatly-arranged chapel, at one side of which is said to be the rock of Calvary. By removing a large gold plate, we thrust our hand through a hole in a marble slab and feel the sides of a hole in the natural rock, which is said to be the excavation in which the cross stood at the time of the crucifixion. By removing another long, narrow plate, about two feet to the right of the first, we thrust our hand down in the fissure of the rock, which, it is said, was made when "the earth did quake and the rock rent" at the time of the crucifixion. While examining these, Lily sits down on the marble slab while she thrusts her hand in the hole of the cross, seeing which a Greek priest, standing near, becomes very indignant and splutters around furiously, but what he says we neither know nor care. It is, in his eyes, doubtless, a terrible sacrilege to sit down on this marble slab, but, in our eyes, it presents no more of sanctity than any other piece of marble hewn and fashioned by human hands. The fanaticism of the priests and monks of the Church of the Holy Sepulchre is wonderful to behold, and detracts much from the sanctity and interest of the place.

As a further illustration of the fanaticism of the monks, and that our readers may learn something of their doings at the Church of the Holy Sepulchre during festive occasions, we beg to transcribe, from a work called "THREE WEEKS IN PALESTINE," the following graphic account of the celebration of " *Good Friday:*"

" On this night the monks of the Latin convent performed the ceremony of the crucifixion. The doors were open at an early hour for a short time and then closed for the night, so that we were obliged to be there two or three hours before the ceremony began. Most of the pilgrims had prepared against the tediousness of waiting by bringing with them their beds, mats, and coverlets; and all around the floor of the church, men, women, and children were taking an intermediate nap. The proceedings commenced in the chapel of the Latin convent, where priests, monks, and the prior with his gold mitre and black velvet cloak trimmed with gold, and some other dignitaries of the church, were present, all very richly dressed.

"On a large cross was a jointed figure representing the Saviour—the crown of thorns on his head, nails in his hands and feet, blood trickling from them, and a gaping wound in his side. Before setting out on the procession the lights were extinguished; and in total darkness a monk commenced a sermon in Italian. After it the candles were relighted, banners and crucifixes raised, and the procession moved round the church toward Calvary. Stopping at the Pillar of Flagellation, at the prison where they say Christ was confined, where the crown of thorns was put upon his head, where his raiment was divided, etc., and giving a chant and an address by one of the monks at each place, they wound round the church till they came back to the staircase leading to Calvary, and leaving their shoes below, mounted, barefoot, to the place of crucifixion. Here they first went to an altar on the right, where, as they have it, Christ was nailed to the cross; and laying the figure down on the floor, although they had been bearing it aloft for more than two hours, they now went through the ceremony of nailing it; and, returning to the adjoining altar, passed the foot of the cross through the marble floor, and with the bleeding figure upon it, set it up in the hole in the natural rock, according to the tradition, on the very spot where, eighteen hundred years ago, Christ was crucified. At the foot of the cross a monk preached a sermon in Italian, warm, earnest, and impassioned; frequently turning round, and, with both hands extended, apostrophizing the bleeding figure above him. In spite of my skepticism and incredulity, and my contempt for monkish tricks, I could not behold this scene unmoved. Every attendant upon the crucifixion was represented; for the governor of Jerusalem was present, with a smile of scorn upon his handsome features, and Turkish and Mussulman soldiers breaking the stillness of the scene with loud laughs of derision; and I could almost imagine that I heard the unbelieving Jews with gibes and sneers crying out, 'If he be the King of Israel, let him come down from the cross!'

"After the body had remained for some time suspended, two friars, personating Joseph of Arimathea and Nicodemus, approached the foot of the cross; and one of them on the right, with a long pair of pincers, took the crown of thorns from the head, waved it around slowly with a theatrically mournful air, kissed it, and laid it down on a table before him; he then drew the long spikes from the hands and feet, and moving them around one by one slowly as before, kissed them and laid them also on the table. I never saw anything more affecting than this representation, bad as it was, of the bloody drama of the crucifixion; and as the monks drew out the long nails from the hands and feet, even the scoffing Mussulmans stopped their laugh of derision. I stood by the table while they laid the body upon it and wrapped it in a clean linen cloth; followed them when they carried it down from Calvary to the Stone of Unction; and stood by the head of the stone while they washed and anointed it and prepared it for burial. As soon as the image was deposited on the slab, numbers of pilgrims came and prostrated themselves before it in the lowliest posture of Oriental abasement, rubbing their foreheads in the dust of the pavement, and imprinting kisses on the image and the marble on which it lay, with crossings, prayers, and tears, evincing every mark of sincerity. A Franciscan then came forward to address the surrounding multitude in Arabic.

"At this period of the service the pictorial effect was magnificent and sublime. The scene was such as Rembrandt would have excelled in, and such as Rembrandt alone could have painted. The lights and shadows cast by the numerous torches were equal to the finest effect of his imagination. In the centre stood the prominent figure of the group, the preacher,—a tall, handsome, but austere-looking Spaniard, whose eyes of the darkest hue flashed fire as he warmed in his subject. His Franciscan garb, bound not indeed with a leather girdle about his loins, but with the knotted cord of his order—the Oriental tongue in which he spoke—his vehement, impassioned, but not ungraceful action—all combined to bring the Baptist vividly before the fancy. His audience too were strictly in keeping, and in costume and appearance admirably represented those who flocked to hear the voice of him that cried in the wilderness. The turbaned heads, the bearded faces, the flowing robes—the wealthy Maronite and Armenian in garments of fine cloth and rich silks, standing beside the wild Arab in his simple shirt of blue cotton, and the fierce-looking Bedouin in his woolen burnoos, alternately striped white and brown—the Greek caloyer, with his raven locks flowing over his shoulders from beneath the quadrangular black cap, and a noble black beard; and his lay countryman in his close red skull-cap, ornamented with a blue tassel, surmounting the same profusion of hair, richly embroidered vest and jacket, white petticoat and scarlet greaves, still 'the full-haired and well-greaved Greeks,' with various others, formed a group at once diversified and harmonious, with which our angular and scanty European habiliments did not assimilate."

Descending from Calvary either by the Latin or the Greek stairs—for such is the enmity between the two that they have separate stairways by which to reach Calvary— a few steps bring us to the Holy Sepulchre, immediately under the large dome. This consists of two chambers, the outer of which is about six feet by ten, and the inner about six feet square. In the centre of the outer is an upright polished stone representing the spot where the angel stood when he said to the Marys, "Fear not ye: for I know that ye seek Jesus which was crucified. He is not here, for he is risen, as he said. Come, see the place where the Lord lay." Passing through this, we enter the tomb itself, the entrance to which is about two and a half feet wide by four high. On one side, and occupying nearly one-half of the width of the tomb, is a shelf, about two feet higher than the floor. On this the body was laid, and this we may add, from observations in Egypt and elsewhere, was the usual form of rock-hewn tombs. This rocky shelf is now covered with a marble slab, which was no part, however, of the original tomb. Overhead and about the tomb are forty-two gold and silver lamps suspended, many of which are kept constantly burning. Indeed, the whole of the tomb is so bedizened with gewgaws—beautiful 'tis true, but, as we think, entirely out of place—that no part of the original walls of the tomb are visible. Without, as well as within, the tomb is richly ornamented. Sixteen handsome columns surround it and support a gallery above; while every part is overlaid with rich marbles and fashioned in the most beautiful style of art. We can understand and appreciate the devotional feeling which led to such profuse ornamentation of the tomb of our Saviour; and yet we cannot but feel that if the "sepulchre that was hewn in stone, wherein never man before was laid," had been left just as it was when Joseph, the counselor, finished it, and just as it was when the body of Jesus lay therein, it would excite far more veneration and interest.

Russian and Greek pilgrims, before entering the tomb, usually take off their shoes, which they leave in charge of some one of their company at the outer door; and some of them even crawl upon their hands and knees from the outer entrance to the stone within the tomb, and, once there, kiss and drop their tears upon it, while others rub their faces and hands, over and over again, upon the marble slab, as if they expected to retain for ever a portion of its sanctity; but we do neither, though feeling and realizing the sanctity of the place, perhaps, quite as much as those who are more demonstrative. Indeed, such is the excess of fervor shown by many of the pilgrims who visit the tomb, and by the Greek priests and monks who have it in charge, that one becomes disgusted, rather than impressed, by their demonstrations. These excesses, as we think them—since God is a spirit and must be worshiped in spirit and in truth, rather than in outward observances—may be seen at almost any hour of the day when the church is open to visitors; but they increase greatly in intensity upon certain festive and fast occasions, when Greek, Catholic, Syrian, Maronite, and Armenian seem to vie with each other in what they regard as demonstrative holiness or devotion.

One of the most remarkable of these demonstrations, connected with the Holy Sepulchre, is the fast in the Greek church, which occurs on the Saturday following the guilt of the crucifixion, and preceding the hope of the resurrection; on which occasion the Greek priests profess to call down from heaven, and impart to their followers, the "*holy fire.*" This fast happens not to come within the period of our sojourn in Jerusalem, and hence we shall not be able to witness it ourselves; but, that our readers may know something concerning it, we will append the account given by Monro, who was himself an eye-witness of one of these anniversaries.

He says: " Entering the great church at nine o'clock, A. M., I found some of the congregation singing, dancing, and shouting round the Stone of Unction, while others on their bare knees bowed their bare heads to the stone. The crowd round the sepulchre itself was dense and disorderly; nevertheless, through the centre of them a passage was kept always open for the processions of fanatics who were continually dancing and rushing round the sepulchre in bodies, and raising, at the same time, hideous cries, among which even the wild Nubian yell might be distinguished. In each procession some of the foremost of the party bore others standing erect on their shoulders, and as these latter were thrown over by the jostling and the rapidity of the motion, others quickly succeeded to their places, and he who could stand the longest seemed to be counted the best mountebank. The revelry of an English fair is a scene of tranquillity and decorum compared with the deeds of these benighted Christians.

" As I passed round the sepulchre, along the alley that was left vacant for the fanatical procession, a crowd of these frenzied enthusiasts were coming on behind us, one bearing another on his shoulders, and, chancing to push against my Catholic conductor, the latter instantly felled two of them to the ground with his fist. I returned to my den in the convent to await the hour when the holy fire was to play its part, of which the following is a short notice.

" When the Church of the Holy Sepulchre was exclusively in the hands of the Roman Catholics, it was their custom, on the anniversary of the crucifixion, to extinguish the lamps throughout the church; and on the Saturday, the eve of the resurrection and the day of preparation, the bishop, entering the church with a solemn procession, replaced new fires in the lamps. Now it chanced, upon a day in the primitive ages of piety and fervor, that the procession came down from Mount Calvary and entered the Holy Sepulchre; some of the lamps were found already burning—kindled by miraculous fire; and the miracle was vouchsafed every year after this to the Roman Catholics, and was fully displayed in the time of Godfrey of Boulogne. At a subsequent period, when that Church had lost the ascendancy and the Greeks succeeded to it, the latter, conceiving their faith to be as much entitled to supernatural sanction as that of the Romans, and having received certain information that the miracle would not take offence and throw them over, but would still keep its engagement though they should put it off to a week later, did so; and the miracle still waits upon the Greeks as it used to do upon the Romans, but at two o'clock on the following Saturday. Gibbon says (chap. lvii.), 'This pious fraud was first devised in the ninth century.'

"Soon after twelve I returned to the church. The crowd had considerably increased, but, preceded by a scourge-bearer, the way was cleared, and I reached the door leading to the gallery above. It was some time before the guardians would admit me, but, being persuaded that the applicant was really *un' Signore Inglese*, the door was at length opened. On the inside four monks were posted for its defence, but the number of candidates for admission was numerous. One of these rushing in, the foremost monk met him in the face with a cudgel, and he staggered out again ; another made a similar attempt and was stopped by the same process.

"It should be remarked that on the north and south sides of the little chapel which covers the sepulchre, in either wall, is a hole of an oval form, through which the fire issues for the two rival parties, the Greeks and Armenians. The Copts, Syrians, and Abyssinians are obliged to obtain it as they can in the general scramble, or buy it of the former at a high price, as they have no private holes of their own.

"As the crisis approached, the skirmishes between Greeks and Armenians became severe. Toward two P. M. the Turkish governor entered, attended by his train and preceded by scourges, courbashes, and staves, all busily employed. The conflict throughout the church now grew general, and sticks and fists were engaged between the contending zealots. The Mutesellim having given notice that *he was ready*, the Greek Patriarch, called 'the Bishop of the Fire,' was next introduced, heading a procession of order in their best clothes, who walked at a slow pace thrice round the sepulchre. At the end of the first round, as the mystic fire began to warm his intestines, his outer robe was removed; at the second round his jacket and shirt were unbuttoned, and he appeared to be suffering under considerable increase of *coke;* at the third round the jacket was taken off, and, with his cheeks swollen as if pregnant of fire, and groaning like Stromboli, he was locked into the chapel. What he did within I know not for certain, but I conjecture that he drew a phosphorus box from the pocket of his breeches (which had been advisedly left on him), and therewith lighted some tow and turpentine.

"Without, expectation and expectants were on tiptoe, and every one was provided with a bunch of tapers, tied fast round the wrist. Close to the Armenian hole, three men were posted in light-blue dresses, from whom, to a side door, an avenue was kept clear through the mob. They were provided with ten lamps, and, having received the fire before any of the other devotees, hurried out of the church, ducking down their heads to avoid the blows that were dealt at them, and surrounded by three or four others as protectors. The fire, thus filched, immediately appeared among the women stationed above in the Armenian gallery and chapel, who lighted their tapers and crossed themselves with them in every direction. Some of them pressed the fire against their bared breasts, and when their tapers were thus extinguished presently lighted them to repeat the same action. Others thrust them into caps and handkerchiefs, which they carried for that purpose, and, lighting them again and again, continually extinguish them in the same manner.

" Below, the fury of the combatants was at its height, and the church presented one general and ferocious conflict. He who had obtained the fire of his party, and was not strong enough to secure his retreat, was severely beaten, and either his tapers were taken from him, or the fire put out ; and for this reason, some time elapsed before it was generally diffused throughout the church. It seems that the torches soonest lighted possess the greatest virtue, and, on that account, large sums are sometimes paid for the privilege of the first ignition. The torches are then extinguished, carried home by the pilgrims, and preserved for burning round their bodies after death.

" At last the chapel and the Greek church beyond presented one blaze of light, and the uproar subsided. Turkish guards had been posted in different places as moderators, to protect the lives of the combatants ; for, on previous occasions, this ceremony had been attended with distressing casualties. In former times, in order to increase the delusion practiced upon the devotees, a dove was let loose from the cupola of the tomb at the moment the sacred fire appeared, to represent the Holy Ghost! This latter part of the impious farce has been discontinued for some years past.

"After the fire function a little Spanish monk afforded much amusement by producing a phosphorus box, and showing up the trick to the Mutesellim, to whom the thing seemed quite new and unintelligible. The Spaniard was, in consequence, chaired and cheered through the gallery by the Franciscans, who bear no good feelings toward the Greeks.

"Ten years ago a horrible catastrophe happened at the enactment of this ceremony. The air of the church had become so contaminated by the exhalations from the bodies of thousands crowded within it that many persons fainted; terror, confusion, and a rush for the door ensued; but as it turned inward it was impossible to get it opened, owing to the extreme pressure of the bewildered crowd against it. The governor of the city, who was present as a spectator in the Frank gallery, ran down and endeavored to restore order; but he, too, was borne down by the pressure, and was, with great difficulty, saved, being, at last, carried out senseless over the heads of the people by a strong body of soldiers. By great exertion the guard forced back some of the crowd with the points of their weapons and opened the doors; it has been ascertained that not fewer than three hundred persons perished on that fearful night. Those concerned in the jugglery of this miraculous fire endeavored, by all possible means, to cloak the matter, and to prevent the exact number that were killed from being made public; but the impression made on the minds of the people was so great that on the next day the very same Armenian bishop who had assisted at the ceremony preached openly against its continuance, and strongly urged the people not to require the performance of what they had been taught to believe was miraculous. The Greeks, however, persuaded him afterward to resume the farce which is found so profitable to the convents. The Latins, at present, hold the ceremony in great contempt; but, as we have already stated, it was originally their own invention."

This same tourist and author was also present at another of the anniversaries celebrated at the Church of the Holy Sepulchre, and so vividly does he describe it, that we know our readers will be interested, as we have been, in reading his description.

He says: "On Sunday morning, being *Easter or Palm Sunday*, I visited for the last time the Church of the Holy Sepulchre. It was more crowded than I had ever yet seen it. The court-yard literally swarmed with venders of amulets, crucifixes, and holy ornaments; and within the church were tables of oranges, figs, dates, etc. The Arab baker was walking about with a large tray on his head crying his bread, and on each of the altars was a sort of shop, in which Greeks were making and selling chaplets and wreaths of palm leaves. It was altogether a lively image of the scene when Christ 'went into the temple and cast out them that bought and sold, and overturned the tables of the money-changers.' The ceremonies of the day were in commemoration of that on which our Saviour entered Jerusalem riding upon an ass, when the multitude followed him, strewing their garments and branches of palm-trees in his path, and crying 'Hosannah to the son of David!' When I entered, the monks of the Latin convent were celebrating grand mass before the Holy Sepulchre; and in the mean time the Greeks were getting ready for their turn. Their chapel was crowded, and all along the corridors the monks were arranging the people in procession, and distributing banners, for which the young Greeks were scrambling; and in one place a monk with a standard in his hand, which had just been handed down from above, with his back against the wall, was knocking and kicking away a crowd of young Greeks, struggling to obtain it for the procession.

"As soon as the Latins had finished, the Arab soldiers, whom I always found regular attendants of these scenes, as if they knew what was coming when the Greeks began, addressed them with loud shouts of 'Yellah, yellah—come on, come on.' A large banner was stationed at the door of the sepulchre, and the rush of the pilgrims to prostrate themselves before it, and to touch it with their palm branches, was tremendous. A tall young Greek with a large turban on his head, while his left hand supported the banner, was laying about him with his right as if he were really defending the sepulchre itself from the hands of the infidels. The procession advanced under a loud chant, preceded by a body of Turkish officers to clear the way; then came the priests wearing their richest dresses, their mitres and caps richly ornamented with precious stones, and carrying aloft sacred banners, and one of them sprinkling holy water. Wherever he came the rush was terrible; the Greeks became excited to a sort of frenzy in their eagerness to catch a drop; and one strapping fellow, bursting through the rear ranks, thrust his face over my shoulder and bawled out, 'Papa, papa,' in such an agonizing voice that the 'papa' aimed at him a copious discharge, of which my face received the principal benefit. When the largest banner came round, the struggle to touch it with the palm branches was inconceivable. A Turkish officer had until this time covered me with his body, and by dint of shouting, kicking, and striking furiously about him, saved me till the procession passed by, but after this the rush became dreadful. I could feel my ribs yielding under the pressure, and was really alarmed, when a sudden and mighty surge of the struggling mass hurried me into the stock in trade of a merchant of dates and oranges. Instead of picking up his goods, the fellow grappled at me, but I got out of his clutches as well as I could, and setting up for myself, kicked, thumped, and scuffled until I made my way to the door; and that was my last visit to the Church of the Holy Sepulchre."

But enough for the present of these scenes of fraud, folly, and shame, and let us now proceed to inspect other parts of this vast edifice.

From the front of the Holy Sepulchre we enter the Greek chapel, which is much the largest and best finished of any of the chapels connected with the church. Near the centre of the audience floor, and somewhat elevated, is a small marble globe, which, the Greeks say, marks the "centre of the world." Exactly how a "centre" can be found on the outside of a globe, or exactly what this "centre" signifies or typifies, we are not informed. A Greek service is being performed during one of our visits to the chapel, and we cannot but observe its beauty and solemnity.

There are nine other chapels and five altars connected with this church, over which Latins, Greeks, Armenians, Copts, Syrians, and Franks have separate and exclusive jurisdiction; but simply as chapels and altars they have no special interest, and hence we shall not stop to describe them, except incidentally as they may be connected with the death and resurrection of Jesus.

The place "where the Virgin Mary's body was anointed" is shown near the stairway leading to the Armenian chapel and lodgings. How her body came to be anointed just here, while as yet it was only a bleak and barren spot outside of the city walls, and then carried to a tomb far down in the Valley of Jehosaphat, is not explained.

Near the "Altar of Franks" the precise spot is pointed out where Jesus and Mary Magdalene stood when the former appeared to the latter as a "gardener" after his resurrection; and where, by the utterance of that one simple yet touchingly beautiful word, "Mary," he was revealed unto her in his true character as the risen Redeemer.

In the church or chapel of the Latins a part of the pillar of flagellation is pointed out; but as in this instance the holy object cannot be reached by the lips of the faithful, it is deemed equally efficacious to kiss it through another medium. A monk stands near the rail, and touching the pillar with a long stick that has a piece of leather at the point of it, like a billiard cue, stretches it toward the lips that are ready pouting to receive it. Here, also, the precise spot is shown where Christ appeared to his mother after resurrection; and the place of recognition of the true cross. The "Church of Flagellation," which is said to be erected over the spot where Jesus was scourged, is some distance from the Church of the Holy Sepulchre; but how it came to pass that a part of the pillar at which he was scourged found its way to the Latin chapel in the Church of the Holy Sepulchre, we are not informed.

"The organ of the Latins is a sore annoyance to their neighbors the Greeks, from whose religious service all instrumental music is excluded; but they make up for that defect by the most discordant nasal singing imaginable, each vying with his neighbor, and braying with a forty-nose power that would be really deafening by itself, were it not overcome by the noise that is produced by the beating of copper drums, about the size of boilers, belonging to the Armenians. There are so few Copts in the place that the sounds they make amount to little more than occasional whines. The chapel in which the organ stands is called the Chapel of the Apparition, where Christ appeared to the Virgin."

Across a dark entry-way, to the left of the Greek chapel, the "place of Christ's bonds" is pointed out; and immediately to the rear of this is a chapel dedicated to the Virgin. Returning to the passage-way, and going around the half circle in the rear of the Greek chapel, we come to the Chapel of the Centurion, who, at the moment when Jesus gave up the ghost, was constrained to cry out, "Truly this man was the Son of God;" and near this, and within the same semi-circle, are the chapels of Parting the Garments, and of the Mocking, both of which are said to mark the spots where these events occurred.

From this circular passage-way we descend forty-nine steps, cut in the solid rock, where we reach what is called the Chapel of St. Helena. This is a room excavated in the rock far below the floor of the church, and dedicated to Helena, the mother of Constantine. The chapel is fitted up in the usual gewgaw style, and has suspended from its roof a large number of lamps, some of which are kept constantly burning.

From the Chapel of St. Helena we descend another flight of thirteen steps, cut in the rock, to the "Chapel of the Finding of the Cross." Just here, it is said, the indefatigable empress found the true cross, deeply imbedded in earth and rock; and so rejoiced was she that she at once ordered the excavation of a chapel in the solid rock, to commemorate the event. The place where the cross lay is marked by a marble slab, over which lamps are suspended; and immediately to the right of this is another "Altar of the Franks."

While we think some of the holy places about this church are worthy of credence, others are, no doubt, the mere localizing of monkish superstition, and only worthy of notice, or of mention, as illustrating the extent to which credulity can be carried. Thus we are shown a stone which is said to mark the exact spot where Abraham was about to sacrifice Isaac, and the monks state that when the cross was laid down, before it was raised, our Lord's head rested upon this spot; and they seem to consider the establishment of this fact necessary to the complete fulfillment of the type. In another place we are shown a small door opening to a dark gallery, which leads, as the monks say, to the tombs of Joseph and Nicodemus, between which, and that of the Saviour, there is a subterranean communication. The tombs are excavated in the rock which here forms the floor of the chamber. "Without any expectation of making a discovery," says Stephens, "I remember that once, in prying about this part of the building alone, I took the little taper that lighted the chamber and stepped down into the tomb; and I had just time to see that one of the excavations never could have been intended for a tomb, being not more than three feet long, when I heard the footsteps of pilgrim-visitors, and scrambled out with such haste that I let the taper fall, put out the light, and had to grope my way back in the dark." And in still another, beneath one of the altars, lies a stone having a hole through it, and placed in a short trough, so that it seems impossible for anything but a spectre to pass through the hole. Nevertheless the achievement was a customary penance among the Greeks, and called by them "purgatory;" until a lady, *enceinte*, in laboring to drag herself through it, came to some mischief; and ever since that accident the Turks have in mercy guarded the stone by an iron grating.

Thus we close our description of the Church of the Holy Sepulchre—a description which might have been lengthened to a dozen chapters had we felt so disposed, but which we have condensed in the smallest possible space, for the reason that only such parts as relate to the death and burial of Christ have any real value in our eyes. And even these parts are so obscured by the gauze and tinsel of over-zealous religionists that, to us, much of their original grandeur and interest is destroyed. As well might one attempt to "gild refined gold or paint the lily" as to place marbles and lamps, and pictures and tapestry, around the tomb of Jesus!

As to the identity of the tomb, we have only to say that, after carefully reading the arguments for and against it, and after examining the spot and surroundings for ourself, we are content to believe that this is the identical tomb in which the body of the Redeemer lay; and the rock near by the identical one in which, or upon which, the cross stood at the time of the crucifixion. As to the spots pointed out where this, that, and the other event took place at the crucifixion, and after the resurrection, we think them all conjecture, though quite as likely to be right as wrong; and whether right or wrong, makes no difference whatever, since all interest is concentrated in two and only two localities—namely, the place of crucifixion and the place of burial.

Excavations are now going on near the Damascus gate, under the direction of an officer of the British army, which may throw new light on the question of localities; but until new facts are presented sufficient to destroy a well-defined tradition of only about three hundred years from the time of Jesus to the time of the Empress Helena, and unquestionable historical records from that time until the present, we shall be content, as before stated, to regard the Church of the Holy Sepulchre as containing within its walls the two great landmarks of Christianity—namely, the place of crucifixion and the place of resurrection.

We have neither time nor space at present to present any facts or arguments bearing upon this vexed question of locality, but after a somewhat careful consideration of the subject and an examination of the localities in dispute, we have arrived at the convictions above stated.

CHAPTER III.

IN AND ABOUT JERUSALEM.

AS incidents of travel, we may mention that the first place at which we call, on reaching Jerusalem, is at the office of the American Consul, where we find sixteen letters and three packages of American newspapers awaiting us, and in the reading of which we have a feast such as only a traveler, more than six thousand miles away from home and without news from there for a month, can appreciate; that our tents are pitched near the Jaffa gate, amid some twenty others, several of which bear the American flag; that on the night following we have a most fearful rain and wind storm, which comes very near overthrowing our tents, and the repetition of which, on the following night, forces us to take shelter in the Russian convent, near by, where we remain until we start for the Jordan and Dead Sea, a few days after; that the number of American travelers now in Jerusalem, and traveling through Syria, is far greater than ever was known before, and far exceeds in number those of any other nation, and who, so far as we have formed their acquaintanceship, are generally such as represent American thrift, enterprise and intelligence.

Next to the Church of the Holy Sepulchre, our steps are naturally directed to the Garden of Gethsemane and the Mount of Olives, than which no two spots about Jerusalem are of greater interest to the Christian traveler.

The Garden of Gethsemane is situated on the easterly side of the Valley of Jehoshaphat, and nearly opposite the St. Stephen's gate. It is enclosed with a high stone wall, and has but one entrance, through a low doorway, near the south-east corner. The enclosure is about one hundred and fifty feet square, and laid out in four plats, each surrounded with a paling fence and tastefully planted with flowers and shrubs. Eight very old olive trees still stand within the enclosure, and the monk, in attendance, says they are of the time of the Saviour, but which one may well be excused for doubting. Around the walls, inside, are praying stations, each designated by a small picture; and at the north-east corner is a small building in which the monks take shelter, in stormy weather, while in the garden. At each of our visits the old monk in attendance kindly gathers for Lily a beautiful bouquet of flowers, and on our last visit he presents her with some bulbous roots from the garden for transplanting in American soil. Should we succeed in having flowers in our home garden from roots taken from the sacred soil of Gethsemane, it will be one of the most interesting souvenirs of our visit to Palestine.

Outside the wall, about ten paces from the doorway, the places are designated where Jesus, John, and Judas stood at the moment of betrayal. This, of course, is merely conjectural, though the faith of some is shown in the fact that when they approach the place they kneel and kiss the central stone, which is supposed to mark the exact spot where the Saviour stood when he said, "Judas, betrayest thou the Son of man with a kiss?"

That these walls enclose a portion of the ground which was known in the days of our Saviour as the Garden of

GARDEN OF GETHSEMANE.

Gethsemane, and that these olive trees have grown up from the roots of the very ones under which he prayed, and where "his sweat was as it were great drops of blood falling down to the ground," we have no doubt. Mr. Wild, a scientific observer, thinks there is nothing unreasonable in imputing an existence of nineteen centuries to these trees. Tradition and history have always been uniform in fixing this as the identical place; and though the Greeks have an enclosure on the other side of the road which they claim (in opposition to the Latins) as the garden, none but themselves give the least credence to the claim.

"This garden of Gethsemane occupies the very spot one's eyes would turn to, looking up from the page of Scripture. It was very near one of the most thronged and busy parts of Jerusalem, and yet it lies so low in the Valley of Jehoshaphat that not a sound from the busy hum of life could have reached its profound depth. On the west, the city walls and the high battlements of the Temple almost overhang the garden, while on the east the still loftier heights of Olivet cast their dark shade over the scene of the divine agony. Fitly had Judas chosen this gloomy scene for the perpetration of his black crime."

We linger long and thoughtfully in this holy and beautiful spot, and endeavor to bring before our mind's eye the agony and shame of the scenes here enacted. Oh what agony of soul was that which could have wrung from the Saviour's lips those sad and solemn words: "My soul is exceeding sorrowful, even unto death!"

"O my Father, if it be possible, let this cup pass from me: nevertheless not as I will, but as thou wilt."

"O my Father, if this cup may not pass away from me, except I drink it, thy will be done."

And then the shame of his betrayal by one who had been called, and loved, and trusted; by one of whom the Saviour had said, "he dippeth his hand with me in the dish," as indicating the greater baseness of the betrayal; by one who could only use that most sacred emblem of love, a kiss, to cover up the perfidy of an act baser and blacker than hell itself!

Leaving Gethsemane, we ascend still eastward a very rough path, until we reach the summit of the Mount of Olives. Here we find a small village called Tur, and several Moslem edifices, one of which covers a rock, in which there is an indentation resembling somewhat the form which a human foot would make in soft clay. This, the monks say, is the imprint of the foot of Jesus as he ascended to heaven; while the Moslems claim, with equal tenacity, that it is none other than the footprint of their own prophet, Mohammed. The Moslems who show us the place seem much impressed with the sacredness of the footprint, and insist that we shall place our own foot upon it, in order, we suppose, to make us more holy in the future. The Empress Helena erected a church upon this spot to commemorate the final ascension of our Lord, though many now think this may not have been the place of final ascension; and the church itself has been superseded by a mosque.

Close by this supposed imprint of a footstep—whether of Jesus, or Mohammed, or neither, the reader can form his own conclusions—there is a high tower or minaret, which we ascend, and from which we have a finer view of Jerusalem and the surrounding country than from any other point. At our feet runs the deep valley of Jehoshaphat, in which the well-cultivated garden-plots, and even the rough stone houses of the natives, look picturesque and beautiful; the wall which surrounds the city can be seen in its entire circuit, and the buildings within the wall—especially the Mosque of Omar, on Mount Moriah —look at this distance ("distance lending enchantment to the view") like a picture set in a frame; away off to the eastward the Dead Sea is plainly visible, while the Valley of the Jordan can be traced for miles above the sea; to the northward, Mount Scopus, where Titus encamped his army prior to his attack upon the doomed city, rises majestically from the deep valley below; while southward the mountains of the desert stretch far away until lost in, or blended with, the final view of the mountains of Moab, beyond the Jordan. Our view from this tower is not our first or last from the Mount of Olives, but it is certainly the most extensive, and, in many respects, the most satisfactory.

There are still some olive trees on the sides and summit of the mount, some of which are very old, and doubtless have sprung up from the roots of those which existed in the days of Jesus. The number then, however, was probably much greater than now, and hence its name.

The Mount of Olives must ever remain a place of peculiar interest to the followers of Jesus. Here it was that the Saviour frequently resorted, alone, or with his disciples, to meditate and pray, after having "taught the people in the temple," and been sorely tried by the waywardness of the Scribes and Pharisees; over this mount his weary footsteps tended as he ofttimes sought the quiet home of Mary, Martha, and Lazarus in the village of Bethany, part-way down on the other side from Jerusalem; it was as he descended this mount, toward Jerusalem, that the "whole multitude of the disciples began to rejoice and praise God with a loud voice for all the mighty works that they had seen, saying, Blessed be the King that cometh in the name of the Lord: peace in heaven and glory in the highest;" it was from this mount that he "beheld the city and wept over it;" and from some place on this mount, near unto Bethany, he left his final blessing and ascended up into heaven.

As to the identity of the Mount of Olives, there never has been and never can be any doubt. It towers heavenward to-day as it did in the days of our Saviour; the rocks are now as then, and as we tread its sacred soil and gaze from its summit, we cannot but feel that we may be treading the very path, and gazing at the very objects, on which he trod and gazed. God made Mount Olivet!—man built Jerusalem; and though the latter may be torn down and rebuilt a thousand times, until the exact locality of every sacred place within its walls may become a question of doubt, the former must for ever remain as a witness to the goodness, and power, and glory of a risen Redeemer.

A little below and on the opposite side of the road from the Garden of Gethsemane, in descending Mount Olivet, we reach the "Tomb and Chapel of the Virgin." The structure is of considerable size and looks ancient. We reach its front by a long flight of steps from the road, and then, after entering, we descend another long flight of steps to the chapel. About half-way down the inner flight of steps two recesses are pointed out—one on either side—the one is said to be the tomb of Joachim and Anne, the father and mother of Mary, and the other that of her husband, Joseph. There are altars in both of these niches, with the usual surroundings of gauze and tinsel.

The chapel itself, which is hewn in the rock, is some thirty feet or more below the level of the surrounding earth, and probably sixty feet square. Numerous lamps are suspended from the ceiling—some of which are of gold and silver, and very handsome—while pictures and damask surround the walls. The tomb of the Virgin rises from the floor of the chapel, a little to the right of the main entrance. It is probably ten feet square, and is said to be cut out of the solid rock. At each side and behind the tomb a small portion of the rock is left exposed, which pilgrims may kiss; all the other portions are covered with thin marble slabs, and the front is quite handsomely ornamented.

That the body of the Virgin was ever laid in this tomb is questionable; but as no other tomb is pointed out, it is as well perhaps to give credit to the belief. According to the Church of Rome, it was from this identical spot that the assumption of the Virgin took place.

A little to the east of this is another chapel or grotto, in which the Greeks locate the Passion of the garden. Here is also an excavation in the rock, though not so large or so well finished as the first. The old monk who shows us about this place seems impressed with the sanctity of the spot, and lights candles at the altar for our special benefit. Of course, he expects and receives, bucksheesh for his trouble, though not probably impressed with the "soundness" of our faith.

Passing over the dry bed of the Brook Kedron, and up the steep hill which leads to St. Stephen's Gate, we are shown the spot, where, it is said, St. Stephen suffered martyrdom, and "fell asleep," while calling upon the Lord "not to lay this sin to their charge." The spot is marked by a large limestone rock on the roadside, through which red veins are visible, and, strange to say, there are some who believe these veins were caused by the blood of the martyr.

Entering the city by St. Stephen's Gate, we find ourselves upon what is known as the Via Doloroso, the road by which Christ was led to crucifixion. A little within the gate, on the left of the street, Pilate's house is pointed out, or, rather, the site on which it stood, as the present structure is used for soldiers' barracks. Pilate's house, as such, possesses no interest whatever; but Pilate's house, as the place to which Jesus was led, and in which he had his mock trial and final sentence, and from which he was finally led to crucifixion, possesses great interest.

A little further on we reach the "Church of Flagellation." This we enter and examine with some care and interest. The record says that from the presence of Pilate "the soldiers led him away into the hall called Prætorium," where, after offering him other indignities, they "smote him on the head with a reed, and did spit upon him, and, bowing their knees, worshiped him." This hall was doubtless near and, possibly, a part of Pilate's house ; and as the Church of the Flagellation is situated directly opposite Pilate's house, both of which may, at one time, have been connected or had an arched passage-way over the street from one to the other, we see no reason to doubt the identity of its location.

A little further on we reach a high arch, built over the street, called the "Ecce Homo." Above the arch is a room, from which a window looks out upon the street. Tradition has fixed upon this as the place from which Pilate presented Jesus, wearing the crown of thorns and purple robe, with the words, "Behold the man!" though but a moment before he had said to that same bloodthirsty multitude, "Behold, I bring him forth to you, that you may know that I find no fault in him." This arch is very quaint and old, and looks as though it might have stood from the days of Noah.

On the same street, and not far from the Ecce Homo arch, the places are pointed out where Christ fell while bearing his own cross; and a little way from this, at a bend in the street, the spot is marked where Simon the Cyrenian was compelled to take the cross from the shoulders of Christ, and bear it himself to the Hill of Calvary.

Next we are shown the spot where Lazarus lay while the dogs "licked his sores," and not far from this the house of Dives, "the rich man," who, when he lifted up his eyes in hell, only asked that Lazarus might be sent to dip the tip of his finger in water to cool his tongue, as he was in torment. Nothing, perhaps, in or about Jerusalem proves more strikingly the lengths to which monkish superstition has been carried than the fixing of these localities, as it is evident from the record that Christ only intended what he said as a parable by which to illustrate a great principle.

Next to this, the house of Veronica is pointed out, who, according to monkish tradition, handed Jesus a handkerchief to wipe the sweat and blood from his face as he passed her door, and on the return of which the impress of his features was fixed upon it. This handkerchief, it is pretended, is still kept in St. Peter's Church at Rome, and such is its sanctity that it is only exhibited on great Church festivals.

This closes the noted places on the *Via Doloroso*, but there are several others within the walls of the city which may be visited; and as we are disposed to see everything which has been, or can be, seen by any one else, of course we visit them.

The supposed site of the Virgin Mary's residence, where she lived and where she died, is upon a narrow street near the Armenian convent. The present structure has nothing about it to attract special attention.

The Armenian convent chapel—which is said to have been the residence of the high-priest Caiaphas—contains two relics which are held in high repute, viz.: the stone which closed the door of the Holy Sepulchre, and the stone on which the cock crew when Peter denied his Master. Here, also, is shown a small room or closet which is called Christ's prison, in which it is said the Saviour was confined while awaiting the action of the high-priest. Visitors are permitted to enter this little room, which is tastefully fitted up with altar, lamps, etc. The stone of the sepulchre forms the principal altar of the chapel; it is so covered up, however, that but little of it can be seen—only two small kissing-places. The altar of St. Peter, where the cock crew, is outside of the chapel and at one side of the inner area, and near it are the tombs of an Armenian bishop and several priests.

While within this chapel we notice two very old books, written in Coptic, lying on a stool, which we take the liberty of examining. At this the old priest in attendance becomes very indignant, and splutters around at a fearful rate, though he mollifies completely when, on leaving, we hand him some bucksheesh.

The Armenian convent itself is a very large building, and capable, it is said, of accommodating over three thousand pilgrims. The gardens of the convent on the opposite side of the street are quite extensive, and cultivated with much care. Near this is the English hospital and dispensary, and the residence of the English physician.

CHAPTER IV.

PAST AND PRESENT OF THE HOLY CITY.

SIGHT-SEEING in and about Jerusalem is quite as wearisome as in any other part of the Old World. If you go on foot, you are constantly annoyed by the bad walking and the filthy streets, and in danger of breaking your neck or being run over by the crowd; and if you go on horseback, the danger is scarcely less, while the getting off and on your horse so frequently is difficult and troublesome. We have horses constantly at our disposal, and try both plans from day to day, as inclination suggests.

Thrice we make the circuit of the walls of the city, and examine each gate with special care. The walls are high and strong, and in several places they are built upon natural rock foundations. They ascend and descend with the slopes of the hills and valleys, and the passage around them is not without difficulty, because of the roughness, and in many places the steepness, of the path.

Ancient Jerusalem was built upon several hills, the names of which must be familiar to every reader: they are easily distinguishable, though the natural surface has undergone great changes. We learn from Josephus that some of these elevations were cut down and the valleys between them filled up by the Asmonean kings; whilst the decay of ancient buildings and the accumulation of rubbish through so many ages have probably done yet more to encumber and conceal the original features of the site. The present town is full of inequalities; you are ever ascending or descending; there are no level streets; and houses are built upon mountains of rubbish, which are probably twenty, thirty, or fifty feet above the original soil.

On the easterly side of the walls the Valley of Jehoshaphat slopes down to a great depth. On the westerly side of this valley, near the wall, is the Moslem burying-place, in which are a great number of roughly-built tombs. On the easterly side is the burial-place of the Jews, and here we notice hundreds, if not thousands, of tombs with Hebrew inscriptions. Devout Jews from all parts of the world come to Jerusalem to end their days, that their bones may rest in this, to them, sacred valley.

Both Jews and Moslems believe that the scene of the Last Judgment Day will take place in this valley; and the Moslems point out the identical stone (jutting out somewhat from the city walls, and near the Mosque of Omar) on which they say their Prophet will sit to judge the people of the whole earth.

But we will return to our description of "Holy Places" within and without the city walls. The next place we visit is the "Cœnaculum," which is situated on the Hill of Zion, and is said to contain the tomb of David and the "large upper room" in which Christ instituted the Last Supper. This room, upon the second story of the building, is large and dingy, with columns in the centre and arches running therefrom to form the roof, and has nothing ancient about it, except some of the materials with which it is constructed. The columns vary in style and age, and the same is true of the stones of the arches

VALLEY OF JEHOSAPHAT.

and walls. It is evident, at a glance, that the building is of Moslem construction, formed of materials gathered from ancient structures. That these columns, and some of the stones in the arches and walls, once constituted a part of the building in which was located the "large upper room," may be possible; and since tradition has fixed upon this as the site of the building, and none other is pointed out, we are content to believe it.

The tomb of David is said to be underneath the building, to which a stairway leads from this upper room. This the Moslems consider too sacred for Christian eyes. We make a movement as if to go down the stairway, at which the Moslem guards present raise such a hullabaloo that we have to desist, nor would the offer of any amount of bucksheesh change them. Had a half-dozen other Americans been present, each with a revolver in hand, we should have liked to force our passage to the tomb, and laughed at the guards in their efforts to prevent us. That such miserable fallaheen, backed only by a government the weakest and meanest on earth, should forbid the entrance of a Christian (only because he is such) to any place of biblical interest, is a disgrace to the civilization of the age; and the Christian nations of the earth owe it to themselves to correct this state of things, either by diplomacy or the sword, at the earliest possible moment. The Turkish government should be offered the alternative —either free access for persons of every clime and every creed to every place of biblical interest in Palestine, or utter extinction as a government; and if they did not speedily accept the first, the second should be applied without hesitation or delay. While we would not interfere with the Moslem's faith, we have no patience with his bigoted exclusiveness, especially in matters relating to holy places, nor would we suffer it an hour had we the power to change it—peaceably if we could, forcibly if we must.

The Jews' Wailing-place next demands our attention. This is a small street, or court, alongside a part of the original wall of the Temple of Solomon. We examine this wall with care, and from the size and character of the stones, differing entirely from any other parts of the wall, we have no doubt of its being a part of the old wall of the temple.

On Friday of each week the Jews of Jerusalem assemble here in great numbers to lament over the destruction of the temple and to pray for its speedy restoration. The stones are worn smooth with their tears and kisses. It is the nearest approach to Mount Moriah, upon which the temple stood, and where the Mosque of Omar now stands, that the Jews are permitted to make.

We could not be there on a Friday on account of other engagements; but while there, on another day of the week, we witnessed the bewailings of some, who, regardless of the day, offer up continual supplication for the return of their ancient glory as a people.

It is a very sad sight, and one that we should not care again to witness. To see the representatives of a people once so glorious, and once the possessors and rulers of this land, now so abject and down-trodden that only by permission dare they lift their eyes toward the outer walls of their once glorious temple; to see them weeping and wailing over their departed glory, and with agony of soul beseeching the God of their fathers to return to them once more; to see them contemned, and buffeted, and spit upon, even by the half-civilized Moslem, in their own city of David; to see them crouching along the street, and crawling as it were amidst the shadows of their rulers and oppressors; and to know that not only in Jerusalem and throughout Palestine, but everywhere throughout the civilized globe, this people, once the chosen of God, are now wanderers and sojourners on the earth, without a distinct nationality and without a Redeemer,—oh! who can but pity and sympathize with them in their hard affliction?

"Were I asked," says one writer, "what was the object of the greatest interest that I had seen, and the spectacle that made the deepest impression upon me, during my sojourn in other lands, I would say, that it was a Jew mourning over the stones of Jerusalem."

> "Oh! weep for those that wept by Babel's stream,
> Whose shrines are desolate, whose land a dream;
> Weep for the harp of Judah's broken shell;
> Mourn—where their God hath dwelt, the godless dwell!"

But God is merciful as well as just, and in due time he will bring even this people within the pale of Christianity. The English mission to the Jews which is located at Jerusalem is doing a good work, and converts are constantly being added; and a large hospital has recently been erected, through the munificence of a gentleman of New Orleans, for their special accommodation.

From the Jews' Wailing-place we go to another portion of the old wall, or rather to a portion of an old arch connected with the wall, now called "Robinson's Arch," so named in honor of the man who first noted and described it in 1842. The stones which remain of this arch are immense. We measure two, and find one to be twenty and a half feet long by three and a half feet in thickness, and another twenty-four feet in length by five and a half feet in thickness. Their breadth, of course, we could not measure. There are others of equal size, but these are the only ones convenient for measurement.

In the works of Josephus, there is a great bridge described as connecting the palace of Solomon, on Mount Zion, with the temple on Mount Moriah, and these stones are, no doubt, a part of the archway of this bridge. The size, situation, and general appearance of the stones render this conclusion inevitable.

Continuing our course toward the Zion gate, we soon reach the long row of low stone huts, near the gate, specially assigned as the residence of lepers. These poor creatures are not permitted to live in any other part of the city, and can scarcely be said to " live" here. We had seen them before as beggars by the roadside, but did not realize their abject, utter poverty until seeing the hovels in which they are compelled to live. These lepers intermarry only with each other, and as the disease is hereditary and must increase by each subsequent transmission, the wonder is that they have not long since all died out.

While looking at these voiceless, toothless creatures, with outstretched hands, from which a part, and, in some cases, all the fingers have dropped off, we cannot but wonder which, if any of them, are the legitimate descendants of the ten who, when they saw Jesus, lifted up their voices and said, "Jesus, Master, have mercy on us," and to whom the Saviour replied, " Go show yourselves unto the priests. And it came to pass that as they went they were cleansed."

The pools and fountains of Jerusalem which we visit at different times, and some of them again and again, next demand description at our hands.

Passing out of St Stephen's gate, on our right hand,

near but within the gate, are the remains of the pool of Bethesda. In the days of our Saviour this pool was probably covered with a beautiful structure, as St. John describes it as having "five porches," in which "lay a multitude of impotent folk, of blind, halt, withered, waiting for the moving of the water."

Now it has no covering, and its waters are no longer sought by the sick or well. It is about three hundred and fifty feet in length, one hundred and fifty feet in width, and contains but little water, and even this little is not used for any purpose.

Here it was that Jesus saw and had pity on the man who had had an infirmity thirty-and-eight years, and to whom he said, "Rise, take up thy bed and walk!"

Farther down the side of the valley is the "Fountain of the Virgin." We reach the fountain by descending a long flight of steps running under the hill. Its name is derived from a tradition that when the Virgin Mary was accused of adultery, she established her innocence by drinking of the waters of this fountain, there being a tradition then, as now, that any one guilty of adultery who drank of this fountain would immediately die. This fountain is connected by a subterranean passage with the Pool of Siloam, some thousand feet or more down the valley. Of its great antiquity there can be no doubt. Its waters are used by such of the natives as live near it, nor do they seem to have any fears of drinking it, whether adulterers or otherwise.

"The Fountain of the Virgin," says Schubert, "is a deep excavation in the solid rock, into which one descends by two successive flights of steps. The water flows hence by a subterraneous passage under the hill Ophel to the Pool of Siloam; but whence does the pool itself derive its supply? The oft-repeated quotation,

"Siloa's brook that flowed
Fast by the Oracle of God,"

is hardly consistent with the idea that the head of the stream should be so remote from the temple as is this fountain; but there is a tradition among the inhabitants of the neighborhood that the latter is connected by an artificial channel with a well placed within the enclosure of the Mosque of Omar. Mr. Wilde even gives the dimensions of the passage, though it does not appear he himself explored it. He rests his proof of its existence on a story current in Jerusalem that the rebellion of that city against Ibrahim Pasha was begun by the Arabs of Siloam, who made their way into the interior by creeping through this subterraneous conduit. The fact may have been so, and less likely tales figure unquestioned in grave histories; but we have heard another solution of the mystery. The governor of Jerusalem at the time the rebellion broke out was the son of the Sheikh of Siloam; he probably left one of the gates open to his father's tribe, and then set the story afloat to cover his own treason."

The Pool of Siloam, as before stated, is some thousand feet or more farther down the Valley of Jehoshaphat. It was once probably covered with a beautiful building, as several columns are still lying about it. It is, at present, entirely open and only walled up with rough stone. It is about fifty feet long by twenty in width, and has a large supply of water. Its waters are cool and palatable. On one of our visits we dismount and bathe our eyes and forehead in its soft waters, and, though not blind, we feel refreshed from its effects.

Here it was that Jesus ordered the blind man to bathe his eyes, after he had applied the clay and spittle unto them; and "he went his way and washed and came seeing."

Dr. Robinson, in describing the lower Pool of Siloam, says: "The water has a peculiar taste, sweetish and very slightly brackish, but not disagreeable. A very remarkable circumstance is related of this pool and fountain : It is reported that the water in them is subject to a daily tide ; and by some writers it is stated to ebb and flow under lunar influence. A woman of Siloam, who was accustomed to frequent the place every day, informed us that the flowing of the water occurs at irregular intervals, sometimes two or three times a day, and sometimes in summer once in two or three days. She said she had seen the fountain dry, and men and flocks, dependent on it, gathered round and suffering from thirst, when all at once the water would begin to boil up from under the steps, and (as she said) from the bottom in the interior part, and flow off in a copious stream.

"In order to account for this irregularity, the common people say that a great dragon lies within the fountain ; when he is awake he stops the water—when he sleeps it flows. So much for Arab philosophy ; that of the West has been exhausted upon ingenious arguments to account for this extraordinary phenomenon, the wonder and the admiration of the pilgrim and the traveler. After all, the simple explanation offered by Mr. Wilde is very probably the true one : The stream or outlet from the lower pool is conducted by artificial channels through the gardens and parterres that lie immediately beneath it in the valley ; and it is the chief source of their fertility. Now, as there is little water in the pool during the dry season, the Arabs dam up the several streams in order to collect a sufficient quantity in small ponds adjoining each garden ; and this they must all do at the same time, or there would be an unfair division of the fertilizing fluid. These dams are generally made in the evening, and the water is drawn off in the morning or sometimes two or three times a day; and thus the opening and closing of the dams produce the appearance of an ebb and flow in the fountains."

That portion of the valley of Jehoshaphat in which the Pool of Siloam is situated is sometimes called the Valley of Siloam, and on the easterly side of the valley is a small, miserably built, and no less miserably tenanted, village, which is also called Siloam. This village is located on the side of a steep hill, and many of its dwellings are grottoes or catacombs, which were formerly occupied as burial-places. While passing this village and clambering around and among its ancient tombs, we observe a good many savage scowls, both from men and women, but these persons make no attempt to molest us, and we pay no heed to their frowns. All travelers, however, do not get through this village so comfortably; and the experience which one gives is so strikingly descriptive and amusing that we cannot refrain from quoting it.

He says: "Proceeding onward through the valley, we found the whole face of the precipitous rock, upon its eastern side, excavated into one vast and almost continuous catacomb, consisting of chambers of various sizes. Some of them were simple square apartments, formed to contain a single corpse, and closed by a stone door fitted into a groove round the entrance so accurate that a seal might have been applied at the joining to secure the sepulchre; and the first of them I visited at once explained to me the form of the tomb of the Arimathean nobleman. The sepulchral grots are continued all down the valley of Siloam, having galleries, stairs, and small terraces cut out of the rock, leading from one to the other. They are all now inhabited, and they, with some mud-built huts at the bottom of the valley, constitute the village of Siloam, which contains upward of fifteen hundred Arabs—a vicious, quarrelsome, and dishonest set of people, and noted for such propensities for centuries past. On my first visit to this place, happening to poke my head into one of the cryptæ, I was startled not a little by the wild, unearthly scream of an old Arab crone who inhabited the interior. The noise she made became the signal for a general outcry; the dwellers in the different caves popped their heads out from their holes like so many beavers reconnoitering an enemy; the children ran shouting in all directions; curses fell fast and heavy on the Giaour and Nazarene; and had I got into the harem of the pasha the alarm could not have been greater than that which I excited among the whole troglodyte population of this cemetery of the living. I made a hasty retreat amidst the general uproar, and took good care never to venture again so far upon a tomb-hunting expedition into Siloam."

There is within the city walls a large body of water, which our guide points out to us as the " Pool of Hezekiah;" but from its location, muddy appearance, and the fact of its being entirely surrounded by houses, we should rather think it was prepared to serve the purpose of a large reservoir for the rain-water which falls from the surrounding houses. It may, however, be the remains of the pool which King Hezekiah constructed when, as we are told, he brought water into the city by stopping the upper water-course of Gihon.

There are still two other pools outside of the walls and up the valley of Gihon, known as the Upper and Lower Pool of Gihon. The former is of considerable size, walled up with rough stones, and doubtless very ancient; the latter, lower down the valley, is interesting as marking the place where " it came to pass in an eventide that

David arose from off his bed and walked upon the roof of the king's house; and from the roof he saw a woman washing herself; and the woman was very beautiful to look upon." This woman was Bathsheba, the wife of Uriah the Hittite, and she through the perfidiousness of David, subsequently became his wife, and the mother of Solomon. At the time David first saw her she was bathing in this Lower Pool of Gihon. Not far from this is the Potter's Field, where Judas went and hanged himself.

Notwithstanding the fountains and pools mentioned, Jerusalem is now, and doubtless always has been, very poorly supplied with water. The inhabitants within the walls depend mainly upon their cisterns of rain-water, caught during the rainy season. Skillful engineering and a comparatively small outlay would bring the sweet and abundant waters of the Pools of Solomon into every dwelling of the city, but it is not at all probable that this will ever be done while Jerusalem remains under its present rulers.

It is a bright and beautiful morning as we mount our horses to ride to the Tombs of the Kings, the Tombs of the Judges, and the Tombs of the Prophets.

We have examined the beautiful tomb of Absalom, situated far down in the Valley of Jehoshaphat, and marked the heap of small stones around its base, one of which has been thrown by every passing Jew and Moslem, as showing their contempt of a son who would rebel against his father; we have seen the tombs of Jehoshaphat and St. James immediately beside that of Absalom; the open tomb of Zacharias in the hillside, northward of the city wall; and the scores of other open nameless tombs, hewn in the rocks around and about Jerusalem; and now we propose to visit the more extensive ones of the Kings, the Judges, and the Prophets.

A ride of about an hour, over a rough and stony path, brings us to the Tombs of the Kings. Following a path down the side of a rock, and entering a doorway cut through the rock, we find ourselves in an open area of probably fifty feet square. From one side of this is the entrance to the tombs, and, lighting our candles, we explore them thoroughly. They consist of several small chambers, hewn in the rock, from which other and still smaller chambers run off at different points. The walls are rough, without sculpture or finish of any kind; and in comparison to the tombs we saw in Egypt, these are hardly worth looking at.

Though this is known as the Tomb or Tombs of the Kings, it is now generally conceded that the bones of no king or kings ever rested within its walls; but that it was built for Helena, the widow of Monobazus, king of Adiabena, who died in Jerusalem in the reign of Claudius Cæsar.

We next ride to the Tombs of the Judges, some distance to the westward. This is more extensive and upon a better plan than the other, having rows of niches for bodies in the sides of the larger rooms. The fact that there are about seventy of these niches has induced the belief that it was built for the seventy Judges of the Sanhedrim, though beyond this there is no proof whatever that it was ever used for such a purpose. There is no sculpture or inscription of any kind within the tomb, and the sculpture over the outside entrance is merely fanciful.

Next we direct our course to the Tombs of the Prophets, to reach which we have a long and tedious ride over stony fields, down the steep slopes of the Valley of

Jehoshaphat, along the valley, and up the steep and stony path nearly to the top of the Mount of Olives. We find the opening of the tomb on the side of a grassy mound, in an unfenced field, and, but for our guide, we certainly would never have found it at all.

Crawling through a small hole, we find ourselves in a good-sized chamber, to which light and air are admitted from a hole above. From this chamber a semi-circular passage-way runs off for a long distance, and other passage-ways cross and recross this at different points. We can easily understand how one might get confused and lost in traversing these irregular passage-ways, and yet the tomb is not so extensive but that a loud call can be heard in any part of it. The chambers are irregular and small; no sculpture or inscription of any kind marks its walls; everything about the tomb is rude and unfinished; and, but for its curious construction and size, it would hardly be worth a visit—especially to persons who had previously seen the extensive and well-finished tombs of Upper Egypt.

Though these are called the Tombs of the Prophets, there is no evidence whatever to show that a single prophet was ever buried within them; and in the absence of any such proof, neither of the tombs mentioned possess even a historical, much less a biblical, interest.

We have yet to describe the Mosque of Omar, which of itself has no interest to the Christian reader; but, standing as it does upon the site, and indeed upon part of the very foundations, of Solomon's Temple, it possesses much interest. Formerly, this was forbidden ground to Christians, but now it is open to any one who is willing to pay a liberal bucksheesh—about one dollar each—to those who have it in charge. We visit it on our fourth day in Jerusalem, and note carefully every part and

MOSQUE OF OMAR

Past and Present of the Holy City. 91.

parcel of the grounds and buildings; but only in such parts as were probably connected with the temple, do we feel any sort of interest.

This is undoubtedly the Mount Moriah on which the temple stood; and the identical "threshing-floor" for which David gave the "fifty shekels of silver." Here stood the wonderful temple built by King Solomon to the glory of the Great Jehovah, and just here was the "veil of the temple rent" when Jesus gave up the ghost! The enclosure, surrounded by the city walls on the outside and a corresponding wall within, is said to be about one thousand five hundred feet in length by one thousand in breadth. Near the centre stands the Mosque of Omar, and southward from this is the Mosque of El Aksa. Both are fitted up in the usual Moslem style, with marble floors, stained-glass windows, and Arabic gewgaws. In the centre of the first is a very large natural rock, called by the Moslems Es Sukhrah, in which they show the footprint of Mohammed as he mounted to heaven. By many, this rock is believed to have been in the old temple, and to have constituted what was known as the "Holy of Holies." The fact that a subterranean passage leads from underneath this rock to the Valley of Jehoshaphat, would seem to indicate that it was the rock, or altar, on which the sacrifices were made, and that this passage-way was intended to carry off the blood and offal.

In the Mosque of El Aksa are several old columns, which were probably parts of the temple. Two of these stand pretty close together, and the Moslems say that only those who can pass between these columns ever reach heaven. We have considerable sport in trying the experiment, and find that every one of our company can squeeze through, except the old sheikh (our conductor), who, being very corpulent, will not try it.

But the part which interests us most is the immense subterranean archways, underneath the surface of the ground not now built upon. We have some difficulty in getting down to these through a hole near the outer wall, but, once here, the view is grand and imposing—arch after arch, and passage-way after passage-way can be seen for a great distance. That these were a part of the old temple we have no doubt whatever. The Golden Gate is also shown, but its identity is very questionable.

Thus we finish our description of Jerusalem and its surroundings, and to-morrow we shall start for the Jordan and Dead Sea.

CHAPTER V.

OFF FOR THE JORDAN AND DEAD SEA.

"IS everything ready for a start, Mohammed?"
"Ready, sir."
"Have you seen that the canteen and tents are properly packed and well secured on the baggage mules, and are they, too, ready to start?"
"Everything is ready, sir."
"Then lead off for the Jordan by the way of Bethany and Jericho."

Mohammed is a faithful servant and a passably good dragoman when he is in his "right mind;" but he will drink to excess when he gets in "coffee-shops" and among his fellow-dragomen, and only yesterday we were obliged to give him a severe horse-whipping, in front of our own tent, and in the presence of other dragomen and scores of lookers-on, because, being drunk, he was insolent and refused to obey us.

It was something new in Syria to see a *Howajji* flog his own dragoman, and the lookers-on seemed astounded and paralyzed at the sight, but it taught him and them a lesson which they will not soon forget, viz.: that an American traveler will not take insolence nor suffer disobedience, even from a dragoman, with all his fine dress and lordly pretensions. Since then he has been a much wiser and a much better man.

But others of our company have gone on, and our Bedouin sheikh, on his beautiful Arab mare, is eager to be off, so now we must away to the Jordan.

Passing around the northern wall of the city, by the Damascus gate, deep down in the Valley of Jehoshaphat, up a rugged path, we find ourselves upon the summit of Mount Olivet, and our eyes are again wandering over the mysterious city, and the hills and the valleys around and about it. We say mysterious, for on all this wide earth there is not a city with such a strange and eventful history, nor one which, having been so nearly exalted to heaven, is now so nearly cast down to hell.

Passing through the narrow, dirty streets of the village on the top of Olivet, we soon emerge on the other side, and from this point we have another very distinct view of the Dead Sea. It seems but a little way off, only over the next hill-top, and no one would hesitate to say (without a knowledge of the facts in the case) that he could reach it in a half hour's ride, and yet it will take some seven or eight hours of hard riding before it can be reached. So rarefied is the air of this country that distances are very deceptive, and woe be to him who attempts to measure his footsteps with his eye!

Another half hour's ride over a descending and very stony path brings us to the village of Bethany, and close along the roadside we find the tomb of Lazarus.

The village itself is now miserable and dirty, like all the Arab villages of Palestine; but its beautiful situation on the easterly slope of Mount Olivet, and its surroundings of olive, pomegranate, fig, and almond trees, show that it may at one time have been a most delightful place of residence and rest.

To reach the tomb of Lazarus we enter a narrow doorway, formed by the piling up of rude stones, and descend twenty-six steps, which brings us to a chamber about eleven feet by nine in size, and about twenty feet below the level of the doorstep. This is the reputed tomb of Lazarus. Through a small doorway at the side of this chamber we descend another short flight of steps, and reach another chamber about the same size as the first. This is said to be the tomb of Mary and Martha, the sisters of Lazarus.

Both these chambers are hewn from the rock, as is also a part of the steps leading thereto, but all is rough, rugged, and dismal. The Moslem villagers who have charge of the tomb only take such care of it as the bucksheesh of travelers induces them to do. How it came to pass that the Empress Helena did not have a church erected over this tomb, as she did over so many other places of less biblical interest, is a wonder to us.

It was here at Bethany that Mary "anointed the Lord with ointment, and wiped his feet with her hair;" here it was that Jesus often repaired to rest for a while amid the companionship of friends, and to commune with those who loved him for his very work's sake; here it was that he cursed the fruitless fig tree and it withered at his word; here it was that "Jesus wept," and here it was that he spoke with a "loud voice," which was heard even unto the spirit land, and said, "Lazarus, come forth." "And he that was dead came forth, bound hand and foot with grave-clothes," when Jesus added, "Loose him, and let him go."

Did time permit, we could linger long and thoughtfully in this sacred place, every stone of which has been made holy by the Saviour's presence; but we must again remount and away for Jericho and the Jordan.

The road from Bethany to Jericho is terrible, horrible, indescribable. Down, down, down paths of rock where you would hardly believe a gazelle could go without breaking its neck, and up paths scarcely less difficult. There is much more going down than up, however, from Jerusalem to Jordan, as the latter lies about four thousand feet below the former.

These bleak mountains and barren valleys constitute the "wilderness" in which Jesus wandered for forty days and forty nights; and just before reaching Jericho our guide points out an exceedingly high mountain, which has the reputation of being the place from which the devil showed Jesus all the "kingdoms of the world and the glory of them," all of which he offered the Saviour if he would but fall down and worship him.

Time and patience, it is said, accomplish all things, and so it proves in this case, for ere the sun has set we see from the mountain side our tents pitched on the plain of the Jordan near Jericho, and thither we hasten, though not without first making a detour of a mile to visit the "Fountain of Elisha," the waters of which, it is said, Elisha "healed" by changing its bitter to sweet. This is indeed a noble spring, bursting out from the base of the mountain in great quantity, and we can attest to the sweetness of its waters now from frequent and copious draughts.

Ancient Jericho, it is thought, stood near this spring, and was a city of much renown in the days of our Saviour. The present Jericho, called by the natives El Riha, is one of the most miserable and filthy of Arab villages, and has nothing about it to interest a traveler.

Our tents are pitched near the village burial-place, and just as we arrive the natives are engaged in committing one of their number to his mother dust. We dismount and draw near to witness the ceremonies of an Arab funeral. Two men are digging the grave, and probably twenty others are standing around giving directions, sometimes in a loud and almost querulous voice; a little way off the corpse lies on the ground wrapped up in a white muslin shroud, tied at the head and feet; and not far from this sit probably fifty women on the ground, some bemoaning in a loud voice, while others seem to be comforting them. Occasionally ten or a dozen of the younger women form a ring and dance around probably a sister of the deceased, uttering meanwhile a dolorous song.

While they are digging the grave we notice no less than six human skulls, with a corresponding number of other bones of the body, thrown out with the dirt at the side of the grave.

When all is ready, several men pick up the dead body and carry it to the grave, in which they lay it upon its side, with the face turned toward Mecca. Stones are then fitted around and above the body, and these are covered over with mortar and dirt; then the bones which are taken out are thrown in, and finally every man present, with his hand or foot, scrapes in dirt until the hole is filled up. Stones are set at the head and foot, upon which one of the men pours a little powder and rubs it with spittle until a black mark is left upon each. The significance of this we do not understand, though it doubtless means something. The men keep up a sort of chant while all this is being done, and, in conclusion, all the men approach and salute two of the men present, probably brothers of the deceased, by pressing their own foreheads against those of the brothers, twice in succession. The women, during the burial, continue seated on the ground some distance off, and at no time do they approach the grave. One old woman, probably the mother of the deceased, when the men are gone away, crawls upon her hands and knees to the foot of the grave, and with uplifted hands and streaming eyes bemoans the loss of her darling boy. This is the saddest sight of the whole proceeding, and in witnessing it our own eyes are made to weep. Miserably poor and degraded as she is, she still loves her darling boy, and bemoans his loss with all of a mother's love.

Standing near the grave while the grave-diggers are doing their work, some ask us for bucksheesh and others for tobacco. We give of both—of the latter all we have in our pouch, and think nothing more of it; but when we get back to our tents and feel in our side coat-pocket for our rubber tobacco-pouch and handkerchief, we find them both missing. Not content with what we had given them, these rascals had stolen both our tobacco-pouch and handkerchief while we were standing among them at the grave-side—thus illustrating in our own case what Christ had said of the man who went down to Jericho and fell among thieves. Our conclusions are that the Jerichoians of to-day are no better than they were in the days of our Saviour; and perhaps they are even worse, since it is not reported of that man that he was attending a funeral at the time he was robbed.

In the Old Testament Scriptures, Jericho is frequently mentioned as one of the cities with which the ancient Israelites had much to do. It was by Jericho that Joshua saw and communed with the "Captain of the hosts of the Lord;" it was the walls of this city which fell at the blowing of the trumpets of rams' horns; and it was here, too, that the blind Bartimeus sat by the wayside begging, and when hearing that Jesus of Nazareth passeth by, he cried out, "Jesus, thou son of David, have mercy on me!" and received the answer, "Go thy way; thy faith hath made thee whole."

Next morning, bright and early, we start for the Jordan, and about one hour's ride over the level plain brings us to the banks of that sacred stream, at the point where its waters were thrice divided—once to permit the children of Israel to pass over to the promised land, once at the command of Elijah, and again at the command of Elisha; and at the point, too, where Jesus was baptized of John, when "there came a voice from heaven, saying, Thou art my beloved Son, in whom I am well pleased."

Shortly after reaching its banks, Lily, Lu, and myself all bathe in its waters, and feel greatly refreshed therefrom.

The width of the Jordan at this point, and at this time, March 28, is not over one hundred feet, though during the rainy season, when its waters are swollen, it is much wider. Its waters are very muddy—so much so that where it enters the Dead Sea, a few miles below, the color of its water can be distinctly traced for a long distance before its final intermixture with the deep, dark, beautiful blue waters of the sea. Its length is said to be about two hundred miles, and its fall, within a distance of eighty miles, exceeds one thousand three hundred feet. The rapidity of the fall and the clayey soil through which it passes account for its turbid, yellow appearance. Aside from its biblical associations, it is not a stream that would excite any interest in any country.

It is not our good fortune to have so timed our visit as to be present at the great baptismal ceremony which takes place every Easter; we must, therefore, be content, for the reader's sake, to borrow from others a description of this strange spectacle. Fancy, then, a vast encampment thronged with thousands of pilgrims of all ages and sexes, a bewildering medley of strange tongues and costumes. The order having been given to march from the encampment near Jericho two hours before sunrise, soon after three o'clock the camp is all bustle and confusion, and the beacons of bitumen are seen slowly moving toward the river.

The river forms an angle at the bathing-place, and has its bank covered with long coarse grass, tall reeds, willows, oleanders, tamarisks, and low brushwood. The width at this point may be about thirty-five yards, and when the stream is somewhat swollen, as is usual about Easter, it runs with the precipitous fury of a rapid. The bank in some places is steep, shelving off abruptly to deep water. The first who prepares himself is a Russian, with hair of enormous length, who, having stripped and enveloped himself in a long new shirt, drops carefully in; and, holding on to the grass, dips and shakes himself, and dips again, much after the manner of a duck that presages wet weather.

The baptismal robe worn on this occasion is preserved by each pilgrim to be used as his winding-sheet; and they believe that if they are cast into hell, it will not catch fire.

The sun, says another eye-witness, has risen over the tops of Abarim, and the river bank presents one of the most *unprejudiced* scenes which it has ever been my lot to witness. The main body of the pilgrims have arrived, and a general undressing commences. There are men of all sizes and climes, from the tottering octogenarian to the crawling bambino, who, being immersed with its head back and its mouth open, fills and bubbles like a bottle: ladies of all ages and angles, colors and calibres, from the Caireen Copt to the fair-skinned Russian. Of the men, some creep cautiously in, and reflect a moment before they go under; others leap, spinning in like wheels, and, returning to the land, repeat again and again the same performance. Of the lovelier creatures, some bounce dauntless in, and, holding fast between two men, are well ducked, and come smiling out again; others go in delicately, and, standing ankle-deep in mud upon the brink, are baptized with basins full of the sacred stream. Nor is it enough that their bodies are consecrated—all their clothes are plunged, and they drink the unconscious element, not each out of his or her own hands, but out of those of a fellow-pilgrim, the two palms being joined together to form a a cavity for the liquid; while bottles of every form and material are filled for distant markets.

Close to the scene of the hallowing rite is a tamarisk tree, which, bending over the water and brushing the surface with its trunk, heads back the current where it is rushing with the greatest velocity. Many of the votaries, being carried with violence against it, come up on the other side; and, if they have sufficient strength to hold on by the branches, they escape a similar encounter from another tree that overhangs the stream five yards lower down. We observe one man likely to be carried in the above direction, but, retaining his presence of mind, he strikes into the mid-stream, and, swimming down like an arrow, lands upon a shelving gravelly bank, a quarter of a mile below. Soon after a Russian, either unable to swim or unprepared to resist the torrent, is dashed against the tree, and, rising on the other side, attempts to hold fast by the branches, but is carried against the second, and, passing under it, appears no more, every one supposing that he is lost. He is afterward thrown on shore below, exhausted, but not dead. Immediately after him another follows in the same direction, and is drowned. This man has a very dark complexion, and it is at first asserted that he came from the interior of the desert, where, never having seen a river, he had no idea of the power of water. But the pilgrims afterward mustering, and finding none of their party missing, conclude that he must have been a Mohammedan who has met his just reward for defiling their ceremony.

The time may come when the body of that same execrated Paynim, thrown up from its asphaltine bed beneath the waters of the Dead Sea, shall be regarded with pious reverence, and fragments of it sought as relics by a race of pilgrims yet unborn. The conjecture is not unwarranted by precedent. About thirty years ago a human body, or what had the form of one, was discovered floating not far from the shore of the Dead Sea, and on taking it out it was found to be encrusted all over with bitumen and salt, in consequence no doubt of its having lain a long while in the lake. It happened to be the time of Easter, and the pilgrims hearing of it broke the body into innumerable pieces with infinite eagerness, believing it to be one of the ancient inhabitants of Sodom, who had risen from the bottom. It was probably the body of some unfortunate Arab who had fallen in.

The baptismal ceremony being concluded, the pilgrims return to Jerusalem. But all do not return. In this barbarous country multitudes cannot undertake a journey even of eight hours without leaving part of their number behind. Remembering that the number that came was nearly three thousand, the list of accidents is not proportionally great. But not one life need have been lost if the pilgrims had been less impatient and less inhuman.

On our way from Jerusalem to the Jordan we meet quite a number of Greek and Russian pilgrims returning from the latter place, many of whom have sprigs of thorn bush in their hands, such as are supposed to have been used in making the crown of thorns with which the Saviour's brow was encircled. Some of them are barefoot and miserably clad, while all seem weary and footsore. We salute each of them respectfully as we pass them by; for, though we pity their ignorance and fanaticism, we cannot but respect the Christian zeal which causes them to leave their homes, thousands of miles away, to make what they regard as a sacred pilgrimage to the tomb of the Saviour and to the river in which he submitted himself for baptism at the hands of John.

Who can stand on the banks of this sacred stream and read the simple, yet touchingly beautiful, account given by St. Matthew of the baptism of Jesus, without feeling that it is indeed a spot which every Christian eye may well delight to look upon?

The record reads: "Then cometh Jesus from Galilee to Jordan unto John, to be baptized of him. But John forbade him, saying, I have need to be baptized of thee, and comest thou to me? And Jesus answering said unto him, Suffer it to be so now, for thus it becometh us to fulfill all righteousness. Then he suffered him. And Jesus, when he was baptized, went up straightway out of the water; and, lo, the heavens were opened unto him, and he saw the Spirit of God descending like a dove, and lighting upon him; and, lo, a voice from heaven saying, This is my beloved Son, in whom I am well pleased."

Think you not, kind reader, that many a weary pilgrim who, after weeks of travel from his home on the steppes of Russia, the plains of the Danube, or the sunny vales of Italy, finally reaches this spot and bathes himself in the sacred river, feels, in a like but circumscribed sense the Holy Spirit descending on his sin-sick soul, and from thenceforth, and ever after, thanks the great God for the privilege of having seen and bathed in the waters of the Jordan?

The tribe of Bedouins who occupy the eastern bank of the Jordan are of rather a lawless character, and in Jerusalem it is not thought safe for strangers to visit the Jordan and Dead Sea without having with them one or more sheikhs and a posse of Arabs who belong to the restless tribes beyond the Jordan, or are on friendly terms with them. Omitting this precaution, some travelers have been robbed and grossly maltreated while visiting the Jordan and Dead Sea, and, even with this precaution, the traveler is not always free from danger.

Our own escort from Jerusalem consists of a sheikh, his son, and some half dozen Arabs on foot, each carrying a matchlock, which looks as if made in the year One; and seems far more likely, if fired off, to kill the holder than an enemy. The sheikh and his son also carry scimetars, of Turkish construction, and both are mounted on splendid Arab mares. The sheikh's son is specially attentive to Lily, riding most of the time close by her side, and constantly gathering flowers for her by the wayside. She has but to smile and point toward a flower to secure it in an instant, for the young sheikh does not have to dismount to pick a flower. Such is his agility that, riding along beside it, he throws his body sideways, and plucks the flower without ever stopping his horse. The attentions of the young sheikh toward Lily become so marked and demonstrative that we begin to fear he may want to carry her off to the desert, to be the light of his own home, as she long has been of ours; but so soon as we strike upon the level plain of the Jordan our fears all vanish away, for the love of the Bedouin for his bonny gray mare supersedes that of his love for woman, and desiring to show both Lily and ourselves that he has a steed of which he may well be proud, he dashes away at a fearful rate, bidding Mohammed, our dragoman, to follow. Away they both go like shafts from a bow, but Mohammed's horse falls so far behind the Bedouin's that the latter laughs the former to scorn, and wheels around and around him, like a hawk about to pounce down upon its prey.

The horsemanship of the Arab, and the love he bears toward his steed, are two characteristics of the Bedouin which fail not to attract the eye of every one who travels among them; and should you believe a hundredth part of what they tell you, you would conclude that many of the horses are more intelligent than their masters, and have the reasoning faculty quite as thoroughly developed. Thus they will tell you that a troop of Druses on horseback attacked a party of Bedouins in Haurân in the summer of 1815, and drove them into their encampment, where they were in turn assailed by a superior force, and all killed except one man, who fled. He was pursued by several of the best-mounted Bedouins; but his mare, though fatigued, continued her speed for several hours and could not be overtaken. Before his pursuers gave up the chase they cried out to him, promising quarter and safe-conduct, and begging that he would allow them to kiss the forehead of his excellent mare. Upon his refusal they desisted from pursuing; and blessing the generous creature, they exclaimed, addressing her owner, "Go and wash the feet of your mare and drink up the water." This is a well-known phrase among the Bedouins, and intended to express their boundless admiration of such noble animals. Another will relate to you a tale of which the following is the substance:

"An Arab and his tribe had attacked the caravan of Damascus in the desert; the victory was complete, and the Arabs were already occupied in loading their rich booty, when the troops of the pasha of Acre, coming to meet this caravan, fell suddenly upon the victorious Arabs, slew a great number of them, made the remainder prisoners, and, having tied them with cords, conducted them to Acre to present them before the pasha. Abou-el-Marsch, one of the Arab prisoners, had received a ball in his arm during the combat; as his wound was not mortal, the Turks fastened him on a camel, and having obtained possession of his horse, led off both horse and horseman. The evening before they were to enter Acre they encamped with their prisoners in the mountains of Saphad; the wounded Arab had his legs bound together by a leathern thong, and was stretched near the tent where the Turks were sleeping. During the night, kept awake by the pain of his wound, he heard his horse neigh amongst the others which were picketed round the tents according to Oriental usage. Roused by the familiar sound, and unable to resist the desire of caressing once more the companion of his life, he dragged himself with difficulty along the ground on his hands and knees, and came up to his courser. 'Poor friend,' said he, 'what wilt thou do amongst the Turks? Thou wilt be immured under the arches of a khan, with the horses of an aga or a pasha; the women and the children will no longer bring thee camel's milk, or barley or doura in the hollow of their hands; thou wilt no longer run free in the desert, as the wind of Egypt; thou wilt no more cleave the waters of the Jordan with thy breast, and cool thy skin as white as their foam; therefore, if I remain a slave, remain thou free!—go, return to the tent thou knowest well; say to my wife that Abou-el-Marsch will return no more, and put thy head under the curtains of the tent and kiss the hands of my little children.' Whilst thus speaking, Abou-el-Marsch had gnawed through with his teeth the cord of goat's-hair with which the horse was fettered, and the animal was free; but seeing his master wounded and bound at his feet, the faithful and sagacious creature understood by instinct what no language could explain to him. He stooped his head, smelt his master, and, seizing him with his teeth by the leathern belt round his body, went off in a gallop, bore him to his tent, laid him on the sand at the feet of his wife and children, and then dropped down dead. All the tribe wept for him, the poets have celebrated him, and his name is constantly in the mouths of the Arabs of Jericho."

Anecdotes of equine fondness are great favorites with the Arabs, and they have an inexhaustible stock of them— some highly poetical like the one we have just related, and others not a little droll. The following was recounted to us at Tripoli on the narrator's "own knowledge:" An officer who had gone round to collect taxes for the governor of Hammah was attacked and slain by banditti as he was returning from his expedition. His favorite mare, *knowing that he had a large sum of money about him*, fought over his body for some days, and would not have been vanquished at last but that she died of starvation.

An Arab commandant, who offered a horse for sale to an Englishman, boasted as one of the great virtues of the animal that, under his protection any one could lie down to sleep in the desert in perfect security; for if the Bedouins should approach, and the horse should fail to wake his master in time for escape by biting his shoulder, he would pick him up in his mouth and gallop away.

That our readers may have a still better idea of these Bedouins, and learn something more of their peculiarities, we beg to make one other quotation from the interesting work of Lord Lindsay. He and his party were returning from the Jordan to Jerusalem, and, by some mishap, became belated on the way: " It was," he says, " near one in the morning, and we were some five hours' distance from Jerusalem. We rode forward as fast as the nature of the ground would allow, but after three hours' continual ascent both horses and men were so weary that we were obliged again to make a brief halt, for which Suleiman selected a small gully tolerably sheltered from the wind, and containing scattered fuel enough to enable us to make a fire. The promise of a little bucksheesh sent all our Bedouins in search of twigs and brushwood; a great heap was collected and fired, and the blaze shot up as high as a house amidst the loud shouts of the Bedouins. Every one lay down to enjoy the cheerful glow, only a few of our people going out from time to time to bring in fresh food for our fire. The restless temperament of the Arabs would not suffer them, however, to remain sitting there so quietly, notwithstanding their previous fatigue. They began to play tricks and tumble each other about on the ground, and to whoop aloud; and when Suleiman told them that if they got up a dance we would be sure to give them a bucksheesh, they were all ready for it in an instant. We ratified the bargain, and had no reason to regret it; for though the promised dance turned out nothing very graceful, still there was something exceedingly picturesque and captivating to the fancy in the group formed by the Bedouins by the flickering fire in the wild ravine. Some thirty of these people—for several of our mounted Bedouins took part in the dance—arranged themselves in a wide semicircle on one side of the fire, while we lay on the other, and began a peculiar song. We understood nothing of the words, which were repeated over and over again without variation; the melody too was quite monotonous, and the song had little to deserve the name, except the measure, which, as it appeared to me, may be expressed somewhat thus: Al—lay—allahla—al—lah—allahla. At first the whole line stood motionless; they then began to nod their heads, then to bow slightly, then gradually more and more, whilst the singing grew faster and wilder as their bodies bent deeper, till at last their faces almost touched the ground; the singing then gradually became more slow as with diminished bendings they brought their bodies once more to an erect posture. When this was done they suddenly clapped their hands, and scampered round and round like mad for a few minutes, and so the ballet ended.

"Meanwhile our fire had been neglected and had died away; one of the Bedouins took a curious way to rekindle it. Bestriding the embers, he sank down nearly into a sitting posture, his burnoos forming a sort of funnel, as it were, over the ashes; he then suddenly started up erect, and this manœuvre he repeated several times, until the working of this extemporaneous air-pump at last revived the flame.

"After the dancers had lain down a while to recover from the effects of their exertions, Suleiman pointed to the dawning east, and gave the word to march. We mounted our horses again, and in a short while reached Bethany.

"From Bethany we had but a short distance to travel to Jerusalem; and we reached the foot of the Mount of Olives just as the morning sun was shedding its first beams on the high terraces of the temple that rose above us, on the beautiful cypresses that rear their pyramidal heads over the porticoes of the mosque of El Aksa, and the domelike orange trees overshadowing the temple source called the Orange Fountain. The scene recalled to my memory one of the most beautiful Oriental traditions invented or preserved by the Arabs. It is thus they recount the circumstances that determined Solomon in his choice of a site for the temple:

"'Jerusalem was a ploughed field; and that part of the ground where the temple is now erected was in the possession of two brothers, one of whom was married and had several children, the other lived alone; they cultivated in common the field which they had inherited from their mother. The time of the harvest being come, the two brothers bound their sheaves, and placed them in two equal heaps, which they left on the field. During the night, the one who was unmarried said to himself, "My brother has a wife and children to support; it is not just that my portion should be as great as his; I will take some sheaves from my heap and add them to his; he will not perceive and so will not be able to refuse them;" and he did as he had determined. The same night the other brother awoke, and said to his wife, "My brother is young, and is without a helpmate; he has no one to assist him in his labor, or comfort him when he is weary; it is not just that we should take from the common field as many sheaves as he; let us rise and carry secretly to his heap a certain number of sheaves; he will not take notice of them to-morrow, and therefore cannot refuse to take them." And thus they did. In the morning each of the brothers went to the field, and was much surprised to see that the two heaps were still equal; neither of them could account to himself for this prodigy. They did the same thing for several nights in succession; but as each of them bore to his brother's heap the same number of sheaves, the heaps always remained equal, until one night they met together, each carrying the sheaves destined for the other.

"'Now, the place where so good a thought had entered the heads of two men at one time, and had been so perseveringly pursued must be a place agreeable to God, and men blessed it, and chose it to build God's house thereon.'"

What a charming tradition! how redolent of the simple goodness of patriarchal manners! How ancient and natural is the impulse that prompts men to consecrate to God a spot where virtue has bloomed on the earth!

After quitting our camp near Jericho, and while riding over the plain toward the Jordan, we keep a sharp lookout for the terrible Bedouins hereabout, who, we were told at Jerusalem, might pounce down upon us at any moment; and we were also informed that if they found us unprotected or unprepared for resistance, they would rob us of our money, steal our horses, and, perhaps, murder us outright. We examine our fire-arms to see that they are ready for instant use, and keep our little company close together; but we neither see or hear of an enemy, and we feel rather chagrined at ourselves for allowing such bugaboo stories to have induced us to pay the expense of a guard.

That outrages have been committed by the Jordan and Dead Sea Bedouins upon travelers, in times past, there can be no doubt; and that they still have a disposition to repeat them, as often as they can with safety to themselves, is, we presume, equally true, though now-a-days travelers usually go so well armed that a Bedouin, with his old matchlock and long spear or pole, would stand but a poor show in a fight, and none know this better than themselves.

The experience of one traveler, in this particular, is so drawn to the life that we cannot refrain from repeating it.

Like ourselves, he and his friends took their lunch on the banks of the Jordan, having, in the mean while, guards stationed at different points, on the lookout for those terrible bloodthirsty Bedouins, about which they had heard so much at Jerusalem. "Two or three times," he says, "during our meal we were disturbed by the shouts of our outposts, but we could not perceive anything that wore a suspicious appearance. But just as we had finished our repast and were getting out our flasks, that we might fill them from the water of the Jordan, the cry of *Arabee! Arabee!* burst upon us from all sides, and Suleiman (chief of the guard) came thundering upon us, sword in hand, shouting *Arabee! Arabee!* as loud as he could bawl, and motioning us to mount and make ready. The bustle and confusion that ensued may easily be imagined. Shots were fired among the bushes around us; blows were heard as of swords ringing on the trees; and our Bedouins set up a screeching as if they were all spitted. Presently figures were discernible all round us, and we soon found that we were beset by a gang of at least thirty or forty half-naked rascals, armed only with stout poles. There was no telling exactly which party was getting the best of the fight, for our Bedouins were completely intermingled with the assailants. Sometimes one of the latter rushed to the spot where we stood, but immediately started back on seeing our horses and weapons. The baron now mounted, and at the same moment three Arabs, somewhat better dressed than the others, made at us from the bushes, one of them armed with a pistol, another with a sabre, and the third with a matchlock. Our little doctor singled out the man with the sword, and charged down upon him; the fellow seemed disposed to stand his ground at first, but seeing the prince galloping up to join us, he wheeled round and ran back into the jungle. The fellow with the pistol let fly at the baron and me, and we heard the ball crash upon the branch of a tree behind us. The other had rested his matchlock on a sort of fork; but giving him no time to send us the contents, we struck the stirrups into our horses' flanks and rode him down. He of the pistol had taken to his heels immediately after firing at us; but before he could reach the shelter of the bushes, the painter had sent a ball after him that wounded him slightly in the leg; and a young Greek pilgrim, who had accompanied us from Mar Saba, fell upon him before he could recover himself, and gave him a sound thrashing with his stick; whilst the baron whacked away in like manner with the flat of his sword at the fellow we had ridden down. The whole fight had now luckily become more grotesque than formidable; and Suleiman and his Bedouins soon put an end to it; for, taking their swords in their teeth, and their pistols in their hands, they drove the Arabs before them like a herd of wild animals to where we stood, and in a few minutes we had them all at our feet begging lustily for quarter. Suleiman made them a thundering harangue, and ordered them to sit down in a circle. The matchlock man, whom we had ridden down, and who was the sheikh of the party, humbly approached Suleiman, the hem of whose caftan he thrice pressed to his forehead in sign of submission.

"After some parleying, in which the whole gang of Arabs occasionally took part with loud screeches, Suleiman asked the baron what he intended to do with the fellows; they were poor devils who had only a mind to help themselves to a little bread to stay their hunger. We knew that well enough; but what was to be done? If we gave them a few kicks and sent them about their business, we might expect that they would again waylay us that evening in the mountains in still greater numbers.

Our wisest course, therefore, was to follow Suleiman's advice, that we should let them partake of our bread and salt, and keep them with us till we reached Jerusalem next morning. Accordingly we turned out the contents of our provision-bags and gave them to our vanquished foes. Thereupon our own Bedouins smoked a pipe with the seniors of the gang, and peace was established between us."

Having finished our inspection of the Jordan—bathed in its waters—lunched on its western shore—gathered two bottles of its water to take to our far-distant home—and talked over the incidents which have given to it such a world-wide interest, we again mount our horses, and a ride of about one hour over a level plain brings us to the shores of the Dead Sea. In the mean time the clouds have gathered blackness, and a sharp shower is upon us. We have our small tent—which we had brought along for the convenience of bathing—hastily pitched, and while Lily and some lady friends remain therein, Lu and I go off some distance along the shore to take a bath, as our time will not permit of our waiting until the shower is over.

Having read of Mr. Prime's sufferings from too hastily plunging into these waters, we take the precaution to go in very carefully, and keep our head, and especially our eyes, clear from the water; but notwithstanding our intended carefulness, some of the water gets in the hair on the back part of our head, and smarts and burns intensely for some time. The only unpleasantness to our skin is a slight smarting sensation, and a greasy feeling, which remain several hours after the bath. Oh, how we wish for another plunge in the Jordan just now, to neutralize the effects of the Dead Sea bath! and if we were visiting these parts again, we would come the other way—that is, by the way of Bethlehem, if for no other reason than to have a bath in the Jordan *after* the one in the Dead Sea.

The buoyancy of these waters is very considerable, and one finds no difficulty in floating leisurely upon them. Its specific gravity is great, consequent on the large amount of the chlorides which it holds in solution—analyses having shown that, in one hundred parts of water, over twenty-four are chlorides of calcium, magnesium, potassium, sodium, and manganese.

From the report of Lieutenant Lynch, of the United States Survey, we learn that the entire length of this sea is forty-six miles; greatest width, eleven miles; medium depth, one thousand feet; level below the Mediterranean, thirteen hundred feet; and below Jerusalem, nearly four thousand feet.

The historical and biblical interest of this sea is centred in the fact that upon the surface, or part of the surface of earth which it now covers, once stood the flourishing cities of Sodom and Gomorrah, upon both of which " the Lord rained brimstone and fire from out of heaven ; and he overthrew those cities and all the plain, and all the inhabitants of the cities, and that which grew upon the ground"—Lot and his family alone being excepted from the destruction.

This whole plain of the Jordan, once so rich and flourishing, is now a scene of desolation, and one cannot but feel that the curse of God has visited, and is still resting upon, it.

Perhaps no body of water on all the earth's surface has attracted so large a share of scientific research as this. Travelers have visited it from almost every civilized nation of the globe, and even governments—including our own—have thought it not unworthy of careful investigation. To notice what some of these travelers have said of this remarkable body of water will not occupy much of our time, and will, we think, prove interesting.

Josephus, whose account necessarily embodies the information possessed by those who had for ages been inhabitants of the country, and by whom it must have been intimately known in every part, after giving its length and breadth—corresponding very nearly with those of later travelers—adds: "The shores are unfruitful; the waters very bitter, and so dense that they bear up the heaviest things thrown into it; nor would it be easy for any one to sink therein, even if he wished. Accordingly when Vespasian (the great Roman emperor) visited the lake, he made experiment of this by causing some men who could not swim to have their hands tied behind them and to be cast into the lake, when it was seen that they were buoyed up by the water, even as light bodies are impelled upward by the wind."

In speaking of the black bitumen, of which large quantities, then as now, were thrown up to the surface of the lake, he compares these masses, quaintly enough, to " headless bulls, both in shape and size ;" adding that " men went out in boats to collect it, which was a work of some labor from the tenacity of the mass, which rendered it difficult to proportion the quantity taken on board to the burden of the vessel. It was used for calking ships and in embalments, as well as for various medicinal purposes."

" This land of Sodom," he says, " was once a blessed and happy country ; but, for the iniquities of its people, was burned up and consumed by the fires of heaven. Of this divine judgment the land still offered abundant traces. Even some remains of the ruined cities might still be perceived. The fruits which grew there were

Off for the Jordan and Dead Sea.

also appropriate monuments of its condition; for, while to the eye, they seemed pleasant and good for food, they were crushed in the hand that plucked them, and offered nothing but dust and ashes."

We may add, with reference to the apples of Sodom, *en passant*, that while riding from the Jordan to the Dead Sea, Lily, Lu, and ourself examine every tree, and bush, and twig on the way, hoping to find something of the kind, but our search is in vain.

The best and most probable description of this curious production is given by Dr. Robinson:

"One of the first objects," he says, "which attracted our notice on arriving at 'Ain Jidy was a tree with a singular fruit, which, without knowing at the moment whether it had been observed by former travelers or not, instantly suggested to our minds the far-famed fruits

'Which grew
Near that bituminous lake where Sodom stood.'

"This was the *ösher* of the Arabs, the *sclepias agigantea vel procera* of botanists, which is found in abundance in Upper Egypt and Nubia, and also in Arabia Felix, but seems to be confined in Palestine to the borders of the Dead Sea. We saw it only at 'Ain Jidy; Hasselquist found it in the desert between Jericho and the northern shore; and Irby and Mangles met with it of large size at the south end of the sea, and on the isthmus of the peninsula.

"We saw here several trees of the kind, the trunks of which were six or eight inches in diameter, and the whole height from ten to fifteen feet. Irby and Mangles found them measuring, in many instances, two feet or more in circumference, and the boughs at least fifteen feet in height; a size which far exceeded any they saw in Nubia. The tree has a grayish, cork-like bark, with long oval leaves; and in its general appearance and character it might be taken for a gigantic perennial species of the milk-weed or silk-weed, found in the northern parts of the American States. Its leaves and flowers are very similar to those of the latter plant, and when broken off it in like manner discharges a milky fluid. The fruit greatly resembles externally a large smooth apple or orange hanging in clusters of three or four together; and when ripe is of a yellow color. It was now fair and delicious to the eye, and soft to the touch; but on being pressed or struck it explodes with a puff, like a bladder or puff-ball, leaving in the hand only the shreds of the thin rind and a few fibres. It is, indeed, filled chiefly with air like a bladder, which gives it the round form; while in the centre a small slender pod runs through it from the stem, and is connected by thin filaments with the rind. The pod contains a small quantity of fine silk with seeds, precisely like the pod of the silk-weed, though very much smaller; being, indeed, scarcely the tenth part as large. The Arabs collect the silk and twist it into matches for their guns; preferring it to the common match, because it requires no sulphur to render it combustible.

"The most definite account we have of the apples of Sodom, so called, is in Josephus, who as a native of the country is a better authority than Tacitus or other foreign writers. After speaking of the conflagration of the plain and the yet remaining tokens of the divine fire, he remarks that 'there are still to be seen ashes reproduced in the fruits, which indeed resemble edible fruits in color, but on being plucked with the hands are dissolved into smoke and ashes.' In the account, after a due allowance for the marvelous in all popular reports, I find nothing which does not apply almost literally to the fruit of the ösher as we saw it. It must be plucked and handled with great care, in order to preserve it from bursting. We attempted to carry off some of the boughs and fruit with us to Jerusalem, but without success.

"Hasselquist finds the apples of Sodom in the fruit of the *Solanum melongena* (night-shade mad-apple), which we saw in great abundance at 'Ain Jidy, and in the plain of Jericho. These apples are much smaller than those of the ösher, and when ripe are full of small black grains. There is, however, nothing like explosion, nothing like 'smoke and ashes,' except occasionally, as the same naturalist remarks, 'when the fruit is punctured by an insect (*tenthredo*), which converts the whole inside into dust, leaving nothing but the rind entire, without any loss of color.' We saw the solanum and the ösher growing side by side; the former presenting nothing remarkable in its appearance and being found in other parts of the country, while the latter immediately arrested our attention by its singular accordance with the ancient story, and is moreover peculiar in Palestine to the shores of the Dead Sea."

Antonius Martyr, another ancient writer, merely speaks of the bitumen and sulphur of the lake, and the absence of any living thing in its waters, or of trees or verdure on its shores. But he adds that in July and August it was usual in his time for lepers to resort to the lake, and bathing in its waters it sometimes pleased God that they were healed.

Bocard confirms the account of its sterile shores. A hideous vapor, he says, rises from the lake, so that the smoke and darkness by which it was invested made it no inapt type of hell. This vapor, he adds, is so deleterious, that the barbarians inhabiting the neighborhood took care to fix themselves beyond the point to which it continues to be injurious when driven before the wind.

Other old writers describe the water as an abominable infusion of nitre and sulphur, so offensive and nauseous to the smell and taste, that the salt of the lake was never applied to any use. Arculfus notices the saline deposit on the borders of the lake, caused by the absorption by heat of the water thrown high up the shores by tempests, or that is left when the lake has sunk to its usual level after the periodical overflow.

We cannot but think that these old writers must have drawn somewhat on their imagination, or else that the character of the waters and the shores must have changed considerably since their time. The waters are certainly very bitter, and while tasting it we think that a solution of epsom salts and the tincture of quassia would make a compound of somewhat similar taste, but we observe nothing nauseous or offensive in the smell; and as to the shores, while their general appearance is that of desolateness, the small trees, and shrubs, and tufts of grass near them prove that the soil is not wholly sterile. We observe no fish, nor do we think any are to be found in the lake, and this is easily accounted for by the chemical constituents of the water. We notice large quantities of drift-wood on the shore, and any quantity of small shells, but both of these, no doubt, come from the waters of the Jordan. All the shells we see are of the fresh-water species. In regard to the smoke and the noxious vapors which the old writers speak of as arising from the Dead Sea, we observe nothing of the kind, though we can easily understand that in a basin so confined, and in which the air becomes so intensely heated, and where, moreover, the water is of such peculiar quality, the process of evaporation, or the incumbent vapor, may oftener·appear visible than under other circumstances.

The description and explanation of these phenomena given by Stephens accord precisely with our own views. He says : "One of the most singular circumstances in the character of the Dead Sea is the deep depression of its level below that of the Mediterranean, amounting, according to the recent survey by Lieutenant Symonds, to thirteen hundred and eleven feet, a circumstance which must have a remarkable effect on the mean temperature of the region. The phenomena witnessed here are such as might naturally be expected from the constitution of the waters and the nature of the surrounding district—a naked, solitary desert. The sea lies in its deep trough, flanked by lofty cliffs of bare limestone rock, and exposed for seven or eight months in each year to the unclouded beams of a burning sun. Nothing, therefore, but sterility and death-like solitude can be looked for upon its shores; and nothing else is actually found, except in those parts where there are fountains or streams of fresh water. The stories of the pestiferous exhalations and the bursts of smoke that rise from this dreaded expanse are a mere fable: there must naturally be an immense evaporation from it in consequence of its low position and exposure to the summer heats; but the character of this evaporation cannot well be different from that of any other body of water in similar circumstances.

The Egyptian heat of the climate, which is found throughout the whole ghor, or lower valley of the Jordan and the lake, is in itself unhealthy; and in connection with the marshes gives rise in summer to frequent intermittent fevers; so that the inhabitants are a feeble and sickly race. But this has no necessary connection with the Dead Sea, as such; and the same phenomena might probably exist in an equal degree were the waters of the lake fresh and limpid, or even were there no lake at all."

CHAPTER VI.

OVER THE HILLS TO BETHLEHEM.

YOU would have laughed, and laughed right heartily, to have seen our little party on the shores of the Dead Sea. Would you not like to have a pen-and-ink-sketch? Certainly, certainly you shall have it.

You see that little tent about twenty yards from the shore; well, that is our traveling kitchen generally, but to-day we have made a traveling bath-house of it: first we pitched it on the banks of the Jordan and now it is here; that is to say, we had intended to make the same use of it here that we did at the Jordan, but the sharp shower which has come suddenly upon us spoiled this calculation completely, so that it is now occupied, as you see, by Lily and two other ladies, to protect them from the storm, instead of being used as a bath-house for ourselves. The tent is only large enough for the ladies, and the half dozen gentlemen of our party go wandering around on the desolate shore, each muffled up as best he may be, like so many ghosts just risen from the waters of the deep Dead Sea!

Major F. and Harvey —— say they would like to go bathing with us, but they don't know what to do with their clothes in such a storm; and then the ladies, too, they fear, may see us from the tent door. Nonsense! say we; come to the Dead Sea and not float upon its waters? No, sir, if the rain came down twice as hard as it does, and the entire shore was lined with ladies, we would go in bathing—" peaceably if we could, forcibly if we must!"

Come, Lu and Charley, we will go in anyhow; and with one umbrella between us three, away we scamper up the shore until we reach a pile of drift-wood, and then, fixing the open umbrella as a roof, and the drift-wood around it in the shape of a patent corn-crib, we hastily undress, throw our clothes under the umbrella, and are in the sea in a jiffy. How we flounder around like porpoises, and how dearly we pay for the pleasure by subsequent pain from the effects of the water, has not all this been told in a preceding chapter, and why repeat it here?

" Tāāl hennee, tāāl gei, Mohammed!"

" Eiwa, ānā gei, Master!"

" Coming, are you? then move along faster, and down with the tent as soon as possible, and let's be off for Mar Saba."

" Praised be the Prophet for evermore!"

From the Dead Sea our course lies in a south-westerly direction, though for a half hour or more after starting we continue along the north-westerly shore of the sea, until we reach a high bluff, near the water's edge, and from thence we commence to ascend the rugged mountain-path which leads toward Mar Saba. This place we reach about a half hour before sunset, after a tedious ride over most terrible roads, and here we encamp for the night.

Leaving Lily in the tent—for females are not allowed to enter this convent under any circumstances, there being a tradition with its monks that the walls will tumble down whenever a woman enters its portals—we hasten to the convent to examine it before the night sets in.

It is a curious old structure, and well repays a visit. Founded by St. Saba in A. D. 439, and then consisting of a single chamber and chapel, excavated in the solid rock, at the side of a deep ravine, addition after addition has since been made until it now embraces many rooms and chapels, some excavated in the rock, and others of masonry. Around the whole is a high, thick wall, to keep out intruders, and to protect it from the gaze of the curious.

Our guide takes us from chapel to chapel, and from room to room; shows us the forty-four skulls of the monks who were murdered by the Persians at the time they plundered the convent in the seventh century; the large and well-executed picture which professes to give the features of each; the tomb of St. Saba himself; and the identical room and chapel which the saint occupied for many years, and of which, it is said, he dispossessed a lion upon his first occupancy of it.

There are now thirty-six monks and some three or four hermits occupying the convent; and from the sleek, lazy appearance of those whom we meet, we should judge that they have good living, and but little to do. This convent has the reputation of being the richest, as it is the oldest, in Syria.

Short extracts from what Olin, Stephens, and Châteaubriand say of this convent will, we think, be appreciated by our readers.

"Few situations on the surface of the globe," says Olin, "are better adapted to the tastes of an anchorite, or ensure more complete seclusion from the world, than the convent of St. Saba. The dominion of sterility and desolation is here complete and undisputed. Beside this general recommendation, the structure of the rock which forms the steep banks or rather walls of Kedron afforded peculiar facilities for the formation of cells for the residence of a vast number of hermits. The channel is here three hundred feet or more in depth. It may be sixty feet wide at the bottom by one hundred and fifty at top, the sides being perpendicular, but broken by a number of offsets, and forming a succession of steps, of various but inconsiderable width, ascending from the bottom quite to the top of the chasm. These towering cliffs are perforated in every direction with a multitude of cavities formed by the displacement of some of the strata, which are as regular and distinct as the layers of stone in a pile of masonry. Nearly or quite all the apartments within the monastery are formed of these natural cavities, that immense structure which stretches from the top of the bank to the very bottom of the deep abyss being only a vast front, including a multitude of cells, with staircases, corridors, and covered ways, etc. I must not forget to mention a large palm tree growing in a wall on one of the terraces, and which was planted, as they say, by St. Saba himself in the fourth century; I am sure that every traveler will notice it as I did; one must be surrounded on all sides by such appalling sterility as here prevails in order to feel the full value of a tuft of verdure."

"The chapel, like all other Greek chapels," says Stephens, "was full of gaudy and ridiculous ornaments and paintings; and among the latter was one that seems to attract the particular admiration and reverence of the devout. At the top of the picture sat the Father, surrounded by angels, and patriarchs, and good men; and on his right hand was a range of two story-houses, St. Peter standing before them with the key in his hand. Below the Father was a large, powerful man, with a huge pair of scales in his hand, weighing sinners as they came up, and billeting on each the weight of his sins; below him were a number of naked figures, in a sitting posture, with their hands spread out and their legs enclosed in long boxes extended horizontally. On the left a stream of fire was coming down from the Father, and collecting in the mouth of a huge nondescript sea-monster, while in front stood a great half-naked figure pitching in the sinners like sticks into a furnace, and the damned were kicking about in the flames. On the right was Elias doing battle with Antichrist; and below was a representation of the last day, and the graves giving up their dead in almost every conceivable variety of form and situation."

"In another chapel, dedicated to John of Damascus," says Châteaubriand, "behind an iron grating in a grotto of the rock, was a most extraordinary assemblage of human bones, the remains, as the monks assert, of fourteen thousand martyrs, who were slaughtered in the valley.

"The principal, who was polite in his attentions, conducted us to the cell which formed the germ of this immense establishment, and in which its founder, St. Saba, spent many years of his life. It was remarkable above the rest for nothing but its greater rudeness and more neglected state, and for the interesting tradition belonging to it, which the venerable monk related to us with the air of a man who fully believed what he spoke, and who expected to be believed. This cave was originally a lion's den, and was in the actual occupancy of the monarch of the wilderness when the holy Saba first visited this sequestered spot with the pious design of founding a religious house. He was in a moment satisfied with its admirable adaptation to his purpose, when he walked into the den of the lion, and told him that one of them must forthwith evacuate the premises. The magnanimous beast quietly and courteously retired, and left his noble lair to its higher destination.

"In addition to its own strong, high walls and massive iron doors, which give this convent the aspect of a feudal castle filled with bustling warriors, rather than that of a hermitage of peaceable, praying men, there are two towers occupying higher ground a short distance from the main edifice. They seem from their position to be designed to guard against surprises, as the convent itself is proof against any open assault. The monks stand in sore dread of the Bedouins, who, when any cause of irritation exists, often lurk about the high cliffs that overlook the convent on the opposite side of the ravine, and sometimes fire on the inmates from that commanding position."

From Mar Saba we go direct to Bethlehem. The road is rough and very hilly, and the time required to pass over it is about four hours. The town looks beautiful at a distance, but the enchantment vanishes as soon as you reach its streets, which are narrow, dirty, and exceedingly rough. The town is principally located on a side hill; the houses rise one above another, and nearly all of them are built of rough stone without any finish on the outside, and possessing few of the comforts of civilization within. The people are comparatively civil to strangers, as their chief profits consist in the beads, shells, and other trinkets which they keep for sale, and which strangers are expected to buy. We purchase a considerable quantity of these as souvenirs of the place and as presents for friends at home. The number of its inhabitants is put down at two thousand five hundred. We hardly think there are so many.

The country round and about Bethlehem is stony and

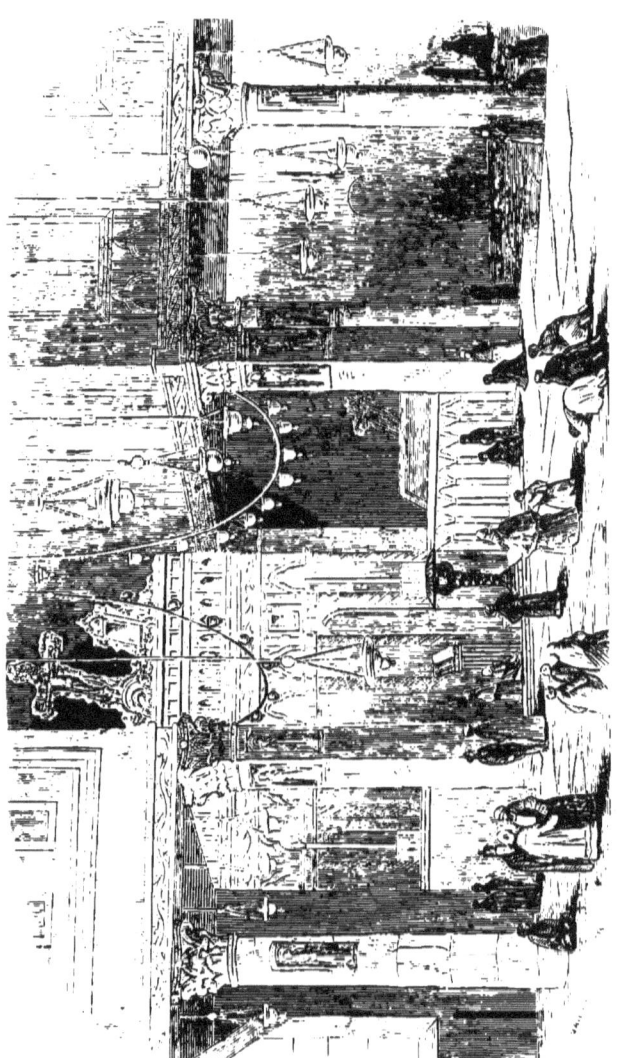

CHURCH OF THE NATIVITY.

only partially cultivated, though it is easy to be seen that under the care of an industrious and enterprising people it might be made, as it once was, very productive. Near here were the rich fields in which Ruth, the Moabite, gleaned after the reapers of Boaz; here it was that Boaz said to his reapers, "Let her glean even among the sheaves, and reproach her not :—and let fall some of the handfuls of purpose for her, and leave them that she may glean them, and rebuke her not;" and here, too, it was that the good old man whispered those gentle words to the kind, loving, confiding Ruth, "Blessed be thou of the Lord, my daughter .... for all the city of my people doth know that thou art a virtuous woman."

One of the reasons given—and a very good one—why the country about Bethlehem is so little cultivated is, that the Bedouins, who are always in the vicinity, seize the growing fruit and corn, and the incursion of a single night is often sufficient to frustrate the industry of a whole year. Even in broad daylight, says Dr. Olin, these barbarians do not hesitate to drive their beasts through fields of wheat under the owner's eye, and to graze their animals upon them without scruple. Under such discouragements the people of Bethlehem naturally turn their attention to other employments than agriculture.

Once within the town the first place we visit is the convent. This is a large collection of imposing buildings, located near the outer edge of the village. The original church was built by the Empress Helena in the early part of the fourth century, portions of which still remain. We particularly notice the beams of cedar, brought from the forests of Lebanon, which seem as sound to-day as they were when first put here, some fifteen hundred years ago. So many additions and alterations have been made to the old church, and so many Catholic embellishments added, that it is now difficult to determine what was the form and finish of the original structure.

Our guide—a Greek priest—first conducts us to the Chapel of the Nativity, to reach which we descend fourteen steps. It consists of a room, excavated in the rock, about thirty-eight feet in length by twelve in width. At the side of the room is a recess, which is said to mark the exact spot of the manger in which the young child was laid. On the floor of the chapel, underneath this recess, is a silver star, around which are engraved the words, " Hic de Vergine Maria Jesus Christus natus est." Here Jesus was born of the Virgin Mary.

On the ceiling of the chapel is another star, which is said to be under that part of the heavens in which the star appeared which directed the wise men of the East to the birth-place of the Saviour; and on the side of the chapel, opposite the place of the manger, an altar marks the spot where the wise men knelt " when they opened their treasures and presented unto him gifts; gold, frankincense, and myrrh."

A little farther on is an altar to Joseph—this being the spot, it is said, to which he retired at the moment of the nativity; and a little farther, is the Altar of the Shepherds; and still farther, the Altar of the Innocents, which is supposed to mark the opening to the tomb or grotto in which the bodies of the children were thrown (twenty thousand) after the terrible massacre ordered by Herod. Other grottoes and tombs are pointed out, the most noted of which is that of St. Jerome. In the room or chapel where the tomb is located this saint spent the greater part of his life, and here he died. One of the finest pictures in the Vatican, at Rome, is that of St. Jerome taking the sacrament on his death-bed, in this chapel. It and Raphael's " Transfiguration" and " Madonna de

Foligno" occupy a room by themselves, and are regarded by many as the three masterpieces of the world.

To reach these several chapels, grottoes, and tombs, we are taken through dark, narrow passage-ways, underneath the floors of the larger chapels or churches; and when we have finished our examinations below we visit the churches above. These structures are of considerable size, and finished off with altars, pictures, etc., in the usual style of Catholic churches. They belong respectively to the Latins, Greeks, and Armenians, each of whom claim a joint proprietorship in the Chapel of the Nativity, and in the altars, grottoes, and tombs heretofore mentioned.

Near the convent is a burial-ground, concerning which one traveler gives his experience as follows:

"We passed the night in the convent, where we met with hospitable treatment. I was roused at daylight in the morning by a loud wailing beneath the window, which on rising I found overlooked the burial-ground, where all the women of Bethlehem seemed to have assembled to call on the dead, as is customary among them on certain days after the decease. I immediately went down to the gathering, and drew fresh tears and louder shouts by my presence, while many inflicted severe blows on their breasts. One old woman bared her bosom, which required no great ceremony indeed, for she had but one garment on, and, throwing herself on the grave, thumped in good earnest. They had brought flowers and herbs to strew. There would have been much interest in a quiet moan; but so dire a yell set all sympathy to flight in a moment."

Leaving the convent, a ride of ten minutes through a narrow street brings us to what is known as the "Milk Grotto." A middle-aged Syrian woman, who occupies a room at the side of the entrance-way, receives us kindly, and points the way to the grotto, to reach which we descend a number of steps. The building erected over the grotto has quite a tasteful appearance, but the grotto itself is nothing more than a cave hewn out of the white limestone rock; though, strange to say, the whiteness is not attributed to the character of the rock, but to a few drops of the Virgin Mary's milk which she is said to have spilled while nursing the "young child" in this cave; and, stranger still, it is even now believed that pieces of this stone, carried about the person, have the power of supernaturally increasing a woman's milk, and pieces are carried to all parts of the world for this identical purpose. The woman in attendance very kindly offers us a handful of these pieces of stone as we are leaving, but not having faith in their virtue, we respectfully decline to encumber our pockets with them.

Tradition points out this grotto as the one in which Mary and the child were concealed during the slaughter of the "innocents" by Herod; and prior to the time when Joseph "arose and took the young child and his mother by night, and departed into Egypt."

Neither Bethlehem, nor the convent, nor the milk grotto, nor anything else in or about the town, would excite the least interest in the mind of any one but from the fact that here—yes, just here, "in Bethlehem of Judea"—Christ was born! Here the "day-star" first had an existence—a star that never has had, nor will have, a setting!

Whether or not Jesus was born in the rock-hewn grotto pointed out as the place of nativity matters not a whit to us. It is enough to know that he was born in Bethlehem, and that this is Bethlehem. As tradition, however, for the first three hundred years pointed this out as the identical spot, and history has ever since recognized it as such, we are content to believe that not only in this town, but in this very rock-hewn cave (then used as a stable), Jesus was born of the Virgin Mary!

In which of the fields near by the shepherds watched their flocks when "the angels of the Lord came upon them, and the glory of the Lord shone around about them," we do not know; but we do know that the field is somewhere in this "same country," and that is quite sufficient!

From Bethlehem we go over a rough but not very hilly road, and after one hour's travel we reach the Pools of Solomon, where we encamp for the night.

These pools are located in the slope of a narrow valley, where Solomon, in his time, probably had a palace or country-seat. They are three in number, and so arranged that the surplus waters of the upper pool run into the next, and the surplus waters of the second into the third —the water, in all, being supplied from a splendid fountain about one hundred yards above the upper one.

The entire measurements, as given by Robinson, are as follows:

Upper pool, length three hundred and eighty feet, and width one hundred and sixty feet at the west end, and two hundred and fifty feet at the east. Depth twenty-five feet.

Middle pool, length four hundred and twenty-three feet, by one hundred and forty-eight feet at the west end and two hundred and fifty feet at the east end. Depth thirty-nine feet.

Lower pool, length five hundred and eighty-two feet, by one hundred and forty-eight feet at the west and two hundred and seven at the east end. Depth fifty feet.

The walls of the pools are of good masonry, and built

to conform somewhat with the slope of the valley—narrow above and wider below. The lower pool has recently undergone repairs, and all three are in a good state of preservation, considering that their original construction dates back nearly three thousand years.

The fountain from which these pools receive their water is in the side of the hill above, considerably under ground, and has a substantial structure erected over and about it. The water flows from three clefts in the rock to a common centre, and from thence it is conducted to the upper pool, through an underground aqueduct. The water is very sweet and clear, and flows out in great quantities.

An aqueduct was built from these pools to the temple in Jerusalem, and the place is still pointed out by the side of the inner wall where the water formerly flowed, but at the time of our visit none was flowing. As stated in a former chapter, it would only require a reasonable amount of skill and engineering, and a comparatively small amount of money, to make the water in these pools supply every house in Jerusalem with fresh, pure water; and in the hands of any other government than the present one this would speedily be done.

A little to the east of the pools, toward the region of the Dead Sea, is a very large grotto, supported by great pillars of the natural rock, perfectly dry, without petrifaction or stalactites; it is a complete labyrinth within, and, as in many of the ancient catacombs, a man might easily lose himself for ever in its windings. It lies in the mountainous wilderness of Engaddi, and is supposed to be the Cave of Adullam, where David received the mutinous and discontented spirits of his days, and where, when Saul was in pursuit of him, he cut off the skirts of his garment, and suffered him to go away unharmed.

Leaving our tents pitched at the Pools of Solomon, we

visit Hebron on the following day and return. This is a hard day's ride, over a rough road, and accompanied with more vexation of spirit than profit, as the sequel will show.

On the way we visit Abraham's oak, and lunch under its widespreading branches. Under this oak, it is said, Abraham pitched his tent, and here the angels visited him. The oak is certainly very large and very old, but that this identical tree has stood for about four thousand years is neither probable nor possible.

An hour's ride from the oak brings us to Hebron, a miserable Syrian village, of rough stone houses, with narrow, filthy streets. Its inhabitants are nearly all Mohammedans of the most bigoted sort, who look upon Christians with an eye of jealousy, if not of hatred.

We ride directly to the mosque (formerly a Christian church, built by the Empress Helena) which is erected over the cave of Machpelah, in which lie buried Abraham and Sarah his wife, Isaac, Rebecca, and Leah, and, it is claimed, though we think it doubtful, the bones of Joseph, which were brought up out of Egypt. A crowd of Moslems, men, women, and children, are in the street leading to and about the door of the mosque, who receive us with scowling faces. For the bucksheesh which they expect to get they are willing to admit us about ten feet within the gate of the outer court; but to admit the eye of a Christian to gaze upon the tomb of Abraham would be too great a sacrilege for a follower of the Prophet to think of. Our blood boils with indignation at this additional specimen of Moslem bigotry, and we feel that if we had a dozen other Americans with us, each with a revolver in his hand, we should like to clear our way—by threats, if possible, but by bullets, if necessary—to the tombs of the fathers. We wonder not now at the zealous and holy enthusiasm of the Crusaders, and had we lived in their day we should have liked to join them in ridding Palestine of these bigoted Mohammedans.

Our experience at Hebron, however, is only a counterpart of that of all other travelers who have visited it. One tourist says of it:

"Hebron, one of the oldest cities of Canaan, David's capital before he conquered Jerusalem, is now a small town, containing seven or eight hundred Arab families. The present inhabitants are the wildest, most lawless, and desperate people in the Holy Land; and it is a singular fact, that they sustain now the same mutinous character with the rebels of ancient days, who armed with David against Saul, and with Absalom against David. The place bears no traces of the glory of its Jewish king; earthquakes, wars, pestilence, and famine have passed over it, and a small town of white houses, compactly built on the side of the mountain, a mosque and two minarets, are all that mark the ancient capital of Judea.

"There is little to detain the traveler at Hebron. The great mosque is said to cover the site of the Cave of Machpelah, nor does there appear to be any reason for doubting this tradition. In different parts of the enclosure the Mohammedans have built tombs for the patriarchs, while their actual place of sepulture is held to be in a cavern below, which even the faithful are not permitted to enter. The Moslems of Hebron are exceedingly bigoted; and when, with a Jewish companion, I stopped for a moment to look up at the long marble staircase leading to the tomb of Abraham, a Turk came out from the bazaars, and with furious gesticulations gathered a crowd round us; and a Jew and a Christian were driven with contempt from the sepulchre of the patriarch whom they both revered."

The "Valley of Eshcol" in which Hebron is situated is still celebrated for its grapes, as in the day when the spies sent by Moses "*cut down from thence a branch with one cluster of grapes, and they bare it between two on a staff.*" We notice a large number of vineyards near Hebron, and are especially struck with the great thickness of some of the vines. They train them by running three vines together, in a pyramidal form, that each may rest upon and support the other. We also notice some fields of wheat and barley in this valley, though all around the hills are rocky, barren, and desolate.

Hebron, next to Damascus, is said to be the oldest city in the world, though it has not, like wine, improved from age. It is frequently mentioned in the Old Testament Scriptures, and seems to have been one of the most important and distinguished cities of the ancient Israelites. Here King David for a long time kept his court; it was this city which Joshua gave to Caleb the son of Jephunneh, "*because that he wholly followed the Lord God of Israel;*" and it was here that John the Baptist was born.

We are so out of patience with the bigoted Hebronites, for their refusal to admit us to the tombs of the fathers, that our visit is anything but satisfactory, and our ride back to the Pools of Solomon seems long and dreary. In this ride, however, we pass some ruins which are said to be the remains of the house of Abraham; also a large fountain with ruins near it, the history of which is not known; another large ruin called Beit Gala; and still another called Beit Oumar; but we are weary and we hasten on to our tents.

Early next morning we have our tents struck and hasten toward Jerusalem, for it is the Sabbath, and we are anxious to reach there in time to attend service at the English church.

In about three-fourths of an hour we reach the tomb of Rachel, at which we halt for a few moments. It is a stone structure, probably twenty feet square, having a round roof or dome, and an open space or room next to the road. The door to the tomb is locked, but by peeping through the large key-hole we can see that there is nothing within save the bare walls, and a wall partition which seems to extend half-way up, with a door at one end.

Mr. Carne, who visited this tomb, records his reflections thereupon in language as follows:

"I thought of Jacob's words in his last hour, when dwelling on the only indelible remembrance that earth seemed to claim from him. The long exile, the converse with the angels of God, the wealth and greatness which had gathered round him, all yield to the image of the loved and faithful wife—'And as for me, Rachel died by me, in the way from Bethlehem, and I buried her there.'

"The spot is as wild and solitary as can well be conceived; no palms or cypresses give their shelter from the blast; not a single tree spreads its shade where rest the ashes of the beautiful mother of Israel. Yet there is something in this sepulchre in the wilderness that excites a deeper interest than more splendid or revered ones. Other tombs the traveler looks at with careless indifference; beside that of Rachel, his fancy wanders to 'the land of the people of the East;' to the power of beauty, that could so long make banishment sweet; to the devoted companion of the wanderer, who deemed all troubles light for her sake. No one can stand by this spot without an earnest wish, and almost a conviction, that it is one of those about which tradition has not erred; and whether this be Rachel's tomb or not, I could not but remark, that while youth and beauty have faded away, and the queens of the East have died and been forgotten, and Zenobia and Cleopatra sleep in unknown graves, year after year thousands of pilgrims are thronging to the supposed last resting-place of a poor Hebrew woman.

"The Moslems have surrounded most of the burial-places of the chief characters of the Old Testament with more pomp and stately observance than this; but the tribute they pay to Rachel's remains is far more sincere and impressive than walls of marble or gilded domes: the desire the Turks feel that their ashes may rest near hers is singular and extreme. All round this simple tomb lie thickly strewn the graves of the Moslems. A trait such as this speaks more for the character of this people than many volumes written in their praise; for it cannot be for any greatness, or wisdom, or holiness, in her who sleeps beneath (for which qualities they show so much respect to the sepulchres of Abraham, of David, and of his son), but simply for the high domestic virtues and qualities which belonged to Rachel: she was a devoted wife and an excellent mother, as well as the parent of a mighty people; and for these things do the Turks venerate her memory.

"It is a scene of no common interest when a funeral train issues from the gate of the city, and passes slowly over the plain of Rephaim to the lonely sepulchre. Were a Jew to cross the procession at this moment, he would be treated with deep scorn and hatred by the very people who are about to kneel round the ashes of one of his ancestry. Deeply fallen nation! forbidden even to draw near or bow down at the place that is full of the remembrance of its ancient greatness."

But notwithstanding the scorn and contempt with which the Moslems thus treat the Jews, they will not be, and cannot be, driven from venerating this tomb of Rachel, and visiting it in person as often as they can. We meet several of them at the tomb, and pass, on our way to Jerusalem, a number who have been there. Indeed, there is no one trait of the Jewish character more strongly marked than love of ancestry, and the attachment they have for the country once their own. All travelers in Palestine observe this, and several have written concerning it in terms at once truthful and beautiful.

"Independently of that natural love of country," says Mr. Wilde, "which exists among this people, two objects bring the Jew to Jerusalem—to study the Scriptures and the Talmud, and then to die, and have his bones laid with his forefathers in the Valley of Jehoshaphat, even as the bones of the patriarchs were carried up out of Egypt. No matter what the station or the rank, no matter what or how far distant the country in which the Jew resides, he still lives upon the hope that he will one day journey Zionward. No clime can change, no condition quench, that patriotic ardor with which the Jew beholds Jerusalem, even through the vista of a long futurity. On his first approach to the city, while yet within a day's journey, he puts on his best apparel; and when the first view of it bursts upon his sight, he rends his garments, falls down to weep and pray over the long-sought object of his pilgrimage; and with the dust sprinkled on his head he enters the city of his forefathers. No child ever returned home, after long absence, with more yearnings of affection; no proud baron ever beheld his ancestral tower and lordly halls, when they had become another's, with greater sorrow than wrings the heart of the poor Jew when he first beholds Jerusalem. This, at least, is patriotism."

"It is curious," says Milman, "after surveying this

almost total desertion of Palestine, to read the indications of fond attachment to its very air and soil scattered about in the Jewish writings; still, it is said, that man is esteemed most blessed who even after his death shall reach the land of Palestine, and be buried there, or even shall have his ashes sprinkled by a handful of its sacred dust. 'The air of the land of Israel,' says one, ' makes a man wise ;' another writes, " He who walks four cubits in the land of Israel is sure of being a son of the life to come.' ' The great Wise Men are wont to kiss the borders of the Holy Land, to *embrace* its ruins, and roll themselves in its dust.' ' The sins of all those are forgiven who inhabit the land of Israel.' He who is buried there is reconciled with God, as though he were buried under the altar. The dead buried in the land of Canaan first come to life in the days of the Messiah."

Of this tomb of Rachel the record simply says, "And Rachel died, and was buried in the way to Ephrath, which is Bethlehem. And Jacob set a pillar upon her grave : that is the pillar of Rachel's grave unto this day." Tradition has always marked this as the spot, nor do we see any reason to doubt it.

From this point we gallop along as fast as possible, and having crossed the " Hill of Evil Counsel," and a well-cultivated valley—the only one of any extent near Jerusalem—by ten o'clock we find ourselves at the Jaffa Gate, and a half hour after we are seated among the congregation in the English church, where we have the pleasure of joining in the service and listening to a most excellent sermon from the Rt. Rev. Bishop Gobat.

This church was established and is still maintained by the "London Society for Promoting Christianity amongst the Jews." The church building itself, located on Mount Zion, is of good size and well finished. It, together with other buildings devoted to a Hospital and Dispensary, House of Industry, Jewesses' Institution, Boys' School, Bible and General Book Depôt, and Inquirers' Home, all belong to the Society.

The Missionary Instructors consist of Rev. Dr. Gobat, Lord Bishop of Jerusalem, Rev. Dr. Barclay, Rev. E. B. Frankel, and Rev. W. Bailey, with two Lay Agents. The number of converts now residing in Jerusalem is about one hundred and fifty; number baptized in 1865-6, nineteen. Services are held in Hebrew, Spanish, German, and English, and prayer-meetings on Tuesday and Friday of each week.

The Sabbath-morning services (in English) are largely attended. This morning every seat is filled, and the service is of the most solemn and impressive character. "Pray for the peace of Jerusalem: they shall prosper that love thee."

CHAPTER VII.

NORTHWARD THROUGH SAMARIA.

AFTER our return from the Jordan and the Dead Sea, we spend nearly four more days in Jerusalem, but as these are spent the same as the previous ones have been, viz. : in sight-seeing, and as in previous chapters we have given a pretty full description of the "sights" in and about the Holy City, we shall not detain our readers with any further account now.

On the afternoon of Wednesday (April 3d) we leave Jerusalem for a tour through Northern Palestine. In about one hour from the time we leave the Damascus Gate we reach the summit of Mount Scopus, where we stop for a few moments to take one last, long, lingering look at the Holy City; for, though we were greatly disappointed in our first view of it, and though all our subsequent examinations have been accompanied with a feeling of sadness akin to disappointment, still we cannot turn our back upon it without a feeling of regret.

Like as one may say of his own country, "With all thy faults I love thee still," so we may say of Jerusalem. Its whole history is so connected with the biblical record that one cannot examine it without feeling that he is reading anew the pages of Holy Writ; that he is seeing what King David saw, and something of what King Solomon did; that he is treading, it may be, in the very footsteps of Jesus—where he lived, and moved, and wrought, and died, and had a resurrection; that he is wandering over hills and through valleys, and possibly over the very paths, in which the apostles trod while they continued their labors of love, even among those who had rejected and crucified their Master; that he is looking upon the very site, and possibly upon some of the very stones, of the city which, having been accursed of God because of its rejection of the Saviour, was subsequently overthrown and utterly trodden under foot by the victorious army of Titus; and that he is treading the very streets and looking upon walls once trod and defended by the Crusaders, who, to rescue the cross from the hands of infidels, were willing to sacrifice the comforts of home and friends, and even life itself if necessary!

With thoughts like these passing through our mind, can you wonder that we leave Jerusalem with regret, and that our last look is long and lingering, notwithstanding the disappointment and sadness we have experienced in seeing and examining it?

In about two hours from the time of leaving the summit of Mount Scopus we reach El-Bir, the ancient Beeroth, one of the cities of the Gibeonites. However much of a city it may have been in ancient days, at present it is only a miserable stone-wall village, with nothing attractive about it, save a fine fountain near by, at which we stop for a few moments to water our horses and refresh ourselves.

Mr. Skinner's experience, while halting at this place, gives us an insight into the manners and customs of the modern Syrians which cannot be better learned from any other source; and as he has told it in a very pleasant and amusing manner, we cannot do better than copy his account verbatim. He says:

"We finished our day's journey about a mile eastward of Ram Allah, and stopped an hour before sunset at the entrance of the village of El-Bir, so called from a clear fountain at the foot of the hill on which the houses stand. It is probably the Beeroth of Scripture, and not Michmash, as usually supposed. We took possession of a ruined arch that serves as a khan, and stands among many at the bottom of the town. It is open at both ends, and the wind blew through it, while the rain drizzled from the broken roof. We swept the floor, and spreading our carpets upon it, placed the cattle against the upper entrance, while the villagers crouched in the mouth of the other. Thus with a blazing log of wood, which we soon arranged, all promised very well, when the colonel, who thought his dignity compromised by this humble retreat, sent his interpreter to trumpet our arrival through the village, and obtain, if possible, a house.

"I have a horror of such civilities as the Arabs of a village are able to afford, and could not sympathize with the Frenchman in his joy at the discovery of a building for our accommodation. We would not divide our fortunes, however, and followed Monsieur Souf through the miserable streets to the highest point of the hill, where, exposed to the full violence of the wind, we found a solitary house, close to the remains of a large church which was built by the Empress Helena over the spot where tradition says the Virgin Mary sat while, having missed our Saviour, after a day's journey, Joseph sought him among their kinsfolk and acquaintance before they returned to Jerusalem.

"These ruins were walled round, and our cattle occupied such shelter as they gave. As we came on foot through the streets, leading our horses, the gentle dames of the village levied a tax upon our property in a very ingenious manner, by pulling the bedding, which hung loose over the saddles, into their huts. Anticipating a clamor when we should make the discovery, they took their husbands into their confidence, who acted their parts most admirably.

" When we reached the airy castle we were to possess for the night, lo! our beds were gone. Hassan made an oration upon their inhospitality to the men who surrounded us. They affected to be shocked, and hoped we did not think it possible that they could have encouraged so scandalous an act. 'You shall have your property,' they all cried, ' but will you not reward us?' They were promised a reward, and in a short time returned with the stolen blankets; then, telling the story, laughed at the success of the stratagem.

" The door of the khan was so low that we were forced to crouch to pass through it. The room was full of smoke; so dark and so close that I fancied we had sunk into the infernal regions. 'Open the window, if there be one!' we all exclaimed, and one of the party pushed a wooden shutter that let in a glimmer of day at the top of the wall, when a loud shout of "Wullah! what dogs are these?" burst from the centre of the chamber as the light rushed into it, where, round a deep hole wherein lay a log from which all the smoke proceeded, about thirty men were seen squatted in a circle, smoking, and wrapped up in their large cloaks. They were like owls disturbed in their favorite darkness, and floundered and flapped about in a most ungentle humor. They insisted upon closing all up again, and we for a while submitted.

" ' There is a mat in the corner; sit down there; take off your shoes, and thank God that you are allowed to come in at all,' cried a fellow bearded like the Saracen's Head upon a sign-post, with a large knife at his girdle, 'What brings you here?' 'Our own business,' replied our interpreter; 'and we wish to have as much room as possible, so you had better be gone and leave us to ourselves.' This modest request was near bringing affairs to a crisis with a vengeance. 'Off with your shoes, unbelievers!' exclaimed a little shriveled Arab, with the most intolerant expression of countenance I ever saw. 'Out with them, in the name of God!' shouted another; while 'Wullah, Yullah,' and all the different variations and invocations of the name of Allah, escaped from the lips of the crowd.

"We drew up into a corner and stood firm; the sailor half drew his sword, we handled our pistols, and the French colonel began to chatter a mixture of languages that promised to perplex the matter as much as words could do for us. Monsieur Souf, who was of a peaceable turn of mind, kept aloof; while Hassan whispered to me, 'Fa niente, signore—don't fight.'

"The colonel's address had rather a composing effect, although I believe not one word of it was understood. When it was over the men sank down to their sitting posture, and allowed the window to be opened, that they might contemplate us at their leisure. We were by this time all in tears from the pain of the smoke in our eyes. I was forced to bandage mine with my handkerchief, and peeped from under it every now and then at the group. They eyed us very minutely, and in a low tone among themselves discussed our appearance, which was not unlike that of a party of children crying at being kept in the corner. I hope this notion did not occur to the Arabs, for the Franks will scarcely be elevated in their judgments from our visit among them, if it did.

"As we could neither get rid of the smoke nor enjoy the air while the crowd remained, we again proposed their departure, when the calm at once grew into a worse tempest than the first. Up they sprang, and cursed us most dismally, repeating constantly, 'Wonderful! Are we not men? They come here to beard us in our own dens!' A loud clatter at the door, which was not calculated to resist much, broke it from its hinges, and in poured a fresh supply of people from the village, screaming out, 'Bucksheesh, bucksheesh!' The wind and the rain, too, drove in upon us, and the sparks from the fire in the centre flew about the room. The adventures in Don Quixote's inn were nothing to those promised to us. We gathered together, and stood in front of our baggage piled up in a corner, and resisted by pushing and pulling every attempt to approach it. 'Out with the dogs! Down with the infidels!' and such agreeable expressions, rang through the multitude. There was now no space to move, and we stood at bay; one hand holding a handkerchief to our eyes, while with the other we used what defence we could to keep our ground.

"We had not yet come regularly to blows, and were all anxious to avoid them. We were nevertheless in full expectation of a furious struggle every moment, when an old man, who had been conversing with M. Souf, called out, 'Silence, my children, and let us hear them speak!' The colonel, who had just whispered to me, 'I wish we had one of his highness' six-pounders here,' advanced with his drawn sword into the centre, and commenced an oration, but in such an outrageous passion that no two words could be connected together. 'Choich, choich—gentle, gentle,' was all that we could say to control the impatience of his hearers, which I repeated till my throat was as dry as possible.

"At length a most fortunate scheme struck the interpreter, who cried out in Arabic to the principal man, 'What is your name?' 'Abd-ul-Kerim,' said he. 'Then write it down, I pray you,' continued the interpreter, turning to the colonel, 'that Ibrahim Pasha may know how his chief engineer has been received while traveling on his service.'

"This speech fell like a thunderbolt among them. The colonel sheathed his sword and drew out his note-book; I presented him a pencil, and we all gathered round to assist in making the muster-roll. It was not necessary, however; the threat was enough, and one by one the crowd began to drop away, till the head man alone remained, who assured us that all that had occurred was meant most civilly; that while the women were making bread, the men usually came up here to smoke, for their wives shut the doors upon them until the sun sets.

"We could not fasten the door during the night, and kept watch alternately by the large fire which the head man of the village, to make amends for our uncourteous reception, supplied most bountifully with fuel from the shrubs around, for wood is scarcely to be seen. Occasional attempts were made by the villagers to enter our resting-place, but we firmly resisted them. The necessity of combating these attacks, and the still more tantalizing one of the numerous insects in the place, prevented the possibility of sleeping. We were glad to be up when the day broke, and escape from so uncomfortable a confinement."

The hills hereabout—and, indeed, generally throughout Palestine—are treeless and shrubless, though we have frequently remarked to Lily, while riding along, that they must have been thickly wooded some day, and now, while reading of this ancient city and its people in the ninth chapter of Joshua, we are confirmed in this belief, for there it is recorded that as a punishment for the deception which the Gibeonites had practised upon Joshua and the princes of Israel, they (the Gibeonites) were condemned to be the "hewers of wood and drawers of water for the congregation," and why should they have been condemned as " hewers of wood," if then, as now, there was no wood to hew? The fact, no doubt, is, that in the days of the ancient Israelites the hills and mountains of Judea, now so barren, were thickly wooded; but there being no coal or other combustibles in the country, save wood alone, the use of it for fuel and building purposes, during thousands of years, has caused the hewing down of almost every tree from off these hills, except olives and other fruit-bearing species.

To such extremities are the natives of these regions now reduced for securing fuel, that they cut down, or rather dig up by the roots, every twig and shrub growing on the mountain side, and not unfrequently have we met dozens of young girls carrying bundles of these twigs on their heads from the mountains to the villages. Not only so, but they dig up for fuel the small thorn bushes growing upon abandoned fields, and, to add still farther to their stores, they gather horse manure from the roads and wherever else they can find it, which, after drying in the sun, they use as fuel. It is curious to observe a family's " wood-pile" consisting of small brush or twigs piled on the house-top, and a heap of sun-dried manure cakes beside the door, and yet such sights are common in all the villages of Lower Palestine. In Middle and Upper Palestine trees are much oftener met with, though even here fuel is very scarce, and twigs and dried manure are extensively used.

From El-Bir we go direct to Bethel, occupying about

two hours, traveling over a very stony, rough path. Here we find our tents pitched, in company with those of two other American parties, with whom we exchange civilities, and then look around to see if there are any ruins of ancient Bethel, but none are to be found except some large Arab ruins, the stones of which may have been of more ancient buildings.

The Bible record says "the name of Bethel was called Luz at the first," from which it may be inferred that a city stood upon this spot in the days of Jacob, but at present a small Syrian village is all that marks the place. The natives, however, call the Arab ruins hereabouts Bourg Bethel.

The only interest in this spot is, that it was here that Jacob "dreamed, and beheld a ladder set up on the earth, and the top of it reached to heaven; and he beheld the angels of God ascending and descending upon it;" and then followed the promises which God made to Jacob, and the account of his rising up early in the morning, and taking the stone which he had put as a pillow, and setting it up as an altar to the Lord.

Lily, following the example of Jacob, has one of the servants bring in a large stone and place it under her pillow—or rather, under the head of the iron bedstead on which she sleeps—but whether she, too, saw a vision of angels, or slept more soundly because of it, we have not been able to ascertain. Because we laughed at her for doing it, she refuses to tell us anything of her dreams last night.

Early in the morning we leave Bethel for Nablous, passing on our way a number of interesting places.

The first we stop to examine are the ruins of the Mosque of Settein, a square stone building. Over the doorway of this is an urn between two wreaths, and within lie the broken pieces of three Corinthian columns. The former use of this building is not definitely known, but from its general appearance we should judge it to have been used for sepulchral purposes.

Near this, on the slope of a hill opposite, is the site of the ancient Shiloh. We were about to write ruins instead of site, but the fact is that no ruins of Shiloh remain, unless we count as such the stones of former buildings, lying in great quantity all over the hillside. The walls of one old, square stone building remain standing, but the arched doorways and general style of architecture show it to have been of Roman origin.

There are numerous tombs in the mountain-sides hereabouts, now all empty and in ruins, which, with other evidences, prove it to have once been a place or city of considerable size; and that this is the identical site of ancient Shiloh there cannot, we think, be any doubt, since it so accurately agrees with the location as given in the last chapter of Judges, and tradition points out no other.

It was here that the children of Benjamin were commanded to "Go and lie in wait in the vineyards; and see, and behold, if the daughters of Shiloh come out to dance in dances; then come ye out of the vineyards, and catch you every man his wife of the daughters of Shiloh, and go to the land of Benjamin."

This was certainly a novel way of getting wives; but, under the circumstances it seemed to be the only chance left for the poor Benjaminites. We doubt if there is a single woman hereabouts now whom even a Benjaminite would care to catch.

Leaving Shiloh, we pass Khan Luban; the village of Luban (ancient Lebonah); the village of Sawich; and after a tedious ascent of a high ridge, we look down upon a long and broad valley coming down from Galilee, and far beyond it we see the snowy summit of Mount Hermon, grand and glorious! This is our first but not our last sight of Hermon.

A long ride up this valley, over a comparatively good road, brings us to Jacob's Well, at which we stop to make examinations. It is located near the junction of this valley with another coming down from Nablous, and not far from the base of Mount Gerizim. The ruins of a heavy wall still surround it, and to reach the mouth of the well we descend into an arched vault, of probably ten feet in diameter. We have no line to measure its depth, but by dropping a few small pebbles into it, and marking the time which it takes before they strike the water, we readily determine that the well is very deep, and contains considerable water. We had hoped to have a drink from this well, but having no line with which to let down a cup, we are compelled to forego the pleasure.

This, then, is the parcel of ground which Jacob gave to his son Joseph; this is the well that Jacob dug, and this the well at which Jesus sat and conversed with the woman of Samaria.

"Jesus saith unto her, give me to drink.

" Then saith the woman of Samaria unto him, How is it that thou, being a Jew, askest drink of me, which am a woman of Samaria; for the Jews have no dealings with the Samaritans?

"Jesus answered and said unto her, If thou knewest the gift of God, and who it is that saith to thee, Give me to drink, thou wouldest have asked of him, and he would have given thee living water."

This is indeed holy ground—sanctified by the footsteps of Jesus, and not less so by the great lesson which he here taught, not to the woman of Samaria only, but to all mankind, that "God is a spirit; and they that worship him must worship him in spirit and in truth."

Stephens, in writing of this region and this well, says: "We were now entering the region of Samaria, and though the mountains were yet stony, a beautiful country was opening before us. Our ride lay principally along the edge of a wide valley, well watered and gloriously fertile. The green expanse of the wheat-fields was refreshing to an eye accustomed for some time to the glare of the streets and surrounding rocks of Jerusalem. We passed several villages, among which I remember was that of Cowara, beautifully situated on the side of the mountain, overlooking a fertile valley, and all the women of the village were in the field picking the tares from the grain. Here I took a guide to conduct me to the Patriarch's well, where our Saviour talked with the Samaritan woman.

"In about two hours we were winding along the side of Mount Gerizim, whose summit was covered with the white dome of a sheikh's tomb; and passing on the declivity of the mountain going down to the valley at its base, we came to Jacob's well, or the Beer Samarea of the Arabs, distant rather more than a mile from the eastern gate of Nablous. It bears evident marks of antiquity, but was now dry and deserted; it was said usually to contain living water, and not merely to be filled by the rains. We had no line with us at the moment to measure the well; but by dropping in stones we could perceive that it was *deep* (John iv. 11), a thing very unusual in Palestine, where the water is generally preserved in superficial cisterns, from which it issues in a fountain; or else a few stairs are placed for descending into it. The depth, as measured by Maundrell and recently by Homes, is about 105 feet."

"I think," says Dr. Robinson, "we may rest with confidence in the opinion that this is Jacob's well, and here the parcel of ground which Jacob gave to his son Joseph. Here the Saviour, wearied with his journey, sat beside the well, and taught the poor Samaritan woman those great truths which have broken down the separating wall between Jews and Gentiles: 'God is a Spirit, and they that worship him must worship him in spirit and in truth.'"

Only a little way from Jacob's well is the site of the tomb of Joseph, now covered over with a small Mohammedan wely. We ride over to examine this, and, when within the enclosure, we notice a curiously-shaped tomb near the centre, with Hebrew inscriptions on the side walls. In one corner of the enclosure somebody has planted a grape-vine, which reaches up and over the wall, and which to our eye is both typical and beautiful.

There are some who say that the tomb of Joseph is in the mosque at Hebron; but since seeing this spot and its surroundings, and considering the arguments pro and con, we are satisfied that this is the parcel of ground which Jacob bought from the father of Shechem, and gave as a special inheritance to his son Joseph; and that just here, and nowhere else, the children of Israel laid the bones of Joseph, which they brought up out of Egypt.

From the tomb, our route lies up the Valley of Nablous, with Mount Gerizim on the one side and Mount Ebal on the other. The plain is not wide, and the two mounts rise beautifully from the valley and face each other. Their slopes are within calling distance, and at one time they presented a scene in Israelitish history grand and wonderful.

Moses doubtless saw these mountains from the summit of Pisgah, when he directed that when the Israelites were brought in the land of promise they should "put the blessing upon Mount Gerizim and the curse upon Mount Ebal."

And now, as we look upon these two mounts, and picture the scene then presented, of a portion of the tribes upon the slope of the one mount and a portion on the other, we can hear (in imagination) the Levites calling out: "Cursed is the man that maketh any graven image, an abomination unto the Lord, the work of the hands of the craftsmen, and putteth into a secret place."

And then from the tribes on the opposite mount the loud response, "Amen!"

"Cursed be he that setteth light by his father or his mother."

And the loud response from the other mount, "Amen!"

"Cursed be he who removeth his neighbor's landmark."

And the loud response, "Amen!"

"Cursed be he that maketh the blind to wander out of the way."

And the loud response, "Amen!"

"Cursed be he that perverteth the judgment of the stranger, fatherless and widow."

And the loud response, "Amen!"

Fearful were the cursings, benign the blessings; and who dare say that they are not as applicable to the present generation as to those who uttered them?

In a little while we reach Nablous and pitch our tents on its western border, amidst the tents of fourteen other Americans and four Englishmen—all, like ourselves, travelers and sight-seers in Palestine.

This town of Nablous (anciently Neapoli) is of very ancient date, its history being traceable for some four thousand years. It was here, or near here, that Abraham first pitched his tent in the land of Canaan; it was the inhabitants of this city who suffered such terrible punishment at the hands of Simeon and Levi (sons of Jacob) for dishonoring their sister Dinah; and it was here that Rehoboam was declared king over all Israel.

Stephens, who traveled over this same route, says: "Turning the point of the mountain, we came to a rich valley lying between the mountains of Gerizim and Ebal. Crossing this valley, on the sides of the mountain of Ebal is a long range of grottoes and tombs, and a little before coming to them, in a large white building like a sheikh's tomb, is the sepulchre of Joseph. I dismounted and entered the building, and it is not an uninteresting fact that I found there a white-bearded Israelite, kneeling at the tomb of the patriarch, and teaching a rosy-cheeked boy (his descendant of the fourth generation) the beautiful story of Joseph and his brethren.

"It was late in the evening when I was moving up the valley of Nablous. The mountains of Gerizim and Ebal, the mountains of blessings and curses, were towering like lofty walls on either side of me. A beautiful stream, in two or three places filling large reservoirs, was running through the valley, and a shepherd sat on its bank playing a reed pipe, with his flock feeding quietly around him. The shades of evening were gathering fast as I approached the town of Nablous, the Shechem or Sychem of the Old Testament, and the Sychar of the New. More than a dozen lepers were sitting outside the gate, their faces shining, pimpled and bloated, covered with sores and pustules, their nostrils open and filled with ulcers, and their red eyes fixed and staring; with swollen feet they dragged their disgusting bodies toward me, and with hoarse voices extended their deformed and hideous hands for charity."

The town of Nablous is at present a miserably dirty place of about six thousand inhabitants, consisting mostly of Mohammedans. Its streets are execrable, as we have reason to know from nearly breaking our neck while passing over them on horseback when searching for the Samaritan synagogue; and its inhabitants are exceedingly hostile to Christians, as we have further reason to know from seeing a boy throw a stone at Lily while quietly riding along on horseback, and for the catching of which boy we offered another boy a dollar, that we might give him such a flogging as would teach him for all time to come to respect the rights of travelers.

The valley in which this town is located is one of great beauty and fertility, and being so near another large valley, it must in times past have been a place of considerable trade and importance.

Early next morning we commence the ascent of Mount Gerizim, which is by no means an easy task. The path from Nablous is so steep and stony that no other than a Syrian horse could ever go up it. In the day of its great glory, when a magnificent temple crowned its summit and thousands went up to worship on this mountain, there must certainly have been a better road or path.

Dr. Robinson ascended Mount Gerizim under the guidance of one of the younger Samaritans, an honest, simple-minded man. When about two-thirds of the way up, they heard, he says, a woman calling after them, who proved to be the mother of the Samaritan guide. He was her only son, and had come away, it seems, without her knowledge; and she was now in the utmost terror at finding that he had gone off as a guide to Franks, to show them the holy mountain. She had immediately followed the party, and was now crying after them with all the strength of her lungs, forbidding him to proceed lest some evil should befall him. The young man went back to meet her, and tried to pacify her, but in vain; she insisted upon his returning home. This he was not inclined to do, though, he said, he could not disobey his mother, and so transgress the law of Moses. This touching trait gave the travelers a favorable idea of the morality of the Samaritans. After reasoning with her a long time without effect, he finally persuaded her to go with them. So she followed the strangers up the mountain; at first full of wrath, and keeping at a distance from them; yet, at last, she became quite reconciled and communicative.

Twenty minutes of ascent in the direction south-west from the city leads the traveler to the top of Gerizim, a tract of high table land, stretching off far to the west and south-west, and covered with rich herbage and wild flowers. Twenty minutes more toward the south-east, along a regular path upon the table land, brings him to the holy place of the Samaritans, which is still some distance from that shown as Joshua's altar. The ground here is rather depressed to a centre, so that a larger assemblage than the Samaritans can now muster might conveniently witness the sacred rites as from an amphitheatre. A few stones formed into an altar, and a paved trench to carry off the victim's blood, are all the tokens of the place and its purposes. A little farther on the extreme and most elevated summit which overlooks the valley are some very extensive remains of a Roman fortress, with large tanks and much masonry of massive and regular construction.

Just under the walls of the castle, on the west side, are a few flat stones, of which it is difficult to say whether they were laid there by nature or by man. Under these are laid, as they allege, the twelve stones brought from Jordan by the Israelites; and there they will remain till the Muhdy (the Messiah) shall appear.

Beyond the castle, toward the south, is the alleged altar of Joshua, the holiest spot, where the Samaritan guide reverently takes off his shoes. It is the kibleh of that people. On whatever side of it they may be, they
14

always turn their faces toward it in prayer; but when upon the spot itself, it is lawful for them to pray in any direction. Round it are slight traces of former walls, possibly those of the ancient temple. The spot itself is a sort of table, level with the surrounding ground, and at first sight appearing to be nothing more than the natural face of the rock from which the surface soil has been removed, and divided into compartments by natural accidents of fracture and fissure. Such Lord Francis Egerton at first considered it, but on closer inspection he was induced to adopt the opinion that it was artificial. "It slopes," his lordship says, " at an angle fully sufficient for the sacrificial purpose of allowing blood to drain off toward the cavernous mouth of a deep well. Of these wells there are several near, and in two, at least, of them I thought I perceived that the stones of the orifice had been arranged artificially, and if so, with consummate skill, and to be, in fact, specimens of that kind of architecture best known by the term of cyclopean—stones, namely, unhewn, but fitted to one another with a felicity which, on a small scale, is often exhibited by the dyke-builders of Scotland. Now, Joshua was directed to build his altar of whole stones, untouched by iron tool; and, on looking at the altar itself, and comparing it with the wells in the neighborhood, I was much inclined to the opinion that all were of the same construction, and of one which would answer this description."

Near the same place the Samaritans show an altar as that on which Abraham was commanded to offer up Isaac; and further south, and, indeed, all round upon this eminence, are extensive foundations, apparently of dwellings, as if the ruins of a former city.

On the summit we find a small encampment of Samaritans, who are here to celebrate their annual passover, and a little farther on we find the ruins of their once magnificent temple.

Around the ruins of the temple proper are very thick walls, with a tower at each corner, which were probably erected and used for defensive purposes, and outside of these walls are the foundation-stones of many other buildings.

Recent excavations by Capt. Wilson, of England, show the temple to have been of great beauty, both as to architecture and the use of materials. The bases and caps of beautiful columns have been found, and the stones, even of the foundation walls, are carefully cut. The view from the summit is grandly beautiful.

No people, perhaps, ever committed so many crimes, or endured so many reverses and persecutions in defence of their religion and its ancient usages, as the Samaritans; and, though there be little to commend in their annals, who can contemplate unmoved the lingering death of an ancient people, now dwindled to a mere handful, but still clinging with a love stronger than death to the memory and laws of their fathers? Only about twenty families now remain of this once numerous people. "I was presented," says Mr. Farren, then British Consul-General in Syria, "in acknowledgment of some little service I rendered them, with a copy of a letter addressed to them about two hundred years ago from a body of Samaritans in India (of whom they have no other trace), beseeching to know the fate of their brethren in Samaria; and when at Sychem and passing at sunset near their tombs, which lay upon a sterile bank within a wild recess at the foot of Gerizim, two Samaritan women, who were seated there and seemed mournfully to be numbering the graves into which the remnant of their ancient race was fast declining, broke their silence as I approached, and, in accents of deep feeling, implored me, if I knew where any of their people were now scattered, to tell them that their few remaining brethren, who still dwelt in the land of their forefathers, besought them to return and close the exhausted record of their fate with kindred sympathies and rites."

Much curiosity has existed among the learned, both in this country and in Europe, with regard to this singular people, and several most eminent men of their day, including Scaliger and De Sacy, have had correspondence with them, but without any satisfactory result. The descendants of the Israelites who remained and were not carried into captivity, on the rebuilding of the second temple were denied the privilege of sharing the labor and expense of its reconstruction at Jerusalem; and in mortification and revenge they built a temple on Mount Gerizim with the permission of Alexander the Great; and ever since a deadly hatred has existed between their descendants, the Samaritans, and the Jews. Gibbon, speaking of them in the time of Justinian, says, "The Samaritans of Palestine were a motley race, an ambiguous sect, rejected as Jews by the Pagans, by the Jews as schismatics, and by the Christians as idolaters. The abomination of the cross had been already planted on their holy Mount of Gerizim, but the persecution of Justinian offered only the alternative of baptism or rebellion. They chose the latter; under the standard of a desperate leader they rose in arms and retaliated their wrongs on the lives, the property, and the temples of a defenceless people. The Samaritans were finally subdued by the regular forces of the East; twenty thousand were slain, twenty thousand were sold by the Arabs to the infidels of Persia and India, and the remains of that unhappy nation atoned for the crime of treason by the sin of hypocrisy."

They pretended to embrace Christianity in the year 551, as the only means of recovering a few trifling privileges. Soon after that period they disappear from the historian's view; crushed down without the power of resistance under the heavy yoke of the Moslems, their number has ever since continued to decrease.

The Syrians tell many marvelous tales about the isolated and mysterious Samaritans: they assert that the number of heads of families among them is invariably forty, and can neither augment nor diminish, being irrevocably fixed by the demons, who are the protectors of the race. Setting aside all such fables, the following is an abstract of what appears best authenticated respecting this people.

They intermarry only with each other, never stray beyond their mountain, and hold no familiar intercourse with their neighbors of a different creed. Cut off from the whole world, ages pass over their heads, leaving them unchanged in all but numbers.

Their synagogue is a small, plain arched room, with a curtained recess on the left hand as you enter, wherein they keep their manuscripts, of which they profess to have about a hundred: one of these, a copy of the Pentateuch, they allege to be three thousand four hundred and sixty years old, having been transcribed by Abishua, the son of Phineas, and great-grandson of Aaron. They demand payment beforehand for showing this, and then produce an old roll, which, however, is not the right one. If the traveler is skilled enough in such matters to detect the fraud, the priest and his hopeful flock only laugh and bring out the other. "This," says Dr. Robinson, "was certainly very much worn, and somewhat tattered with much kissing, and here and there patched with shreds of parchment; but the handwriting appeared to me very similar to the former, and the vellum seemed, in like manner, not ancient." They regard the genuine manuscript, whatever that may be, as a palladium with which are bound up the lives and destinies of Samaritans; but they are possessed, it is said, with a sad foreboding that the precious deposit will one day be wrested from them, and then will the days of the last of their race be numbered. According to their account, their two families of priests are still of the stock of Aaron. Until recently these families had kept their blood pure from all alien mixture; but in consequence of their continual diminution, the males among them, now five in number, have been obliged to take wives from other houses. The place where they sacrifice [on ordinary occasions] is an altar of dry stone, erected behind their village, on an artificial mound, which serves them as a representative of the famous Mount Gerizim. They keep the passover in the manner of the ancient Hebrews.

In child-birth the Samaritan woman remains shut up in her house for forty days, and no one is allowed to see her but the midwife or the nurse. Were any one else, even her husband, to see her during that time, the whole house would be rendered unclean, and it would be necessary to burn every article in it that was incapable of being purified by fire or by running water. Her chamber is closely shut, and talismans are hung on the door to drive away the demon *Leilat*, a formidable being, ever on the watch to steal into the lying-in chamber, and cast a malignant spell upon the mother and her child. Above the talismans the name of *Leilat* is inscribed in large red letters, with an imprecation against the fiend; for of all magic charms his own name is thought most potent to repel him. On the fortieth day the woman quits her prison, Leilat no longer having any power to molest her; but it it is not till twelve days after this that she performs her solemn ablutions, and a festival is held in the house to celebrate her readmission into the family circle.

Like the Jews, the Samaritans carefully avoid all contact with a dead body or with a tomb, lest they should be rendered unclean: they wash their whole bodies and change their raiment before presenting themselves at the altar for prayer or sacrifice.

As a reason why the Samaritans never quit Nablous, the following incident is related:

Some members of their community were accused before the atrocious Djezzar, pasha of Acre, of having blasphemed the Mohammedan faith, by declaring that they alone, as possessing the true ancient religion of God, were entitled to Paradise. Djezzar instantly summoned the chief men of the Samaritans, who entered his presence with dismay. Leaning on his hatchet and surrounded with his cut-throats and executioners, he stared for a long while with the aspect of a tiger on the Samaritans, whose terrors he beheld with delight. "Filthy miscreants!" he cried at last, in a voice of thunder, "what is the exact number of your people?" "A hundred and sixty," they replied, half dead with fear. "A hundred and sixty! and Paradise is for you alone! Well, then, sons of dogs, leave the earth to those against whom Paradise is barred, and go straight to heaven." Thereupon the pasha made a fatal gesture with his right hand, and the wretched men were hurried out for execution. But presently Djezzar appeared to change his mind. "Send those dogs back to their dens," he said; "and if a single one of them ever ventures to show himself beyond them, let him be killed like an unclean beast." He then, by way of commuting their punishment, increased the taxes paid by the Samaritans six-fold, and saddled them with the cost of constructing and maintaining a fountain at Kefr Nuohr, two leagues from Saffad, that, as he said, they might do some good in this world to those who were to be deprived of Paradise in the next. The Samaritans returned home, rejoiced at having got off so well from this interview with the ferocious pasha, who, fortunately for them, happened on this day to be in unusually good-humor. "Ever since that day," say the oldest Samaritans, "none of us have gone into the plain, and we die without ever quitting the walls of our quarters."

Djezzar Pasha has been many years dead, but the lesson still works, and the Samaritans keep close to home, dreading to expose themselves to the outrages of the rude Nablousian mountaineers.

CHAPTER VIII.

DESOLATION AND BEAUTY.

BEFORE leaving Nablous we go and see the Samaritan synagogue, and the copy of the Books of Moses which the Samaritans have, and which is said to be the oldest in the world.

After coming down from Mount Gerizim, we enter the city gate, and after wending our way through dark and narrow streets, and under arches, some of which are so low that we have to dismount before going under them, we reach the door of the house, in the second story of which the synagogue is located. The room is rather small, with arched ceilings, and is furnished much after the style of Jewish synagogues. We ask to see the copy of the old Law, which they claim was written by Abishua, the son of Phineas, some three thousand five hundred years ago, and straightway the young men in attendance produce it. It is upon rollers, in the usual style of Hebrew manuscript copies of the Law, and certainly looks very ancient, though we doubt the antiquity which they give to it. Handing the young men some bucksheesh for their trouble in showing us the synagogue and manuscript, we remount, and after another difficult and hazardous passage through the street, we find our way out of the gate and to our camping-place, and from thence we proceed on our journey.

After about two hours' ride over a comparatively pleasant road, we reach the site of ancient Samaria—now called Sebustieh—where we find our tents pitched for another night's rest.

The site of this ancient city is the long ridge of a lofty hill, around and about which are extensive and beautiful valleys. The present village is of no account, but the ruins which remain of Samaria, and those of a more recent date, are quite extensive and of great interest.

We first visit the ruins of the Church of St. John, which was erected by the Knights of St. John, over what they believed to be the sepulchre of John the Baptist. The ruins show that the edifice was one of much beauty, though at present it is in a very dilapidated condition. To reach the reputed tomb of St. John we descend some fifteen feet below the floor of the church, and once here, we find a room of some twenty feet square, excavated in the rock, with recesses for burial-places. The heavy stone door which was used to close the tomb is now unhinged and sits against the wall.

Notwithstanding the almost universal belief that this is the identical burial-place of St. John the Baptist, Josephus relates expressly that John was beheaded in the castle of Machaerus, on the east of the Dead Sea; and it is hardly probable that his disciples who " came and took up the body and buried it" (Matt. xiv. 12), first transported it all the way to Samaria.

The eastern end of the church is rounded in the common Greek style, and resting as it does on a precipitous elevation of nearly one hundred feet, it is, or rather has been, a noble and very striking monument. Common tradition, as in so many other cases, falsely ascribes this once magnificent church to the Empress Helena; but the style of the architecture necessarily limits its antiquity to the period of the Crusaders, though it is possible that a portion of the eastern end may be of earlier date.

Next we visit and examine what remain of the columns of the beautiful colonnade built in the time of Herod. This extended around, or nearly around, the hill, about one-third of the way down, and must have been very grand and imposing. A large number of the columns—probably one hundred—remain standing, or lie near where they once stood, and being surrounded by rough stone walls and cultivated fields, they look sadly strange.

In a fig orchard, just above the present town, a number of beautiful columns remain standing, which probably belonged to a temple; not far from these columns the remains of fortifications may be seen, though of these but little remain. The remains of a great gateway may also be traced on the western side of the hill.

The situation of the place, the careful terracing of the hill, the beautiful and once well-cultivated valleys which surround it, with the remains of ancient structures, fully prove it to have been a city of opulence and enterprise. But what a change! How desolate and dreary, and God-forsaken everything about the town now appears.

This was the hill which King Omri bought of Shermer for two talents of silver, and built thereon a city which he called Samaria; this was the city in which King Ahab was besieged, and where the people were reduced to such extremity that mothers boiled and ate their infant children for food; this was the city in which the prophet Elisha predicted the deliverance in due time, " and it came to pass as the man of God had spoken to the king:" here it was that the Assyrians again surrounded the walls, and after a lengthy siege, took the city; and this was the gift which the Emperor Augustus bestowed upon his favorite Herod the Great, who rebuilt it in great splendor.

"Sebustieh," says another traveler, "is the Arabic form of Sebaste, another foreign Greek appellation, which, since the days of Herod, has continued to usurp the place of the earlier name, Samaria. The neighborhood is qûite a forest of truncated columns, bearing witness to Herod's magnificence; and it would be difficult to find in all Palestine a situation to equal, in strength, fertility and beauty combined, this site of the later capital of the Ten Tribes. In all these particulars it has greatly the advantage over Jerusalem. The whole hill consists of fertile, cultivated soil; on the summit is a broad level, apparently artificial, from which a view is obtained, extensive and beautiful almost beyond comparison. All around is a noble valley, watered by murmuring streams, and covered by a rich carpet of grass sprinkled with wild flowers of every hue; and beyond, stretches like an open book before me, a boundary of fruitful mountains, with their deep, green ravines, and the fig, vine, olive and waving wheat rising in terraces to their very summits. I sat down on a broken column under the shade of a fig tree; and near me a fellah was turning his plough round a column, the mute witness, perhaps, of the revels of Herod, 'his lords, and high captains, and chief estates of Galilee.' I asked the man what were the ruins we saw; and while his oxen were quietly cropping the grass that grew among the fragments of the marble floor, he told me they were the palace of a king—he believed of the Christians. What a comment on the vanity of worldly greatness! While pilgrims from every quarter of the world turn aside from their path to do homage in the supposed prison of Herod's victim, this Arab, who was driving his plough among the columns of his palace, knew not the proud monarch's name."

On the high hill beyond Samaria we stop a while and have a magnificent view of the site of the former city, the valleys surrounding it, and Mounts Gerizim and Ebal in the distance; and away off in the opposite direction hill after hill rises up in barren grandeur. Riding along through a succession of beautiful valleys, nearly all the way close to the banks of a running stream, with numerous villages in sight, we come to Sanûr, seated on an insulated hill, commanding an extensive view of the country, and once a strongly fortified place, but now totally demolished. The notorious Djezzar, with five thousand men, once ineffectually besieged the sheikh of this place for two months in his stronghold. More than thirty years afterward it was again invested by the late Abdallah Pasha of Acre, assisted by the troops of the Emir Beshir. It was taken after a siege of three or four months; the insurgent inhabitants were put to the sword, and their houses burned and razed to the ground. The plain on the east of Sanûr is a beautiful tract, oval or nearly round in form, three or four miles in diameter, and surrounded by low, picturesque hills. Having no issue for its waters, this plain becomes a lake in the wet season, whence it has received the name of Merj-el-Ghuruk, or Drowned Meadow.

Passing Jerba on our left and Kufeir on our right, we ascend a slight rocky eminence, and reaching its top are suddenly gratified with a wide and glorious view extending across the lower hills to the great plain of Esdraelon and the mountains of Nazareth beyond. The impression at first almost overpowers us. Just below us, on the left, is a lovely little basin or plain, a recess shut in among the mountains, and separated on the north from the great plain only by a slight ridge. We look eagerly for the round summit of Tabor, but it is not visible; the mountain of Duhy, the Little Hermon, rises in desert nakedness between, and shuts out Tabor wholly from the view.

Further west the mountains rise boldly along the north side of the great plain, and the Mount of Precipitation is conspicuous, bearing north by east.

We have now a considerable descent on the other side of the ridge; we soon pass Kubatieh, a large village in the midst of very extensive and beautiful olive groves, and at about six o'clock we leave the beautiful country of Samaria and enter the little town of Jenin, standing on the borders of Galilee, at the commencement of the great plain of Jezreel. This town, the Ginæa of Josephus, has usually passed for the site of ancient Jezreel, an error corrected by Dr. Robinson, who has identified the latter with Zerin, a small village about seven miles further north.

Here we find our tents already pitched, and our dragoman and muleteers anxiously awaiting our arrival; but as it is a pleasant afternoon and not yet sundown, before dismounting we ride into, through, and around the town, looking at and chatting with its inhabitants, and seeing whatever else is to be seen. With the exception, however, of a passably good mosque, and a very fine fountain just within the town, we find nothing about it of special interest.

The next day being the Sabbath, we decide to spend it as a day of rest in camp; and having Rev. Dr. Burt, of Cincinnati, as one of our company, a committee is appointed to wait upon him and ask him to hold religious service in one of the tents. To this he consents, and at half-past ten o'clock about a dozen Americans and three Englishmen assemble in one of the tents, to worship the only living and true God. The prayers, the singing, and the discourse are all excellent and appropriate to time and place.

While we are thus assembled for worship in the Holy

Land at the usual hour for divine service in America, our friends at home are sleeping their soundest—it being about three o'clock in the morning by the time with them. We think of this, but it lessens not the pleasure of the service to us. God is everywhere, at all times, and is ever ready to hear the prayers of those who call upon him in sincerity and truth.

Early on Monday morning we strike our tents, preparatory to a move forward; but just as we are ready to start, a sudden and violent shower comes on, which forces us to take shelter in the tent of a neighbor for the time being; and as our tents are wet and the ground thoroughly soaked, we afterward decide to occupy the upper room of an Arab house, in the village, for the balance of the day. This is a new experience, and, though bad enough, it is the better choice of evils. Showers continue, more or less, all the day, and we stick to our little Arab room and try to make the best of a bad predicament.

The clouds look somewhat threatening next morning, but the air is soft and balmy, and we conclude to make a start for Nazareth.

From the time of leaving Jenin we enter upon the great plain of Jezreel, which is a branch of the still greater valley of Esdraelon. Both of these plains are not only large in extent—the latter being no less than twenty miles from east to west, and about thirteen miles in breadth—but capable of the highest cultivation, though, at present, grass forms the principal product. When large cities, with immense populations, were scattered hereabouts, these plains were doubtless cultivated to the greatest possible extent, and must have yielded large crops. Now, not a fence, nor house, nor scarcely a tree, can be seen on all these broad and beautiful lands; only here and there is seen a miserable Syrian village, whose inhabitants are the very impersonations of indolence, ignorance, and poverty.

While looking upon the desolation which is at present observable in almost every part of Palestine, some travelers have been led to doubt whether, indeed, the biblical and early profane historical-records, as to the once great fruitfulness of this land, can be true. This thought, or doubt, impresses the mind painfully while traveling through Judea and the lower part of Samaria ; but as one comes northward, and especially after reaching the rich valleys, of which this of Esdraelon is one of the largest and richest, the doubt gradually vanishes, and even the most skeptical may believe that all which has been written of the fruitfulness of the land may be true. As to what it might be under a good government and with proper cultivation, there is much diversity of opinion ; and as upon this point we cannot better express our own views than by giving the views of another, we beg to quote the following from the excellent work of Rev. Dr. Olin :

He says: "Having now traversed the Holy Land nearly in its length and breadth, I can form my own judgment of its soil, a subject on which, above all others connected with the country, I had found my previous information most defective. The statements which I had seen were contradictory and irreconcilable. My own experience leads me to regard it as quite certain that some portions of Palestine, once fertile, are now irreclaimable. The entire destruction of the wood that formerly covered the mountains, and the utter neglect of the terraces which supported the soil on steep declivities, have allowed the rains to lay bare many tracts of rock formerly clothed with vineyards and corn-fields. It is likely, too, that the disappearance of trees from the higher grounds, where

they invited and arrested the passing clouds, may have
diminished the quantity of rain, and so have exposed the
whole country, in a greater degree, to the evils of drought,
and doomed some particular tracts to absolute sterility.
Except these, I do not recognize any permanent and
invincible causes of barrenness, or any physical obstacles
in the way of restoring this fine country to its pristine
fertility. The soil of the whole country has certainly
deteriorated under bad husbandry and the entire neglect
of the means of improvement; but a small degree of
skill and industry would be sufficient to reclaim it, as
must be evident to every traveler who has observed the
vineyards near Hebron and Bethlehem, and the gardens
of Nablous. Except the tracts about the Dead Sea,
which must always have been barren, the worst part of
Palestine is now in the 'hill country' of Judah; yet
this was precisely adapted in soil and climate to the
growth of those important staples, the grape, the fig, and
the olive, and they made it perhaps the most wealthy and
populous part of the land. The innumerable remains of
terraces and cisterns, and the ruins of large towns and
villages thickly scattered over this romantic region, would
clearly demonstrate, even if both sacred and profane history were silent on the subject, that it has been densely
peopled and highly cultivated. Now by far the largest
portion of this mountain tract is susceptible of being fully
restored to its ancient fertility. The valleys produce
wheat very well at present, and the tops of the mountains, though utterly neglected, are covered with fine
pasturage.

"Any practicable attempt to restore Palestine to its
former prosperity must be based on the revival of agriculture. There is now really no basis for any extension
of commerce, and a colony of tradesmen, such, for in-

stance, as the Jews would give the country, would only increase its poverty and wretchedness. The Duke of Ragusa advised Mohammed Ali to make Palestine and Syria an immense sheep-walk, and this should probably be the first object of a colony here. Large additional tracts might also be tilled in wheat, with no greater labor of preparation and improvement than that of turning up the soil with the pough. The product of cotton and tobacco, which are already articles of export, might be doubled or trebled at once. Plantations of vine, olive, fig, and other fruit-bearing trees would require more time and return slower profits; but they would be indispensable to the complete renovation of the country and the full development of its resources.

"It fills me with surprise to see some of the best men of England laboring to promote the colonization of Jews in Palestine, and that under existing governments. The Jews are precisely the last people on earth fitted for such an enterprise, as they are a nation of traffickers, and know nothing of agriculture. It would be worth while also for the Christian philanthropist to inquire whether the probabilities in favor of their conversion to Christianity would be multiplied by this restoration to their fatherland, where a thousand circumstances would perpetually remind them of the glorious days of their nation and its religion. And surely the form of Christianity which a Jew may behold in Jerusalem is not such as can ever win him to forsake the cherished faith of his fathers."

About two hours and a half over level road bring us to the site of ancient Jezreel. There are no ruins here save an old square tower, probably of Roman origin; the town itself is a small collection of rough stone huts, with flat mud roofs. Its situation is on a gently rising mound or hill, the apex of which is probably two hundred feet above the average level of the surrounding plains. The view from this point is grand and beautiful. East and west the valley stretches out as far as the eye can reach, or until it rests upon the blue hills of Moab on the one side, and Mount Carmel on the other; on the south stands the mountains of Gibeon, where the followers of Saul cast away their shields, whilst he and Jonathan fell slain in the hands of their victorious foe; far to the northward the heights of Little Hermon rise gently in view, to which the snow-capped heights of the Great Hermon form a fitting background.

Standing upon a watch-tower at this point, it was easy enough for the watchman to see the intrepid Jehu, driving "Jehu-like," as he came up from the eastward, and in sufficient time to report it to Joram and Ahaziah, who were in the palace.

This was the city of King Ahab, and hereabouts was the vineyard of Naboth; here it was that the infamous Jezebel was thrown from the window by the eunuchs, and when they went to bury her "they found no more of her than the skull, and the feet, and the palms of her hands," as had been spoken by the prophet Elijah; and from this place went forth the terrible order of Jehu, that of the seventy sons of Ahab all should be slain; and "they took the king's sons, and slew seventy persons, and put their heads in baskets, and sent him them to Jezreel."

A short ride brings us to the Fountain of Jezreel, bursting out in great force at the base of the hill, around which the army of Saul encamped, and on which his body was found after the battle. We drink from the spring, and find the waters sweet and refreshing.

At this time (April) the plain of Jezreel has no sign

of cultivation about it; but another traveler, who passed over this same route at a later season of the year, says: "We found harvest going on in many places. The grain, as soon as cut, is brought in small sheaves to the threshing-floors on the backs of asses, or sometimes of camels. The little donkeys are so often covered with their load of grain as to be themselves hardly visible; one sees only a mass of sheaves moving along as if of its own accord. A level spot is selected for the threshing-floors, which are then constructed near each other, of a circular form, perhaps fifty feet in diameter, merely by beating down the earth hard. Upon these circles the sheaves are spread out very thickly; and the grain is trodden out by animals, or a coarse sledge is driven over it, the under surface of which is set with sharp flint-stones that force out the grain and cut up the straw into chaff. The whole process is exceedingly wasteful, from the transportation on the backs of animals to the treading out upon the threshing-floor."

Another short ride across the plain, in a diagonal direction, brings us to the site of ancient Shunam, now called Sulem. A score of lazy idlers sit upon the outskirts of the village as we approach it, and wonder, no doubt, what in the world can cause such an influx of "Franks" to their miserable, dirty town.

Not one of them, probably, has ever read or heard of the Shunammite woman to whom, for kindness received, Elisha first promised a son, and when disease had laid that son low in death, restored him to life, and presented him once again to a mother's love.

Not far from Shunam is the village of Nain, on the northern slope of Little Hermon. It contains but few houses, and these few are very poor. A little beyond the village we reach the present burial-place, and near this are rock-hewn tombs of very ancient date. The path from Capernaum to Nain goes near these ancient tombs, and it is not difficult to trace, in imagination, the weary footsteps of Jesus, as, coming from the place where but the day before he had healed the centurion's servant, he meets the mournful procession, carrying to the tombs "the only son of his mother, and she was a widow." "And when the Lord saw her, he had compassion on her, and said unto her, Weep not. And he came and touched the bier, and they that bare him stood still. And he that was dead sat up, and began to speak. And he delivered him to his mother."

What could be more touchingly beautiful than this simple narrative of the compassion and power of Jesus? And do you wonder that we feel a deep interest in viewing even this little Syrian village, with all its poverty and wretchedness, after knowing that Jesus once hallowed it with his presence, and restored from death to life, near its gate, the son of the widow of Nain?

On a hillside, to the east of Nain, is the site of ancient Endor, now called Endoor; and but a little way off are caves in the rocks, in one of which the witch probably dwelt to whom Saul went for divination prior to the fatal battle of Gilboa. Saul would know his fate even from the lips of Samuel; and when the "old man, covered with a mantle," stood before him, and with deep, sepulchral voice inquired, "Why hast thou disquieted me, to bring me up?" and when the same voice said to Saul, "Wherefore then doest thou ask of me, seeing the Lord is departed from thee, and is become thine enemy?" need we wonder at the subsequent recital, that "then Saul fell straightway along on the earth, and was sore afraid because of the words of Samuel?"

Directly opposite where Endor was situated, Mount

Tabor looms up from the valley, but of this more hereafter when we climb to its summit and "view the landscape o'er."

At the foot of Mount Nazareth, near a little village called Saleh, we commence the ascent of a very difficult path, though we finally succeed in reaching its highest point; and turning our horses' heads around, we have another magnificent view of the plain of Esdraelon and the hills and villages around and about.

On, still on, we travel, over a rough path, until we come within sight of Nazareth. It stands upon the slope of a hill opposite to the one we are descending, and from almost every point of descent we have the whole town in full view. Its white stone houses, looming up one above the other, look beautiful in the distance, though a closer inspection, we regret to say, takes away much of the enchantment.

As we descend the long, steep hillside, we have time to reflect that here—yes, just here—the child Jesus spent most of his early years; upon this very mountain, and over this hillside, his feet often wandered; under the shadow of some of these rocks he probably sat and pondered over the work which his Father had given him to do; in the streets of the town now before us he in his early years was only known as the "carpenter's son;" here he commenced his ministry, but when the words which he uttered in the synagogue pleased not the Nazarenes, they "rose up and thrust him out of the city, and led him unto the brow of the hilll whereon their city was built, that they might cast him down headlong. But he, passing through the midst of them, went his way."

It is nearly sundown when we reach Nazareth, and here we will rest for the night; but before closing this chapter we know our readers will be gratified if we add the experience and observations of another traveler (Skinner), who, not many years since, visited this same city of Nazareth. He says:

"It was just five o'clock when we came to Nazareth, which was not visible till we were immediately above it. The capital of Galilee is now a little town containing three thousand inhabitants, chiefly Christians. Its white houses are delightfully situated on a gentle acclivity, hemmed in by mountains on all sides but one, which opens on a valley about two miles and a half in length. The Greek church, the high minaret of the Turkish mosque, and the extensive, broad walls of the Latin convent, were the first objects that caught our eyes.

"We proceeded at once to the Latin convent; the inner door was closed; and passing through a small arch at the upper end of the court and raising a curtain, I stood in the Church of the Annunciation. It was the hour of the the vesper service, and the monks were all on their knees, with their arms stretched, in the manner of the Franciscans, toward heaven. It was dark, and no light came from without, but candles and lamps innumerable gave a rich color to all around. The procession was over, and the monks were immovable in prayer; their devoted attitudes, their bald heads and long beards had a most imposing effect. The solemn notes of the organ, the odor of incense, and the handsome building itself, with the sudden manner in which I had descended into it from the hills, had an air of mystery about it that seemed not of this earth. It was not profane, I hope, in so holy a neighborhood, to remember the Scotch knight in the subterranean chapel of Engaddi: just such a surprise did it all seem to me. Beneath the altar, which stands in the centre of the church, was a flight of steps leading into a cave, over which a soft stream of light was cast from several lamps that hung within it. I could then only conjecture the character of these evidently most sacred places, for all the monks were so absorbed in their devotions that I could not inquire. I do not think any one perceived me.

"At length they rose from their knees, and in a solemn procession, headed by the superior, wound along the aisles, their heads bowed down and their arms crossed upon their breasts. At certain parts of the church they paused, and kneeling for a moment, touched the pavement with their foreheads, and again rising, moved on, till all being finished, they gradually disappeared through a small door beneath the organ loft; the last of the devout line closed it after him, and I was left alone in the church, doubtful almost whether I had witnessed a scene of reality or not."

CHAPTER IX.

ONWARD THROUGH GALILEE.

THERE are but few places in Palestine of more general interest to the tourist than Nazareth—not only because of the associations connected therewith, but because the location of the town itself, and the extensive view one can have from the summit of the hill immediately behind it, are among the finest in Syria.

The first place we visit in Nazareth is the Latin convent, in which are located the Church of the Annunciation and the house of Joseph and Mary.

The convent is of considerable size, very old, and fitted up in the usual convent style. The central portion is arranged as a church, with altars, praying-places, etc., and adorned with damask, silk, and other gewgaws. A descent of a few steps brings us into what are shown as the kitchen, parlor, and bedroom of the Virgin; and in front, or rather to the right, of the altar are two granite pillars, about three feet apart, which are said to mark the precise spot where Mary and the angel stood when the latter said to the former, "Fear not, Mary, for thou hast found favor with God. And behold thou shalt conceive in thy womb, and bring forth a son, and shalt call his name Jesus."

One of these columns has at some time been severed, and the upper part is now suspended from the roof—not by Divine interposition as the monks pretend, but by good, strong mason-work in an arched ceiling. These monks declare that the column was hacked through by the swords of the Mohammedans. Below the suspended portion, leaving a space of probably a foot, the fragment of another column has been placed, of different kind of stone from the first. How even the most credulous can be made to believe in the miraculous suspension of the upper portion of the column is most marvelous! The other two rooms are mere excavations in the rock and without adornment.

From this church we are conducted through another street to a small chapel, which is pointed out as the workshop of Joseph. The chapel is neatly fitted up, and over the altar hangs a well-executed picture, representing Joseph resting from his labors, while the child Jesus is reading to him from an open book on his lap, and Mary, in the background, is listening attentively.

Near this is another chapel, which is pointed out as the synagogue, or the site of the one, in which Jesus taught the people, and from which he was thrust out by the provoked Jews. Worship is being held in this chapel at the time we visit it, and the worshipers seem wholly absorbed in their devotions.

Another traveler writing of this incident in the life of Jesus, says : " The little Maronite church of Nazareth stands quite in the south-west part of the town, under a precipice of the hill, which here breaks off in a perpendicular wall forty or fifty feet in height. We notice several other similar precipices in the western hill around the village. Some of these, perhaps that by the Maronite church, may well have been the spot whither the Jews led Jesus ' unto the brow of a hill whereon their city was built, that they might cast him down headlong ; but he, passing through the midst of them, went his way.' There is here no intimation that his escape was favored by the exertion of any miraculous power; but he made his way fearlessly through the crowd; and probably eluded their pursuit by availing himself of the narrow and crooked streets of the city.

"The monks have chosen for the scene of this event the Mount of Precipitation, so called; a precipice overlooking the plain of Esdraelon, nearly two miles south by east of Nazareth. It appears to be seventy or eighty feet to the first shelving place, but to the very bottom three hundred. A stone four feet and a half high stands on the edge of it as a parapet, in which are some small round cavities, believed to be the marks of our Lord's fingers when he struggled against those who would have thrown him over. A little altar below, cut in the rock, formerly stood within a chapel built by St. Helena, the foundations of which remain, together with two cisterns of great depth.

"Among all the legends that have been fastened on the Holy Land none are more clumsy than this; which presupposes that in a popular and momentary tumult they should have had the patience to lead off their victim to an hour's distance, in order to do what there was an equal facility for doing near at hand. Indeed such is the intrinsic absurdity of the legend that the monks themselves, now-a-days, in order to avoid it, make the ancient Nazareth to have stood on the summit of the precipice in question. But the good fathers forget the dilemma into which they thus bring themselves; for, upon that supposition, what becomes of the holy places now shown in the present town?"

On another street, and farther up the side of the hill on which the town stands, is another chapel, recently reconstructed, in the centre of which is a large, flat stone, which is represented as the table on which Christ frequently ate, both before and after his resurrection. On a tablet of marble is the certificate of the Pope, certifying to the identity of the stone, and granting an indulgence to such pilgrims as visit it.

At the other end of the town the Greeks have a convent, erected over what is known as the Fountain of the Virgin, where, they say, the Annunciation took place while Mary was drawing water. Near the mouth of the fountain is an altar profusely decorated, over which hangs a picture representing Mary standing by the fountain, and the angel near her, announcing the glad news of her acceptance as the chosen instrument through which the Messiah was to be born into the world. The church is neatly fitted up, and the structure of the whole convent is much superior to the Latin.

The weight of evidence, as derived from long tradition, rests with the Latins, and but few tourists give any credence to the pretensions of the Greeks.

With reference to these two convents, and of convents generally throughout the Holy Land, Lamartine says: " Travelers" (Catholic travelers he means, and perhaps Châteaubriand especially) " have given a romantic and false representation. Nothing is less poetic or less religious, when inspected narrowly. Their conception is beautiful and grand. Men tear themselves from the delights of Western civilization to put their existence in jeopardy, or to lead a life of privations and martyrdom amongst the persecutors of their faith, on the very spots where the mysteries of their religion have consecrated the earth. They fast, they watch, they pray, in the midst of the blasphemies of the Turks and Arabs, in order that a little Christian incense shall still burn on each piece of ground where Christianity had birth. They are the guardians of the sacred cradle and sepulchre ; the angel of judgment shall find them alone at these places, like the holy women who watched and wept near the empty tomb. All this is beautiful and sublime in thought, but in actual fact these ideas must vanish. There is no persecution, no martyrdom ; all around these retreats there is a Christian population, ready for the service and orders of the monks of the convents. The Turks annoy them in no respect whatever ; on the contrary, they protect them. They are the most tolerant people on the earth, and understand better than others religion and prayer, in whatever language and under whatever form they are expressed. Atheism alone they detest, as they esteem it, with reason, a degradation of the human intellect, an insult to humanity much more than to the undoubted Being, God. These convents, besides, are under the respected and inviolable protection of the Christian Powers, represented by their consuls. On a complaint of the superior, the consul writes to the pasha, and justice is done on the very instant. The monks whom I have seen in the Holy Land, far from presenting to me the image of the long martyrdom with which they had been credited, appeared to me the most happy, respected, and feared of the inhabitants of these countries. They inhabit a sort of strong castles, similar to those of our own Middle Ages. Their residences are inviolable, surrounded with walls, and closed with gates of iron. These gates are only opened for the Catholic population of the neighborhood, which comes to assist at the offices, to receive a little pious instruction, and to pay, in respect and devotedness to the monks, the dues of the altar. I never went out accompanied by one of the fathers into the streets of a Syrian town but the children and women came and bowed to the monk, and kissed his hand and the bottom of his robe. The Turks, even, very far from insulting them, seem to partake the respect which they everywhere command as they move along.

"Now, who are these monks? In general, Spanish and Italian peasants, who have entered young into the convents of their country, and growing tired of the monastic life, are anxious to diversify it by the aspect of new countries, and seek to be sent to the Holy Land. Their residence in the house of their order established in the East does not in general continue for more than two or three years. A vessel comes to take them back, and brings others in their place. Those who learn Arabic, and devote themselves to the service of the Catholic population of the towns, stay longer, and often pass there the whole of their lives. They follow the occupations and life of the country curés in France, but they are encircled with more veneration and attachment. Others remain shut up within the precincts of the convent, or pass from one house to another in order to complete their pilgrimage—sometimes to Nazareth, or to Bethlehem, to Rome, to Jaffa, or to the convent of St. John in the desert. They have no other employment than the offices of the church, and the promenade in the gardens or on the terraces of the convent. No books, no studies, no useful function. They are devoured by listlessness; cabals are formed in the interior of the convent; the Spaniards decry the Italians, and the Italians the Spaniards. We were not much edified by the relations the monks of Nazareth gave of each other. We did not find a single individual amongst them who could sustain the slightest rational conversation, even on subjects which their vocation should have rendered familiar to them. No knowledge of sacred antiquity, of the fathers, or of the history of the places they resided in. The whole is reduced to a certain number of popular and ridiculous traditions, which they transmit amongst themselves without examination, and which they deliver to travelers as they have received them from the ignorance and credulity of the Christian Arabs of the country. They all sigh for the moment of their deliverance, and return to Italy or Spain without any advantage to themselves or to religion. As for other points, the granaries of the convent are well filled; the cellars are stocked with the best wines this earth can produce. They do it all themselves. Every two years a ship arrives from Spain, bearing to the superiors the revenue supplied by the Catholic Powers, Spain, Portugal, and Italy. This sum, increased by the pious alms of the Christians of Egypt, Greece, Constantinople, and Syria, furnishes them, it is said, with an income of from £12,000 to £16,000 sterling per annum, which is divided amongst the different convents, according to the number of monks and the wants of each community. The edifices are well supported, and everything indicates comfort, and even relative luxury, in the houses which I have visited. I have never witnessed anything flagitious in the monks' abodes in the Holy Land. Ignorance, idleness, and listlessness are the three plagues which they should and could eradicate."

Nazareth is said to contain about three thousand inhabitants, most of whom are Christians. They are civil to travelers, and the monks and priests at the convents are particularly polite and attentive to visitors. The houses of Nazareth are better than those in most of the Syrian towns, and there seems to be more trade and enterprise among the people.

Buckhardt observed, and so have we, that the inhabitants of Nazareth differ somewhat in features and color from the Northern Syrians; their physiognomy approaches that of the Egyptians, while their dialect and pronunciation differ widely from those of Damascus. In Western Palestine, especially on the coast, the inhabitants seem in general to bear more resemblance to the natives of Egypt than those of Northern Syria. Toward the east of Palestine, on the contrary, especially in the villages about Nablous, Jerusalem, and Hebron, they are evidently of the Syrian stock in features, though not in language. It would be an interesting subject for an artist to portray accurately the different features of the Syrian nations; the Aleppine, the Turkman, the native of Lebanon, the Damascene, the inhabitant of the sea-coast from Beyrout to Akka, and the Bedouin, although all inhabiting the same country, have distinct national physiognomies; and a slight acquaintance with them enables one to determine the native district of a Syrian with almost as much certainty as an Englishman or American may be distinguished at first sight from an Italian or an inhabitant of the south of France.

The view from the high hill-top back of Nazareth is grandly beautiful. On the summit stands a Mohammedan wely or tomb, from the top of which the view is still more extensive. Away off to the west, Mount Carmel rises majestically in view and reaching to the blue waters of the Mediterranean; south-eastward Mount Tabor lifts its lofty head, with its green mottled sides and ruin-capped summit; behind this are the blue hills of Moab, with Little Hermon and Gilboa intervening; away to the southward stretches the Valley of the Jordan; while, over the intervening mountain, you look down upon the plain of Esdraelon, stretching far to the eastward and westward. The view is such that once seen it can never be forgotten.

From Nazareth our course lies direct to Mount Tabor, which mountain we propose to ascend. The path from Nazareth to Mount Tabor is rough, but we finally reach its base and commence to ascend. We had been told that the path up Mount Tabor was difficult, but, whatever it may have been in times past, at present it is one of the best mountain-paths in Syria. The side of the mountain where the path goes up is dotted over with Syrian oaks and shrubs of various species, and special pains have been taken to plant them along each side of the path. The recent erection of a Greek convent on the summit of the mount may account, in part, for the better condition of the road at this time.

As we zigzag up the mountain-path the view at each new facing and elevation grows more and more extensive and grand; and when we fairly reach the summit and stand upon the topmost point of the old ruins, it seems as though we could see all over Palestine. As we sit upon these old ruins, exclamations of surprise burst forth again and again from the different members of our party, so magnificent is the view from this point. Two Scotch tourists are with us, who are no less interested than ourselves in the prospect around and about us.

The ruins upon the summit are quite extensive, and show great strength and solidity in their construction. Some have been fortifications, others churches and chapels, and still others may have been temples of date more ancient, but all are now in a ruined and desolate condition, save the new Greek convent, which, though small, seems to be neatly and substantially built.

We are not a little interested in looking over the great plain of Esdraelon at our feet, and trying to locate some of the many great battles which have taken place from time to time upon it. The Hebrews, the Romans, and the French have all marshaled their forces upon this plain at different periods of the world's history.

The battle of Mount Tabor, in which the First Napoleon, with six hundred men, rescued General Kleber and his fifteen hundred from twenty-five thousand of the enemy, is well known to all modern historians; while ancient history and the Bible inform us of many other great and bloody battles fought within view of where we we are now sitting.

The descent of Mount Tabor is quite as easy as the ascent, and in due time we find ourselves once more upon the broad plain, with our faces directed toward the Sea of Galilee.

At the foot of Mount Tabor is the small and wretched village of "Deborah," where she who judged Israel is reported to have dispensed her decrees to the people who "came up to her for judgment." It is worthy of remark that at the present day the Arabs assemble at the foot of the same Mount Tabor every Monday, to hold a bazaar and dispose of their merchandise, the governor of Taberiah, in whose jurisdiction it is, either attending in person or sending a deputy to dispense justice. There is no village at the place, but the meeting is held in the open plain, as it might be, "under the palm tree of Deborah;" and close to the spot are some ruins, at which all those who are debtors for tributes or duties are accustomed to pay them. Although it is merely related in the Book of Judges that the people "came up for judgment" to stated places at different periods, it is yet by no means improbable that they did at the same time transact other business, and that the meeting was also taken advantage of for the sale of merchandise, out of which ancient practice the present one seems to have grown.

On our way to Galilee we pass the ruins of two old Saracenic khans, and see several Bedouin encampments, with their black camel-hair tents and extensive herds of horses, donkeys, cattle, and sheep; but beyond these we see nothing of interest until we reach the high hills which surround the Sea of Galilee and look down upon its placid waters and the town of Tiberias located on its shores.

From this moment all the sacred associations of these waters and these shores commence to impress themselves forcibly upon our mind; and it takes but a little stretch of the imagination to see Jesus of Nazareth delivering the sermon from the Mount of Beatitudes, near by; to see Jesus walking by the sea, and calling the "two brethren, Simon called Peter, and Andrew his brother," to make them "fishers of men;" to see the Lord upon a vessel, in the midst of the sea, and a great storm abroad, and to hear his voice rebuking the winds and the sea, when immediately follows a great calm; to see Jesus seated in a vessel, a little way from shore, and teaching the multitude the way of eternal life; to see Jesus taking the man who was deaf, and had an impediment in his speech, aside from the multitude, and hear him speak the words "be opened;" and straightway his ears were opened, and the string of his tongue was loosed, and he spoke plain; to see the four thousand seated on the slopes of the sea-shore with Jesus in their midst, feeding them miraculously with seven loaves and a few small fishes.

These, with many other works which Jesus did on and near the Sea of Galilee, press upon our mind, and make us feel that we are indeed looking upon one of the most hallowed spots of all God's footstool.

The Mount of Beatitudes, which we see on the way, is a beautiful spot, and just such an one as the Saviour might have chosen for the occasion. Stephens, in writing of it, says:

"Not very much farther is the Mount of Beatitudes, whence our Saviour delivered his sermon. It stands very little above a green plain of the stillest possible appearance. There is a gravity about the scene that would have struck me with peculiar awe, even though I had not known the peculiar solemnity attached to it. Whether the tradition be true or not, it was just the place where, in those primitive days, or even in the state of society which exists now in the Holy Land, such an event might have taken place—the preacher standing a little up the hill, and the multitude sitting down below him. Indeed, so strikingly similar in all its details is the state of society existing here now to that which existed in the time of our Saviour, that I remember when standing on the ruins of a small church supposed to cover the precise spot where Christ preached that compendium of goodness and wisdom, it struck me that if I or any other man should preach new and strange things, the people would come out from the cities and villages to listen and dispute, as they did under the preaching of our Lord."

Dr. Robinson gives his impressions of this route, and his first view of the Sea of Galilee, as follows:

"Farther on we passed the scene of the miracle of the loaves and fishes. These and other localities, marked out for the veneration of the pious, may be and perhaps are mere monkish conjectures; but one thing we know, that our Saviour and his disciples journeyed on this road; that he looked upon the same scenes, and that in all probability somewhere within the range of my eye these deeds and miracles were actually performed. At all events, as I reached the brow of the height above Tiberias, before me in full view was the hallowed lake of Gennesareth. Here we cannot be wrong: Christ walked upon that sea, and stilled the raging of its waters, and preached the tidings of salvation to the cities on its banks. To me, I confess, so long as we continued round the lake, the attraction lay more in these associations than in the scenery."

It is about five o'clock when we reach our tents, pitched on the sea-shore near Tiberias; and as we propose to remain here a week, we shall have ample time to examine everything of interest about the sea. There are eighteen tents here beside our own, the occupants of most of which are Americans, showing the great interest which our own countrymen feel in the history and associations of the Holy Land.

From what we had heard and read of this sea, we had expected to find an encampment on its shores uncomfortably warm, even at this season of the year (April 12), but in this we are happily disappointed. Indeed, if there is any fault at all to be found with the temperature, it is from the cold rather than from the heat. As the waters of this lake lie in a deep basin, surrounded on all sides by lofty hills, except at the outlet and entrance of the Jordan, the heat upon the shores is, at some seasons of the year, no doubt very oppressive. Lord Francis Egerton, who visited this lake in the month of May, thus relates his experience:

"We pitched our tents on the margin of the lake, determining to prolong our stay over the morrow. We found bitter reason to repent this arrangement. All my previous conceptions of heat were inadequate to the reality of a hot wind which set in during the night from the desert, and which at this season I was told was without precedent. At Jericho the sun was powerful; but it was honest heat, tempered by the breeze and mitigated at night. Here the night scarcely lowered the thermometer a degree below 104. The wind, confined by the conformation of the surrounding mountains, blew strong down the valley like a furnace-blast through a funnel.

The ineffable luxury of a morning and evening bath in the lake was dearly purchased by the miseries of the day and night. I could observe while enjoying this temporary relief that the water actually swarmed with fish, generally of small size, near the shore, but large ones were taking the fly at a little distance. One of the two boats on the lake passing near the shore in front of our encampment, I longed for a sail, and desired our janissary to hail her and make the proposal. The boat at first pursued her course; but I presume that Hassan in his zeal resorted to threats, for she soon came to, and landed her master, a Prussian Jew, who accosted me in bad German, and deprecated my supposed wrath with excuses as profound as though I had any right to command his services. As he was standing with bated breath and uncovered head in the burning sun, I desired him to put on his broad-brimmed hat. The astonishment he displayed at this common act of civility, or rather humanity, convinced me that he expected to be knocked down as a preliminary to further conversation. I of course soon relieved him from longer anxiety, and he quitted me to prosecute his mercantile voyage—I hope under no bad impression of Christian dealings, or of our mode of employing the pasha's firman, which I suspect had been made the most of by our zealous official.

"We found the kiosk scarcely more supportable than our tents as to heat, and far worse as to noise; for parties of men and women were using the public bath alternately through the night, maintaining an uproar such as I never heard. We could make no attempt to explore the shores or look for the lost site of Capernaum. No physical lassitude, however, could deprive the scene of its impressions. The hot red haze which obscured the distant mountains by day, melted into a deep purple toward evening. At night the fires of Arab charcoal-burners on the opposite hills looked like the bivouac of some Sennacherib. The waters, agitated by the hot wind, broke with a soothing sound upon the shore."

At night, while the stars look down from heaven, just as they did when Jesus and his disciples walked upon these shores, Lily and I walk down the sea-shore and take our first bath in the clear, blue lake. The waters are cool, and at first chilling, and the shores are covered with large pebbles, which hurt the bare feet, but still we feel better for our bath, and sleep more soundly because of it.

The following day we mount our horses and ride down to that point of the sea where the river Jordan flows out. It is about six miles from our camping-ground, with a good road all the way. And here occurs an accident, or incident, by which we get a second bath in the Jordan, rather unexpected to ourself. The horses of Lily, Lu, and myself are standing quietly in the Jordan, while all of us are examining and talking about its exit and onward flow. Looking down, Lily sees a white pebble on the bed of the stream which she desires to have, and, calling to one of our servants, desires him to get it for her. He rides his horse in the stream, but no sooner does his horse approach mine than both rear, and mine wheels suddenly around to kick his. The suddenness of the movement lands me at the bottom of the Jordan, the waters of which cover me completely. A double-barrel shot-gun, which I have slung across my shoulders at the time, helps materially to the rapidity of my descent, and interferes somewhat with my rising, but still I do rise and wade to the shore, looking more like a drowned rat than a live American. The horse's fore feet did not, fortunately, come down upon me as I lay there on the bottom of the stream, or I might not have been here to write this. The danger and annoyance being past, we all laugh heartily at the incident, while I feel none the worse for having had a second bath in the river Jordan.

Our return trip leads us close by the hot springs, over which Ibrahim Pasha erected a very comfortable, and, in its time, a very luxurious, bath-house; and here we all stop to take another bath.

The bath-room is circular, with dome roof. The excavation in the centre—into and out of which the hot water flows from a spring on a higher level—is about twenty feet in diameter and five feet deep. Around the edge, about half-way down, runs a step of about two feet in width, while at three points are regular steps leading from the platform to the bottom of the bath. The platform around the bath, running from the edge of the bath to the wall, and inclining slightly inward, is about six feet in width, with a seat running all around the wall. Six composite columns run up from the edge of the bath and support the dome, the latter of which is perforated with holes, through which the birds fly in and out. The bath itself and the platform all around are covered with slabs of polished marble. Other rooms open from this circular room, which were originally intended for undressing and lolling-places, and for the use of the family in charge. At present they are only used by the latter.

The water as it first comes into the bath is very hot—too hot for any one to endure until it has cooled from standing. It is quite salty, and has considerable of a sulphurous taste and smell. The steam which rises from it is about like that from boiling water, and it is exceedingly debilitating to the system at first.

To enjoy a bath here, the first thing is to secure the room exclusively to yourself, as there are so many coming all the while that it is rarely empty. A small gratuity to the superintendent will secure this, and upon its receipt or promise, he will clear every man, woman, and child out of, and away from, the bath but yourself. He will then furnish you with matting, upon which to stand and lay your clothes while undressing; and, with all this, if you don't have one of the most luxurious hot baths that the mind can conceive of, then our judgment is at fault.

There are several other hot springs, of like character, along the base of this hill, not far from the shore of the sea, and at least two others have had buildings and bathing-houses connected with them; but that of Ibrahim Pasha is now the only one in general use. The Jews of Tiberias, it is said, still bathe in one of the old houses, because they are not permitted to use the new one, but we know of no other distinction.

These springs have long been celebrated for the cure of rheumatic complaints; and since we have tested the kind of water which flows from them, containing, as it does, heat, salt, and sulphur, we have full faith in its general efficacy, though it may fail, of course, in some cases, in doing any good whatever.

To thoroughly test the efficacy of these waters we have our tent, next day, removed from the old camping-ground to a spot near the bath-house, with the door of our tent within a few feet of the sea; and our plan is to go over to the bathing-house every morning before breakfast, and then, immediately after coming from the hot bath, take a plunge in the sea. The latter produces a chilling sensation at first, but its general effect is delicious, and for the balance of the day we feel like a new-made man. Occasionally we repeat the bath late in the afternoon, just before dinner-time; and on one occasion we take a third bath between nine and ten o'clock at night.

Thus we spend six days on the shores of the Sea of Galilee, riding, reading, writing, and bathing; and, certainly, no one ever enjoyey six more pleasant days.

We visit, in the mean time, the sites of the ancient towns and cities once around its coast—Magdala, Capernaum, Bethsaida, etc., but of these more hereafter.

CHAPTER X.

THE SEA OF GALILEE.

THE Sea of Galilee, or, as it is sometimes called, the Lake of Tiberias, is about fourteen miles in length, by about seven in breadth at its widest part. Its waters are exceedingly clear and sweet, except near the hot springs, where they have a slight saline and sulphurous taste. It contains an abundance of fish, and having ate of them we can attest to their fine flavor. Many are daily caught with hook and net near our tents, and they form an important addition to our morning meals.

This sea lies six hundred and fifty-three feet below the level of the Mediterranean, and ten thousand seven hundred and sixteen feet below the summit of Mount Hermon, which is in plain sight all the time except when obscured by clouds. This difference of elevation readily accounts for the fact that, while upon the shore of the sea the earth is quite warm, the summit of the mountain is capped with snow, looking joyously beautiful in the distance. Indeed, the hills immediately about the sea are of considerable height, ranging from six hundred to eight hundred feet above its surface.

Through the day its waters are very smooth, unless disturbed by wind or storm; but, about, and for several hours after, sundown, quite a heavy surf breaks upon its western shore, accompanied with considerable wind. We would scarcely have believed that this little sea, so deeply imbedded in mountains, could have gotten up such a commotion, had we not seen it for ourselves. It must have been during just such a storm when "there arose a great tempest in the sea, insomuch that the ship was covered with the waves," that His disciples cried out, "Lord, save us, we perish;" and when Jesus arose and "rebuked the winds and the sea, and there was a great calm." The little inconvenience which we ourselves suffer from the storm is far more than repaid by this vivid illustration of one of the most interesting passages of Holy Writ.

Some of our readers may ask, why this body of water is sometimes called a sea, and at other times a lake. It was usual for the Jews to call every natural expanse of water *a sea*. Accordingly, the Evangelists Matthew, Mark, and John, being native Jews, invariably call the Lake of Tiberias a "sea;" but Luke, who was a native of Asia Minor, and whose geographical terms are always more distinctive, calls it generally a "lake." The present inhabitants, like those of ancient times, still call this water a sea, and reckon it and the Dead Sea to be the two largest known except the great ocean. If some of these Syrians could have a glimpse of the great northern lakes of America, their ideas as to the relative magnitude of their own would be greatly changed.

The beauty of this lake has been a theme for writers from the earliest days of historic record until the present. The Jewish writers enlarge in the most glowing terms on the excellency of this lake; and, considering their limited means of comparison, they had reason to do so. "Seven seas," says the Talmud, "have I created, saith God, and of them all have I chosen none but the Sea of of Gennesareth." Josephus dwells on the sweetness and softness of its water, on its pebbly bottom, and, above all, on the salubrity of the surrounding atmosphere. Dr. Clark says: "In picturesque beauty it perhaps comes nearest to the Lake of Locarno in Italy, although it be destitute of anything similar to the islands by which that majestic piece of water is adorned. It is inferior in magnitude, and, perhaps, in the height of the neighboring mountains, to the Lake Asphaltites; but its broad and extended surface covering the bottom of a profound valley, surrounded by lofty and precipitous eminences, when added to the impression under which every Christian pilgrim approaches it, gives it a character of unparalleled dignity."

In these vivid descriptions some allowance must be made for the enthusiasm of the writers; for, while it is indeed true that the lake itself and the surrounding hills are somewhat beautiful and intensely interesting, yet the stillness and desolation which brood over all has a saddening rather than a pleasing effect on the eye and mind of the traveler. You may stand upon its shores and gaze for hours without seeing a single boat upon its surface, and scarcely a human being upon its borders; and, with the exception of the mean town of Tiberias and one or two miserable villages, you may look in vain for signs of habitation.

In this respect how different is the view now from what it was in the time of Christ! Then the borders of the lake were thickly populated, and the eye rested in turn upon fortresses and cities, towns and villages. Here stood not only the royal city of Tiberias, but the woe-doomed cities of Chorazin and Capernaum, both the frequent witnesses of his "mighty works," and the latter his most usual place of residence. Then they "were exalted unto heaven," but now they are so utterly "cast down" that men know not exactly where they stood. Here also were Bethsaida—"the city of Andrew and Peter"—Hippos and Gamala, Tarichea and Beth-Meon, Ammaus and the strong Magdala, with many other places of less note, the names of which history has found no occasion to preserve. Then, also, the surface of the lake was enlivened with the numerous boats passing constantly across, and from town to town, with passengers and goods, while the fishers launched forth to cast their nets in the deep waters. Then, the shores were everywhere richly planted and cultivated, and afforded many delightful gardens and paradises, while numerous people, busy or unoccupied, were seen passing to and fro; and then, instead of this silence, were heard the voices of men calling to each other, the joyous shouts of happy children, the sound of the song and harp, the noise of the millstones, and the lowing of the herds on the sides of the hills. Amidst the present vacancy and silence the mind can better fill out of the details of such a picture than if the scene actually occupied other and different objects than those which the imagination wishes to supply.

On one of the days, while stopping on the shores of the sea, we take a ride along its western coast, to see the ruins or sites of its ancient cities; and, if possible, to reach the point where the Jordan flows into it; for we may here remark that the Jordan flows not only out of, but into this sea or lake, and at one time (and even still, by some) the sea itself was only regarded as a broad expansion of the river.

Leaving our tents about eight in the morning, we pass by the town of Tiberias, and in about an hour after we reach Magdala, a small, miserably-built Syrian village, with nothing of interest about it except its being the place of Mary Magdalene, who, as it is recorded in St. Luke, "brought an alabaster box of ointment, and stood at Jesus' feet behind him weeping, and began to wash his feet with tears, and did wipe them with the hairs of her head, and kissed his feet, and anointed them with the ointment;" of whom Jesus said, "Her sins, which are many, are forgiven; for she loved much; but to whom little is forgiven, the same loveth little;" and to whose name the immortality of faithfulness will for ever remain, as having been " last at the cross and first at the sepulchre."

After leaving Magdala we enter upon a small plain or cove, with the sea upon the one side and high hills on all the others. It embraces an area of several hundred acres, which at one time, doubtless, was highly cultivated, but now it is all grown over with grass and weeds. Several small streams run through it in their course from the surrounding mountains to the sea. This is the plain of Gennesaret, from which the sea itself is sometimes called the "Lake of Gennesaret."

At the northern end of this plain, not far from the sea, and near where the road commences the ascent of the high hills, is the Fountain of the Fig, or, as the natives call it, *Ain el Tin*. This, until recently, has been supposed to mark the site of ancient Capernaum; but recent excavations made by Captain Wilson of the British army on the sea-shore, about one mile further north, prove (as far as proof is possible now) that Capernaum was located there instead of near the Fountain of the Fig, as heretofore supposed. The very few remains of buildings about the fountain go still further to confirm this opinion, while the ruins at the newly-discovered site are of considerable extent and of some beauty.

Capernaum, simply as a city—whether large or small,

or wherever located—has nothing in its history of special interest, except so far as the Saviour is connected with it; and, in this respect, it was and is of very great interest to the inquirer after biblical localities.

Here it was that Jesus, after being thrust out from Nazareth, came and "taught them on the Sabbath days; and they were astonished at his doctrine, for his word was with power;" here it was that Jesus cast out from the man "a spirit of an unclean devil," which in agony of defeat cried out, "I know thee who thou art, the Holy One of God;" here it was that the centurion's servant lay sick, to whom Jesus extended his healing power, because of the great faith of the master; and this was the place of which Jesus uttered that awfully solemn prediction, "And thou, Capernaum, which art exalted unto heaven, shalt be brought down to hell; for if the mighty works which have been done in thee, had been done in Sodom, it would have remained until this day." Fearfully has the prediction been verified—deep in the nethermost "hell" has that proud city sunk—until, at present, not only its walls and inhabitants are among the things that were, but even its site is a question of debate.

The site of ancient Bethsaida is midway between what was formerly thought to be the site of Capernaum and the place more recently pointed out; in either case but a short walk from the latter city. To reach it we climb a narrow path cut in the rock, leading up from near the "Fountain of the Fig." Its location was upon a hill overlooking the sea, and having a fine view of the surrounding hills and mountains. Nothing of the ancient city remains, unless we count as such the stones of buildings lying loosely about the hillside, and what seem to have been the foundations of two buildings, near the water's edge.

The Sea of Galilee. 207

It was at Bethsaida that Jesus " took the blind man by the hand and led him out of the town ; and when he had spit on his eyes, and put his hands upon him, he asked him if he saw aught. And he looked up, and said, I see men as trees walking. After that he put his hands again upon his eyes, and made him look up, and he was restored, and saw every man clearly ;" and it was of this city Jesus said, " Woe unto thee, Bethsaida ! for if the mighty works which were done in you" [Chorazin and Bethsaida] " had been done in Tyre and Sidon, they would have repented long ago in sackcloth and ashes." Woe, indeed, has befallen to Bethsaida, until scarcely one stone has been left upon another ; and where hundreds, and perhaps thousands, once dwelt in peace and plenty, now the owl and the lizard are monarchs of all they survey.

As to the sites of Chorazin, Hippos, Scythopolis, Tarichea, Gamala, and other cities which once stood upon the borders of this sea—of which we read in Holy Writ and in the works of Josephus—everything is in doubt; and each tourist is privileged to locate them as may best suit his ideas of probability. The small villages of Aaj, Dukah, Kufeir, Adweiriban, and Semakh, on the other side of the lake, are supposed by some to occupy the sites of those ancient cities, but it is all conjecture. There is no tradition even to fix these localities, and the judgment of one man is quite as good as another in determining where these ancient cities stood.

We find the point where the Jordan enters the sea too far to reach in one day's ride ; though from the farthest point to which we go we can see the clefts of the mountain through which the Jordan comes into the sea, and can distinctly trace the long, muddy, yellow waters of the river far out in the lake, before the final commingling of the waters.

On our return we ride, for some time, close along the water's edge, to pick up some of the shells, which lie in bushels upon the shore. These shells are of the *Buccinum* species, mostly small and of not much variety, though some are rather pretty. Lily and Lu remain behind to select shells, while I ride on to take another look at Magdala. In the town, through the town, and around the town we ride, while every man, woman, and child of the village seems to be staring at us, and wondering, we suppose, what in the world the howajji can want or mean by thus closely inspecting their mud huts; but we see nothing to repay us for our pains, in the way of ruins or ancient mementoes of any kind. There is, on the outer edge of the town, the remains of a stone building, of recent date and of considerable size, which bears evidence of having once been beautiful. It is now entirely abandoned, and the grounds about it are covered with thorn and brier bushes, as we have occasion to remember from having attempted to pass through them.

The sun is near its setting as we reach our tents; and though somewhat fatigued from our ride, we cannot but feel that the day has been profitably spent in trying to trace the footsteps and resting-places of Jesus during the three years of his ministry and pilgrimage upon earth. This is, indeed, holy land, and, as compared with the whole, the Sea of Galilee may, not inaptly, be called the Holy of Holies.

While stopping on the sea-shore, we one day visit and ride through the town of Tiberias, to see what is to be seen within its once stately walls.

During the occupancy of this country by the Romans this was one of their principal strongholds. The walls

which surrounded the place upon all sides, except that
next the sea-shore, appear to have been of excellent
masonry and very strong; and parts of several of the
towers along the wall still remain. At the north-eastern
corner of the wall was a very large and strong fortress,
or citadel, the walls of which still remain, in part, for the
study and admiration of tourists. As we wander from
room to room, and underneath its many stately arches,
we cannot but think of the many who have lived, and
loved, and hated, and died within these walls—now so
wholly abandoned that not even an owl or a bat takes
refuge within them.

A frightful earthquake befell this place on the 1st of
January, 1837. The walls of the town were thrown
down; the castle suffered severely; very many of the
houses were demolished, indeed few remained without
injury. Out of a population of twenty-five hundred, there
perished probably seven hundred persons, the larger proportion of whom were Jews. A native relates that he
and four others were returning down the mountain west
of the city in the afternoon when the earthquake occurred.
All at once the earth opened and closed again, and two
of his companions disappeared. He ran home terrified;
and found that his wife, mother, and two others of the
family had perished. On digging next day where his two
companions had disappeared, they were found dead in a
standing posture.

Burckhardt says—and the same is true now—that "the
Jews occupy a quarter in the middle of the town, ad-
jacent to the lake; this was formerly surrounded by a
wall with a single gate, which was closed every night.
Tiberias is one of the four holy cities of the Hebrews,
and here, as at Jerusalem, Hebron and Safed, the unhappy remnant of a fallen people still hover round the

graves of their fathers, and though degraded and trampled under foot, are still looking for the restoration of their temporal kingdom. They are divided into two classes, Asiatic and European, with distinct rabbins, synagogues, and schools. The Europeans are Muscovites, Poles, and Germans, a poor, haggard, and filthy race, the shadows of those that may be seen in the fairs of Leipsic. The Asiatic Jews are more thriving, and so, too, are the Spanish and Portuguese, who everywhere associate with their Eastern brethren, most of whom speak their language. They observe a singular custom here in praying. While the rabbin recites the Psalms of David, or the prayers extracted from them, the congregation frequently imitate, by their voice and gestures, the meaning of some remarkable passages; for example, when the rabbin pronounces the words, ' Praise the Lord with the sound of the trumpet,' they imitate the sound of the trumpet through their closed fists. When 'a horrible tempest' occurs, they puff and blow to represent a storm; or should he mention ' the cries of the righteous in distress,' they all set up a loud screaming; and it not unfrequently happens that while some are still blowing the storm, others have already begun the cries of the righteous, thus forming a concert which it is difficult for any but a zealous Hebrew to hear with gravity."

For neither love nor money will the Jewish population open their doors to a stranger after dark. An English party arriving at a late hour, sent a servant to buy some wine of the Jews, who sell a very good sort; but he found all the houses closed against him. "They were afraid," he said, "of being made Turks if they opened their doors in the night-time." Truly a most awful calamity to arise from selling a bottle of wine! To account for the fear by which the Hebrew damsels of Tiberias are oppressed—for the conversion is peculiarly destined for them—it seems that some time ago a Turk was captivated by the beauty of a Jewess, and did all he could to obtain her. She was not to be won by fair means; so, watching an opportunity, when one night there was eating and drinking in her father's house, he rushed in with a party of servants, and carried away the prize. When called on to make some defence for the outrage before the governor, he had merely, he said, had pity on a maiden whose charms might add fresh delight to Paradise; and, as "God is merciful," had converted her to the faith of Mohammed. "It is the will of heaven," said the governor, "and fate is not to be resisted." There was an end therefore of the matter; and the chance of being made a Turk has been ever since a very natural fear in the city.

Once within the walls of the town, we inquire for the Convent of St. Peter, and, funny enough, the boy of whom we inquire, and whom, from his actions, we suppose understands what we want, takes us direct to the hotel, the proprietor of which opens his door to receive us with all the urbanity of a Sir John Falstaff; but as it is not the place we are looking for, we decline to enter. Even had we been seeking a hotel, a single glance within the door and upon the courtyard of that one would have determined us at once to sleep in the open air rather than in such a place. From this point another boy undertakes to pilot us to the convent, which, after a few twists and turns through the narrow, rough and dirty streets of the town, we succeed in reaching.

The convent stands on the sea-shore, and consists of a chapel, several rooms, and a small outer court. It is said to mark the spot where Peter lived, and where, or opposite to which, the miraculous draught of fishes was made.

The old monk who lets us in at the gate and leads us into the chapel seems so intent upon his book and beads that he can give us no further attention, and thereby misses the bucksheesh which he would have got had he remained at our elbow. This church is said to have been built in apostolic times, but the style of its architecture and the Arabic letters in an inverted position on one of the stones composing it, prove that it cannot be older than the time of the Crusaders.

Some idea of the former grandeur of this once proud city of Herod may be guessed from the quantity of broken columns that strew the shore beyond the southern walls. They extend for more than a mile, and there is no doubt that this ground was covered by the ancient city. The plain runs back half a mile to the foot of the mountain, in the sides of which are long ranges of tombs. It was from one of these tombs, it is said, that the man possessed with devils rushed forth when our Saviour rebuked the unclean spirits and made them enter into a herd of swine, which ran violently down a steep place into the sea and were drowned.

As illustrating this incident in the life of Jesus, a traveler relates the following as happening to himself at just this place. "One day," says he, "while I was exploring these caves, a Bedouin, to my great surprise, started from the floor of one of them and rushed to the entrance; he had probably been sleeping and was enraged at my intrusion. That part of valor which is called discretion I put in practice on the present occasion, took to my heels, and never looked behind me till I arrived at the foot of the mountain, where I had left my guide in charge of the mules. The first thing I did was to seize the gun, which was slung across my saddle; and I had just time to cock it, when I saw my pursuer about ten yards off, gesticulating violently and pointing his musket at me. He was alone, and might have fared badly had we proceeded to extremities, for it was ten to one if his rusty matchlock was in order, and my servant was now beside me, sword in hand. I simply kept the gun to my shoulder, regarding him steadily. He retreated a few steps and cried out, '*Magnoun enti?*'—'Are you mad?' My Arab roared in reply, '*Eiwa magnoun kitir*'—'Yes, we are very mad!' The Bedouin seemed to believe him, for he ran up the side of a mountain like a goat, and we soon lost sight of him."

But to return from this digression in our narrative: From the Convent of St. Peter we ride by the house of the governor, on whom we had made a business call a few days previous; then through the bazaar of the town, which is small and poor; then up to the ruins of the old castle; and from thence to our tents by the sea-side.

Two little incidents occur while we are at Tiberias, which forcibly illustrate the Moslem respect for power and position; while, as every one knows, they hold in utter contempt all whom they can make to cringe to their authority.

From other travelers, or in some way, the governor had learned that we were a United States Commissioner, accredited by our government to the Paris Exposition. While quietly sitting in our tent one day, smoking, thinking, and writing, and in our shirt-sleeves, one of our servants comes running to the door to say that the commandant of the Turkish troops of the town is approaching, with dragoman, guards, etc., and, as he thinks, with the intention of calling upon us. Hastily putting on our coat, we step out of the tent door, and there, sure enough, is the commandant, dressed in full uniform, with a broad Turkish scimetar at his side, and accompanied by several servants, approaching our tent. We shake hands, bow, touch our foreheads to each other, but beyond this neither can understand a word of what the other says. It is rather an odd predicament, but we resolve to make the best of it. Once in our tent, however, with our own dragoman as interpreter between us, we get along very well in a conversation of an hour, and in the mean time we drink coffee and smoke together as familiarly as though we had known each other for years. We offer him wine, but this he declines, as every follower of the Prophet must who is faithful to his creed.

He says to us that he starts this afternoon on a tour, on business of the government, and fearing we might leave before his return, he does himself the honor of calling upon us before he goes. All this is said, and much more, in true Oriental style, but without any affectation in speech or manner. He is certainly a very agreeable gentleman, and doubtless a good officer. The usual salaams are exchanged on parting, and with hearty good-will on our part.

About an hour after a servant again rushes to our tent door to say that the governor and all his suite are approaching, and, as he thinks, to call upon us. Again we hastily put on our coat and step to the door, and find, as the servant surmised, the governor approaching our tent, and with him his son and a large guard of mounted soldiers. We had sent our own dragoman to town about a mile distant only a little while before, and now indeed we are in a fix, since we have no one to interpret for us. Hastily despatching Lu for our dragoman, we prepare to receive the governor as best we can, and in a few moments thereafter welcome him and his son to the tent with the usual shake of hands, bows, and salaams. He talks and we talk, but neither can understand a word that the other says, except from signs and gestures.

We order coffee, cigars, and a bottle of wine, which our servant at once brings us; for, since we cannot understand each other's language, we can communicate, at least, through our palates until our dragoman returns from the town. Of the coffee and cigars he partakes freely, but the wine he declines, with the polite explanation (which we understand from gesture rather than from the words he speaks) that "no true Mohammedan ever drinks wine."

The governor's dress is in true Turkish, Oriental style—dark cloth, profusely embroidered with gold; while his dragoman and guards are also dressed in great style, each with a huge scimetar hanging at his side.

At length our dragoman arrives, and from thenceforth the governor and I keep up a brisk conversation until his departure. We learn from him much concerning Syria, Damascus, and Constantinople, which will prove of value to us in our future travels. He kindly offers to send a guard with us as far as Banias, but this we decline, telling him we have no fears of robbers or trouble on the way. He finally urges us to do him the honor of a call before leaving Tiberias, and, as we propose to start to-morrow morning, we cannot, of course, do less than promise to call upon him in the afternoon at five o'clock.

It is now our turn to do the "agreeable," so, mounting our horses about half-past four, we ride toward the town, and on reaching the wall we find one of the governor's servants watching for us, to guide us through the streets to the residence of His Excellency. On reaching the governor's house, we find a guard drawn up on either side of the passage-way to the door, each of whom, with a wave of the sword, salutes us as we pass. The governor, dressed in full official uniform, comes out to meet us, and conducts us into a large room, in the centre of which is a table covered with beautiful glass and porcelain vases filled with flowers; and around which are divans on which to sit cross-legged. Lily and Lu manage to quirl themselves up much better than ourself; for being rather fleshy, our legs much prefer horizontal or perpendicular lines to anything like a twist.

A few moments after being seated a servant approaches with a very pleasant Turkish drink, the name of which we have now forgotten; then coffee is passed in small cups and in silver holders, and then cigarettes, *ad infinitum*, all of which we enjoy and appreciate.

Lily asks to see the ladies of the household—a privilege never granted to gentlemen—and for about a half hour she is delightfully entertained by them. The dress, she tells us, of the wife and three daughters of the governor was Oriental throughout and exceedingly beautiful. We should have liked to see them ourself, but civility among the Turks forbids even our asking after the health of wife or daughter, much less looking upon their unveiled faces! Had we dared to look behind us when mounted and about leaving, we might, perhaps, have seen them in the doorways or peeping out at the windows, but even this politeness forbade us to do.

When our call upon His Excellency is ended, we pass out through a line of guards as when entering, and waving an adieu to the governor with our hand and to the soldiers with our cane, as if it had been a sword, we remount, and, passing through the narrow, dirty streets of the town, we are soon again at our tent door, heartily glad that official civilities are ended, though not regretting their occurrence, since it has given us an insight into the manners and customs of the higher and better class of Turkish officials, such as we otherwise might not have had.

Another incident occurred to-day, illustrating another phase in Eastern life, and showing, especially, the hard conditions to which the Jews of Palestine are subjected by their Moslem rulers.

In the course of our conversation with the governor as he is seated in our tent, our dragoman happens to mention that, as we start to-morrow on our tour northward, it would be desirable if we could have the half or the whole of a sheep for food on the way, and that while up in town he tried to induce the butcher to kill one for us, but this the butcher had declined to do, as it was not his day for slaughtering.

The governor at once replies that he will order his servants to kill one from his own flock, and have it sent to us immediately on his return to town.

We thank the governor for his proffered courtesy and kindness, and add that we cannot think for a moment of accepting such a gift at his hands; but if he can persuade the butcher to slaughter one for us, we would be greatly obliged, and would pay for it liberally.

His only answer is, "It shall be done."

We think nothing more of the matter until near dark, when Mohammed returns from the town, having with him a servant, bearing the coveted mutton; and then he relates to us what occurred between himself and the butcher, in language somewhat as follows:

"I went, sir, as you directed me, to the butcher, and found that he had received an order from the governor to kill a sheep at once for the howajjii. The butcher is a dog, sir—a Jew; and though he dared not disobey the governor, he did the job in a slovenly manner and delayed me beyond a reasonable time. I threatened to complain of this to the governor, but the dog only became the more surly and impudent. Thereupon I seized him by the beard and pulled every hair from the accursed dog's chin. He roared like a bull, when a score of other Jewish dogs came rushing up to aid him, but when they saw that I was a Moslem and a dragoman, they dare not lay so much as a finger upon me. The butcher, when I let him go, went straight to the governor to complain of me, and I went too; and with us both came fifty or more Jews. He told his story and I told mine, to which the governor only replied that I had served him right; adding, however, that if the sheep, nicely dressed, was not at your tent door within one hour, he would have him bastinadoed—and here the sheep is, within the hour."

"You paid him the money I gave you, did you not, Mohammed?"

"I did, sir, though the dog deserved no pay, nor would he have got it but for your positive order."

Thus is it here, and thus, indeed, is it everywhere, with the poor, down-trodden Jew. The curse of God still follows him wherever he may be and whatever he may do. Even here, upon the soil once possessed by his ancestors; here, where King David ruled and Solomon uttered his words of wisdom; here, almost within sight of the temple, "the glory of which filled the whole earth;" yes, even here, the Jew is treated as the veriest " dog" by his Moslem rulers!

One would think that this fact alone—if no other—would so impress the Jewish mind that they would be forced to acknowledge the divinity of our Saviour—that they would see in all this the just indignation of an offended God, and would be led to seek forgiveness and mercy from Him who alone can save them. How long, how long, O God, shall this land, once thy chosen habitation, but now so accursed, continue under thy fierce displeasure? How long, how long, O God, shall this people, once thine "own chosen," but now so down-trodden and oppressed, continue to wander into by and forbidden paths?

CHAPTER XI.

DESOLATE PLACES.

OUR six days near Tiberias, on the shores of the Sea of Galilee, with hot and cold baths every day, and the cool and invigorating breezes from the snow-capped summit of Mount Hermon blowing down upon us, will ever be remembered as among the most pleasant of all our days in Palestine; but, as all things earthly, however pleasant, must have an end some time, and as we have many other places yet to visit, we must now strike our tents and away.

At half-past seven on Wednesday morning, April 17th, we leave our camping-ground by the seaside, and start on our tour northward. We again pass by Tiberias, by Magdala, by Gennesaret, and by the Fountain of the Fig, and soon after reach an old khan, which is thought by some to mark the spot where Joseph was cast into the pit by his brethren before they sold him to the Ishmaelites.

Stephens, in writing of this spot and of this event, says:

"Turning away from the consecrated lake, we fixed our eyes on the end of my day's journey, the towering city of Safed. About an hour from the lake, we came to the great caravan road from Jerusalem to Damascus, and a little off from this to a large khan, in which there is a well-known tradition, as the pit into which Joseph was cast by his brethren before they sold him to the Ishmaelites. In all probability the legend establishing this locality has no better foundation than most of the others in the Holy Land; but I cannot help remarking that I do not attach the importance assigned by others to the circumstance of its distance from Hebron, at that time Jacob's dwelling-place. We know that Joseph's brethren were feeding their father's flock at Shechem; and when Joseph came thither, 'wandering in the field, he inquired after his brethren, and a man told him, They are departed hence, for I heard them say, Let us go to Dothan.' If there be any good reason for calling this place Dothan, to me it does not seem at all strange that in the pastoral state of society which existed then, and still exists unchanged, Jacob's sons had driven their flocks to a pasture-ground two days further on. It happened, just as if to afford a striking illustration of the scene supposed to have taken place here, while we were loitering around the khan, a caravan of merchants came up on their way from Damascus to Egypt; and the buying and selling of slaves, white or black, being still a part of the trade between these places, I had no doubt that if I had offered my servant for sale, they would have bought him and carried him to Egypt, where perhaps he would have risen to be a grand vizier."

The city of Safed, to which Stephens alludes, we can see far off on the mountain-top, but as we have chosen another route for Damascus, we will not visit it. We must therefore content ourself to give to our readers a description of it from the sight-seeing of others, rather than of our own. Its elevated position, and the fact that it can be seen from a great distance and from almost every point of the compass, has led travelers generally to believe that this is the place to which Christ alluded when 'he spoke of a "city set upon a hill, whose light cannot be hid." At one time it was a city of no small importance, and, perhaps, of considerable beauty; but the misrule of the country, and the earthquakes with which this town has been visited on several occasions, have worked its complete overthrow, until at present it is little more than a heap of ruins. When Stephens visited it in 1839, about eighteen months after the calamitous earthquake of 1837, he says: "The frightful spectacle of human misery had of course passed away, but the place was still little more than one great mass of ruins. In the eastern quarter many of the houses had been again built up, though more still lay around us level with the ground. The southern quarter was perhaps the least injured of all; here the rubbish has been cleared away, and this was now the chief seat of the Mohammedan population. Here, too, the Mutesellim had taken up his abode. The castle remained in the same state in which it had been left by the earthquake—a shapeless heap of ruins; so shapeless, indeed, that it was difficult to make out its original form. In the Jews' quarter many houses had likewise been temporarily rebuilt, but the rubbish had not been removed from the streets. We passed throughout the whole quarter, and found the poor Jews still wandering amid the ruins, among which we could scarcely wend our way. Many of them were employed in digging among the rubbish, each apparently before what had once been his dwelling."

And so, we are told by travelers whom we have met recently, it remains, in a great measure, even unto the present day. The present ruinous and desolate condition of this city, and, indeed, of all others throughout Palestine, affords striking evidence of the weakness and vices of the Ottoman rule, as their vast dimensions and solidity of structure do of the efficiency and magnificence of that of their founders. No element in the Mussulman character is more remarkable, or more unfavorable to national prosperity, than the indifference to the progress of decay, the unwillingness to repair the ravages of time. Even when a little attention or a little expense would prevent a building or an establishment from falling to ruin, nothing is done to arrest the march of destruction. If an edifice be shaken by an earthquake, it is abandoned—it is seldom or never raised again on its foundations; a ruined building, like a felled oak, remains in the dust for ever. Even in the populous parts of some of the great cities of Syria the heaps of ruins which have been left in the pathways by successive earthquakes have not been removed. A few hours' labor would clear the wrecks away, but the inhabitants prefer to clamber up and down the piles of stones and fragments rather than to displace them.

For hours after we climb, climb, climb, and yet all the while the waters of the Sea of Galilee seem lying almost at our feet; and when we stop, at noon, to lunch, at an elevation from which the last look of the sea on this road is to be had, it seems but a stone's throw from us. The air in this country is so rarefied that one is constantly at fault in measuring distances by the eye; and the usual way of measuring distances in this country is by the hour, that is, by the time it takes to make the trip on horseback. If you ask a man how far it is from this place to that, his answer will be, So many hours. The people seem to have no conception of distance, except by time. So far as we can judge, their usual estimate is about three miles per hour, and by multiplying the number of hours by three, we can usually get at about the number of miles.

From the high hills, far to the southward, we have a fine view of the lake El Huleh, which, in a direct line, is only about ten miles from the Sea of Galilee. This little lake is regarded by some as the head waters of the Jordan, as it receives from large springs immediately surrounding it, and from several small streams, the waters which afterward form the Jordan, and this is the only river flowing from this lake. Others trace the source of the Jordan to springs and streams still farther north; but in this matter, as in many others concerning Palestine, each tourist is privileged to exercise his own whim or judgment.

This lake of El Huleh is called, in the Old Testament, " the waters of Merom," and is celebrated chiefly from the defeat of the confederate kings of Canaan by Joshua, on its borders. The record says: " And when all these kings were met together, they came and pitched together at the waters of Merom, to fight against Israel. And the Lord said unto Joshua, Be not afraid because of them, for to-morrow about this time I will deliver them all slain before Israel: thou shalt hough their horses, and burn their chariots with fire. So Joshua came, and all the people of war with him, against them by the waters of Merom suddenly; and they fell upon them. And the Lord delivered them into the hand of Israel, who smote them, and chased them unto Mizrephoth-maim, and unto the valley of Mizpeh eastward; and they smote them, until they left them none remaining."

This lake is not mentioned in the New Testament at all, from which we infer that Christ and his apostles never visited it. Josephus calls it the Lake Samochonites, which appears to be a Greek rendering of the native name Samaco, which it bears in the Jerusalem Talmud. But in the same Talmud it is sometimes called " the Sea of Cobebo," while the Babylonian Talmud names it " the Sibbechean Sea." Its dimensions are about eight miles long by four in breadth, though one-half of its upper end

PLOUGHING IN SYRIA.

is but little, if anything, more than a marsh, covered with tall reeds. The banks of the lake are very low; but the lake itself is on a considerably higher level than the Lake of Tiberias, and for this cause, together with the narrow and rocky character of its channel, the Jordan flows from Lake Huleh to Lake Tiberias with considerable rapidity and noise. The lake abounds in fish, and its south-western shore bears the name of Melaba, from the ground being covered with a saline crust.

The valley in which this little lake is located is broad, and seems to be quite fertile. We notice, as we pass along, fourteen cow and young steer teams ploughing on one piece of ground; though, if all they did in a day were added together, it would not amount to as much as one plough and a pair of horses would do in the same time in America. Their plough is nothing more than a sharpened stick, which tears up the ground about four inches wide, as it is pulled along by the cows; and we notice that for every hour they work they seem to rest about two. A more indolent, lazy set of creatures than these Syrians never existed, and but for the necessities of nature not one of them would do a stroke of work from one year's end to another.

Near where we encamp is a fine fountain, from which flows a large body of water, quite sufficient to turn the two stones of an old mill, situated some ten feet below the pond formed from the waters of the fountain. And as this mill of Malaha is one of the institutions of Syria, and evidently regarded by its owners, or those who tend it, as a little superior to any other mill in the world, we cannot do better than spend a few moments in describing it.

Its walls are of stone, one story high, and about two feet and a half thick—its size, say 20 by 40 feet. It has two run of stone, the lower ones stationary, while each of the upper ones rests upon a wooden centre-post, ten feet long, with the lower end of the post pointed with iron and resting on a stone at the bottom of the waste-weir. In the posts, below the mill floor and near the water, are wooden arms, which look much like the spokes of a wagon wheel, only a little broader. The water, which comes through a narrow sluice-way above, dashes against these spokes or arms in its rapid rush outward, and thus the stones, which are affixed to the posts above the floor, are turned. This is all the machinery there is about the mill—not a wheel, cog or strap is anywhere to be found.

The three men who show and explain to us the operations of the mill, and who evidently take great pride in doing so, as if we had never looked upon its equal before, first turn on the water, then take hold of the stone and give it a start, and then, with folded arms, gaze upon the slowly revolving stone as if it were the most wonderful of man's inventions.

Of course we say *tieb! tieb!* (good, good), and thank them for the pains they have taken to show and explain to us the operations of their mill, though scarcely suppressing a laugh, not only at the simplicity of their mill, but at the men who tend upon it and admire it so much.

When it is recollected that this is found in a country which had reached its highest civilization more than twenty-five hundred years before ours was discovered, the retrograding of this people and the rapid advancement of our own will be duly appreciated.

Next morning we leave the Mill Malaha and cross the plain of El Huleh at its western end. The many small streams which flow from the hills to the plain make the ground soft and marshy, and difficult to cross. Several times our horses mire so deep that we fear for their and our safety; but finally we get across the marsh safely and reach a dark ravine, where the Hasbeiyah river comes down from the mountains of Lebanon, and passing up this ravine some distance, we reach an ancient bridge of a single arch, through which the waters of the Hasbeiyah dash furiously onward and downward. Here we lunch, and while lunching we observe on the other side of the stream quite a cavalcade about to move forward. It consists of about a hundred Mohammedans, who have been to the tomb of a sheikh, on a mountain opposite, to hold a festival. They are dressed in holiday attire, are of both sexes and of all ages, and seem in the best of humor with themselves and the rest of mankind.

Crossing the old bridge, we pass through groves of oaks and olives, and in about one hour thereafter we find ourselves at Banias, the ancient Cæsarea Philippi.

Here we order our tents pitched; but as the sun is still high in the heavens, we conclude, before dismounting, to visit the ruins on the summit of the mountain, immediately behind the town.

This summit is probably a thousand feet above Banias, and to reach it we ascend a narrow, rocky path, which, at times, is difficult, if not dangerous, to both horse and rider. The north-eastern side of the hill, far up toward the ruins, is terraced and planted with olive trees, which have evidently, at one time, been nurtured with great care and have yielded abundantly.

The ruins of the castle of Banias, or Suibeh, or, as it is sometimes called, Khulet-el-Banias, look grand and imposing as we see them from the valley below and as we approach them from the hillside; but once within, we find nothing but an immense mass of stones, piled one upon the other, with scarcely a trace of their former beauty remaining. We find one large cistern cut in the rock and arched over with pointed arches, and near this a large arched passage-way, with rooms contiguous; and at the south-western and north-eastern corners are the remains of large and strong towers, but beyond this all is inextricable confusion. A portion of the outer wall remains, which bears evidence of having once possessed great strength as a means of defence; and the wonder is how, in those early days, without the use of gunpowder, a castle so defended could have been taken at all except by siege. And yet history informs us that it was taken and retaken, time and again, during the wars which in early and more recent periods swept over this part of Palestine.

The eastern end of the ridge, on which the castle is located, is the highest, and this was taken advantage of by the projectors to form an upper citadel commanding the rest of the castle. It is separated from the lower western portion by a regular interior cross-wall, with towers and trench, and is without entrance or approach except through the lower fortress. Here, more than anywhere else, the beetling towers and ramparts impend over the northern precipice and look down into the chasm of Wady Khushabeh, six or seven hundred feet below. Within this citadel are the loftiest and strongest towers, and this portion is the best preserved of all. Not less than one-third of it is ancient beveled work, exhibiting a better and more finished bevel than is perhaps to be found elsewhere out of Jerusalem.

The Saracens and Crusaders while in possession of this castle made, Dr. Robinson says, no additions to the fortress. They did nothing in the citadel but patch up a few portions of it where this was necessary for defence, leaving all the rest as they found it. Their repairs are easily to be distinguished from other parts of the work. Nor did they do much more in the lower or western part; though there are quite a number of Arabic inscriptions, mostly dated A.H. 625, equivalent to A.D. 1227, recounting that such and such a prince, with a long pedigree, built up this or that tower at a certain time.

"The whole fortress," adds Dr. Robinson, "made upon us a deep impression of antiquity and strength, and of the immense amount of labor and expense employed in its construction. It has come down to us as one of the most perfect specimens of the military architecture of the Phœnicians, or possibly of the Syro-Grecians; and whoever will make himself acquainted with the resources and prowess of those ancient nations, must not fail to study the ruins of this noble fortress."

The view from the ruins is very fine, extending over the plain of El Huleh, and far beyond to Mount Tabor and Gilboa. At our feet lies Banias, surrounded by olive orchards, with the waters of the great fountain rushing furiously at its side; while, looking northward and eastward, mountain upon mountain rises grandly and gloriously in view. Crossing some of these mountains afterward, however, we find that "distance lent enchantment to the view," and that, once face to face, they are quite as rugged and uninviting as many others we had seen in the more southern parts of Palestine.

The town of Banias itself is small, poorly built, with rough streets, and does not contain, we should think, over five hundred inhabitants. That it has been a place of importance, however, is evidenced from the ruins on the outer edge of the town, some of which are still quite imposing. Its chief attraction consists in the magnificent fountain, which gushes out at the base of a hill near the town. The waters come out from a space probably a hundred feet in width, and, flowing to a common centre, form a stream sufficiently large to turn the largest mill in America. Soon after issuing from the fountain the waters commence a rapid descent, and go dashing and foaming over the rocks below at a most furious rate. A large excavation has been made in the rock under the hill, immediately above where the waters issue, and on each side of this are sculptured niches in which sylvan deities have some time stood.

While the Greeks occupied Syria, this cave or grotto was made a sanctuary in which they worshiped their sylvan deity, Pan; and some portions of the temple built near this by Herod the Great, in honor of Augustus, still remain.

The town is of very ancient date, and possesses some historical and biblical interest. By the Greeks it was called Panias, and this name it continued to bear until Philip the Tetrarch enlarged and beautified the place and named it Cæsarea Philippi. Afterward it was called Neronias, in honor of the tyrant Nero. Still later it resumed the old name of Cæsarea Philippi; and such was its importance during the occupancy of Syria by the Romans that Titus selected this place in which to celebrate triumphant games after the conquest of Jerusalem. How many of his Jewish prisoners destroyed each other while fighting as gladiators for the amusement of the people is not stated, but probably a great number. During the time of the Crusades it became the north-eastern key of the Holy Land, and here were fought several of the fiercest and bloodiest battles between Christians and Mohammedans. It finally fell before the superior forces of Salah-e'deen, and has ever since remained in the possession of the Turks.

The history of this place during the Crusades is thus epitomized by Dr. Robinson: "It first came into the possession of the Christians in A.D. 1129 or 1130, along with the fortress of Es-Subeibeh on the mountain ; being delivered over to them by its Ishmaelite governor after their unsuccessful attempt upon Damascus in behalf of that sect. The city and castle were given as a fief to the Knight Rayner Brus. In A.D. 1132, during the absence of Rayner, Banias was taken after a short assault by the Sultan Isma'il of Damascus. It was recaptured by the Franks, aided by the Damascenes themselves, in A.D. 1139; the temporal control restored to Rayner Brus, and the city made a Latin bishopric under the jurisdiction of the archbishop of Tyre. Banias fell afterward by inheritance into the possession of the Constable Houfroy, who called in the aid of the Hospitalers for its protection ; in A.D. 1157 it was besieged by the formidable Neireddin, who succeeded in taking and burning the town, but was not able to master the fortress situated in the city itself. The place was relieved and the fortifications immediately rebuilt by King Baldwin III. But in A.D. 1165, Neireddin again attacked Banias during the absence of Houfroy, and with better success ; after a short siege it surrendered, and never came again into the power of the Franks. In A.D. 1172, King Almaric besieged Banias for fifteen days in vain. The place, with others, was dismantled by Sultan Mu'adh-dhem in A.D. 1219. The Christians once more, in A.D. 1253, made an expedition from Tyre against Banias, under the command of Seneschal Joinville, and got possession of the town for the moment ; but not being able to subdue Kul-at-es-Subeibeh on the mountain, they immediately abandoned their conquest and retired to Sidon."

But its greatest interest to the Christian tourist is, that Jesus, during his pilgrimage on earth, once honored it with his presence ; and here occurred that memorable conversation between the Saviour and his disciples, in which he first acknowledged himself in his true character as "the Christ, the Son of the living God."

The record reads, "When Jesus came into the coasts of Cæsarea Philippi, he asked his disciples, saying, Whom do men say that I the Son of man am? And they said, Some say thou art John the Baptist, some Elias, and others Jeremiah, or one of the prophets. He saith unto them, But whom say ye that I am? And Simon Peter answered and said, Thou art the Christ, the Son of the living God. And Jesus answered and said unto him, Blessed art thou, Simon Bar-Jona; for flesh and blood hath not revealed it unto thee, but my Father which is in heaven."

It is thought by some, that inasmuch as the records of the sublime mystery of Christ's transfiguration occurred immediately after this, it may have occurred at this place, but we can find no evidence to confirm this opinion. The fact that the transfiguration did not occur until six days after this conversation with his disciples, and that it occurred on a "high mountain," points, we think, more probably to Mount Tabor, or possibly to the Mount of Olives; and the argument used against the former of these places, that its summit was built upon at the time, has but little weight, we think, since the transfiguration may have taken place upon either of its slopes as well as upon its summit. Since the record does not give the precise spot, and since so many places in Palestine claim the distinction, each tourist is left free to fix it where his own best judgment may direct.

We have now reached the farthest point northward to which the footsteps of Jesus ever led him, so far as we have any knowledge from the Sacred Volume. We have visited the place of his birth at Bethlehem; the place of his early childhood and boyhood and manhood at Nazareth; the places where he spent three years and upward in teaching in the synagogues, healing the sick, walking upon the waves, and bidding the winds and the waters "be still," along the shores of the Sea of Galilee; the place of his baptism in the river Jordan, and the wilderness in which he fasted for forty days and forty nights; the places where he called back to life the widow's son, raised Lazarus from the grave, and gave to blind Bartimeus his sight; the place where in agony of spirit he prayed, and sweat, as it were, great drops of blood; the places where he was betrayed, where he was cruelly crucified, and where he was laid in the new-made tomb; and the place, too, where he burst the bonds of death asunder and arose triumphant from the grave!

From henceforth we shall no longer follow his earthly footsteps; but God grant that we may be able to follow him in a spiritual sense more closely than ever heretofore.

CHAPTER XII.

AMONG THE DRUSES.

FROM Cæsarea Philippi (Banias) our course lies over the mountain, and the paths here, as elsewhere in Syria, are horrible, though somewhat relieved by the glimpse of valleys we get in the distance, and the occasional ones we cross.

All the forenoon we ride within close view of the snow-capped Hermon, and on reaching the summit of the mountain opposite, the winds become so strong and cold that we are obliged to put on shawls and overcoats. And at lunch-time so cold are the winds that we seek the shelter of a friendly rock to protect us from the blasts while we lunch and take rest.

About 2 P.M. we reach Beit-jin ("the abode of an evil spirit," as translated in English), a considerable village, situated at the head of a deep valley or gorge, and occupied principally by Moslems, though in the heart of the Druse country. Before descending the steep hill which leads down to the village, two Druses with guns on their shoulders come up to us and seem disposed to be very chatty; but having heard of the murderous disposition of these disciples of the crazy Kalif El-Hakim, we keep a close eye upon them, and give them to understand that we are fully prepared to protect ourselves in case of necessity. They trot along beside our horses for about a mile, and then finding they can get no bucksheesh from us, either through fear or favor, they suddenly disappear.

As this is our first acquaintance with the Druses, and as they are regarded as the most singular, most courageous, and most warlike body of men in Syria, we cannot do better than devote a few moments to their history and peculiarities of character as a people.

Everything belonging to this singular little nation is calculated to excite curiosity and interest—its manners and customs, its bravery, its rare stability of character, and, above all, the mystery that has so long hung over its moral history, and which has only begun to be penetrated within a very few years past. Even at this day it is not easy to speak positively and precisely of the Druse doctrines; and though some of their religious books found their way long ago into Europe, and several of them fell into the hands of the Egyptian soldiery during the last insurrections against the authority of Mohammed Ali, these have not fulfilled the hopes founded upon them of arriving at a complete knowledge of the principles and practice of the Druse religion.

The Druses occupy the southern portion of Lebanon, the western slopes of Anti-Lebanon, and the Jebel Sheik. There are thirty-seven large towns and villages in Lebanon inhabited solely by Druses, and two hundred and eleven villages of Druses mingled with Christians. In Anti-Lebanon there are sixty-nine villages or towns belonging exclusively to the Druses; and there are several others having a mixed population of Druses, Maronites, and schismatic Greeks.

Ammatur and Bachlin in Lebanon, Hasbya, and Rysheya in Anti-Lebanon, are capitals as it were, regarded by the Druses in the same light as Jerusalem was by the Jews, and Samaria by the kingdom of Israel. Each of these towns is a rallying-point for the nation, and possesses a religious edifice (khalueh), in which are deposited their sacred books and their war standards.

In the last century five hundred or six hundred Druse families withdrew to the mountains of the Haourân, on the borders of the desert. This emigration began in the year 1757, the same in which the civil wars began of Sheikh Omar-el-Daher.

Like all the other races of Syria, the Druses are distinguishable by a peculiar cast of features: the people of the country recognize a Druse, a Metuali, etc., at the first glance, as easily as the children in our streets do a Jew. The physiognomy of the Druse is noble, grave, and sometimes even characterized by an expression of high spirit, not untinctured with ferocity. "Haughty, sanguinary, and vindictive by nature, they conceal these defects," says Perrier, "under an exquisite suavity of demeanor, and they fairly compensate for them by their unbounded hospitality, generosity, and loftiness of soul. Their code of morals is extremely rigid, and the greatest good faith prevails in their mutual dealings; their word, once passed, becomes a sacred oath as binding as the most solemn legal contract. No people are more nice than they upon the point of honor; with them the least insult is instantly requited with the khanjar or the rifle; whereas, among the people of the plains, it only provokes abusive retorts. From this delicate susceptibility has arisen among them that politeness of manner which a gentleman, with the prejudices of his European education not yet modified by much contact with Orientals, is astonished to discover among peasants. It is carried even to dissimulation and falsehood, especially among the chiefs, whose greater interests demand a greater wariness of speech and conduct. Circumspection is imperatively requisite where retaliation is so prompt and so formidable."

We must not omit stating *per contra* that, according to Burckhardt, the Druse is thus nice only in the defence of his public honor, and that he will tamely submit to injurious treatment, and even to blows, if there be no witnesses of his disgrace. The Syrians, too, say that the good faith observed by the Druses, as regards each other, does not govern them in their transactions with men of other sects, toward whom their religion teaches them it is no sin to violate the most solemn engagements. But both these assertions appear exaggerated and to need further investigation.

Though the Druses inhabit many villages in common with the Christians, they have little intercourse with the latter, never enter into family alliances with them, and hold them in sovereign contempt. Still, the outward harmony between the two classes is seldom disturbed by any open broils. The Druses despise the Franks; and the worst insult one Druse can offer to another is the exclamation, "May God put a hat on you!" Yet these very people are unbounded in their kindness to the Frank stranger who claims their hospitality. Their national character is, in truth, a compound of seemingly contradictory principles, and cannot be fairly estimated from the hasty inductions travelers have drawn from partial observation or hearsay. A general disregard of religious observances would naturally render the Druses hateful to fanatics of all persuasions; and, surrounded as they are on every side by zealous professors of other creeds, it cannot excite surprise that they should be made the subjects of misrepresentation and calumny.

These men carry the virtue of hospitality to a romantic pitch. Whoever presents himself at their doors as a suppliant or a wayfarer is sure of being entertained with lodging and food in the most generous and unaffected manner. "I have often," says Volney, "seen the lowest peasants give the last morsel of bread they had in their houses to the hungry traveler; and when I observed to them that they wanted prudence, their answer was, 'God is bountiful and great, and all men are brethren.'" When they have once contracted with their guest the sacred engagement of bread and salt, no subsequent event can make them violate it. Many instances of this are related to their honor. An aga of the Janissaries having been engaged in a rebellion toward the close of the eighteenth century, fled from Damascus and retired among the Druses. The pasha was informed of this and demanded him of the emir, threatening to make war on the latter in case of refusal. The emir demanded him of the sheikh Talhook who had received him; but the latter indignantly replied, "When have you known the Druses deliver up their guests? Tell the emir that as long as Talhook shall preserve his beard, not a hair of the head of his suppliant shall fall." The emir threatened him with force: Talhook armed his family. The emir, dreading a revolt, adopted a method practiced as juridical in this country: he declared to the sheikh that he would cut down fifty of his mulberry trees daily until the aga were given up. He proceeded as far as a thousand, and Talhook still remained inflexible. At length, the other sheikhs became incensed and took up the quarrel, and the commotion was about to become general, when the aga, reproaching himself with being the cause of so much mischief, made his escape without the knowledge even of Talhook.

The Druses have long been divided into numerous factions, often at war with each other, but which always unite when there is a common foe to fight. When war is resolved on, every man, whether sheikh or peasant, able to bear arms, is called on to march. He takes with him a little bag of flour, a musket, some bullets, and a small quantity of powder, and repairs to the appointed rendezvous. If it be a civil war, each man rallies around the standard of his chief. A strict spirit of clanship prevails in Syria, and, above all, in Lebanon, among the Druses. The father bequeaths his opinions and his party to his son; and there is hardly an example of a Maronite or a Druse espousing a quarrel or adopting a party other than that of his ancestors. In civil feuds the incensed adversaries often seem on the point of proceeding to the last extremities, but they seldom engage in mortal strife; mediators always interpose, and the quarrel is appeased the more readily as each patron is obliged to provide his followers with provisions and ammunition.

The gathering of the clans, as described by Volney, an eye-witness, forcibly reminds one of the speeding of the fiery cross, in former days, along the braes and glens of Scotland. "When," says he, "the emir and sheikhs had determined on war at Deir-el-Kammar, criers went up at night to the summits of the cliff, and cried aloud, 'To war! to war!' Take your guns—take your pistols! Noble sheikhs, mount your horses—arm yourselves with the lance and the sabre—rendezvous to-morrow at Deir-el-Kammar. Zeal of God! Zeal of combats!' This summons, heard in the neighboring villages, was repeated there; and as the whole country is nothing but a chain of lofty mountains and deep valleys, the proclamation passed through its length and breadth in a few hours. These cries, from the stillness of the night, the long, resounding echoes, and the nature of the subject, had something awful and terrible in their effect. Three days after, fifteen thousand armed men were assembled at Deir-el-Kammar, and operations might have been immediately commenced."

The clannish disposition of this people, and their hereditary feuds, make them averse to forming matrimonial alliances out of their own families. They invariably prefer their relations, though poor, to a rich stranger; and poor peasants have been known to refuse their daughters to wealthy and thriving merchants of Beyrout. They observe, also, to a certain extent, the custom of the Hebrews, which directed that a brother should wed his brother's widow; but this is not peculiar to them, but one of many ancient usages which they retain, in common with other inhabitants of Syria and all the Arab tribes.

The Druses take but one wife. Their young men usually marry at the age of sixteen or eighteen, and the girls at thirteen or fourteen. Three days before that fixed for the celebration of the marriage, the bridegroom, accompanied by some young men of his own age, all well armed, proceeds formally to demand his bride at the hand of her father, who awaits the party, armed *cap-a-pie*, on the threshold of his door; and there gives his final sanction to the conditions of the contract. The young man fixes the dowry (*maahr*) to be settled by him on his intended, and promises her family that he will render her happy. The betrothed girl appears for a moment, but closely veiled, and accompanied by some female relations and by her mother, who guarantees the unblemished honor of her child. Upon this the young man pops the question to the fair one herself, who replies *neble tak* (I accept you), presenting him, at the same time, with a khanjar (a broad and slightly curved dagger) sewed up in a red and white handkerchief, or *kefieh*, generally of

DRUSE MARRIAGE PROCESSION.

wool, and wrought with her own hands. The khanjar is a token of the protection she expects from her husband; but it is likewise the instrument destined to expiate her guilt if she has trifled with her maiden honor, or if she ever violate her marriage troth, or even fail in her duty as an obedient and duteous wife.

All parties then enter the house; the bride afterward proceeds slowly to the bath, where she spends the day with her companions, whilst the men mount their horses and amuse themselves with their favorite games, or remain smoking and drinking coffee in the house of the bride's father: the same ceremony is twice repeated. On the wedding-night, the women conduct the bridegroom to the nuptial-chamber, where the bride awaits him covered from head to foot with a red veil spangled with gold; removing this, he presents her with the tantoor (a sort of skull-cap) and places it on her head, where it is to remain for the rest of her life. The moment the husband snatches off the veil, the women run out of the room screaming, or rather gabbling very like turkeys. This is the signal for the commencement of a tremendous uproar in the house; the women never leave off screaming and gabbling in their own apartment for several hours, and the men assembled in another room perform the *dance of arms*. They caper about and put themselves into all sorts of ludicrous attitudes, clashing their sabres or their yataghans together, and feigning to be in a towering passion. All this hubbub is made to drive away the jins and the evil spirits, who are thought to be particularly busy about the house on such occasions.

"Every Druse," says Burckhardt, "possesses an absolute and uncontrolled power to repudiate his wife on paying the stipulated dowry; nothing can be simpler than the form of pronouncing her divorce; it is enough that the husband show her the door and say, 'Go!' Nay, if a wife asks permission of her husband to make a visit to her relations, and he grants it without adding an injunction to her to return, even that omission is tantamount to a divorce." But, notwithstanding this facility, divorces are not frequent among the Druses, and hardly ever occur without grave reasons. The woman who is convicted of conjugal infidelity is invariably punished with death—not by her husband, who only sends her back to her relations with the khanjar he received from her when they married —but by her relations themselves; her guilt reflects shame not on him, but on them, for *dishonor follows the line of blood*, say the Druses, and does not devolve on a man or on a family of other blood. The khanjar sent back without its sheath apprises the family of their disgrace. Upon this the father and the brother of the guilty woman assemble at the husband's house to investigate the case. If proofs be wanting, the husband's oath is held sufficient; the relations, on their return home, put the unhappy woman to death. Usually they cut off her head, and send her tantoor to her husband with a lock of her hair dyed in her blood, as a proof that justice has had its course. The more a father loves his daughter the less hope she can have of pardon. "An execution," says Perrier, " of this kind took place in 1839, in a small Druse village near Jeyzin. The victim, who was hardly fourteen years of age, was put to death in a council of her kindred; her eldest brother was her executioner. Her mother and sisters, shut up in an adjoining apartment, in vain appealed for mercy with shrieks of despair; nothing could soften the inexorable brothers, not even the pardon granted by the aged father of the culprit. As for the accomplice of her guilt, he instantly disappeared and was never more heard of. The rumor was industriously propagated that he had fled to Turkey to escape the chastisement of a severe bastinado, to which he had made himself liable; but the neighbors and the inhabitants of the village were not deceived by this report. They knew that the torrents that roll near Jeyzin are deep, and that the caverns of the mountains are mute as the grave."

Death is likewise the fate of the unmarried girl who has forfeited her honor; in this case only the father may grant forgiveness, if he has no other children; brothers are always implacable. The pashas and governors of Syria cautiously abstain from interfering with the right assumed by families thus to avenge the jealous honor of their blood.

The Druses are perhaps the only people who do not love music, vocal or instrumental. Rarely, if ever, is the ballad, or legendary song, or mountain air heard in their cottages or at their festivals. They have no sort of musical instruments, and they march to battle without trumpet, pipe or song. Their pleasures are very simple; in the evening they sometimes assemble in the court-yard or house of the chief of the village or family. "There," says Volney, "seated in a circle, with legs crossed, pipes in their mouths and poniards in their belts, they discourse of their various labors, the scarcity or plenty of their harvests, peace or war, the conduct of the emir, or the amount of the taxes; they relate past transactions, discuss present interests and form conjectures on the future. Their children, tired with play, come frequently to listen; and a stranger is surprised to hear them, at ten or twelve years old, recounting, with a serious air, why Djezzar declared war against the Emir Yousef, how many purses it cost that prince, what augmentation there will be of the miri, how many muskets there were in the camp, and who had the best mare." This was written sixty years ago. There are other persons and things than Djezzar and his wars to talk of in the mountains at the present day; but, making allowance for such changes, the general truth of the picture remains unaltered.

Like many other heterodox sects subjected to Moslem sway, the Druses found it expedient from the very first, and, indeed, necessary to their self-preservation, to stoop to dissimulation. They have express warrant for this in their religious books, which say, "Embrace the religion of those who have power over you; for such is the pleasure of our Maoula, till he to whom the best times are known shall unsheath the sword and display the power of his unity." Acting on this principle, the Druses affect in public to speak well of all religions. Outwardly, they are professors of Islamism, and they perform all the rites prescribed by it whenever they mix with Mohammedans. In private, however, they break the fast of the Ramadan, curse Mohammed, indulge in wine, and eat food forbidden by the Kur-an. Some of them feign a great veneration for *Kadra Mariana*, the Virgin Mary, in order to gain favor with their Christian neighbors. If you press them closely to tell you what are their real notions of religion, their answer is invariably, "God alone sounds the depths of the heart of the believers in his law; but men may be deceived by outward appearances."

It is almost superfluous to remark of men so indifferent as to religious matters that they evince no disposition to make proselytes. But if they do not seek to spread their tenets through other lands, they are yet persuaded that numbers of their co-religionists exist, unknown, in various countries of the world, above all, in China! There are ackals, they say, in the mountains of Scotland as sage and pure as any in Lebanon; only their European brethren are compelled by the fear of persecution to assume the outward appearance of Christianity, as they themselves do those of Mohammedanism. From the description they give of the habits and practices of these supposed Druses of the West, more especially of their manner of burying the dead, it seems evident that they allude to the order of the Templars, which they believe still to exist in *Jebel-el-Scouzia*, the Scottish Highlands.

Some among them even lay claim to a European origin, and pretend to be descended from the French. The agents of the French government availed themselves of this notion with considerable effect during the troubles that immediately preceded the expulsion of the Egyptians from Syria by the allied forces. The prevalence of this opinion among Europeans, and its eager adoption by the Druses, is accounted for in the following way:

The renowned Druse Fakr-ed-Deen, in whose family the supreme chieftainship was vested, ruled over the mountain tribes during the early part of the seventeenth century. He at length extended his sway throughout the whole district between Tripoli and Sidon; and it was only after a long and successful career, during which he introduced a great degree of civilization into the mountains, that he fell at last a victim to the jealousy of the Ottoman government. His family soon afterward became extinct, and the Shehab were elected, by popular consent, to succeed it.

When threatened by a formidable armament sent against him by the Porte, Fakr-ed-Deen, who had formed connections at the court of the Medici in Florence, repaired thither in person to solicit aid. The arrival of an Oriental prince in Italy did not fail to attract the public attention, and the origin of the Druses became a popular topic of research. The conclusion was speedily arrived at that a people who had taken refuge in the mountains, and who were hostile to the Mohammedans, could be no other than the offspring of the Crusaders. Fakr-ed-Deen, seeing how favorable to his views was this idle conceit, took care to encourage it, and was artful enough to pretend that he was related to the house of Lorraine. The learned in etymology, struck with the resemblance of the names, insisted that *Druse* and *Dreux* must be the same word; and on this foundation they built their system of a pretended colony of French Crusaders, who, under the conduct of a Comte de *Dreux*, had formed a settlement in Lebanon. This hypothesis, however, is completely refuted by the fact that the name of the Druses is to be found in the Itinerary of Benjamin of Tudela, who traveled before the time of the Crusaders.

"The truth is," says Lord Lindsay, "you meet with traces of the Franks and reminiscences of the Crusaders everywhere in Syria; but while the Bekaris, or descendants of Abubekr, are still flourishing in Damascus, as well as the houses of many of the companions of Mohammed, the descendants of the great Syrio-Norman families have sunk generally into mere *fellahs*, or cultivating Arabs. Some few exceptions there may be. A Frank traveler some years ago discovered, on examining a bundle of old parchments in the possession of a village sheikh, that the owner was the descendant of one of the oldest crusading families in France. Ignorance would have been bliss in this case, poor old man! He started forth on a pilgrimage to Paris, and got as far as Alexandria; but falling ill there, and other obstructions being cast in his way by a kind Providence, he returned to his own village, Gausta, and was living there in extreme old age in the year 1835.

The founder of the Druse religion was the Caliph Hakim-Bi-Amr-Allah, the third of the Fatimites, who became caliph of Cairo in the year of the Hegira 386, or

A.D. 996, when little more than a child. His reign was distinguished by the most ridiculous extravagances; he forbade women ever to go out of doors, and prohibited workmen from making any kind of foot-gear for their use, on pain of death; all the necessary supplies were to be conveyed to them through loopholes in the walls by means of long poles, so that none might ever see them. Not content with these follies, the caliph chose to make himself God, and he gave orders that public registers should be opened for the purpose of enrolling the names of all who were willing to recognize his divinity. Fear or adulation filled the registers in a few days with sixteen thousand names; whereupon the madman proclaimed himself an incarnation of God and the founder of a new religion, which was altogether to supersede that of Mohammed. At last, after an execrable reign of four-and-twenty years, he was murdered by his minister, Hamzi, who became the continuator of the religion begun by Bi-Amr-Allah, and changed that name, which signifies *governing by order of God*, into Hakim-Bi-Amri, *governing by his own order*.

The succeeding caliphs persecuted those who were stupid enough to believe in the divine character of such a monster. Several of the sect fled to Syria, and there they propagated their doctrines, and soon became a strong and bold people. The ground, in fact, was already prepared to receive the seed they cast upon it. The mystical doctrines of Hakim Burka, "the Veiled Prophet of Khorassan" (A.D. 771), and those of Karmath (A.D. 891), had already been widely spread in Syria, and had formed a fit basis for the superstructure of transcendental folly reared by the founders of many sects now existing in this country. Much as the Druses, Metualis, Anzeyrys, Ismeylis, Yezidis, etc., differ from each other, still there is a family resemblance pervading their habits and ways of thinking, as well as those, too, of the terrible Assassins, that clearly points to a common origin. But to the honor of the Druses be it said, their mysticism, however extravagant, has not carried them, like some of the other sects, to the horrible excess of abrogating the moral law. The Karmathians are a sort of Oriental Muggletonians, who hold that faith and knowledge raise men above all distinctions of right and wrong, and the Anzeyrys appear fully to have embraced that opinion; not so the Druses, whose moral character, all things considered, is deserving of high praise.

The leading doctrines of Hakim Burka were the transmigration of souls and the unity of God; but, at the same time, the transfusion of that sole godhead into the person of Adam the first man, into those of the prophets, and of many great men who had appeared at various epochs, and lastly into the person of him, Hakem, the last personification of God. All this is nearly identical with the fundamental doctrines of the Druse creed; and as Hamzi-Ben-Ahmed, the vizier of the impious Caireen Caliph, was a Persian, we are not unwarranted in supposing that he borrowed from Hakim Burka those notions which he suggested to his master, and on which he himself continued to act after the violent death of the caliph.

It is scarcely possible to arrive at a knowledge of the present tenets of the Druses; several of their religious books have been translated by those into whose hands they were thrown by the chance of war; but little can be learned from them, for they are full of cabalistic signs, broken sentences, and disjointed, unintelligible phrases. None but an ackal can ever disclose the mystery, but there are no religious traitors among them, and but one civil traitor, the Sheikh Shubleh Arriam, who took bribes of Ibrahim Pasha, and betrayed his brethren in the revolt of 1838. He, if still alive, might perhaps be induced to betray the secrets of the ackals.

A few fragments from the Druse books, carefully translated by Perrier, may not be uninteresting to the reader:

"The god of the Druses desires not that his ackal children should weary themselves in his worship: he is alone glorious and luminous in himself, and he does not exact the toil and fatigue of his children.

"This god, the ruler of the universe, is Alli-el-Allah (the supreme god); he was called also. . . . .

"But Alli-el-Allah vanquished the creator of the world, who is now only Adam the rebel.

"Now this supreme god is likewise Melek (the sovereign) Hakim-Bi-Amr-Allah, grand prince who was born in Egypt, etc., etc. . . . .

"Here is the transfusion, the transmigration of the god Bi-Amr-Allah; here is the god Hamzi. Hamzi-Ben-Ahmed-el-Farsi (the Persian) was the vizier of the Caliph Hakim. During his reign, in Cairo, Melek-Bi-Amr-Allah had a subterranean passage made to the lake called El Gizeh. He then left this palace secretly, mounted on an ass, and appeared on a sudden issuing from the water with his ass. He announced to men that he thus transported himself to different places, and that he was one day to appear in China; accordingly all owned him as a god.

"Now his vizier was Hamzi the Persian, the son of Ahmed. During the night the vizier strangled the god, and in the morning laid his garments on the waters of the lake El Gizeh. All the disciples of Hakim immediately hastened to the spot; but Hamzi said to them, Your god is gone; await his return in peace and hope, for he will reappear at the great day.

"Hakim and Hamzi built the great pyramids of Egypt! Within those buildings there are secret places which they made the depositories of the laws and of the wisdom of all times.

"All the prophets who have appeared on the earth, Adam, Noah, Abraham, Moses, Jesus, Mohammed, etc., had all had but one same spirit, transmigrated from one body to the other."

Each Druse family religiously preserves and transmits from father to son what is called the "purse of the faith." This is a small sum of money carefully sealed up, which is to serve as a token of recognition on the transmigration of the soul of the head of the family to another body. Should a Druse return to life after several successive transmigrations, he could prove his identity and make himself known as a true believer by means of the purse of the faith. When families divide, the son selected by the father (usually the eldest son) succeeds to the sacred purse, which he is forbidden to open even in his most urgent need. The purse must always be transmitted in a direct line to the individual who is regarded as the head of the family. During the revolt of Hourân there were found some of these purses that had been thus sealed up in parchment for hundreds of years, without ever having been opened.

The other children of the deceased receive each a small black stone of jet or agate, in token of hope, union, and recognition. The stone is rudely carved into the form of some animal; a circumstance which has probably occasioned the Syrians to assert that the Druses adore a small stone calf. This is scarcely true; they are not idolaters, but they do entertain a mysterious veneration for the purse of the faith, or for the *hars*, the black stone. The Syrians in general are unwilling to enter the house of a Druse without first shouting or making a noise to announce their presence, for they are fully persuaded that if they came suddenly upon him, and their eyes lighted by chance on that object of his veneration, which is ever to be sedulously hidden from all the profane, the Druse would be bound by his religion to slay the profaner who had "*blackened his face*" and "*surprised his hidden religion.*"

The Druses have signs of mutual recognition which have much analogy with the forms of free-masonry. The initiated everywhere know each other. When two Druses meet and discover by certain signs that they are both "ackals," they proceed to interrogate each other. One of them inquires, "Dost thou know in thy country a plant of peculiar excellence above all others?" "Yes," is the reply; "it is the aliledj." Upon a second inquiry as to the place where grows this marvelous plant, the respondent answers again, "It grows only in the hearts of the faithful Druses who believe in the unity of the God Itakim Bi Amri." The proof is not yet complete; they have now recognized each other as among the faithful and initiated, and next grasping each other's hands, one giving the left, the other the right, they whisper the names of the five prophets or Itedoubs, and two or three words unintelligible to all but those who have reached high degrees among their ackals. The inquiry is now complete, and they salute each other, laying their hands on their breasts.

This mysterious plant, which they call *aliledj* and the other Arabs *cuscuth*, is a small creeper with blue flowers (*cuscuta repens*, or *cuscuta minor*). The plant seems to have been always held in veneration in Syria. Pliny describes it under the name of the *cassyta* or *cadytas* of Syria. For the Druses it is a symbol of faith and union, and a pledge of hope and happiness. A small bunch of it always surmounts their banners; a branch hangs within the doors of their khaluehs, and some seeds and dried flowers of the plant are worn in a small egg-shaped silver box, which hangs from the neck of their acklat women.

Among no other race, perhaps, is there to be found so strong a faith in amulets (*itedjabs*) as among the Druses; they possess a great number of them, and such implicit confidence do they repose in the virtue of these talismans that, when armed with an *itedjab*, in the most desperate engagements their natural courage is often exalted to an incredible degree of temerity. The wealthiest among them wear signet rings called *Katem Suleymani*, supposed to have been enchanted by virtue of the name of Solomon. They are commonly of silver, with a black swivel stone, on one surface of which is inscribed the name of the owner, and, on the other, stars, constellations, and cabalistic figures.

Those who would know more of this strange people should consult the excellent French works of Perrier, *La Syrie sous Mehemet Ali;* and Sylvestre de Sacy, *Religion des Druses*, 2 vols., 8vo., Paris, 1838.

The situation of Beit-jin, through which village we have just passed, is quite picturesque, and the many tall, straight poplar trees growing along the banks of the stream which runs near it, give to the place and surroundings a pretty appearance. We cross this stream, and for some time after ride along its bank down the narrow valley.

It is nearly 5 P. M. before we reach Kafr-Howaran, and here we order our tents pitched, though first looking around to find, if possible, a sheltered spot, as the winds still blow strong and cold from Mount Hermon, which now seems but a little way off—just over the next hill—

though really several miles away. Scarcely are we within our tents before a strong gust of wind, sweeping down from the mountain side, snaps two or three of the tent cords, and but for the promptness of our servants in seizing and holding on to the side which had given away, we should speedily have had it about our ears. To protect ourselves from another mishap of the kind, we now double the ropes all around, and add another cross-rope from the flag-staff.

The blowing down of one's tent in the day-time, and when no storm is prevailing, can soon be remedied, and is usually laughed at as one of the episodes of tent-life in Palestine; but when it occurs at night, and in the midst of a furious, driving storm, it becomes a serious matter. Twice during our journey we come very near having such mishaps ourselves, but both times a complete overthrow is avoided by timely attention. Not so, however, with some of our American friends, who not only had their tents blown completely down while encamping outside of the walls of Jerusalem, but were obliged to flee, bare-naked, to a neighboring house to save themselves from still more unpleasant consequences. One gentleman, thinking a second deluge and the end of the world had come together, gathered up his clothes in his arms, and as soon as he could extricate himself from the folds of his fallen tent, ran to the nearest house with no clothing on whatever save his night-shirt! That those within the house thought a ghost had suddenly appeared to haunt them, and for a while refused admittance to what they thought an unearthly visitor, is not to be wondered at.

CHAPTER XIII.

"*THE GARDEN OF EDEN.*"

EARLY next morning we leave Kafr Howaran and after a ride of some hours over barren hills we come within sight of the far-famed valley of Damascus, at the north-east end of which lies the city itself, but so completely embosomed in trees that no view of the city can be had from this direction until almost within its gates.

This plain is very large and flat, and at one time, probably, was in a very high state of cultivation, though, at present, it is far from being so. We notice a few fields of barley, very thin and poor; a few fields of grape vines, some very large; and quite near the city, some potatoes and vegetables, but beyond this all is desolation. The indolence which prevails in lower Syria seems not less so here, and hence the almost utter desolation of this once beautiful plain. Divided up in small farms, and in the hands of Yankee farmers, it could indeed be made a "Garden of Eden," as some believe it to have been originally. Through this valley flow the waters of Abana and Pharpar, the far-famed rivers of Damascus. The Abana is led off in dykes to different parts of the valley to irrigate the land, and in skillful hands might be made still more useful in this particular.

For a Christian to get within the walls of Damascus has not always been an easy matter, though, at present, such treatment as earlier travelers speak of need not be feared. It is amusing as well as instructive to read the accounts which some tourists give of their first introduction to this city. Thus Dr. Robinson says :

" I was well aware that Damascus was one of the few places remaining in the Turkish dominions where religious fanaticism drew a strong line of distinction between its Mussulman and Christian population. Many are the humiliations to which the latter are exposed. Here, for instance—and it was the same until lately at Cairo and Jerusalem—they are not allowed to enter the town on horseback. It was my intention to comply with the interdiction at the proper place; but, being tired, I deferred the execution of it until I should reach the gates. My guide and servant, who were Christians, unfortunately betrayed me by alighting. Whilst riding carelessly along some hundred yards ahead of them, absorbed in my reflections, two or three ruffian-looking Turks ran suddenly up to me, and, seizing hold of the bridle of my horse, asked me, in an impetuous tone, if I were not a *Djour*, or 'Infidel.' To avow my faith required no deliberation; but I could not help retorting, '*Ana Nazeron, Djour deyil*'—'I am a Christian, not an Infidel.' No sooner had the words escaped my lips than I was torn violently from my horse, and loaded with a volley of imprecations. In a few minutes some hundreds of the inhabitants had collected round me, and I was apprehensive of becoming the victim of a popular tumult, particularly as my guides, who were better able to explain matters than myself, had become too much alarmed for themselves to interfere in my behalf. I therefore retired to the side of the road, and, sitting down on the bank, I endeavored to disarm the infuriated mob by the attitude of resignation; for as long as their hostility—which arose from religious not personal motives—was confined to words, I knew what value to set upon it. But my pacific appearance had a contrary effect. Seeking a pretext for their conduct, some spots of green, the privileged color, were discovered in my flowered turban, and it was instantly torn off my head. A young urchin—the devil take him—encouraged by this indignity offered me, walked up and spat upon my beard! This last affront for a moment robbed me of my equanimity, but I immediately recollected, and in time, that the slightest attempt at retaliation would be followed by instant death. Every man had a pistol or dirk in his girdle, and it would have cost him little to draw it out, and act upon the impulse of the moment. After appealing in vain to some sheikhs, or elders, who were standing by, I got up and made the best of my way to the gates of the city, followed by a host of boys and women, throwing stones at us as we passed along.

"During the whole of this disgraceful scene, which lasted about half an hour, the women, *horesco referens*, were even more violent than the men. At one time I thought I should have died the death of St. Stephen at the gates of Damascus. Here the conflict subsided; nevertheless, I had the mortification of being myself obliged to pass along the streets, and through the crowded bazaars, on foot, my dress and person covered with mud and other impurities, whilst the muleteers rode our horses before us, Mustapha wearing my turban on his head. This last part of the 'comedie larmoyante' he acted with such consummate insolence that I joined heartily in the laugh directed against myself, to the no small astonishment of those who were looking on."

The experience of the gallant and lamented Major

Skinner possesses still more of the ludicrous, without the danger to life and limb to which Dr. Robinson was subjected. He says: "It is only six months since a European has been able with safety to appear in his own costume, and very few have yet been here to display it. I am, to many, therefore, a most singular exhibition. I appear so mean a figure in comparison with the flowing robes about me that I am miserably out of conceit with my wardrobe, and have no occasion to be flattered with the notice I have attracted. The Turkish women mutter 'God is merciful!' as I pass them, and seem to call for protection from my ill-omened aspect; the Christian women laugh aloud and chatter, with their sweet voices, comments far from favorable to my appearance. As I walked in front of a group of these merry dames, I drew my handkerchief from my coat pocket, and, naturally enough, applied it to wipe the dust from my eyes. I was assailed by such a shout of laughter that I thought I had committed some frightful indiscretion. I stood in great perplexity with my handkerchief in my hand, evidently an object of intense interest, for many women came shuffling from a distance to see the show. This was at length ended by my returning the cause of all the amusement to its place; when, forgetting their propriety, they clapped their hands, and laughed with double enjoyment.

"It is not a difficult matter to become the wonder of a city, and, as yet, unconscious of the way in which I had merited to be one, I followed the crowd, as the evening approached, toward the convent. When we had entered the gate, a little boy, struck by the singular shape of a round hat which I wore, clapped his hands and cried out, 'Abu-tanjier! Abu-tanjier!' 'The father of a cooking-pot! Look at the father of a cooking-pot!' This was echoed from every side; for the resemblance a hat bears to a common cooking vessel, with a rim to it, is too strong to escape, and I was pursued by the shouts of the people till I was nearly out of sight.

"A woman who had heard the uproar came to her door, and, as I had outwalked the crowd, she could not resist the chance of gratifying her curiosity, and begged me to show her my hat. I took it off with great gravity, and put it into her hands; I believe she was disappointed to find that it was not a cooking-pot in reality. I rescued it from her in time to save it, or it might have been lodged in one of the colleges as a perpetual puzzle to the learned of the city."

On the following Sunday our traveler strolled up and down the pavement in front of the convent church as the congregation was coming out; he was soon surrounded by a group of women, among whom were some of the merry ones whose laughter had been so excited by the management of his pocket handkerchief. They requested him, by very intelligible signs, to play the scene over again; and, on his complying, so many fair hands were thrust into his coat pockets that he struggled with difficulty to escape, lest his clothes should be torn to pieces, and distributed throughout the city as relics of some extraordinary monster.

After all, he had no great reason to complain of his fate; for, as we have already seen, he might have met with worse usage than merely being laughed at. The Damascene Moslems have long had the reputation of being pre-eminent for fanaticism and intolerance. The Turks themselves say of them that they are the most mischievous race in the whole empire (but that probably means no more than that they are the most sturdy in resisting Turkish tyranny), and the Arabs, who delight in jingling proverbs, say *Shami, shoumi*—Damascene rascal, just as they say, *Halabi tchelebi*, Aleppine *petit-maître*. Though we may question the truth of this wise saw, there is no doubt that the sequestered position of the city, and the pride inspired by its superior sanctity, have not contributed to render the inhabitants very tolerant toward outlandish giaours. They bear with European monks, because they are used to their dress, and look upon them as Orientals; but, previously to the Egyptian invasion, no Christian dared to show himself within the gates in the Frank habit, nor was he allowed to mount a horse, as we have illustrated in the case of Dr. Robinson, but was compelled to content himself with the humble jackass, and even to think himself fortunate if he was not compelled, by insults, to dismount and lead his donkey by the bridle when passing through the bazaars, whilst every Mussulman thought himself privileged to kick the infidel out of his way. When Ibrahim Pasha first entered Damascus, he was earnestly entreated not to suffer the Christian dogs to ride on horses, whence they might look down on the true believers and "blacken their faces." "Oh," said the conqueror, "there is an easy remedy for that. If the Christians ride on horses, do you ride on dromedaries, and then, you know, you will be above them."

It is not surprising that a Frank, dressed in his own habit, previously so rare an object in Damascus, should create a great sensation, for a being more totally different in all outward appearances from the natives could hardly fall among them. In manner, in figure, in the mode of walking and of sitting down, who can be more opposite than an American and Oriental?

We do not ourselves go within the city walls on first reaching Damascus. Not that there is any hindrance to our doing so, for the Damascenes are very civil to strangers just now; but having learned while at the Sea of Galilee, from the Turkish commandant stationed there, that the most pleasant spot for encampment was on the banks of the river Abana, about a half mile from one of the city gates, we hunt up the place and have our tents pitched as he had recommended. Our tent door is not more than ten feet from the beautiful flowing river, the waters of which Naaman the Syrian thought "better than all the waters of Israel," and which the present inhabitants hold in scarcely less estimation.

The Abana and Pharpar rivers are branches of the Barrada—"the Golden River" of the Greeks—which, after leaving the mountains, divides into seven branches. Some of them flow directly to the city, and supply the public baths and the countless fountains with which it is refreshed and adorned; the others, after being sub-divided into numerous smaller channels for the irrigation of the surrounding gardens, unite on the south-east of the city and continue in a single stream toward the eastern mountains, where they are lost in a marsh called Birket-el-Merdj.

The zone of verdure that encompasses the city consists entirely of gardens profusely watered; the trees planted in them are so numerous and acquire such an extraordinary size and vigor that they more than supply every demand of the inhabitants for fruit, timber and fire-wood; and yet, so bounteous is the climate, they do not at all impair the produce of the beds beneath them. The manner of irrigation and the peculiar features of the landscape strikingly accord with the description of the orchard belonging to the enchanted castle in the story of the third Calendar in the Thousand-and-One Nights:

"This delicious orchard was watered in a very peculiar manner. There were channels so artificially and proportionably cut that they carried water in considerable quantities to the roots of such trees as required moisture; others conveyed it in smaller quantities to those whose fruits were already formed; some carried still less to those whose fruits were swelling; and others carried only so much as was just requisite to water those which had their fruits come to perfection, and only wanted to be ripened. They far exceeded the ordinary size of the fruits in our gardens. Lastly, those channels that watered the trees whose fruit was ripe had no more moisture than what would just preserve them from withering."

The afternoon and evening of the day on which we reach Damascus we spend in looking after the erection of our tents and in watching the gay promenaders, on foot and on horseback, who come out for exercise and for pleasure on the great macadamized French road which runs along the bank of the river, on the outer side of our canvas home, our tents being pitched on a beautiful green sward between the river and the road.

If there is anything at present in or about Damascus entitling it to the name of the "Garden of Eden," it is the pleasant promenades and gardens outside of its walls rather than within them. Very tolerable horses, with gay saddles and crimson housings, are to be procured by tourists for hire, and the rides in the lovely evenings about the different parts of the environs present beautiful points of view and most interesting snatches of Oriental life. As the sun is declining in the west we see little caravans of dromedaries, or a few mules, slowly emerging from the gloomy gateways of the town to gain a few hours' march to some neighboring village, in order to commence their journey in earnest at an early hour on the morrow. From our horse we see over the mud-walls that impede the view of the foot-passenger, into the gardens, where donkeys with panniers are receiving their loads of enormous radishes, gourds, water-melons, grapes, pomegranates, and other produce. By the side of the donkeys stands a grim figure, with one eye, and with a long white stick in his hand, pointed with iron, at the first movement of which the donkeys start off headlong with their load of vegetables, clearing away right and left, and upsetting all who are heedless enough to await their onset.

Here and there, while riding in the outskirts of the city, we meet a string of dromedaries, some weary mookres, and a party of wayworn travelers, exhausted by the heat of the sun and parched with thirst; a woman, perhaps, with a young child screaming for thirst, is nodding in a tackterawan, fastened on the hump of a dromedary. They have made a long journey, as we guess by their jaded looks and by the rapturous eagerness with which they pull up at the first flowing stream they meet. There goes the aga or sheikh of some neighboring village, who has been to town to pay his contribution into the coffers of the governor or to order himself a new scarlet robe. He makes a very gay figure on his Arab charger, accompanied by attendants with long white sticks, who run on either side of his horse's head. If you wander far enough, you may fall in with some great encampment, the Bagdad caravan, for instance, three of which go annually from Damascus, and take from thirty to forty days on the journey each way. The line of camels, several thousand in number, extends to the verge of the horizon; tents are pitched, the merchandise unladen, and guards set to watch it. Innumerable fires glitter in every direction, and round them are groups of wild figures eating their frugal meal or stretched on the ground to sleep.

On Friday, the Mohammedan sabbath, after midday prayers, and, indeed, on the afternoon of almost every pleasant day, the Mussulman population throng the gardens that constitute their paradise. "Nor, indeed," says a quaint old writer, "doth a Turk at any time show himself to be so truly pleased and satisfied in his senses as he doth in the summer-time, when he is in a pleasant garden. For he is no sooner come into it (if it be his own or where he thinks he may be bold) than he puts off his upper coat and lays it aside, and on that his *turbant;* then turns up his sleeves and unbuttoneth himself, turning his breast to the wind, if there be any, if not, he fans himself, or his servant doth it for him. Again, sometimes standing upon a high bank to take the fresh air, holding his arms abroad (as a cormorant, sitting on a rock, doth his wings in sunshine after a storm), courting the weather and sweet air, calling it his soul, his life and his delight, ever and anon showing some visible signs of contentment. Nor shall the garden, during his pleasant distraction, be termed otherwise than *Paradise*, with whose flowers he stuffs his bosom and decketh his turbant, shaking his head at their sweet savor. Sometimes he singeth a song to some pretty flower, by whose name his mistress is called, and uttering words of great joy, as if at that instant she herself were there present. And one bit of meat in a garden shall do him more good than the best fare that may be elsewhere."

Damascus is, perhaps, the most ancient city in the world, and the only one that has enjoyed a continued, though not undisturbed, course of prosperity through so vast a succession of ages. It existed in the days of Abraham, and was founded, it is said, by Uz, the grandson of Noah. Founded before all those that afterward rivaled or eclipsed it, it has seen them perish one by one, and sometimes so utterly as to leave no memorial to mark the place on which they stood. And yet Damascus has had its full share of the buffetings of war and civil violence.

It became the capital of the kingdom of Syria, founded by Rehsin, was taken and sacked by Jeroboam, king of Israel, but soon recovered from the blow, for it was once more the metropolis of Syria long before the Seleucidæ had transferred the seat of their empire to Antioch. Under the Saracens, in the brilliant period of Arabian history, Damascus became, like Bagdad, the residence of the caliphs. After this, sieges and disasters were no rare occurrence in its annals. Repeatedly was it swept with fire and sword, but never did it sustain so fearful a calamity as toward the close of the fourteenth century, when it was beleaguered by the ferocious conqueror Timur Lenk (Timur the Lame, or Tamerlane). For several days the black flag floated in vain on the Tartar's tent; and never had that signal of desolation been hoisted for three days on the same spot without the fulfillment of its fatal presage. At length the city was taken by storm, and the streets were deluged with blood. They still show, near the gate called *Babel Kabi*, the spot on which stood a pyramid of heads, the horrible monument of the victor's ferocity. Timur Lenk carried off with him the ablest artisans after butchering the rest, desiring to enrich his capital, Samarcand, with all the arts of which he robbed Damascus.

Its present population is estimated at from one hundred and fifty to two hundred thousand souls, and though mostly Moslems, still within its walls and upon its streets may be found people representing almost every nation of the earth. Its streets are mostly narrow and badly paved, when paved at all; and its houses are generally of the Oriental style—plastered walls without, and a profusion of gewgaw and filagree work within. The houses of some of the wealthier class are finished with fine marbles within, both for walls and floors, while the richest of damask curtains hang at the windows and about the walls.

The entrance to some even of the finest houses is by a low, mean-looking door in a great blank wall, little according with the luxury and splendor within, and seeming more likely to lead to a cow-shed than to a luxurious mansion. This unpromising entrance admits you, through an outer court occupied by the porter and some other domestics, into a spacious quadrangle, paved with marble, in the middle of which a fountain throws up a continual shower, cooling the atmosphere and refreshing the evergreens and flowering shrubs which are placed around it. In one corner stands a tall, slender pole like a signal-staff, for the purpose of hoisting up an earthen jar full of water, which is cooled by the evaporation that takes place through the porous sides of the vessel. An arcade, supported by low, slender columns, runs round the quadrangle, giving admission to the lower apartments; these are elaborately painted and gilded, and the cornices are ornamented with Arabic inscriptions. Rich carpets and deewans, with cushions of damask or velvet, embroidered with gold, cover the floors; and china plates, jars, basins, and bowls are advantageously disposed in niches in the walls or on shelves. In one of these apartments the stranger is generally received on his first introduction, but the places of common reception are the arcades, one of which is furnished with a deewan, which is shifted as the sun comes round. Here, as the Turk reclines upon softest cushions, the mild air that fans his cheek, the delightful mellowing of the light by the evergreens, the fragrance of the blossoms, and the plashing of the fountain, all weave around him a charm of the most voluptuous repose. Even here the same mysterious solitude prevails as in the streets; the sound of your own footsteps, echoing over the marble pavement, seems to you a rude intrusion on the genius of the place; and you could almost fancy yourself in one of the enchanted palaces of the Arab romances.

The fond attachment to the declining cause and to the ancient usages of Islamism which, in the common people of Damascus, declares itself in acts of insolence and intolerance, appears among the wealthier and more polished classes chiefly in a certain antique sumptuousness, a more gorgeous profusion of "barbaric pearl and gold." The palaces of the agas, the aristocracy of the city, surpass, in the splendor of their internal decorations, anything of the kind to be seen elsewhere in the empire, and seem to realize to our imagination the magnificence of the days of the caliphs, the Saladins, and the Solymans. Many of their apartments are fitted up at a cost of as much as a hundred thousand piastres, and in some palaces there are as many as eight or ten of these lordly halls. One gorgeous apartment in the house of Ali Aga Kazini-el-Katabi cost the proprietor upward of two hundred thousand piastres, equaling about ten thousand dollars.

The ceiling was formed of a species of gold-carved tracery on a glass ground, producing a most splendid effect. The walls, a short distance below the ceiling, were gayly painted in the form of buildings, fantastic porticoes, and columns, through which, in the distance, were glimpses of the sea and blue mountains, and here and there foregrounds of the weeping willow and the cypress, painted by artists from Stamboul. Below these were recesses with folding doors, richly inlaid with different colored woods, and ornamented with light tracery and figure-work. Around them were scroll patterns of clusters of arms and weapons, and portions of the walls on each side were richly inlaid with tortoiseshell and mother-of-pearl.

The house of Mallim Yusseff, the Jew treasurer and secret director of most of the affairs of the pashalic at the time of Mr. Buckingham's visit to the city, had been built by that minister's father, during the latter half of whose life, or about twenty-five years, there had been employed in its construction and embellishment at least fifty workmen of different descriptions, every day excepting holidays. The exterior of this mansion was even more than usually remarkable for poverty and meanness.

The agas are in general the sons or descendants of pashas, who have employed in the decoration of their dwellings the treasures amassed by their fathers. They are a numerous class, exhibiting under another form a counterpart to the nepotism of Rome; they fill the chief civil and military posts in the city under the pashas deputed by the sultan, and have vast territorial possessions in the villages surrounding Damascus. Their pomp consists in palaces, gardens, horses, and women; at a sign from the pasha their heads fall, and their wealth, their palaces, their gardens, their horses, and their women, are transferred to some new favorite of fortune. Such a system naturally invites to enjoyment of the present moment and to resignation; voluptuousness and fatalism are the necessary results of Oriental despotism. In the year 1839 the wealthy Ali Aga, mentioned above, being detected in carrying on a clandestine correspondence with the Turkish seraskier, Hafiz Ali Pasha, the general acting against the forces of Mohammed Ali, an order followed for his execution. His headless body remained a whole day exposed in the bazaar. His death was much regretted, for he was a man of high birth, and respected by all classes.

Almost every one has heard of the English lady, who, from being at one time the wife of an English lord, has finally become the wife of a Bedouin sheikh, and now lives in Damascus, on the income which she receives from the estates of her first husband. The story is a long one —too long for a chapter—though strikingly illustrating the old saying that "truth is sometimes stranger than fiction," and conveying a moral which it would be well for all young ladies to heed. Suffice it to say, that she married for position, not for love—that her husband procured a divorce because of her dissolute habits—that she subsequently contracted several marriages of convenience, which only lasted so long as whim or fancy dictated—that from Italy she came to Damascus, where, for some fancied service of this Bedouin sheikh, she married him, and since then has lived part of the time in her beautiful villa, just without the walls of the city, and part of the time in tents on the desert sands with her last husband.

Having read the strange and eventful history of this woman, we resolve, if possible, to see her, or at least to see the place in which she lives. Knocking at the gate, we are informed by a servant that her ladyship is not at home, but may be found at a coffee-shop on the banks of the Abana; and this reminds us to say that these coffee-shops, in the midst of beautiful gardens, are very numerous in and about Damascus, and are frequented by persons of every class, who here while away their idle hours in eating, drinking, and listening to music. We then ask to be shown the house and grounds of her ladyship, which request is granted, as the servant is given to understand that there is bucksheesh at the end of it. He leads us all through the garden and grounds, which are indeed beautiful, having roses and other flowers blooming everywhere, with a handsome marble fountain and rustic arbor near the centre. He also admits us to two of the best rooms of the house, both of which are finished and furnished in real Oriental style. The pictures on the walls, and some of the books and souvenirs lying about, betray an English origin, and are doubtless mementoes of her early days. Several of the smaller pictures are said to have been painted by herself, and show much taste and skill. She is now, we are told, over fifty years of age, and we could not but think how very sad must be the retrospective view of her life. From the spoiled pet of the Court of St. James, with which her father held high and honorable relations, she is now the wife of a despised Bedouin, and the town-talk of all who know her past history.

An allusion above to a coffee-shop—in which, we were told, the English lady might be found—may make some of our readers desire to know something more concerning them, as they are one of the " institutions" of Damascus, and not among the least, if we accept the estimate placed upon them by the natives.

This city has long been celebrated for the number and elegance of its coffee-houses; they are for the most part built in the kiosk fashion, of wood painted different colors, green and blue predominating, and open on the sides, except where partially closed with plants coiling up the slender columns that support the roof. The softened light that makes its way through the leafy walls forms a charming contrast with the intense glare of the sun glancing upon the waters or reflected from the whitened walls of the houses of the town. Nor are they more remarkable for their picturesque appearance than for their happily-chosen position, being generally situated on the border of some running stream, the view opening out on a pretty cascade, with gardens and orchards lying on the opposite bank. At night, when the lamps, suspended from the slender pillars, are lighted, and Turks of different ranks, in all the varieties of their rich costume, cover the platform just above the surface of the river, on which, and its foaming cataracts, the moonlight rests, and the sound of music is heard, you fancy that if ever the enchantments of Eastern romance are to be realized, it is here.

The pleasures enjoyed in these places are usually of the silent kind; but sometimes they are enlivened by the performances of professional dancers, story-tellers or singers.

The recitation of Eastern fables and tales partakes somewhat of the nature of a dramatic performance. It is not merely a simple narrative; the story is animated by the manner and action of the speaker. A variety of other story-books, beside the Arabian Nights, furnish materials for the story-teller, who, by combining the incidents of different tastes and varying the catastrophe of such as he has related before, gives them an air of novelty even to persons who at first imagine they are listening to tales with which they are acquainted. He recites, walking to and fro, in the middle of the coffee-room, stopping only now and then when the expression requires some emphatic attitude. He is commonly heard with great attention, and not unfrequently, in the midst of some interesting adventure, when the expectation of his audience is raised to the highest pitch, he breaks off abruptly and makes his escape from the room, leaving both his heroine and his audience in the utmost embarrassment. Those who happen to be near the door endeavor to detain him, insisting on the story being finished before he departs; but he always makes his retreat good, and the auditors, suspending their curiosity, are induced to return at the same hour next day to hear the sequel. He no sooner has made his exit than the company in separate parties fall to disputing about the characters of the drama or the event of the unfinished adventure. The controversy by degrees becomes serious, and opposite opinions are maintained with no less warmth than if the fate of the city depended on the decision.

When the charm of novelty is worn off, tourists, especially Americans, are apt to complain of the monotony and want of amusement in these places, where they find no public papers, no political or other gossip, nothing to keep alive that brisk current of national or local interest which enlivens our places of social resort. But the men of the East know nothing of that restless activity that animates the American, and makes exertion of body or mind a craving of his nature which must be satisfied even in his moments of recreation. The habits of their lives present but two phases—excited energy and profound repose. To act is, according to their way of thinking, to suffer, and they cannot understand the possibility of people willfully putting themselves to trouble when there is absolutely no necessity for their doing so. The Mussulman's bliss is expressed in the word *kieff*—a word incapable of being translated, because the peculiar kind of abstraction it signifies is unknown in the Western world. It is not the *farniente* of the Italian, for that amounts to no more than a simple negation of action; but *kieff* implies beside this, a brooding over passive animal enjoyment—a state of feeling like what we may guess the ox to experience when he lies down to ruminate in pleasant pastures, or that sweet consciousness of *un*waking bliss we sometimes feel at morning in bed, when we are just able to entertain one thought —" Now I am asleep."

Here, then, in these coffee-houses the Moslems sit the live-long hours, seemingly as phlegmatic as Dutchmen, smoking, sipping coffee, and conversing after their way; that is, with an interval of a quarter of an hour between every two phrases. Do not, however, conclude too hastily that the thoughts and passions of busy life never molest the somnolent genius of the place. Perhaps at the very moment you are wondering at the listless apathy of the smokers, you are unconsciously assisting at the noiseless birth of one of those revolutions that so often deluge Damascus with blood. The leaven works silently and unseen for a long while, till at length its effects break out when least expected. The people side with one party or another, and fly to arms under the conduct of one of the agas, and the government passes for a time into the hands of the victor. The vanquished are put to death, or escape to the deserts of Baalbec or Palmyra, where the independent tribes afford them an asylum.

CHAPTER XIV.

SIGHTS OF DAMASCUS.

OUR first introduction to the "sights" of Damascus is that of a man hanging by the neck, at the corner of a street where two of the principal bazaars cross each other. What we saw seemed to be a stuffed figure of a man hanging as a sign to some shop; but upon a closer examination it proves to be a real man, who had been hung up at that corner an hour or two before, for having committed the crime of murder. The beam from which the body is suspended juts out from the corner of the building about three feet, and is probably twelve feet from the pavement. The rope about the neck is probably three feet in length, the body about six, and consequently there is only about three feet space between the feet of the hanging man and the pavement. He was hung, we are told, by soldiers in obedience to orders, but no soldiers are about the body now, and hundreds of persons are passing and repassing every hour of the day, scarcely one of whom even stops to glance at the body, so common are sights of like character in this city. The body is kept hanging until sundown, at this one of the most public places of the city, that everybody may see and take warning, and is then taken down and buried by the soldiers detailed for the execution.

Moslems believe that punishment for crime should always be of the most public character, that others, seeing it, may take warning in time to avoid a like fate; while we, in America, have adopted a contrary opinion and practice. Much, of course, can be said in support of each theory, but which is really the best is not so easy to determine. That not only the knowledge, but the actual observance of punishment, as the penalty of crime, may deter some from committing criminal acts, is undoubtedly true; and it is no less true that familiarity with punishment, however horrible, has upon some the effect of blunting and hardening the sensibilities. Much, we think, depends upon the education and civilization of the people for whom the laws are made. From what we have seen of the Arabic character, both in Egypt and Syria, we are well satisfied that the dread of instantaneous and severe punishment as the penalty for crime, and the sight of its infliction, are the best possible preventatives to crime for this people; but we are not at all certain that a like rule would hold good in the United States. On the contrary, our general inclination has been, and still is, in favor of private executions.

Though our first experience of sight-seeing in Damascus is so unpleasant, we still persevere, determining to see all that is to be seen in this far-famed city. The other objects of interest to tourists consist of the mosques, the castle, the convents, the bazaars, the house of Ananias, the place where Paul was let down from the wall in a basket, and the reputed place of his conversion.

Our guide conducts us to each of these, and, in the course of the trip, points out many other objects which he seems to regard as of special interest.

The mosque of St. John, which occupies the site of a

Corinthian temple, and still contains some of the old columns, is the only one worthy of a visit.

This great mosque (St. John) was once a cathedral, and is said to be the largest and most splendid of all the churches erected by the early Christians in this country. The mosque of the Durweeshes has the finest minarets in Damascus, and another is remarkable for having its minarets, which are of great height and grandeur, cased with enameled tiles of a rich green color; the reflection of the sunshine from this iridescent surface produces a splendid effect. Many of the mosques were built by the caliphs as mausoleums; they have courts, porticoes, and fountains, and some are overshadowed by a few green trees, among which sacred doves may be heard cooing.

The walls of the Old Castle are grand and imposing, and from the towers at the corners we have an extended view of the city. The castle is eight hundred feet long by six hundred in width; the walls are thick and laid up with square blocks of stone, and put to shame the flimsy, miserable structures which surround it. It is now occupied as barracks by Turkish soldiers.

Near the castle is a government mill, for the grinding of wheat and corn for the garrison. Its propelling power is a large iron wheel, turned by the waters of the Abana. This mill the officer takes us all through, and shows it to us with evident delight, believing, no doubt, that it is by far the greatest mill in the world. Of course we say *tieb*, *tieb* (good, good) to everything, though in reality it will not compare with the commonest country mill of America.

Of the convents we visit, the Greek, now in the course of renovation and addition, is the only one worthy of note. This, when completed, will be a fine structure for Damascus, though miserably poor as compared with many convents in Europe. The monks have many sad tales to tell of the extortion and ill-treatment of their Moslem rulers. The following is one of the many:

The best paved street in Damascus is that on which stands the front of the Franciscan convent. It was in such bad order some years ago that the monks resolved to repair it whenever their finances would allow them to do so. They at length commenced the work, to the great joy of the Christian population, who would have a capital place to lounge in during the various offices of their festivals. The governor took no notice of the work during its progress, but when it was finished he sent to demand on what authority they had dared to improve a street in Damascus, and ordered them instantly to pay thirty thousand piastres to secure the privilege of walking upon it. The poor monks were in despair, and declared they could never hope to afford so exorbitant a sum. The pasha seized the superior and put him in prison, with the determination to keep him there until he should be ransomed by his brethren. This was at length effected, and fifty yards of pavement were gained to the church.

We had heard and read much of the bazaars of Damascus, and expected to find them far superior to any others we had seen, but in this we are greatly disappointed. They are not to be compared with the bazaars of Cairo, either in extent or in the quality of goods offered. There is not in all of Damascus a single yard of pure silk goods manufactured, notwithstanding the assertions to the contrary. They make fabrics of half silk and half linen, and of such brilliant colors and glossy appearance as easily to deceive the eye of the inexperienced; but their largest silk dealers inform us (after they find deception unavailable) that no fabrics of *all* silk are manufactured in this city or country. Such as they have are imported from France, and these are not of the best quality.

Among the lost arts of Damascus appears to be the manufacture of the splendid silk damask interwoven with gold, which is seen in some of the richest houses, but is not easily to be found in the bazaars. The present manufactures are of red leather shoes and slippers, a variety of silver work, a very durable mixed stuff of silk and cotton, in general wear throughout Syria, some of the patterns of which are remarkably handsome, and some very neat cabinet work, chiefly in the form of boxes and coffers. This latter is a particularly important branch of trade, since the principal furniture of an Arab family consists in one or two chests, in which they keep their clothes and other movables. Most of these boxes are of cedar, painted red, and studded with gilt nails in various devices. Some are inlaid with ivory and mother-of-pearl, or finely carved in relief. The smell of cedar wood pervades the whole bazaar, and mingling with the thousand different perfumes exhaled by the shops of the grocers and the druggists, and with the incessant smoking of countless pipes, fill these places with a peculiar atmosphere of their own.

The manufacture of the celebrated Damascus swords no longer exists. The weapons offered for sale by the armorers are of a very ordinary character. Some specimens of the old manufacture are still met with; they pass as heirlooms, from hand to hand, and are esteemed exceedingly precious. The blade of one presented to Lamartine cost the pasha who had owned it five thousand piastres. Many Turks and Arabs, he tells us, who prize these weapons above diamonds, would give all they had in the world for such a blade; their eyes sparkled with admiration at the sight of it, and they pressed it reverently to their foreheads, as if they adored so perfect an implement of death.

A scimetar, to be perfect, ought to be broad in the blade, and its length, from hilt to point, should be exactly equal to the distance from the tip of the ear to the fist, as you stand upright, with your arm by your side. If the steel gives a clear crystalline sound when you twitch the point with your nail, you may be satisfied of the good temper of the weapon. Such is the keenness of edge of which the best blades are susceptible that it is a common amusement with the Turks to cut through down pillows or silk handkerchiefs as they are thrown at them. Weapons are as frequent a subject of conversation among the men as jewels and fashions are among the women of the Levant. The Turks have a peculiar knack of bringing the discourse to bear upon a topic so gratifying to their vanity. You will often see them unsheath their scimetars in the middle of a repast, and hand them across the table to each other. Their mode of presenting the weapon to the scrutiny of an amateur is exceedingly graceful. Twirling the hilt round in their hands, so as to bring the blade under their arm, they present the hilt to him with a bow and gesture of the hand, signifying the entire sacrifice of their person.

The saddlers are the most numerous and the most ingenious workmen in Damascus. They occupy a long, handsome bazaar at the northern end of the city. The floor or street of the bazaar is covered with skins, on which men, horses and dromedaries walk, and which, after being thus thoroughly trampled upon, are turned into leather by steeping them in an astringent liquid made from the husk of the pomegranate. The scarlet and blue housings, embroidered in gold and silver; the gay bridles, martingales, breast and head-pieces, decorated with beads, bits

Sights of Damascus. 279

of silver, silk, shells, or tassels; the saddles, some of red leather, and some covered with purple and blue velvet, brocaded with silver and gold thread, either finished and exposed for sale, or in the act of being made, give this bazaar a very gay appearance. Nothing can surpass the beauty and splendor of the trappings made to be worn on state occasions by the horses of the Arab chiefs or of the agas. The prices of all these rich articles are greatly below the European standard.

A variety of other manufactures of minor importance are met with; but British goods have now taken the place of many of the inferior native fabrics, and many articles which used to be brought from India by the Persian Gulf, and reached Damascus by the caravans from Bagdad, are now imported direct from London and Liverpool to Beyrout. The principal articles of import are cotton goods, cotton twist, iron, hardware, West India produce, indigo, and cochineal. The bazaar of the mercers displays an extensive assortment of Manchester and Glasgow calicoes, muslins and printed goods, and a few articles of Swiss manufacture.

Among the shopkeepers we must not forget the barbers, those dear old friends with whom the Arabian Nights have put us on so cordial a footing of intimacy. With that easy suavity for which their fraternity is renowned all the world over, they invite the passers-by to enter and submit their heads and faces to their beautifying fingers. Their shops are always full of customers. They are long, narrow rooms, with benches on each side, on which a dozen Turks may sometimes be seen squatting in a line, with their heads, already shaved, poked out in the most patient manner, to be kneaded between the hands of the barber, who rolls them about as if they were balls quite unconnected with the shoulders they belong to. The barbers of

Damascus are celebrated for taste and skill in all the mysteries of the toilette, including the art of imparting to the beard and mustachios that dark glossy hue so anxiously and universally coveted. The important affair of arranging the turban is their daily business, and the becoming variety displayed in the disposition of the turbans worn by the gallants of the city does infinite honor to these meritorious artists. It is pleasant to know that such men continue to enjoy a due share of consideration in the East, and that their talents often raise them to affluence. When Mr. Carne's party wished to hire a separate residence in Damascus, they were recommended to a barber who had become a sort of capitalist and was possessed of some houses. The old gentleman, extremely well dressed, with a goodly length of beard, was always found seated at his ease, smoking or chatting with some of his friends. He wished the Englishmen to take a luxurious apartment of his, situated on a terraced roof; it was profusely gilded, the cushions of the deewan were as white as snow, and it commanded a superb view of the mountains. But the barber's wife was by far the more zealous part of himself, and protested with loud clamor that infidels should never sully the purity and beauty of her deewan; and after a warm dispute the good man was forced reluctantly to give way. He related that when Bonaparte and his army were in Syria, he and many others in Damascus took up arms and marched a great distance to fight with the Giaours for the honor of the prophet. "They were full of zeal; and our forces," said the old man, "soon had an action. We were beat, and I received a severe wound; and when they carried me with them in the retreat, in an agony of pain I cried out, 'What had I to do with Giaours? Go to hell, all the world!'"

The shops of all kinds being open, everything is done

in public. If a merchant is put in a passion by a customer, he jumps up among his bales and storms and raves to his heart's content without the least interruption. Each commodity has its own peculiar mart; if you chance to want boots or shoes, you will be directed, on inquiry, to a bazaar filled from end to end with piles of red and yellow boots, shoes, and slippers for both sexes. There are always very entertaining doings to be witnessed in the ready-made clothes shops, where cheapness is more regarded than fashion; and the poorer classes dress themselves in all the costumes of the East. They try the articles on either in the midst of the thoroughfare or on the board of the tailor, and loungers stop frequently to offer their opinions on the style and fit. There is a singular ostentation in the display of new clothes in the East, from some superstitious feeling, perhaps, for the ticket is never taken off the turban or the shawl round the waist until their novelty is completely worn away. The gayest Turks in Damascus strut with greater pride when the mark of the shop dangles from their heads.

In our wanderings about the city we observe nothing like a book-bazaar, or even book-stand, though we presume there must be some place where books of some sort can be had. We should like to procure a copy of the Kur-an in Arabic, to take home as a curiosity; but after the experience of another traveler, whose account we have read, we should be somewhat afraid to ask for it, even if we came across a book-store. This traveler asked first about other books, and then inquired for a copy of the Kur-an. "That instant," he says, "the eyes of the old Turk flashed fire; his beard wagged with indignation; and he shouted at the pitch of his voice, *Yallah, yallah!* 'Go, go, get you gone!' with sundry uncourteous expressions and rude epithets, among which that of infidel dogs was more than once repeated. Finding all further negotiation broken off for the present, we made as decent a retreat from the spot as we were able. It is considered sinful by the Moslems to allow the sacred book to be profaned even by the touch of an infidel, and no strict follower of the prophet will sell a Kur-an to a Frank; but it may generally be obtained through some less scrupulous agent, who will buy it for you."

The bazaars, like the Palais Royal of Paris, have their restaurants, where the merchants or the loungers may find a dinner. Tables and covers are, of course, out of the question. The purchaser provides himself with a large flat pan-cake, which serves him at once for bread, plate, and napkin, and the cook supplies him with little pieces of baked mutton, about the size of nuts, stuck on a skewer, somewhat in the fashion of our cat's meat. Ices, iced-water, and sherbet are carried through the bazaars by men whose sole occupation it is to make and sell these articles; and several times, while riding along the streets, do we stop to buy from these men a sort of water-ice, made from the snows of Mount Hermon.

The Armenian gold and silversmiths carry on their trade in what was once a Christian church: it is parted off into alleys, where the workmen sit with fire, bellows, anvils, hammers, pincers, drawers, and so forth; and the ear is stunned with the incessant clattering on all sides. Old men with sallow faces and gray beards are seen poring over ingots of gold and silver, melting the metal in pots and pans on charcoal fires, or drawing it out into long wires and hammering it into different shapes.

On one of our shopping excursions we visit the bazaar of the gold and silver smiths, thinking that here, at least, we will find something worthy of the reputation of the place. Judge, then, of our surprise to find what seemed to us much more like a row of ordinary blacksmith shops than of jewelry manufacturers. The tools with which they work are coarse and clumsy, and we do not observe a single piece of machinery in any of the shops. Everything is done with anvil, hammer, tongs, and file, and the work which they turn out is fully in keeping with the implements used in its manufacture. Fine stones are so coarsely and clumsily set as to give them the appearance of the most common brass rings and pins, such as you would hesitate to give a sixpence apiece for if offered you by a jewelry vender in the streets of New York. Brilliancy of color and display are the only noticeable things among the manufactured articles of Damascus. The commonest dress is made to appear showy, and even their horses, and mules, and donkeys, are arrayed in trappings of velvet, fringe, and shells. The question of utility seems to be ignored, if only they can make the article attractive to the eye. Everywhere and in everything this fact is painfully observable.

The direction of the street called "the Straight" corresponds, contrary to Turkish custom, with its ancient name, and leads from one of the gates to the citadel, which has probably always retained its present position. The dwelling of a rigid Mussulman covers a spot in this street venerated as the site of the house of Judas, where Saul of Tarsus lodged. In a different quarter, a curious substructure, resembling the crypt of a primitive church, is reputed to be the house of Ananias, who restored the apostle's sight. A broken staircase descends through a great deal of rubbish to a spacious vaulted chamber, in the form of a Greek cross, which receives no other light than that from the entrance. A strange notion seems to prevail throughout the country, that, in earlier days, people burrowed in the earth; for all the houses exhibited as the abodes of celebrated or pious men are in grottoes or caves below the ground.

We examine these places with some care, and would like to believe that they are the exact spots where these important events of biblical history took place; but, in a city almost wholly Moslem, as this, and of which they boast that the cross never floated over it, it is hardly probable that any pains would be taken to retain the locality of events among the most prominent in Christian history. However, we glance at the places pointed out, and know that if not just here, certainly somewhere in this city the devout Ananias dwelt, when the Lord said unto him, "Arise and go into the street which is called Straight, and inquire in the house of Judas for one called Saul of Tarsus, for behold he prayeth."

The wall which formerly surrounded the city was built of large blocks of stone, and must have been of great strength, but much of the original wall has fallen down, and the blocks of stone have been carried away for other purposes. On the top of what remains of these stones the Turks have built a mud wall, which the smallest cannon ball would penetrate at any point; and no better commentary on the past and present of Damascus could be had than a view of this mud structure upon its stone foundation.

The eastern gate, now walled up, is memorable as the place where the apostle was let down by the wall in a basket. They pretend to show the very house from which he thus made his escape; and whatever faith we may put in this tradition, it is, at least, a curious fact that in a fortification of the present day, houses still stand on the walls with their windows toward the country, and immediately overhanging the ditch in a manner so likely to facilitate escape, and even to afford entrance to an enemy.

This, at any rate, proves how little Damascus has changed from its earliest days.

The Christians have here a large unenclosed cemetery, much visited by them; and near it is a tomb enclosed in a wooden cage, and said to be that of the warder, traditionally called St. George, who, having become a Christian, allowed the apostle to escape, and afterward suffered martyrdom for his zeal and humanity. There is an arch in the burial-ground, where, it is pretended, St. Paul hid himself after his descent from the wall.

In a wide, open road beyond the cemetery, about a quarter of a mile from the gate, is a place still highly venerated as the supposed scene of Saul's miraculous conversion. The present track deviates now from the straight line, leaving a few yards to the right, the precise spot believed to be that where he fell to the earth. This is evidently a portion of an ancient road, consisting entirely of firmly-embedded pebbles, which, having never been broken up, stands alone like the fragment of an elevated causeway. The sides have been gradually lowered by numerous pilgrims, who, in all ages, have sought the pebbles to be preserved as relics. A wide, arch-like excavation through the centre of the causeway, produced by the same superstitious industry, has given it the semblance of a dismantled bridge. Through this aperture it is considered an act of devotion to pass; and the pious may sometimes be seen performing the ceremony with all due solemnity, rubbing their shoulders against the pebbly sides, and repeating their prayers with exemplary earnestness.

Damascus is a true Oriental city, and the least sophisticated of all the Moslem capitals. Here everything is Eastern; there are no Frank quarters, no shabby beings wandering about in black hats and pea-green jackets, no fantastic aping of Frank customs and Frank follies by the command of an innovating sultan. The aspect of its streets certainly does not meet the expectation excited by its romantic appearance as viewed from a distance; they are narrow and irregular, and flanked with ugly dead walls; but broad streets are no luxury in a warm climate; and "here," says Dr. Richardson, "I felt the full force of the remark of Tacitus, that Nero spoiled Rome by broad streets." Those of Damascus are seldom of a width more than sufficient to allow two laden camels to pass each other without crushing the pedestrians, and many are of much narrower dimensions. They are the most noiseless possible; there are no wheeled carriages rolling along them, and the occasional step of a Christian's ass, a camel, a mule, or more rarely of a horse, does not much disturb the mysterious stillness in which the city appears wrapped, until you approach the bazaars and other places of busy resort.

The women of Damascus are esteemed the handsomest in the East; and, though the fame of their charms has no doubt been much enhanced by the difficulty of seeing them, they sometimes, from behind their tantalizing clouds, pour forth a light that might dazzle the most discreet beholder. There is a very graceful style of coquetry in the manner in which an Eastern belle displays her arms, which are the roundest and most perfect imaginable. The fingers, covered with rings and dyed pink under the nails, play about the folds of the drapery, as if anxious to restore it to its place, in which, somehow or another, they can never succeed, when there is a sly opportunity of disclosing the beauty it is meant to conceal. Large blue eyes are common among the Christian women, some of whom are exceedingly fair; and there is a grace in the turban beyond all the arts of a civilized toilette.

We cannot, we think, better close this chapter on sight-seeing in Damascus than by repeating the story which is told of two of its most celebrated governors, Assaad and Abdallah-el-Satadgi:

About the year 1755, one of the black eunuchs of the seraglio of the then reigning sultan of Constantinople, making his pilgrimage to Mecca, took up his quarters with Assaad, then governor of Damascus; but, dissatisfied with the simple hospitality with which he was entertained, he would not return by Damascus, but took the road to Gaza. Hussein Pasha, who was then governor of that town, took care to entertain him sumptuously. The eunuch, on his return to Constantinople, did not forget the treatment he had received from his two hosts, and, to show at once his gratitude and his resentment, he determined to ruin Assaad and raise Hussein to his dignity. His intrigues were so successful that in the year 1756 Jerusalem was detached from the government of Damascus and bestowed upon Hussein, under the title of a pashalic, and the following year he obtained that of Damascus. Assaad, thus deposed, retired with his household into the Desert to avoid still greater disgrace. The time of the caravan arrived; Hussein conducted it, agreeably with the duty of his station; but, having quarreled with the Arabs concerning some payment they demanded, they attacked him, defeated his escort, and entirely plundered the caravan, in 1757. On the news of this disaster the whole empire was thrown into as much confusion as could have been occasioned by the loss of the most important battle. The families of twenty thousand pilgrims who had perished with thirst and hunger or been slain by the Arabs; the relations of a multitude of women who had been carried into slavery; the merchants interested in the plundered caravan, all demanded vengeance on the cowardice of the Emir Hadj and the sacrilege of the Bedouins. The Porte, alarmed, at first proscribed the head of Hussein, but he concealed himself so well that it was impossible to surprise him; while he, from his retreat, acting in concert with the eunuch, his protector, undertook to exculpate himself. In this he succeeded, after three months, by producing a real or fictitious letter of Assaad, by which it appeared that the ex-pasha, to revenge himself on Hussein, had excited the Arabs to attack the caravan. The proscription was now turned against Assaad, and nothing remained to be sought but an opportunity to carry it into execution.

The pashalic, however, remained vacant. Hussein, disgraced as he was, could not resume his government. The Porte, desiring to revenge the late affront and provide for the safety of the pilgrims in future, made choice of a singular man, whose character and history deserve to be noticed. This man, named Abdallah-el-Satadgi, was born near Bagdad, in an obscure rank of life. Entering very young into the service of the pasha, he had passed his early years in camps and war, and had been present as a common soldier in all the campaigns of the Turks against the famous Shah-Thamas-Kouli-Kan, and the bravery and abilities he displayed raised him, step by step, even to the dignity of pasha of Bagdad. Advanced to this eminent post, he conducted himself with so much firmness and prudence that he restored peace to the country from both foreign and domestic wars. The simple life of the soldier, which he continued to lead, requiring no great supplies of money, he amassed none; but the great officers of the seraglio of Constantinople, who derived no profits for his moderation, did not approve of this disinterestedness, and waited only for a pretext to remove him.

This they soon found. Abdallah had kept back a sum equaling twenty thousand dollars, arising from the estate of a merchant. Scarcely had the pasha received it before it was demanded of him. In vain did he represent that he had used it to pay some old arrears due to his troops; in vain did he request time; the vizier only pressed him the more closely, and, on a second refusal, despatched a black eunuch, secretly provided with a khatsherif, to take off his head. The eunuch, arriving in Bagdad, feigned himself a sick person traveling for the benefit of his health; and, as such, sent his respects to the pasha, observing the usual forms of politeness, and requesting permission to pay him a visit. Abdallah, well acquainted with the practices of the divan, was distrustful of so much complaisance, and suspected some secret mischief. His treasurer, not less versed in such plots and greatly attached to his person, confirmed him in his suspicions, and proposed, in order to come at the truth, to go and search the eunuch's baggage while he and his retinue should be paying their visit to the pasha. Abdallah approved of the expedient, and at the hour appointed the treasurer repaired to the tent of the eunuch and made so careful a search that he found the khatsherif concealed within the lining of a pelisse. Immediately he flew to the pasha, and sending for him into an adjoining room, he told him what he had discovered. Abdallah, furnished with the fatal writing, hid it in his bosom and returned to the apartment, when, resuming, with an air of the greatest indifference, his conversation with the eunuch, "The more I think of it," said he, "O Khowaga, the more I am astonished at your journey into this country; Bagdad is so far from Stamboul, and we can boast so little of our air, that I can scarcely believe you have come hither for no other purpose than the reestablishment of your health." "It is true," replied the aga, "I am also commissioned to demand of you something on account of the four hundred thousand piastres you received." "We will say nothing of that," answered the pasha; "but come," he added in a determined tone, "confess that you have likewise orders to bring with you my head. Observe what I say; you know my character, and you know my word may be depended on; I now assure you that if you make an open declaration of the truth you shall depart without the least injury." The eunuch now began a long defence, protesting that he came with no such black intentions. "*By my head*," said Abdallah, "confess me the truth." The eunuch still denied. "*By your head*," he still denied. "Take care! *By the head of the sultan*," he still persisted. "Be it so," said Abdallah, "the matter is decided; thou hast pronounced thy own doom;" and drawing forth the khat-sherif—"know you this paper? Thus you govern at Constantinople! Yes, you are a gang of villains, who sport with the lives of whoever happens to displease you, and shed, without remorse, the blood of the sultan's servants. The vizier must have heads—he shall have one —off with the head of that dog and send it to Constantinople." The order was executed on the spot, and the eunuch's retinue were ordered to depart with their master's head.

After this decisive stroke Abdallah might have availed himself of his popularity to revolt, but he chose rather to retire among the Koords. Here the pardon of the sultan was sent him, and a firman appointing him pasha of Damascus. Weary of his exile and destitute of money, he accepted the commission and set out with one hundred men who adhered to his fortunes. On his arrival on the frontiers of his new government he learned that Assaad was encamped in the neighborhood; he had heard him spoken of as the greatest man in Syria, and was desirous of seeing him. He therefore disguised himself, and, accompanied only by six horsemen, repaired to his camp and demanded to speak with him. He was introduced, as is usual in these camps, without much ceremony; and, after the usual salutations, Assaad inquired of him whence he came and wither he was going. Abdallah replied he was one of six or seven Koord horsemen who were seeking employment, and who, hearing that Abdallah was appointed pasha of Damascus, were going to apply to him; but being informed on their way that Assaad was encamped in the neighborhood, they had come to request of him provisions for themselves and their horses. "With pleasure," replied Assaad; "but do you know Abdallah?" "Yes." "What sort of a man is he? Is he fond of money?" "No. Abdallah cares very little for money, or pelisses, or shawls, or pearls, or women; he is fond of nothing but well-tempered arms, good horses, and war. He does justice, protects the widow and the orphan, reads the Kur-an, and lives on butter and milk." "Is he old?" said Assaad. "Fatigue has made him to appear older than he is; he is covered with wounds; he has received a sabre-cut which has made him lame of his left leg, and another which makes him lean his head on his left shoulder. In short," said he, starting abruptly to his feet, "he is in shape and features exactly my picture." At these words Assaad turned pale and gave himself up for lost; but Abdallah, sitting down again, said to him, " Brother, fear nothing; I am come not to betray thee; on the contrary, if I can render thee any service command me, for we are both held in the same estimation by our masters; they have recalled me because they wish to chastise the Bedouins; when they have gratified their revenge on them, they will again lay plots to deprive me of my head. *God is great; what he has decreed will come to pass.*"

With these sentiments Abdallah repaired to Damascus, where he restored good order, put an end to the extortions of the soldiery, and conducted the caravan, sabre in hand, without paying a piastre to the Arabs. During his administration, which lasted two years, the country enjoyed the most perfect tranquillity. The inhabitants of Damascus long remembered him with gratitude, saying that under his government they slept in security with open doors. He himself, frequently disguised as one of the poorest of the people, saw everything with his own eyes. The summary justice he sometimes inflicted in consequence of his discoveries under these disguises produced a salutary effect, and was long a favorite theme of conversation among the people. It is said, for example, that being on his circuit at Jerusalem, he had prohibited his soldiers from either taking anything or imposing any order without paying. One day, when he was going about in the disguise of a poor man with a little plate of lentils in his hands, a soldier, who had a faggot on his shoulders, insisted on his carrying it. After some resistance, Abdallah took it on his back, whilst the soldier, following him, drove him forward with oaths and curses. Another soldier, happening to recognize the pasha, made a sign to his comrade, who instantly took to his heels and escaped through the cross streets. After proceeding a few paces, Abdallah, no longer hearing his man, turned round, and vexed at missing his aim, threw his burden on the ground, exclaiming, "The rascally knavish dog! he has both robbed me of my hire and carried off my plate of lentils." But he did not long escape; for a few days afterward the pasha, again surprising him in the act of robbing a poor woman's garden and ill-treating her, ordered his head struck off on the spot.

As for himself, he was unable to ward off the destiny he had foreseen. After escaping several times from hired assassins, he was poisoned by his own nephew. This he discovered before he died; and sending for his murderer, "Wretch that thou art," said he, "the villains have seduced thee; thou hast poisoned me to profit by my spoils: it is in my power before I die to punish thee, but I will leave thy punishment in the hands of God." And so it came to pass that the nephew's head soon after paid the forfeit of his perfidy.

CHAPTER XV.

ANTI-LEBANON.

THE time fixed for our departure from Damascus having arrived, we order our tents struck, and at 3 o'clock in the morning we start for Baalbec. Our course lies through Sulghiyeh, the chief suburb of the city, and we notice in passing quite a number of well-built public and private houses. Here we strike into a path which leads up the mountain-side, and for the next hour our horses and mules have a hard time in carrying us and our baggage up the path. The sun shines burning hot, and we feel its power more this morning than at any time heretofore.

Finally, however, we reach the Kubbet-el-Nasr—Dome of Victory—and here we turn our horses' heads to take a last look over the valley and city of Damascus.

There is a tradition current among the Mohammedans, that when their prophet beheld Damascus from this point he was so transported by the beauty of the scene, that he halted suddenly and would not descend to the city. "There is but one paradise destined for man," he exclaimed; "as for me, I am resolved not to choose mine in this world." The story is apocryphal, for Mohammed never had it in his power to enter Damascus: it was not till two years after his death that Khaled and Yezid, the two generals of Aboo-bekr, his successor, defeated Heraclius in a pitched battle near the city, which they took after a siege of six months, A.D. 634. Nevertheless, the fable has much meaning, even though it wants historical truth; and it was to commemorate this event that the Moslems erected the dome upon the summit, and still keep it in good repair. The imagination of an Arab from the parched Hedjaz could hardly have conceived the existence of a more enchanting oasis beneath the heavens.

The view from this dome is indeed very fine. The valley, about twenty miles in length by six in breadth, with the river Abana running through it, and little arms or rivulets leading off from it in every direction, and here and there a stuccoed village dotting the plain, presents a natural panorama such as is seldom met with on earth's broad surface.

And then the city, nestled amid the tall, green poplar trees, with gilded domes and minarets pointing heavenward; and the long lines of yellow-stuccoed houses and walls running hither and thither like threads of gold on a dark green surface; and the silver chords of the Abana and Pharpar flashing out upon the eye ever and anon, as they go dancing and gurgling amid the orange and lemon groves which surround the villas outside of the walls, form a picture of real and enchanting beauty.

Never before have we so fully realized the truth that "distance lends enchantment to the view;" for while we observe and acknowledge all the beauty of the picture as seen from this point, we know full well, from a previous and closer inspection, that the valley is now a comparatively barren plain, while the houses and streets and walls of the city are anything but beautiful.

Another hour's ride brings us to the village of Dumar,

situated far down in a valley, along a stream, and surrounded by poplar trees ; and here we turn off in a path to our right—leaving the direct course—for the purpose of visiting the great fountain of the Barada, of which we have read glowing accounts.

Ere long we reach the village of Messima, situated in a beautiful ravine, through which flow the waters of the Barada, and along the banks of which are a great number of poplars, English walnuts, fig, and pomegranate trees. Little patches of wheat and barley are cultivated near this village, giving to the whole a home-like appearance such as is seldom met with in Syria.

About 1 P.M. we reach the great fountain of the Barada, near the village of Feejee, and great is it indeed in every sense of the word. We were surprised and delighted with the size and grandeur of the fountains at Milaha and Banias, but this far exceeds either. Bursting out from beneath a great rock, it forms, from the very commencement, a good-sized river, which goes dashing and foaming down the valley with great force. Its waters are sweet, fresh, cool, and in every way spring-like, and but for this we should be inclined to regard it rather as the outlet of some large stream, which in some way had found a passage under the mountain, than as a fountain— so great is the volume of water.

In ancient times this fountain was covered with a temple, the ruins of which are still to be seen. The large stones used in its construction, the arch over the fountain, and the niche which remains in the rear wall, in which probably stood a god or goddess, point to a Roman origin. The remains of other buildings near the temple are also observable, proving it to have been a spot not only of note, but of considerable size.

Here we lunch, at the base of a tree, near the gushing waters; and while our inner man is strengthened with cold chicken, eggs, and vegetables, our ears are delighted with the music of the fountain as it gushes out from the mighty rock.

The temple which formerly covered this fountain was called El-Fijeh. Thus Abulefa, in writing of it, says: "The source of the river Damascus is under a temple called *El-Fijeh*. .... Afterward it unites with a river called Barada; and from hence come all the rivers of Damascus." And Edrisa, writing on the same subject, says: "The waters which irrigate the Ghutah come from a source called El-Fijeh, which rises upon the mountain; they flow down from the mountain with a noise and roaring which is heard at a great distance."

Dr. Robinson, in speaking of this locality and the fountain, says: "The course of the valley just here is about from west to east; and the fountain issues from under the northern hill. The road makes a short sweep away from the river, in order to pass above the fountain. The latter bursts forth at once a full, large stream, considerably larger than the Barada higher up, and comparing well in size with the great fountain at Tell-el-Kady; though the water is less beautiful and sparkling than that at Banias. The stream tumbles and foams along its rocky bed to the Barada, a distance of some twenty rods; it is so broad and deep and violent that no one would undertake to ford it." Of the temple erected over the fountain he says: "We could not resist the conclusion that this structure was once a vaulted platform sustaining a small temple, erected over an artificial branch of the fountain. The workmanship is simple and rude, and points to a high antiquity." What he means by "artificial branch" in this connection we do not understand, unless he refers to some other than the principal fountain.

Prime says of this fountain: "It is the finest fountain in the world. I had thought so of Tell-el-Kady and of Banias, but this surpassed them both. It springs out like a living thing. It is strong, furious, noble in its first plunge, and it goes down the ravine as if it had a great work to accomplish somewhere and were hastening to it."

A number of the villagers—mostly women and children —come down to look at the Howajjis, and when we ascend the bank to mount our horses, each of them raises the cry of bucksheesh. To each of the smaller ones we give a piece of money, but the larger ones we try to shame by telling them that they should work rather than beg; but we presume the lesson is lost upon them, as they cannot understand a word we say. Some of the little girls present Lily with bouquets of flowers, expecting, and of course receiving, bucksheesh in exchange.

The village of Feejee, near by, is small, and has nothing about it worthy of note except its delightful situation near this great fountain and its surroundings of luxuriously growing trees.

Soon after leaving the fountain we come within sight of the cliffs of Abila, on the summit of which Moslem tradition locates the grave of Abel, who, they say, was murdered by Cain at Zebdani, a village some fifteen miles further northward. This reported grave of Abel is a mound some twenty-five feet in length, and near it are the ruins of an ancient temple—when, or by whom built, no one can now say.

Somewhere near this—possibly on the table-land of the cliff—once stood the city of Abila, of which not a single trace now remains.

Before leaving Damascus we order our muleteers (from whom we separated at Dumar) to pitch our tents at Zebdani, as we wished to make but two days' journey between that city and Baalbec. Judge, then, of our surprise, on reaching Suk-Wady-Barada, to find our tents pitched here, with the American flag flying beautifully from the flag-staff and the muleteers arranging for a night's repose. It is their first act of disobedience of orders, and might be overlooked on the plea they make that here they have the company of others who have had orders to pitch at this place; but as it will entail on us an extra day's journey if submitted to, we resolve to remedy it at once. Riding down to the tents, we order them taken down and reloaded immediately, and when the head muleteer commences to make explanations and excuses, we raise our cane and threaten to break it over his head unless he obeys us immediately. This has the desired effect, and in less than thirty minutes both tents and baggage are reloaded on the mules and ready for a start. Had we flogged the rascal, it would have done him good, and we regret since that we did not. These Moslem dragomen and muleteers need an occasional flogging to make them know their places, and from none but an American would they ever expect to get it. It is too common with travelers to submit to their impositions as if they were their servants rather than their masters.

From Suk-Wady-Barada the ravine becomes more narrow and picturesque, and the stream along which we pass, and through which we have to wade our horses for some distance, because of the narrow and dangerous condition of the path along its banks, rushes furiously and madly by. Our horses stumble along over the large stones in the bed of the stream, and once or twice we come very near being unhorsed. A bath in the boiling, bubbling waters of this stream, with hard stones to lie upon, would not be half so pleasant as the one we unexpectedly had in the Jordan.

The hillsides along this stream, near where a lofty stone

bridge crosses it, are perforated with the doors of tombs, and below these the remains of a road and aqueduct, cut through the solid rock, can be traced, showing conclusively that a large city once stood somewhere near, though no other remains of it are now traceable.

The long day's march which we have laid out for ourselves will not allow of our stopping to examine either the tombs or the ancient road; but Dr. Robinson, in writing of the former, says: "They are laboriously wrought, and some of them are reached by long flights of steps. The whole cliff is somewhat curved, and forms a sort of amphitheatre. Mr. Robson (his companion in travel) had climbed up to several and examined them in the summer of 1848. One which he entered was a square chamber, having two crypts on each side, with two niches in each crypt; also one crypt with four niches opposite the door, beside four niches (*loculi*) in the floor of the chamber itself. Other tombs are similar, some larger and some smaller. Some are simply a recess cut into the face of the rock, about seven feet long and two deep, arched at the top and in the bottom a single *loculus* for a corpse. All these single tombs had formerly lids of stone, like those of sarcophagi; but all have been opened. In the cliff on the southern bank is a single sepulchral excavation, a little further up the stream. On the top of the north-western cliff, above the sepulchres, are said to be extensive ancient quarries."

In writing of the road he says: "The most remarkable of all the remains is the ancient road, excavated along the face of the north-western cliff, a hundred feet above the modern road and bridge. It begins at the angle of the hill where the valley bends round from the west; and there is no difficulty in climbing up to it in that quarter. The sides of the chasm are here from six hundred to eight hundred feet in height. The road extends along the face of the cliff for about two hundred yards. It is finely cut through the solid rock fifteen feet wide. In some parts on the river-side a thin portion of the rock is left, of various heights, as a guard; in other parts a wall was probably built up. At the north-western end this road breaks off abruptly in a precipice of rock rising from the sloping bank below. If the road was ever continued farther, it must have been sustained on artificial and temporary supports; since the ancient aqueduct which passes just below it, and extends along the face of the cliff beyond, serves to show that there has been no fall of the rock nor change in its general features. It is not easy to see how the road was continued, or, if ended here, what purpose it could have served."

It is near seven o'clock before we reach Zebdani, and although we are ready to stop for the night, our situation is not the most pleasant; we are chilled by the cold winds from the snows of Mount Hermon, which sweep through the valley furiously; the blackness of darkness seems to be gathering about us, portending a fearful storm in the night, and we are all alone, our former companions in travel having stopped at Suk-Wady-Barada. Nevertheless we are here and must abide the issue. We order our tent-cords doubled—the curtains tied down tight and snug—a pan of coals brought in to warm our feet—and, after dinner, we read and write until time to retire.

The wind continues to blow furiously all night, but fortunately no rain accompanies it, and we pass the night with some degree of comfort.

Next morning we are *en route* for Baalbec. The hour was too late, and too many other things demanded our attention, to see Zebdani on the evening of our arrival; but we take a stroll through the town on the morning of our departure.

This town contains about three thousand inhabitants, and is situated in a valley which in many respects has the most American, home-like appearance of anything we have seen in Syria. The fields are square, with gateways and good hedge fences, and are generally well cultivated. The orchards are planted regularly in rows, and all the fruit trees are carefully pruned and cared for. The houses scattered throughout the valley, and even those of the town, are of a better class and look far more comfortable than those generally found throughout this country. Indeed, one might easily imagine that a lot of American farmers had, in some way, got possession of this valley, and were showing the indolent Syrians how things can be done. Why the difference between this and other parts of Syria we have no means of knowing, but that the difference exists any one will at once observe.

Not far from Zebdani is the village of Bludin, where, it is said, the more wealthy citizens of this part of the country make their summer residences. It is located a thousand feet above the valley, and looks picturesque in the distance, though a nearer view would probably reveal the ragged appearance which characterizes other Syrian villages.

Back of Zebdani rise the mountains of Anti-Lebanon, from six to seven thousand feet in height. Our course lies partly over these, and the path by which we ascend is narrow and difficult.

Several times while climbing the mountain we stop and look back at the valley below. It seems like again leaving the old familiar scenes of home, and we think and talk of friends far, far away across the broad Atlantic.

Oh what would we not give just now to be seated for an hour on the broad veranda of one of our Jersey farmer friends, to talk over the familiar affairs of home, and drink such milk and eat such apples as only they can furnish.

Up, and still up—over, and still over—all the time within sight of snow, but never reaching it—our backs burning from the piercing rays of the sun, and our bodies chilled from the cold winds whistling about us—sometimes going along precipitous hillsides and looking down in ravines a thousand feet below—then deep down in a valley, and anon on a summit, looking far away at other summits and mountain-ranges—thus we travel and thus we go until we come within sight of the great plain which lies between the mountains of Anti-Lebanon and the true Lebanon, where the cedars of the temple grew, and where snow-capped summits for ever keep watch over the sunny vales below.

Once fairly in the valley, we seek the first favorable place for lunching, and find it beside a little stream, and beneath the shadow of an overhanging rock.

Lunching over, we again mount our horses and proceed up the valley toward Baalbec. The valley is broad and beautiful, and was once, probably, highly cultivated, though it is now almost a barren. The roads are smooth, and as a storm is threatening, we let our horses gallop along at full speed. Lily and Lu occasionally run a race, while Mohammed and I follow along as out-riders. On our right are the mountains of Anti-Lebanon, and on our left the true Lebanon, the summits of both of which are covered with snow, and the cold winds from which sweep through the valley, occasionally with great force.

We have, now and then, a laugh at Mohammed as we ride along, because of his inability to remember the word Lebanon, though his recollection of names generally is very good. Whenever he attempts to speak of Lebanon, he calls it "de mountain of de trees—what you call him?" He has been to the "cedars" with other travelers, and knows all about the road thither and the mountain itself, but for some cause or other the name escapes him whenever he attempts to speak it.

About four o'clock in the afternoon we approach Baalbec, but instead of going direct to the town we make a detour to the right to visit the fountains near by and the ruins which surround them.

These fountains are about three-fourths of a mile from the town, in a south-easterly direction, and must at one time have been highly prized, as about them are ruins of cut stone which, in the day of their freshness, were probably very beautiful.

The largest of these ruins was a temple, with arched windows, doorways, and roof. Sculptured stones still remain over the doorways within, but the inscriptions are so defaced that nothing can be learned from them. The central doorway, looking eastward, is quite large, with an arch of cut stones, as perfect to-day as when first built, probably two thousand years ago. Through this temple runs a stone aqueduct, supplied with water from the fountains above.

There are several points where the water bursts forth, and two of the principal fountains have a semi-circular wall of handsomely cut stone about them. The waters from all the fountains come together near the larger ruin, and from this point there is formed a considerable stream which flows toward the town.

It is probable that when the temples of Baalbec were

in their glory, the waters of these fountains were held in high repute, and were conducted in viaducts to the temples. At present they waste their sweetness in the marsh below, with none so poor as to do them reverence.

About 5 P. M. we reach the ruins of Baalbec, and have our tents pitched within the very walls of the temple; but for a description of these we must refer the reader to the next chapter.

CHAPTER XVI.

BAALBEC.

THE ruins of Baalbec have long been the wonder and admiration of tourists from all parts of the world, yet little is known of their real history, and so various have been the theories put forth by different authors with regard to them that the traveler of to-day is left as much in the dark concerning their origin as though he had just discovered them himself on the great Desert of Arabia.

Whether the temples, once so grand and beautiful, which stood within this enclosure were built by Solomon for his Egyptian wife, or whether they were erected by the Persians, the Greeks, or the Romans, during their successive occupancy of this country, no one can now say of a certainty.

Jewish, Doric, Tuscan, and Corinthian architecture is found amid the ruins, so that no clue can be had of their origin from this department of science; and the immense stones which are found in one portion of the ruins, and the mystery by which such stones were quarried and raised to their position, makes the problem of the origin of these ruins still more difficult to solve.

The most probable of the theories, we think, is that different portions of these structures were built at different periods of the world's history, and under the rule of

RUINS OF BAALBEC.

different dynasties—each ruler trying to outdo the other in the additions and alterations made. Such is the well-known history of the great temple, or successive temples, of Karnak, on the Nile, and these may have been erected in a similar manner.

The first view of the ruins, though grand and imposing, is anything but satisfactory; and it is only after we have walked around and viewed them from every side, and then made a careful survey and analysis of the structures within, viewing one in relation to the other, searching out parallels and dividing lines, marking the foundation-stones and the relation of one line with another, observing the semi-circular temples around the walls and the relation they probably bore to the great temple, that we arrive at any correct idea with regard to them.

All this we do, first on our arrival in the afternoon and evening, and then again, still more carefully, on the following day; but, notwithstanding all the pains taken, much remains in doubt and perplexity to us, and will for ever thus remain to all future explorers.

The ruins proper embrace an area of about nine hundred feet in one direction by about five hundred in another. The present, and possibly the original, entrance within the high, thick walls which make the outer enclosure to all the temples, is through one of the arched vaults, of which three form the base of the artificial platform on which the temples were built. This platform is raised about thirty feet above the average level of the plain, and is formed by three arched passage-ways—two running in one direction and one in another—which are underneath, having vaulted rooms running out from their sides, and the interstices filled in with earth and masonry.

What was the original destination of these vaulted rooms it is now impossible to tell; but the Arabs, who ascribe the whole structure to the great magician, Solomon, and the jins who wrought his behests, imagine them to be depositories for treasure. Indeed, it is a universal belief among the Turks and Arabs that every great mass of ruins lies over mighty heaps of treasure ; nor can they be persuaded that Europeans visit them for any other purpose than that of carrying off the spoil. The huge structures of Baalbec were reared, they think, by the power of cabalistic words ; and they suppose the Franks, who are known to be great magicians, can uplift them by their spells, and possess themselves of what lies beneath them. Nay, there are natives, too, they say, who can exercise this forbidden power if their admirable conscientiousness did not forbid them to do so. "One of our Arab friends," says Madame Lamartine, "a man of good information and judgment, has frequently assured us, with every possible mark of internal conviction, that a sheikh of Lebanon possessed the secret of the magic words that had been employed in primitive times to move the gigantic blocks of Baalbec, but that he was too good a Christian ever to make use of them or to divulge them." When questioned on the subject at Baalbec, Burckhardt made answer, " The treasures of this country are not beneath the earth ; they come from God, and are above the surface of the earth. Work your fields and sow them, and you will find the greatest treasure in an abundant harvest." " By your life" (a common oath) " truth comes from your lips," was the reply.

The vaults, heretofore described in this volume, as forming the substructure of the large area in front of the Mosque of Omar, on Mount Moriah, Jerusalem, and on which the great Temple of Solomon, no doubt, stood, are very much of the same character as these at Baalbec ; and this fact, more than any other, has induced many to think that both structures were erected under the direction of the same master mind.

The evident object of this raised platform at Baalbec, as at Jerusalem, was to give to the temples an elevation far above the surrounding plain, without marring their architectural proportions. Had the temples themselves been built thirty feet higher than they were, the relative proportions would have been lost and the beauty of design utterly destroyed. Hence the necessity of first making an artificial hill, or platform, on which the foundations, as well as the superstructures, might be laid and built.

On emerging from the passage-way, within the walls, the first objects which strike the eye are the six immense columns which are all that remain standing of the fifty-four which once surrounded the Temple of the Sun. These columns are of Corinthian architecture, seventy-five feet high by about seven in diameter, and the base and caps remain almost as perfect as when first erected. The entablature over these six columns is also well preserved and shows great beauty of design and finish. Each stone of the entablature reaches from column to column, a distance of fifteen feet, and the thickness of each is about the same as the length.

These six columns, in fact, are no larger than those about the Temple of Jupiter, near by, though they look, at first sight, much higher and thicker, because of their more elevated and isolated position.

The bases of many of the other columns which surrounded this temple are still in their original position—some on the same foundation-wall where the six remain standing, and others in the two outer walls, which originally formed a part of this structure. The Saracens, when they converted these ruins into a fortification for defensive purposes, piled other stones on the outer walls and thereby obscured, and partly walled in, some of the column-bases, so that only by close observation can they now be traced.

The foundations of this Temple of the Sun, which can still be traced, show it to have been about three hundred feet in length by about one hundred and sixty in breadth, and so constructed that the western end was somewhat more elevated than the eastern. Of course this elevation was only of the floor within, and not observable without, else it would have greatly marred the architectural beauty of the building. Only a small portion of the entrance-way to this great temple remains, but sufficient to show that it must have been of great beauty. In front of this temple was, and still is, a large quadrangular court, around the outer walls of which are several semi-circular temples, in which the niches, where gods were placed, are still observable. These niches are ornamented with sculpture-work above, and formerly had a small column at each side. Some of them are cut to represent scallop-shells, odd and beautiful.

Various are the conjectures as to the use of these semi-circular temples: Were they chapels or shrines for the worship of subordinate deities? or recesses for the philosophers to sit and lecture in? or lodgings for the priests? or was the great court a forum, and were these sheltered places intended for the convenience of the merchants, the civil functionaries, or the people? It is in vain we toil after a solution of these enigmas; we cannot re-construct in thought, and re-people as of old, the public buildings of an age, or of a nation of whose religious or secular usages we have no thorough knowledge. Nevertheless our ignorance of the purposes for which these chambers were intended cannot mar our admiration of their exceeding beauty and richness of decoration, and of the singularly picturesque effect which results from the mixture of the garlands and the large foliage of the capitals with the living sculpture of wild plants that spring from every chink and profusely adorn the stone.

The quadrangular court is filled with ruins of various smaller buildings, all of which, at one time, no doubt, were connected in some way with the Great Temple.

Following out the same line of direction, and passing through what was once a large door or passage-way, we enter into a hexagonal court, around which are niches for statues, and on each side of which is a square room, probably occupied by the grand wardens of the temple. Passing through this court, with our face still eastward, we reach what has doubtless been the grand portico and the steps leading up from the plain below. On each side of this entrance there has been a square tower, scarcely a trace of which now remains, and of the grand stairway nothing exists.

Retracing our steps through the hexagonal and quadrangular courts, and bearing a little to the left, we reach the Temple of Jupiter, which stands upon a railroad platform ten feet lower than that of the Temple of the Sun, and directly south of it.

This temple is still in good preservation, and the different portions of it can be traced with much satisfaction. Many of its columns have fallen, and much of its sculpture has been broken off or defaced, but from the columns and sculpture which remain its original construction and beauty can be readily understood.

The outside measurement of this temple is two hundred and thirty feet in length by one hundred and twenty in width. A portico surrounded the building, the roof of which was supported by forty columns, many of which remain standing. The shafts of these columns were plain, and of the same height and thickness as those of the Temple of the Sun, except four of the inner front columns, which were fluted. The capitals are of the Corinthian order and of great beauty. The ceiling of the portico is composed of immense stones, which reach from the entablature to the walls of the main building, and on the under side of which are carvings of gods and goddesses, fruits, flowers, etc.

To enter this temple we pass through a hole in the wall, erected by the Saracens, immediately in front of it. This brings us in front of the grand door-way, the jams of which are elaborately and beautifully carved, and on the undersill of the stones which form the top of the doorway is the carving of an eagle, with a cupid on either side. The centre or keystone of these three has been shaken from its position by the earthquake which destroyed the other portions of the temple, and now hangs in a position threatening destruction to whoever passes under it.

Once within the temple, its gorgeous beauty strikes the eye from every point. Its carvings are intricate and of innumerable patterns, and we observe among them many of the styles and patterns used in public buildings of the present day. Around the walls are recesses for statues, in each of which, doubtless, stood a god or goddess of exquisite workmanship.

About twenty feet from the west end, the remains of a curtain of masonry and of two pedestals are observable. On each of these pedestals probably stood a colossal figure of a god, and at the farther end, partly concealed by the side curtains, the statue of Jupiter himself. Behind this curtain was the altar where the priests offered their oblations, and from whence they breathed blessings and curses upon their deluded followers.

Baalbec. 313

On each side of the main entrance to this temple is a square tower, with a circular stairway leading from the bottom to the top. To enter one of these we descend a steep declivity and pass through a narrow doorway. Then up and up for some fifteen minutes, and we reach the top, where we have a fine view of the ruins as a whole, and of the surrounding country.

The injuries which this temple has sustained have most of them resulted from barbarian violence, and the same, we presume, may be said of the others. The columns especially have been destroyed for the sake of the iron bars by which they were held together. Think of the ignorance and barbarism which would destroy a beautiful column, the cost of which must have equaled thousands of dollars, to obtain a few iron bars and a few pounds of lead, the entire worth of which would not equal twenty dollars!

The tottering condition of the beautiful portal of the Temple of Jupiter, however, has been produced by a concussion more destructive than even the mutilating hand of the Moslem—the tremendous earthquake of 1750. The key-stone had sunk eight inches in Volney's time, and has continued to descend, slowly, but surely, until it is now more than three feet below its original position. The least new shock will bring it to the ground, and with it the whole architrave. As we pass underneath this threatening stone two or three times, we cannot refrain from looking up and hastening our steps—just a little.

" The ornaments of this doorway," says Lord Lindsay, " are exquisitely delicate, especially the ears of corn and the grapes and vine leaves. It was not until a second or third visit that we discovered the little elves or genii lurking among the leaves in the lower compartments formed by the intertwining vine. The rolling frieze, the cornice, the graceful scroll, I have no words to express their beauty."

About one hundred and fifty yards from the Temple of Jupiter there is a beautiful little Corinthian temple, circular within and without, and pierced externally with handsome niches, each flanked by two columns, so as to give the building the appearance of an octagon. Wreaths are gracefully suspended from the cornice over each niche. A more elegant little edifice we have seldom seen. Earthquakes have sadly shaken it, and four pillars only are standing. A weeping willow bends over it, like Beauty mourning over Genius. This building was used in Pococke's time as a Christian church.

In coming out of the Temple of Jupiter we turn to the right, and by passing along its southern side, over broken columns and large stones, clambering up here and down there, we finally reach the outside of the walls, and from thence proceed to examine the immense stones, of which so much has been written, and about which so many conjectures have been made.

These stones are twenty in number, and are located on the west and north sides. Those on the north side form a wall by itself upon which no superstructure was ever built. These are ten in number, averaging about thirty feet in length, thirteen feet in height, and ten feet six inches in thickness. There is about ten feet space between this wall and that of the temple, or the raised platform on which the temple stood. Why this wall should have been left thus isolated no one can now tell.

On the west side we find six stones, the total length of which is one hundred and eighty-nine feet, being an average of thirty-one and a half feet each, and of the same height and thickness as the ten on the north side. Another one of these huge stones, about the same size as the others, forms the corner and connecting link between the first ten and last six.

But the stones which have excited the greatest wonder and admiration are the three which lie upon and exactly cover the six on the west side. These three are each sixty-three feet in length, thirteen feet in height, and their width probably the same as the others. The wall of the platform continues upward from these, and of course there is no way to get at their exact width.

There is but one other cut stone in the known world so large as these, and this we see afterward in a quarry about a mile from the ruins; the same quarry, doubtless, from which the other three were taken. This last is about sixty-nine feet in length, seventeen in height and fourteen in thickness. It is accurately squared and trimmed on all sides, save the lower and at one end. This, with other examples of like character, though of smaller size, in the same quarry, proves that it was the custom of the ancients to square and dress their stones while quarrying them, instead of taking them out in the rough and dressing them near where they are to be finally laid, as is the custom at present.

We noticed in the sandstone and granite quarries along the Nile, in Egypt, that a like custom prevailed there.

Lamartine, in writing of these stones and of the walls which encircle the temples, says:

"Beautiful as are the structures we have described, and replete as they are with interest and delight for any person pretending to the slightest taste for works of art, they yield as objects of wonder to the wall which encircles them, or rather upon which they stand, for their base is nearly on a level with its top. The site of the ruins is nearly a dead level, on which has been reared a platform a thousand feet long, six hundred broad, and varying in height from fifteen to thirty feet. This prodigious mass of masonry is wholly composed of huge cut stones, many of which are nine paces long, ten feet broad, and six feet thick; and three of them are more than double that length. They are cut with the beveled edge, exactly like the cutting of the stones in the subterranean columns of the Haram Shereef in Jerusalem, which Dr. Richardson considered to be of Jewish workmanship; and he thinks it highly probable that both structures were the work of the same people, and nearly of the same era. Among the cities enumerated in the eighth chapter of Chronicles, as being built by Solomon, is Baalath in Lebanon. The similarity of name and situation identifies it at once with Baalbec; and Baalath is mentioned by Josephus as one of the places of pleasure erected by that king in Syria, on account of the temperate nature of the climate, the delicacy of the fruits, and the excellence of the air and water. It may possibly be that these are the remains of the House of the Forest of Lebanon, described in 1 Kings, ch. vii. as formed of 'costly stones, according to the measures of hewed stones, sawed with saws within and without, even from the foundation to the coping, *and so on the outside toward the great court*, and the foundation was of costly stones, *even great stones*, stones of ten cubits and stones of eight cubits.'

" The second builders of this enormous pile have built upon the foundations of the former edifice; and, in order that the appearance of the whole might be of one date, they cut a new surface upon the old stones. This operation has not been completely finished, and some of the stones remain half cut, exhibiting part of the old surface and part of the new, so that the different eras of the building are exemplified in the same stone. Three of the blocks lying near each other in the western wall are so enormous that early travelers seemed almost afraid to declare their dimensions. One of them measures sixty-three feet long, nearly fourteen feet broad, and nine feet thick; the others do not differ much from it in size. These are, perhaps, the most ponderous masses that human hands or machinery ever moved into a wall, and here they are between twenty and thirty feet above the foundation. Dr. Richardson doubts, however, that they formed any part of the original wall; they do not harmonize with that which is around them, and the part below them is the repaired, not the original wall. He supposes that they were lowered to the present position by the workmen who found them lying useless on the top of the platform; and Lord Lindsay, who adopts this conjecture, imagines that they may have been the intended material for three pillars of the great temple, no trace of which or even of their bases he could discover. But here we are met by another puzzling difficulty. The existing columns are in three several pieces, whilst these stones are alone of a size sufficient each for the construction of a whole one. The quarry from which these blocks were extracted is about a mile from the ruins; the material is compact limestone. There is now lying in it a block ready shaped, smoothed and planed, which measures sixty-nine feet two inches in length, twelve feet ten inches in breadth, and thirteen feet three inches in thickness. Wood, the architect, who saw this stone in 1751, computes it to contain 14,128 cubic feet, and to weigh, supposing its specific gravity to be the same as that of Portland stone, 2,270,000 lbs., or 1135 tons; and this stone was hewn out by manual labor, and prepared to be transported a mile to be built into a wall!"

The queries which naturally arise in viewing such stones are, why they quarried them of such immense size for building purposes, and how, when quarried, did they ever raise them in position?

The answer to the first probably is, that having no gunpowder or other means of blasting, and being obliged to cut with chisels each separate stone from its native bed, they found it more expeditious to cut one large than several smaller masses. But as to the means of moving and placing them in position no one at the present day can give a reasonable answer. No instrument, sculptures, engravings, plans, or history of any kind remain by which we can learn how they did such herculean work, and certainly no builder of the present day would undertake such a labor; nor with all our vaunted knowledge of mechanics, and of all branches of natural philosophy, are we at all certain that it could be done if undertaken.

Diligent search has been made among the ruins to find inscriptions, hoping thereby, if found, to trace something of the history of the temples, but efforts in this direction thus far have proved of little worth. The Latin inscription quoted in Dr. Robinson's work only reveals the name "Heliopolis" (of the Sun), and then proceeds to salute or laud the Roman emperor in whose time the inscription was chiseled; but it is by no means certain, we think, from this, that the temples were built by the Romans or in their time, while the two Greek inscriptions found by Mr. Prime in one of the small chapels, and which seemed to him only to mark the seats of priests or teachers, are so imperfect that nothing can be determined as to their meaning.

Taken as a whole, these ruins of Baalbec are among the grandest in the world. They do not equal in extent those of Karnak, near Thebes, but in exquisite workmanship they are superior. To an antiquarian they present the study of a lifetime.

We should earnestly recommend all tourists who may visit Palestine to spend the additional time it may take to visit the ruins of Baalbec.

CHAPTER XVII.

AMONG THE MARONITES.

OUR sight-seeing at Baalbec ended, we turn our face toward the sea.

Our hearts bound at the thought of turning our faces once more westward; for, hereafter, every day's journey will bring us nearer home and friends.

Those who are sitting by their cozy fireside, and who, as they read these chapters, wish themselves where we are now, will scarcely appreciate this feeling of ours. They will wonder how it can be that one who is traveling in the far-famed East, and seeing such glorious, time-honored sights as we are seeing, and enjoying what seems an almost perpetual summer, with flowers blooming by the wayside and sparkling fountains bursting out from the hillsides, can possibly wish himself once more amid the blue hills of New Jersey; but let such try the experiment as we have tried it, traveling week after week on horseback, over mountains the most desolate and roads the most horrible of which the mind can conceive, sleeping in tents, and living on mutton and chicken, and chicken and mutton, until their very names seem nauseous, having no letters or papers from home for over a month, and not knowing, in the mean time, whether the world has "turned upside down," or still keeps on the "even tenor of its way," being daily and hourly in contact with men with whom we can have no sympathies in common, and whom we fairly loathe for their lack of civilization and Christian courtesy—let them, we say, try all this as we have tried and still are trying it, and if they don't doubly and trebly realize the value of home and friends, and wish themselves among them, they will have less of the common feelings of humanity than we give most men credit for.

And yet, after saying all this, we cannot but add that, notwithstanding all the hardships of our trip through Palestine, we do not regret having taken it; nor would we have what we have seen and enjoyed effaced from our memory for a thousand times its cost.

It is something for one to remember during the balance of a lifetime that he has looked upon the spot where Jesus was born; where he spent the earlier years of his earthly life, and commenced his ministry; where he was baptized; where he did "many wonderful works" along the shores of the Sea of Galilee, and at other memorable places throughout the Holy Land; where he agonized in spirit while his disciples slept; where he was crucified; where he was buried, and from whence he arose triumphant from the grave!

One can well afford to endure some discomforts to see and feel all this; and yet, having seen, and felt, and realized, the mind instinctively turns toward home—sweet home!—as the place of all places most devoutly to be wished for.

Before leaving Baalbec, however, we take occasion to see the few other ruins which surround the place, and of which we must here add a short description.

We visit what remains of the once beautiful, though oddly constructed, Mosque of Salah-e'deen. We say oddly constructed, for most of the columns used in the erection of this structure were taken from the ruined temples near by, and placed in the mosque without reference to size or material. Hence we find, standing side by side, a large column and a smaller one—one of porphyry, another of granite, and a third of marble—one of Doric and another of Corinthian architecture. The walls are of like intermixture—large stones and small, smooth stones and rough, beveled stones and plain; while here and there the Saracens added something of their own style and workmanship, which makes confusion worse confounded.

The only interest which attaches itself to the ruins of this mosque is, that here, it is said, lie the remains of the great Salah-e'deen; for, Turk and infidel though he was, his genius and generalship are not to be doubted. He it was that fought the Crusaders at the gates of Jaffa, and finally routed them completely and took from them the Holy Cross on the Plain of Hattin. And when he had thus completely subdued his foes and was himself master of the situation, he acted toward them so magnanimous a part that pen and pencil have since been employed by Christian hands to commemorate his name.

His tomb is now wholly neglected, and, unless some friendly hand looks after it soon, its whereabouts will no longer be traceable.

The modern town of Baalbec is scarcely worthy of notice. It contains but a few hundred inhabitants, its houses are small, streets narrow and rough, and, but for the ruins near by, no tourist would think of visiting it.

Our course lies westward over the great plain by which we came. A little way from the town we stop at the quarries to examine the great stone of which we have heretofore given a description; and still, a little farther on, we again stop to examine what, in the distance, seems a small ruined temple, but which, upon closer inspection, proves only a circular structure, made by some Moslem genius, by standing eight granite columns (stolen from the temple near by) on their ends (some of them upside down) and making thereon a sort of architrave or dome. As we have heretofore had occasion to remark, nothing more strikingly illustrates the difference between the ancient and modern occupants of this country than the utter lack in the latter of anything like architectural taste or genius, and the instance now before us is but one of hundreds scattered throughout Syria.

The road over the plain of Baalbec is well marked, broad, and generally smooth, and we let our horses skim along at a bounding pace. Lu's little white horse generally leads the way, while Lily's, Mohammed's, and my own keep within calling distance.

At one P. M. we reach an old mill on a small stream, and here we stop to lunch, on a green sward, around which the waters are flowing. Mohammed's horse, while rolling, breaks the girth, and the saddle rolls off in the stream. The saddle is recovered but thoroughly soaked, and, for the balance of the day, the poor fellow has to ride on a wet seat. We laugh at him for the mishap, though, had it been our own, we should have hardly thought it a laughing matter.

Later in the afternoon we reach the small village of Kerak, where we stop a while to examine the reputed tomb of Noah. It is in an old mosque near the roadside, and the venerable Moslem who has charge of the building seems thoroughly impressed with its identity. The tomb extends from one end of the building to the other, probably a hundred feet. It is about three feet wide and three high, running up to a sharp edge. On it lie a number of shawls, some coarse and some quite fine, which have been donated to the tomb by persons who have thought themselves miraculously cured of disease by visiting it. Near one end we notice a quantity of gum, such as is used in Catholic churches for the " burning of incense," and which the old Moslem tells us is used here occasionally, in like manner, by persons who visit the tomb for devotional purposes. The attendant makes no objection to our taking some of this gum as a memento of the place, on condition of our leaving enough bucksheesh to cover its cost.

Beyond this, a little way, we reach the village of Maalakha, and are surprised at its general neatness and the number of new houses. On inquiry we learn that it is mostly occupied by Christians, and that the large number of new buildings observable is accounted for from the fact that, not long since, the Moslems of the surrounding villages burned the houses of the Christians of Maalakha, and the government, to make good the loss, had these new houses erected for those who had suffered from the fire. Had the Moslem dogs been thrown in the buildings which they set on fire it would only have been a just rettribution for their consummate meanness and bigotry. Oh that we had the power to wipe this people from off the land which they so much disgrace and pollute by their presence! The more we have seen and had to do with Moslems, the higher is our appreciation of the Crusaders.

We are now in the neighborhood of the Maronites, one of the most numerous and most singular body of semi-Christians in Syria; and as they have heretofore excited, and still excite, a large share of attention from tourists in this country, and from Christians generally throughout the world, a short account of their history and peculiarities may not prove uninteresting to our readers.

The Maronites derive their name from Marroun, a holy hermit, who flourished in the odor of sanctity in the fifth century. But his followers were condemned by the general council of Constantinople (A.D. 681) as holding the *monothelite* heresy; and, being driven from the greater part of the cities of Syria, they took refuge on the mountains of Lebanon and Anti-Lebanon. For several successive centuries from that period Lebanon continued to be an asylum from religious persecution for every caste. By no other means can we account for the fact of Pagan and Christian amalgamating for so long a series of ages, and submitting to be governed by a single head.

And still is Lebanon one vast city of refuge. The stranger, pursued by implacable enemies, the Christians of the plain, unable to endure the cruel oppression and extortions of the Turkish governors, fly to the mountain, and neither private malice nor the tyranny of the rulers will venture to seek them there. In 1821, when the disasters of Navarino had excited the intensest hatred in the bosoms of the Turks against everything European, the consuls and the Franks resident in Syria, alarmed for the safety of their lives, sought an asylum among the inhabitants of Lebanon; and during a space of fifteen or eighteen months passed by them in that region, never did the least shadow of danger trouble their tranquillity: the hospitable Lebanon keeps trusty guard over those who confide in its protection. By what a noble instinct, by what an admirable law not written in human books, do the mountaineers thus devote themselves to the defence of the fugitive and the oppressed! " Thanks be to God for the mountains!"

The Maronites adhered to the Latin Church in the year 1182, but still remained under the authority of their own patriarchs. In the course of the events that followed the

Crusades their attachment to the Church of Rome became much diminished; but they were won back to it by able negotiations in the year 1403; and in 1445 the Maronites solemnly renewed their recognition of Roman supremacy under the pontificate of Eugenius IV. Thenceforth they have always piqued themselves on their strict fidelity to the Holy See, which in its turn has favored them with many immunities. Thus celibacy is not strictly imposed on the Maronite priests, who may be ordained though married, but they must not take a second wife if the first die. Only the higher clergy and the monks, and those who are unmarried when they take orders, are compelled to remain single.

They celebrate mass in Syriac, of which the greatest part of them comprehend not a word. The gospel alone is read aloud in Arabic, that it may be understood by the people. The communion is administered in both languages. The host has a small round loaf, unleavened, of the thickness of a finger, and about the size of a crown-piece. On the top is the impression of a seal, which is eaten by the priest, who cuts the remainder into small pieces, and putting it into the wine in the cup, administers to each person with a spoon. In this manner he serves the whole congregation.

The Maronites constitute at this day a community governed by the most purely theocratical system that has withstood the changes of time—a theocracy which, having constantly had the fear of Moslem tyranny impending over it, has of necessity a character of moderation and paternal tenderness toward the governed, so that it has fostered among them some germs of civil liberty, which need only a more favorable season to unfold themselves. The patriarch (*batrak*) is elected by the bishops of the nation, subject to the approval of the pope or of his legate. The patriarch's authority is unlimited; all the Christians of the mountain pay him extraordinary respect and deference. He has but to speak to be obeyed implicitly, and that even in matters not pertaining to his spiritual functions. The influence of the numerous bishops is also very great, and the Turkish authorities are careful to avoid offending them, knowing that a word from their lips would be enough to arouse the whole population.

The bishops are possessed of stated revenues, that enable them to live in comparative affluence; but this is not the case with the inferior clergy, who have no fixed sources of income, but subsist on the produce of their masses, the bounty of their congregations, and the labors of their hands. Some of them exercise trades; others cultivate small plots of land; and all are industriously employed for the maintenance of their families and the edification of their flocks. This poverty is recompensed by the great respect paid them; their vanity is incessantly flattered; whoever approaches them, whether rich or poor, great or small, is anxious to kiss their hands, which they fail not to present; nor are they pleased that Europeans withhold from them this mark of reverence.

It is perhaps to the potent influence of the clergy that we must attribute the mild and simple manners generally prevailing among the Maronites, for violent crimes are extremely rare among them. Retribution immediately follows every offence, however slight, and the clergy are rigorous in preventing every appearance of disorder or scandal among the members of their flocks. Before a young man can marry, he must obtain the consent of his pastor and of his bishop. If they disapprove of the marriage, they prohibit it, and the Maronite has no remedy. If an unmarried girl become a mother, her seducer is compelled to marry her, whatever be the inequality of their conditions; if he refuses, he is reduced to obedience by measures of severity, fasting, imprisonment, and even bastinading. This influence of the clergy extends to every detail of civil and domestic life. The Maronite who should appeal from the decision of the clergy to the civil authority of the emirs would not be listened to by them, and the act would be regarded by the appellant's bishop as a transgression to be visited with condign punishment.

The clergy have at their command a fearful word of execration—a word that excites unbounded horror whenever it is uttered; but its application is rare. This word, applied to an individual, would instantly bar every door against him; he would find himself everywhere cut off from all social intercourse, for no one would have any communication with him, or give or sell anything to an *accursed one* like him. This word, the more terrible, inasmuch as the explanation of its import is always left to the imagination of the mountaineer, is *fra-massoon*, a corruption of *franc-macon* (freemason). A Christian of Lebanon believes in his heart that a freemason is a horrible being, whose soul is doomed to irretrievable perdition, and who has daily dealings with Satan, who is endowed with a thousand infernal qualities, and possesses a thousand atrocious means of working mischief, by casting malignant spells, and inflicting diseases on the faithful, making them succumb to temptation, and dragging them down along with himself to the bottomless pit.

Among the gorges of the little barren mountain of Abaron, a day's journey from Deir el Kammar, there is a spot whither the Maronites repair in numerous small parties with extreme secresy, to venerate the tomb of Moses, the law-giver of the Jews. The discovery of this

sacred tomb is thus recounted: In the year 1655, some
Maronite herdsmen, who were keeping their flocks on
the mountain, frequently found the tale of their goats
defective. The missing animals would return after one
or two days' absence, but, to the great surprise of their
keepers, they always brought back with them a delicious
perfume, which they retained for a long while. Curious
to ascertain the cause of such a prodigy, the men one
day followed the goats that were in the habit of straying
from the flock; and, after many devious wanderings
through broken glens and over precipices, they lost sight
of the goats near a cavern, the entrance to which was
closely screened by thick masses of foliage. The men
boldly entered the cavern after the goats, and immediately
recognized the admirable odor that had previously so
much perplexed them. They found, in the middle of the
cave, a tomb constructed of unhewn stone, and covered
with a marble slab that gave forth a dazzling lustre, and
bore this inscription, *Moosa Cadam Allah!—Moses the
servant of God.* Quitting the sacred spot, they made
all haste to Kanobin, to communicate what they had
seen to the patriarch. The odor with which they were
still impregnated amply corroborated the truth of their
report. This discovery produced an immense sensation
all over the mountain. Latins, Greeks, Armenians, and
Jews, all longed to become exclusive possessors of the
hallowed sepulchre of Moses. The heartburnings, intrigues, and broils that ensued were carried to such an
acrimonious and scandalous pitch that Bekir Pasha,
governor of Damascus, at last caused the entrance to the
tomb to be closed with a wall of solid masonry, and prohibited all approach to it, under severe penalties, in order
to take from the rival factions all pretext for disturbing
public tranquillity. "At present," say the Maronites,

"all that can be seen is the entrance to the grotto; but, at a certain season, a balmy atmosphere still issues from it, despite the thickness of the wall."

The group of mountains extending from the Nahr-el-Kelb to the Nahr-el-Kebir is commonly designated the Kesrouin, though Burckhardt confines this appellation to a much more limited district north of the former river, extending about fourteen miles in length from north to south, and from eight to twelve miles in breadth. The principal and almost sole produce being silk, mulberry trees are the chief growth of the soil; wheat and barley are sown, but not in sufficient quantity for the consumption of the people. The loom is, of course, an indispensable article of furniture in every house, and the manner of plying it is singular enough; the weaver sits in a hole sunk in the earthen floor. A man's wealth is estimated by the number of rotolas of silk which he makes, and the annual taxes paid to the government are calculated and apportioned on the same principle. The *miri*, or land-tax, is taken upon the mule-load of mulberry leaves, eight or ten trees in common years yielding one load. The custom, before the late armed interference of the allied powers, was for the Turks to exact one or two *miris* annually, by way of tribute, from the grand prince of the mountain, who, on his part, levied the same upon the inhabitants, besides several others on his own account. But despite the complaints long made by the Maronites respecting the taxes extorted from them, these were not to be compared in amount with those paid by the inhabitants of European countries. It is not the mere amount of taxation that crushes the energies of a nation, but its arbitrary character and the irregularity with which it is imposed. If the taxes were legally determined, and their proportion fixed in the Turkish empire, their pressure would scarcely be felt; but the first element of national wealth is wanting where no law secures the rights of property or defines the extent of the claims to which it is liable. In Lebanon the amount to be paid by each individual is determined by the several village sheikhs, and it may well be imagined that a part of the sums raised sticks to the fingers of the collectors.

But, after all, the condition of this people is essentially happy. Its rulers fear it, and dare not establish themselves in its provinces; its religion is free and respected; its churches and its convents crown the summits of its hills; its bells, that sound as a welcome token of liberty and independence, peal their summons to prayer night and day; it is governed by its own hereditary chieftains and by the clergy it loves; a strict but equitable system of police preserves order and security in the villages; property is respected, and transmitted from father to son; commerce is active; the manners of the people perfectly simple and pure. Rarely is there seen a population whose appearance bespeaks better health, more native nobility, and a higher civilization than that of these men of Lebanon. Education, though limited to reading, writing, arithmetic, and the catechism, is universal among them, and gives them a deserved superiority over the other tribes of Syria.

But, though the ability to read and write be thus general among the Maronites, it must not be inferred that they are a literary people. Far from it; the book-learning of all classes, both clergy and laity, can hardly be rated too low. There are native printing-presses at work in some of the monasteries, but the sheets they issue are all of an ecclesiastical kind—chiefly portions of the Scripture or mass-books in Syriac, which few, even of the clergy, understand, though they repeat them by rote.

The ignorance respecting even the most ordinary subjects of thought, which is to be found in some of the more retired districts, is really curious. A Frenchman was asked by a Maronite if they had a moon in his country. A European woman having found her way into a village of Lebanon, some Maronite females laid violent hands on her, that they might satisfy themselves whether or not the women of Europe and those of Lebanon belong to the same species. Lady Frances Egerton complains that, in her journey through the mountains, there was no such thing as keeping the women out of her room. "If I fastened my door, they called, and knocked, and battered at it until I feared that it would yield to their efforts, and this at five o'clock in the morning, whilst I was in bed, as well as at other times. If the door was left a moment unfastened, then they flocked in. If I did not admit them, then they peeped through every crevice, and I was obliged to bolster up the door with cushions and curtains. It is sad that in a country where the men are particularly well bred and even polished in their manners, and where they are never intrusive or troublesome, the women should be in so degraded and inferior a state. In fact, until they are educated and permitted to mix with the men, this country can never attain a proper degree of civilization."

The Maronites are gay in their attire. Their turbans, of various forms, are of every color except the forbidden green, the sacred color of the Moslems. They sometimes wear the striped abbas of the Druses, but more generally a short red jacket over a parti-colored vest; embroidery of silk or gold cord is not spared by those who have the means of procuring such finery, and their crimson and yellow sashes sustain a little portable armory of silver-mounted khanjars, yataghans, and pistols.

The usual apparel of the women, both Maronite and

Druse, consists of an outer pelisse, generally blue, and fringed with silk cord: it is open in front, and has sleeves to the elbow; under this is another robe, with sleeves open to the wrist: a shawl round the waist, long and full trousers, with painted toes or yellow slippers, complete the costume. But the most remarkable peculiarities of their dress are the immense silver ear-rings hanging forward on the neck, the large bell-shaped silver bobs they wear upon their long plaits of hair, and above all the tantoor.

The tantoor is a tube of gold, silver, or even tin, according to the wealth of the wearer, measuring in size from the diameter of an inch and a half at the smaller extremity, to three inches at the other, where it terminates like the mouth of a trumpet. If the smaller end were closed, it might serve for a drinking cup; and in Germany glasses of the same form and size are still occasionally used. In some villages the tantoor is a gilded buffalo's horn. But whatever be the material, this ornament is the peculiar and distinguishing sign of the matron condition. Maidens are never allowed to wear the honored emblem, with certain rare exceptions in favor of those belonging to important families; and those privileged young ladies wear their horns "with a difference," so that no native can mistake them for married women. The broad end of the tantoor is fixed to a pad on the top of the head by two silk cords, which, after being wound round the head, hang behind nearly to the ground, terminating in large tassels, that among the better classes are capped with silver. The narrow end commonly projects over the forehead at an angle of 45°, like the horn of a unicorn, and in this position it might indeed serve as a formidable weapon of offence. But the mode of wearing it is subject to endless variations; it points forward, backward, directly upward, to the right or to the left: its shape too is no less diversified; sometimes it assumes the form of a truncated cone five or six inches long; sometimes of two such figures joined at their narrow ends; sometimes it is in the shape of a funnel, more than a foot long, projecting from the side of the head, with the broad end outward, and looking like a very large hearing-trumpet.

There are several convents of nuns in the Kesrouan, as, for instance, the convent at Antoura, opposite to that of the French Lazarists. One of the superiors and two of the sisters formerly were, and, if alive still, are Ethiopian negresses. The Convent of the Bekerke, in this vicinity, is memorable as having been founded by the notorious Hendye, the romantic history of whose crimes is related by Volney.

She was a young Maronite damsel, whose extraordinary way of life attracted general attention about the year 1775. She fasted, wore haircloth, had the gift of tears; everybody looked on her as a model of piety, and many esteemed her a saint. It was but one step more to a reputation for working miracles; and, in fact, a rumor of this kind was soon spread. Availing herself of this general enthusiasm, Hendye aspired to be the foundress of a new order. To build a convent funds were necessary. The foundress appealed to the piety of her partisans, and offerings poured in to so large an amount that in a few years she was enabled to erect two large mansions of hewn stone, the construction of which must have cost twenty-five thousand dollars. The Kourkeh was soon peopled with monks and nuns. The patriarch for the time being was the director-general. Other offices, great and small, were conferred on divers priests and candidates, who were established in one of the houses.

For a long while everything went on as well as possible. It is true that many nuns died; but the blame was laid upon the air, and it was difficult to imagine the real cause. Hendye reigned over her little kingdom for nearly twenty years, when an unforeseen accident threw everything into confusion. A factor traveling from Damascus to Beyrout in the summer was overtaken by night near this convent; the gates were shut, the hour unseasonable; and as he did not wish to give trouble, he contented himself with a bed of straw, and laid himself down in the outer court, waiting the return of day. He had only slept a few hours when he was awakened by a sudden noise of doors and bolts. From one of the doors issued three women with spades and shovels in their hands, who were followed by two men bearing a long white bundle that appeared very heavy. They proceeded toward an adjoining piece of ground full of stones and rubbish, where the men deposited their load, dug a hole, into which they put it, and covering it with earth, trod it down with their feet, after which they all returned to the house. The sight of men with nuns, and this bundle thus mysteriously buried by night, amazed the traveler, and in anxiety and fear he hastily departed to Beyrout before daybreak. He was acquainted with a merchant in that town, who some months before had placed two of his daughters in the Kourkeh, with a portion equaling two thousand dollars. He went in search of him, still perplexed with what he had seen, but burning with impatience to recount his adventure. They seat themselves cross-legged, the long pipes are lighted, and coffee brought in. The merchant makes inquiries respecting his journey, and is told that the traveler passed the night near the Kourkeh. Further particulars are asked; and at length the visitor, no longer able to contain himself, whispers his host what he had seen. The merchant listened with surprise; one of his daughters he knew was ill, and he could not but remark that a great many nuns died. Tormented with these thoughts, and the dismal suspicions they occasioned, he mounts his horse, and accompanied by his friend repairs to the convent, where he asks to see his daughters. He is told they are sick. He insists they shall be brought to him; this is angrily refused; and the more he persists the more peremptory is the refusal, till at last his suspicions are converted into certainty. Leaving the convent in an agony of despair, he went to Deir el Kammar and laid all the circumstances before Saad, *Kiaya*, or minister of Prince Yousef, chief of the mountain, who ordered a body of horse to accompany him, and, if refused admission, to break into the convent by force. The cadi also took part with the merchant: the ground where the bundle had been buried was opened, and a dead body found, which the unhappy father discovered to be that of his youngest daughter; the other was found confined in the convent and almost dead. She revealed a scene of such abominable wickedness as almost petrified the hearers, and to which she, like her sister, was about to fall a victim. The pretended saint being seized, acted her part with great firmness; and a prosecution was begun against the priests and the patriarch. The latter was suspended and deposed. The affair was brought to Rome in 1776; the Propaganda instituted an inquiry, and discovered scenes of the most infamous profligacy and the most horrible cruelty. It was proved that Hendye destroyed her nuns, sometimes to get their property into her hands, at other times because they were not submissive to her will; that this infamous woman not only communicated, but even consecrated the host and said mass; that she had holes under her bed by which perfumes were introduced at the moment she pretended to be in ecstasy and under the influence of the Holy Ghost; that she had a faction that cried her up, and gave out that she was the mother of God returned to earth, and a thousand other extravagances. Notwithstanding all this, she retained a party powerful enough to prevent the severe punishment she merited. She was shut up in several convents, from which she frequently managed to escape. In 1783 she was at the visitation of Antoura, and the emir of the Druses interested himself in her behalf. She died in the year 1802, at the age of seventy—a hypocrite to the very last; and such was the rigor of her penances and mortification that the Maronites to this day revere her as a saint.

There is a large and well-built Latin convent in this village of Maalakha, the doors of which are invitingly open to tourists, but we have no time to stop even to wish them God-speed in their work among this heathenish people. We notice hereabouts that the mulberry tree is cultivated with great care and in great quantity, from which we infer that the pious monks of the convent are endeavoring to encourage the manufacture of silk among the people.

Here at Maalakha we reach a branch of what is known as the "French road," which runs from Damascus to Beyrout. This branch is about six miles in length, and is as well macadamized as any road in Europe. It looks more like civilization than anything we have before seen in Syria.

Six miles farther on we strike upon the great road itself, and notice a number of substantial French buildings, erected by the company for the accommodation of its employés. This road was built a few years since by a company of French capitalists, and, as before stated, runs between Beyrout and Damascus, a distance of probably eighty miles or more. It is constructed with great care, and its engineering shows skill and judgment. Its zig-zag course up and down the mountains which it crosses makes the grade at all times easy, while its surface is smooth and hard as pounded stone can make it. Over this road the company have exclusive right to run diligences and freight wagons. Of the latter we notice great numbers on the road, going to and coming from Damascus, each of which is loaded to its utmost capacity with freight. The diligences make the trip from city to city in about one day, and it is by far the most comfortable way of reaching Damascus from the sea-coast.

Next to a railroad, nothing could be more opportune for the people of Northern Syria than this splendid turnpike, and if its effect upon them should be to open their eyes to the advantages of enterprise and improvement, the large expenditure will prove advantageous, even though the company itself should not reap very large dividends for some years to come.

Shortly after coming upon this road we met the Turkish governor of Maalakha and his suite returning from an afternoon ride. The governor is a fine-looking man, about thirty years of age, splendidly dressed, and still more splendidly mounted. His son rides near him, on a beautiful Arabian horse, with an attendant on either side. Before his excellency one of the guards carries a bunch of black ostrich feathers, on a long staff, which, we presume, is the insignia of his rank and position. About twenty horsemen accompany him as a guard, each with a Turkish scimetar at his side and a brace of pistols in his belt. The cavalcade is quite imposing, and the pleasant smile and bow which our little party receives from the governor on passing impresses us favorably with his good-breeding. Whether he would be as polite to those over whom he has control is another question; we should rather guess not.

About sundown we leave the valley and commence the ascent of the eastern slope of Lebanon, and shortly after this we find our tents pitched on a level plateau, looking down into the valley. We retire early and sleep soundly, for we have had a hard day's ride, and greatly need the wooings of "Nature's sweet restorer, balmy sleep."

Next morning early, we are again in our saddles, *en route* for Beyrout. The road is excellent; we feel jubilant at the thought of being near our journey's end in Syria, and we let our horses gallop along at a good rate of speed. Once, however, we come very near being unhorsed by the force of the winds which sweep over these mountain ranges, and until we can round a point where the winds have less power, we are obliged to move along very carefully.

The views to be had from various points of this French road—running, as it does, for a considerable distance along the crest of the mountain, and then gradually sloping down toward the Mediterranean—are exceeedingly fine, and once daguerreotyped upon the mind, they can never be forgotten.

A long way before reaching Beyrout we have a view of the city and of all the valley stretching between the western slopes of Lebanon and the deep blue sea. Beneath us lies the town with its domes, its minarets, its embattled walls, and its old fortresses overgrown with a forest of creeping plants, blossoms and wild fig trees; then the broad bay, with the anchored barks heaving dreamily on its swelling bosom; and beyond it the sombre masses of the mountain chain stretching away toward Tripoli. Eastward, the mighty wall of Lebanon stands before us in indescribable majesty. Looking up at its gleaming white ridges from this position, we have no difficulty in accounting for the name of Lebanon, that is, the "Milky Mountain." The terrace-plots of cultivation that climb its flanks are here concealed from view, so that the whole mountain side seems composed only of immense masses of naked whitish rock, severed by deep wild ravines, running down precipitously to the plain. No one would suspect among these rocks the existence of a multitude of delicious glens and thriving villages, inhabited by a numerous population of mountaineers, hardy, industrious, and brave.

Between us and the foot of the mountain extends a broad region of undulating greenwood, full of beauty. In the foreground is a richly cultivated plain, overgrown with trees that completely hide the soil, and sprinkled with white houses and roofs, like chalky islands in a sea of verdure; the view is then narrowed in by a graceful hill, crowned with a Greek convent, the blue domes of which are overtopped by the umbrella-like heads of a few spreading pine trees. The sides of the hill descend to the sea by a series of terraces, propped up with stone walls, and thickly planted with olives and mulberries. Beyond the hill there is a second plain, where the river winds its lengthened way through woods of evergreen oak; this plain extends the whole way to the gilded flanks of the mountains. The mountains do not tower up at once from their base; they begin with hills, like huge blocks of stone, some rounded, others almost square, each partially covered with vegetation on its summit, and sustaining a village or a monastery glittering in the sun. Their sides, of cream-colored stone, rent and shattered by earthquakes, gleam and sparkle in the checkered light. Broader masses succeed these lower eminences, topped with platforms of one or two leagues in width, furrowed with the deep beds of torrents and dark precipitous glens. Beyond these platforms the mountains begin to rise almost perpendicularly, but still dotted here and there with black patches of cedars and pines, and now and then exhibiting a convent almost inaccessible, and looking as if suspended on the very verge of the precipice.

Lastly, behind this second chain the true Lebanon rears its lofty head, too remote to enable the eye to judge of the forms of its sides or the character of its surface. Its masses melt indefinitely into the transparent air of which they seem to make a part. The sun appears to rest eternally on the gilded angles of its crests, the varied tints of its rays rendering them undistinguishable now from the snow that remains on their highest points till the middle of summer, and now from the purple clouds of the morning that float like enchanted islands in the blue expanse of heaven. From noon till two or three o'clock the entire summit of the mountain is involved in a blaze of radiance.

From this point we can see that the whole southern and western portion of the promontory of Beyrout is composed of exceedingly fine sand, thrown up into hills by the winds. On this spot, situated a short distance southeast of the town, there exists a grove of pine trees, planted by the celebrated emir of the Druses, Fakr-ed-Deen, (or, as he is commonly called, Faccardine), for the purpose, it is said, of arresting the progress of the shifting sands, which threatened destruction to the town and its rich environs. Thus far the emir's object has been fulfilled, and another good effect has ensued, which he could not have foreseen, for the town, which was previously unhealthy, has ceased to be so since the trees were planted, but the grove is not sufficiently extensive, and the danger threatened by the sands is but partially overcome. The Duc de Raguse, who has looked upon the town with an eye practiced in engineering speculations, asserts that the sands are advancing toward it by a constant and regular progression; they gain every year from four-and-twenty to thirty yards, and yet no one thinks of doing anything to stay them. Houses, and even trees, become completely buried in a few months, gradually disappearing under the continual accumulation of the almost impalpable grains. The same fate awaits the town, and the period when it will be consummated may even be calculated with tolerable precision. This is a melancholy spectacle even for a stranger; yet the inhabitants of Beyrout seem to take no heed of it, and enjoy the present moment without concerning themselves about the future.

This dreary and desolate region is an exact representation in miniature of the Great Desert; it is a strip of the Egyptian waste transplanted to the foot of Lebanon, and surrounded by magnificent oases. To complete the illusion, after you have wandered but ten minutes through its labyrinths, you may find yourself utterly ignorant of your position and bearings. The sandy hillocks conceal the horizon on all sides; no track of man or beast is discernible on the unstable ground that shifts with every breeze, and all around you is as dismal a wilderness as imagination can conceive—the aspect of a storm without its noise, but with its images of wreck and death. This red sand, the Arabs tell you, is not brought hither by the winds nor accumulated by the sea, but thrown up by a subterranean torrent communicating with the deserts of Gaza and El Arish; they hold it for an established fact that there are springs of sand as well as springs of water; and, in confirmation of this opinion, they point to the manifest difference in color and other physical characters between the sands of this desert and those of the sea-shore.

A growth of two centuries and a quarter has reared up Fakr-ed-Deen's grove into a noble forest; the stems of the trees shoot up without a branch to a height of from sixty to eighty feet, and their motionless broad arms locking together form an immense verdant canopy over a soil as soft as velvet to the tread Except upon the beaten paths that wind between the trunks of the trees the ground is everywhere covered with a light downy turf, thickly set with flowers of the brightest red; the bulbs of the wild hyacinths are so large that they do not break beneath the horses' hoofs.

We also have a fine view, from this point, of the Mohammedan burial-ground, just outside of Beyrout, a most lovely spot, where the dead sleep well and are not forgotten by the living.

Few things strike the traveler in the East more than the tender piety of the Moslems toward their dead; their habits, in this respect, present an intense contrast with our own, and one that is wholly to our disadvantage. We, boasting a faith that robs death of its sting and the grave of its victory, habitually violate the consoling spirit of our religion; we picture to ourselves death under the most revolting emblems; we make the last resting-places of our kindred ugly and dismal to the eye, and not to be thought of but with shuddering repugnance. Why is this? Whence this unchristian, this Egyptian parade of death's heads and cross-bones—this perverse brooding over the horrors of the charnel-house? If we hated the memory of our departed friends, how could we more strongly display our aversion than by thrusting away from us their living images, and forcing ourselves to think of them only as what humanity shrinks from with loathing? It is otherwise in the East. There " they bury a friend, and the next day they plant flowers on his grave; and ever afterward they tend and water them, visiting them regularly once a week, and always when they walk out for health or pleasure, turning their steps habitually to the burial-ground." The tenant of the tomb is, to the last, numbered as one of the family; and in every household you may find, among bearded men and aged matrons, the happy faith of the little maid in Wordsworth's well-known lines. It is not the Moslems who mourn as those that have no hope; happier than too many Westerns, they can still believe and pray.

There is something exceedingly touching in the little artless contrivances by which the people of the East endeavor to lighten the gloom of the grave, and to connect it with all that is most beautiful and life-like in nature. They plant on it myrtles, roses, and other fragrant shrubs, and deck it day by day with fresh-culled flowers; they hang over it cages of singing birds, which are fed morning and evening with religious care; they make receptacles for water in the tombstone, that the fowls of the air may drink thence, and thus something living acknowledge the charity of him who sleeps below; and they take care to leave a square opening in the side of the masonry, that the narrow house may not be utterly shut up from the light and the breath of heaven. The women, who are the most regular frequenters of the burial-ground, often carry their food with them; the tombstone is their table; they leave a place for the dead to sit with them, putting the best morsels before it; and they talk with him as if he was living by their side.

Beyrout seen thus from a distance, with quaint houses and green trees dotting the landscape, and the long line of macadamized road twisting and turning down the mountain side, and then running in a straight line through the valley toward the city, is exceedingly picturesque and beautiful.

And then the sea, deeply, darkly, beautifully blue—how it seems to woo us to its embrace—and how the very winds which come from off it seem to whisper of home and friends! For weeks we have been without letters, without newspapers, without a word of any kind from our own native land, and we feel that it will be like begining life anew to get once more among a civilized people.

So soon as we have passed the last descent, and stopped for a few moments to lunch, in a fig tree orchard by the road side, we hasten onward and at about two P. M. reach the city of Beyrout.

CHAPTER XVIII.

BEYROUT.

BEYROUT is the point at which nearly all travelers close their pilgrimage through Palestine; and yet, for many reasons, it is the very point from which it should be commenced.

In commencing at Jaffa and coming northward, you see the worst parts of Palestine first, and the mind is shocked at what seems an irreconcilable difference between the biblical description of this land and its actual condition. Instead of a "fair" land—a land of "watercourses and springs bursting out from the rocks,"—a land "of olives, and pomegranates, and fig trees,"—a land "flowing with milk and honey," you only see mountains of rock and valleys of barrenness, dry beds of brooks and wells without water. The very rocks of the paths over which you travel seem so old, and gray, and worm-eaten—without moss, or tree, or shrub to relieve their hideousness—that you instinctively shrink from them as something accursed of both God and man!

And then in approaching Jerusalem from the Jaffa road every previous conception of its beauty—if not of its holiness—vanishes from the mind. Tired, and weary, and heartsick at what you have already seen, you reach a barren summit of rock, to see in the distance only the old walls of the city, rough, jagged, and uninviting, with here and there a convent, a hospital, and a few straggling houses outside of the city walls. The " holy city"—the " city of the Great King"—the city which you have thought of and dreamt of as one whose

> "Gates are set with precious pearls,
> And streets all paved with gold,"

is nowhere to be seen, and the disappointment which comes over the soul will cleave to it for days and weeks, if not throughout all the remainder of the tour through Palestine.

In reversing the route—that is, in starting from Beyrout and closing the trip with Jaffa—all this would be changed. After visiting Baalbec and Damascus your course would lay southward, over plains, some of which are beautiful to look upon—over mountains, the ruggedness of which is relieved in part by the surrounding plains and a few trees—by flowing brooks and outgushing fountains. And though the country through which you would thus pass would probably not be equal in all respects to the conceptions which you have formed, yet in a measure it will be found to correspond with the biblical record of what Palestine undoubtedly was in the day of its greatest glory.

And then, too, in approaching Jerusalem by the Damascus road, you have, from the summit of Mount Scopus a complete panorama of the city, with the Mount of Olives and the Valley of Jehoshaphat to add to its picturesque beauty. Even from this point you may feel some disappointment in your first view of the Holy City, but nothing in comparison with that which every traveler must feel in approaching it by the Jaffa road.

There is another advantage in starting from Beyrout. The first great object of every Christian tourist in visiting Palestine is to trace the footsteps of Jesus, and in doing this the route from Beyrout southward is far preferable. First you visit Nazareth, where all his youthful years were spent—then Cana, where he performed his first miracle—then Nain, where he gave back to life the only son of a widow—then the Sea of Galilee, where more than three years of his life and ministry were spent—then Jerusalem, where he lived, and suffered, and died, and rose again! From Jerusalem you visit Bethany, and Jericho, and the Jordan, and Bethlehem, and, after returning, spend such further time in the Holy City as inclination dictates.

Travelers usually spend but four or five days in Jerusalem, and then, with the prospect of a long trip before them, they hasten on to complete their journey, and, when completed, spend their surplus of time in Beyrout; whereas, if they went from this city southward, and found on reaching Jerusalem that they could conveniently spend two or three weeks more in Palestine, no better use could be made of this time than by spending it in examining the objects of interest in the Holy City.

The principal objection urged against this change of route is, that the port of Jaffa is not as accessible to steamers as Beyrout, and that one might have to wait there some time for a steamer, which would be more irksome than to wait at Beyrout.

While there is some truth and some force in this objection, yet the advantages of this route are so great that the traveler can well afford to take the risk of waiting a few days for a steamer; and now that there is a telegraph line between Jaffa and Jerusalem, one could easily learn before leaving the latter city what the probabilities of a steamer's arrival were, and if unfavorable, he could remain in Jerusalem until the steamer came along.

From Kelly's "best and most recent authorities on Syria and the Holy Land," we may quote the impressions and experience of another tourist, whose good fortune it was to approach Palestine by the way of Beyrout. He says: "The traveler whose good fortune it has been to make his first approach to Syria by sea, and to land at Beyrout, must always esteem it a happy coincidence that the most frequented port on all the coast is likewise precisely the point where a man of taste and quick feeling would choose to receive his first impressions of the country. Long before the vessel nears the shore, the sunlit peaks and wavy ridges of Lebanon are seen marking the blue sky, while its sides are hid from sight by the haze upon the waters; by and by the craggy masses of the mountain come forth like airy promontories; the eye gradually distinguishes the deep and dark valleys that cleave its flanks; the rocky crests assume a bolder outline; and you half discern villages scattered on the mountain-sides, and monasteries like feudal fortresses crowning their summits. Each object caught sight of is hailed with delight; all hands are on deck; every eye is strained, and each gazer has continually some new discovery to impart to his companions. It is always an exciting thing to have a mountain land in view as the termination of a sea voyage; but here the charm is felt with tenfold strength, for the land before you is endeared by a host of associations linked with your earliest and most hallowed recollections.

"Meanwhile, the vessel holds on its course; the land grows beneath the eye; the white walls of the countryhouses, spread along the plain at the foot of the mountain, peep out with a look of welcome from between their clustering trees, and the air is loaded with the perfumed breath of orange and lemon blossoms. At last the anchor is dropped, and you are riding in the bay of Beyrout in front of a long promontory rising gradually from the water, above which are seen the minarets and towers of the town, and beyond them the summits of the Jebel Sunnin, and the Jebel Kneese, and the long lines of the Jebel el Drus.

"If you have the good fortune to escape being condemned to quarantine (supposing that any is still enforced), a boat conveys you a distance of about a mile to the *marina*, or quay, thronged with Arabs in all the gay diversity of their picturesque costumes and bristling weapons. The scene exhibits all the lively bustle of a European sea-port. Boats are continually plying between the shore and the trading vessels from Europe anchored in the roads; porters are carrying bales of merchandise to and fro; you hear the shrill cries of the Arabs wrangling on the quay, and the uncouth and dismal sounds uttered by the camels as they are made to kneel down to be loaded. Before you can step out of your boat on the wet sands, you are caught up by some bare-legged Arabs, who carry you in their arms to the entrance of a narrow, gloomy street, built on the side of a rapid slope. Everything about you gives you indisputable assurance that you are treading on Eastern ground.

"Your officious friends now beset you with a clamorous demand for *bucksheesh, bucksheesh!* perhaps at the same time significantly rubbing together the tips of their thumbs and fore-fingers. You gather from this pantomime that *bucksheesh* is Arabic for those familiar sounds of Frangistan, 'summat to drink,' 'pourboire,' 'trinkgeld;' and having thus learned the first word of a new vocabulary, you need not fear that you will be allowed to let it slip very soon from your memory."

We have written at some length on this change of route, for it was one that deeply impressed us during our whole tour through Palestine ; and if, from what we have written, other travelers are saved the mistake which we have made, we shall be amply repaid for the pains we have taken to put them upon a better track.

Before entering upon a description of Beyrout and its surroundings, a few thoughts with reference to Syria as a whole may not be out of place.

There is not, perhaps, in the world, a country so remarkable as Syria for the lustre of its early glories, the vicissitudes of its fortunes, and the blood that has drenched its soil. Its admirable fertility, the variety and beauty of its climate, and its advantageous position in the very heart of the ancient world, rendered it the chosen abode of early commerce and civilization ; but these very advantages excited the ambition of conquerors, and many a time brought down on Syria the desolating ravages of war.

The traveler treads at every step on the remains of perished cities, and of monuments of art and industry that testify the vast population, the wealth, energy, and grandeur of the land in days gone by. To Syria we owe the origin of our written characters ; here commerce and navigation began their humanizing career, and here a multitude of useful arts and discoveries had birth, or were carried to the highest degree of perfection ; and—infinitely more momentous thought to the Christian—here was prepared, developed and consummated that stupendous series of events on which man rests his hopes for eternity.

Formerly one of the earliest abodes of almost all religions, Syria still teems with the mute memorials or their living representatives. On the eastern side of the hills of Jordan, and over the plains of Manasseh and Gad, are found monuments apparently of Buddhist origin. They resemble those of the Druid age in England, and carry us back in imagination to the times when the adventurous ships of Tyre and Sidon transplanted into that remote island the elements of civilization and a hierarchical polity.

"The languages of antiquity," says Mr. Farren (Letter to Lord Lindsay), "are the living tongues of Syria, and in their compounds is still familiar the name of Britain, derived from Phœnician origin." *Beret anic*, he says, would imply in Arabic "the land of tin," tantamount to the Cassiterides of Herodotus; and he is inclined to think that the name Νῆσοι Βρεταννικαι is derived from it.

It would be erroneous to suppose that Christianity, Judaism and Mohammedanism monopolize the land between them. The Anzary mountains still shelter in their fastnesses the rites and the descendants of ancient Paganism; there still subsist in Syria the mysterious initiations of the *Druse*, the infamous rites of the *Ismeylee*, the adoration of the devil by the *Yezeedee*, and the practical pantheism of the *Koord;* whilst in a part of Shechem, or the modern Nablous, several families, descended from the revolted tribes, preserve their ancient Pentateuch and still offer upon Gerizim the rites and sacrifices of the Samaritan worship.

It would seem, as though by a perpetual law, Syria were peculiarly marked out as an arena whereon to determine mighty issues, such as involve the destinies of mankind at large. How often has the lot of empires and nations been decided here, from the gray dawn of time down to our own days! Jews, Assyrians, Chaldeans, Macedonians, Romans, Saracens, Western Christians, Tatars, Turks and Egyptians, have all left their bones to bleach upon this common battle-ground of the nations. It was the resistance offered to Napoleon by the petty fortress of Acre which rolled back on Europe the tide of conquest that otherwise had swept over Asia.

Our stay in Beyrout has lasted for nearly a week, waiting for a steamer for Constantinople ; and during the time we have had ample opportunity to see and learn all about the place.

In many respects it is by far the best city in Syria. Its streets are generally good, its houses comfortable, and many of them even luxurious ; its inhabitants industrious, and quite as enterprising as you could possibly expect in a country like this ; its bazaars well supplied with Oriental and European goods, and the merchants about as honest as you could hope to find in a country where the common custom is to ask two prices for everything, and get all they can, especially from travelers. It is said to contain about fifty thousand inhabitants, though we should think this an over-estimate.

Beyrout is a place of great antiquity, having given its name to Baal Berith, a Phœnician deity, to whom there was a temple here ; Augustus made it a Roman colony, and called it, after his daughter, Colonia Felix Julia. It still asserts, by the beauty of its scenery, its admirable climate, and the fertility of its environs, its ancient claim to the epithet *Happy;* but it presents few architectural remains of the greatness it attained to under the emperors, one of whom, Justinian, styled it "the nurse of the law," and conferred on it, in conjunction with Rome and Constantinople, the exclusive right to have professors who should expound the Roman jurisprudence. Some faint trace of the magnificent baths and theatre erected by Agrippa, the grandson of Herod the Great, may still be seen on the north of the town ; portions of tesselated pavements and shafts of columns are found in the gardens and along the sea-shore; and a great part of the quay, facing the harbor, is constructed of fragments of pillars, some of which appear to have been of the largest kind, and highly finished. Though these remains are of little value in the eyes of the antiquary, they may, as old Sandys has it, "instruct the pensive beholder with their exemplary frailtie."

In every Eastern town, the stranger desirous of seeing "life in the streets" turns his steps to the bazaars, where all the retail trade is carried on, and where all who have business and all who have none are continually congregated. If the visitor looks in Beyrout for bazaars answering to the description of those of Constantinople, Cairo, or Damascus, he will, of course, be disappointed; but if his expectations are more moderate he will derive much pleasure from the animated and picturesque scenes exhibited in the throned marts even of this little city. People of all ranks and conditions, clad in all the costumes of the country, are incessantly coming and going; priests, dervishes, Maronites, Druses, Turks, and Arabs, Armenians, and Jews; women like sheeted ghosts, and slaves of both sexes, black, brown, and white, pass in review before him. He finds an endless fund of amusement in watching the occupations, attitudes, and gestures of the ever-changing groups that mingle and cross each other in every direction; the most trivial circumstances of their every-day habits are full of novelty for him. He will not fail, for instance, to be struck with their extraordinary attachment to the sitting, or rather squatting, posture, with their heels tucked under them. With them almost every occupation is sedentary; you may see the blacksmith sitting and hammering his iron; the carpenter sitting and hewing his wood or planing his plank, and the women sitting and washing their clothes. It is for the sake of being able to reach every article of their stock without standing up that the merchants carry on their business in little shops not more than five or six feet square. You are not surprised to see the tailor sitting cross-legged; he does so all the world over; but the Eastern tailor does not even quit his shopboard to measure you, but, stretching out his arm, takes your dimensions with a plummet and line.

The great variety of sects and creeds assembled in Beyrout is nowhere more strikingly observed than in the bazaar. If it rarely happens that all the shops are open, on the other hand it would be almost as extraordinary a circumstance to find them all closed on any one day. It is always holiday with some portion or another of the population, and workday for the rest. Three out of the seven days of the week are Sabbaths—Friday for the Moslems, Saturday for the Jews, and Sunday for the Christians. Besides this, the United and Schismatic Greeks, the Maronites and the Armenians, keep so many saints' days that the merchants and poor artisans who earn their bread day by day are consequently defrauded of much valuable time. But, indeed, time is a commodity nowhere jealously prized in the East.

The shopkeepers of the different races may be distinguished as readily by their manner of doing business as by their dress. The sedate Turk is a man of few words, and seldom utters more than is strictly necessary. He sets his goods before you, names their price, and leaves you to do as you please about buying. You need not think of offering him a lower bidding; he will not bate a para, and the only reply he will make will be to take back the article in question and return it to its place.

The Christian talks more; he is anxious to recommend his goods, and is not offended by the offer of a reasonable price, though it be lower than his first demand. He knows that there are people who take pleasure in higgling and cheapening, and who will never make a purchase unless they can obtain it at a reduced rate; he therefore makes his arrangements accordingly.

But if the customer has a genuine taste for the art and mystery of shopping, the Arab is, by all means, the man for his money. Inshallah! you shall not make any purchase of him, unless it be for a very trifling amount indeed, under half an hour's bargaining, or more. When you have found the article you want, instead of flippantly demanding its price, throwing down the money, and carrying off your purchase, you prepare yourself very deliberately for a long and interesting set-to. You mount upon the *mustabah* or platform, on which the shopkeeper sits, seat yourself at your ease, fill and light your pipe, and then comes the war of words. An offer of half the price demanded is a very good move to begin with on your part. It is, of course, rejected, but it brings your antagonist to somewhat closer quarters; and so you both go on, he lowering his demand and you rising in your offers, with sundry episodes and digressions touching last year's figs, or any other irrelevant topic of conversation, till at last the business is brought to a conclusion, and the bargain is struck for a sum generally half-way between that first demanded and that first offered. When you deal with an Arab, whatever be the subject of the bargain—shop-goods, horseflesh, or personal services—it would be the most impolitic thing in the world to accede to the first price demanded, even though you should think it not exorbitant. If the man accepts your money, it will not be long before he repents of what he has done, and then you will find you have brought down an old house about your ears. The novelty of the thing disconcerts him, and, pondering over the matter, he comes to the conclusion that you are a cheat and himself an injured innocent. Perhaps he will kick off his shoes and run about like a madman, slapping his face and crying out, " Oh my sorrow !" But it more usually happens that, on your imprudently committing yourself by assenting to his first demand, he asks a quarter or a third more ; it will then be too late for you to retrieve your error, for when, after much debate, you again close with him, he again steps back in the same proportion as before.

As for the Jew, he is the same in all countries and under every garb. You may know him at once by his importunate eagerness to obtain custom, his volubility of speech and his grotesque gesticulation, which seems the more strange by contrast with the gravity and sedateness of the Moslems.

The only shops containing native manufactures somewhat worthy of note are those of the silk-mercers. After having seen the coarse machinery in use, one can hardly conceive how such beautiful textures can be produced by such clumsy means. At several of the shops where we stop to examine silk goods, we find in an adjoining room, and sometimes in the same room, an illy-constructed hand-loom, somewhat after the fashion of the old looms on which our great-grandmothers used to weave rag carpets in this country ; and on these we observe native Syrians weaving brocades which in fineness of quality and brilliancy of color equal, or at least rival, those manufactured at Brussels and Lyons. Formerly these silks were more or less employed in the dress of all classes of the population, but lately they have been greatly supplanted by the cheaper goods of Europe. Still the rich gold and silver brocades manufactured in Beyrout and vicinity are in much demand among the wealthy Syrians as the chief material for their gala dresses. Caftans made of this gorgeous material have a most brilliant effect. The silk sashes of Beyrout are also much esteemed, and are exported to different parts of the East. We heard of these before leaving Cairo, through Abd-el-Atti, Mr. Prime's old dragoman, who, one day broadly hinted that on reaching Beyrout we would find sashes which would make "elegant presents to friends"—meaning, of course, that he should not be forgotten in the distribution, as he added immediately that "it would be entirely safe to trust our own dragoman, who would return to Cairo with their delivery."

The money-lenders and traffickers in specie in Beyrout cannot fail to attract the attention of the traveler, and the probabilities are that he will be compelled to have more or less dealings with them, in the settling up of affairs with his dragoman, muleteers, servants, etc. Here, as elsewhere in the East, this kind of traffic is mostly confined to the Jews; and it may be supposed that the obloquy to which they are subjected adds not a little to the exorbitance of their demands. They form a numerous body throughout all Syria—at Jaffa, Jerusalem, Damascus, Beyrout, and in some of the smaller towns of Palestine.

It must not be forgotten that the right of the Jews to lend on heavy interest (usury) to strangers is specifically recognized by the Mosaic law, and it cannot be wondered at that they should avail themselves of it; but it is a main cause of the opprobrium to which they are subjected.

But the sin of usury is not monopolized by the Jews to the entire exclusion of the Moslems. The latter have much degenerated from the primitive fervor of Islamism, particularly in Syria, and have invented a multitude of subterfuges and gross tricks by which they contrive to combine a fanatical reverence for the dogmas of the Kur-an, with a most impudent disregard for its practical morality. The following is the device by which the Moslem usurer quiets his conscience and keeps within the strict letter of the law. The borrower makes himself liable, before the cadi, for the sum lent, together with the interest agreed on; the contract being to this effect, that Abu Thaleb acknowledges himself indebted to Hadji Ismael for so much money on account of value received, to wit, one or more bales of soap, indigo, etc. The matter is thus put upon a perfectly legal footing, and Hadji Ismael figures in the honorable light of a merchant deriving his gain from the fair and open ways of commerce. The contract being settled, the two parties proceed to the hadji's house, who hands over the money in question to the other, after deducting the interest agreed on. He then, with the utmost gravity, takes the first small animal he can lay his hands on (he generally has a stock of cats by him for this purpose), lays two small bundles of the goods mentioned in the bond on the animal's back, and delivers it, thus loaded, to his customer, who, with no less gravity, walks away with his purchase. The sale is thus completed, and the interest comes to be regarded only as a bucksheesh. The loan, it is to be observed, is always for a very short term, and the creditor takes care to secure himself against all contingencies by exacting a pledge from his debtor, often of double the value of the money lent.

The diversity of costume in the streets of Beyrout is augmented by the varied garb of the different sects of Christians, Greeks, United and Schismatic, Armenians and Maronites. Then there are the various *nuances* of the Moslem faith, which are likewise evinced by the dress.

Yonder walks the grave Turk of the old school (and there are still many such in Syria), dressed in his long caftan and his white or green bellying turban; the latter color distinguishes the descendant of the Prophet, who is entitled to be styled emir, or the hadji, who has made the pilgrimage to Mecca. Though *emir* is properly equivalent to lord, or even to prince, the title is now sunk in value, and the majority of those who may claim it in its primitive sense are to be found among the lowest classes, such as porters, water-sellers, etc.

The genuine Moslem pursues his way sedately, with one hand fondling his curling beard and the other resting on the dagger or the writing-case in his girdle. The unfortunate scattered race of Judah has likewise its representatives here. Always on the alert to increase his store, the Jew shuffles through the crowd, dressed in a dirty caftan and dark-colored turban, squinting right and left after any chance of petty gain that may present itself; above all, he throws a sheep's eye at the Europeans wandering about here, and makes up to them at once with offers of all possible services. Delegates from almost all the nations of Europe are here in great numbers, and all true to their respective national characters. The Frenchman saunters about in canary-colored *gants de Paris glacés*; and whilst all the Austrian sailors take off their hats to every well-dressed Frank that looks civilly at them, the wooden-faced Englishman sails right ahead, staring up at the houses and the sky, and runs every one down that does not get out of his way.

Female promenaders are not so numerous here as in Constantinople. All the Moslem women have their faces concealed by a strip of black silk or cotton, fitting like a visor, hanging down to the middle ; beside this, whenever they spy a stranger approaching, they throw also over their heads a piece of white muslin that hangs over their backs, and this manœuvre is practiced with peculiar alacrity by the oldest and ugliest—a proceeding on their part to which there can be no possible objection ; " A man must travel eastward," says Lord Egerton, " duly to appreciate the hag-like hideousness of female antiquity." The young and pretty not unfrequently draw their veils aside and disclose a pair of black, lustrous eyes, for which they are immediately chided by their more rigorous seniors. The Maronite women, who wear a white veil over their horns, drop it now and then to conceal their pretty round faces from the gaze of strangers. Nevertheless, they ave made very tolerable progress in civilization, and they often enough favor one with a good-humored smile. The women of the Arab Catholics, of whom there are many here, go unveiled, and we have seen among them some splendid figures and faces of rare beauty.

Among the institutions of the city are the " coffee-houses" —the word coffee, in this instance, signifying anything a man may choose to call for in the way of drinks. Through the day these places are frequented to considerable extent, but at night, when all the larger ones have music, they are thronged. In passing them at night, one would suppose that half the inhabitants of the city were in the coffee-houses, and a more hilarious set of men is nowhere to be found.

Another of its institutions is the Turkish bath ; and as some of our readers may not exactly understand what this means, we will relate our own experience in one of them :

First, the bath-house itself is of Oriental construction, consisting of a large circular room, surmounted by a dome of elaborate workmanship, with side rooms for undressing, steaming, scouring, etc., etc.

After disrobing in one of the side rooms and reappearing under the central dome, a strong, burly Moslem took us in charge and directed the putting on of wooden slippers, or rather stilts, with which to walk over the marble floor into the adjoining steam-room. We essayed to do as he directed, but soon found (after nearly breaking our neck in the attempt) that though a Turk may walk with such shoes very comfortably, we can do no such thing, and consequently we kick them from our feet in disgust.

On reaching the first room we found the air hot, and in the next room still hotter. Pointing to a marble platform in the centre of the room, he directed us to take a seat, and here we sat until the sweat exuded from every pore while he made preparations for further operations. Next he directed us to lay flat on the marble floor, while he, with his hand encased in a rough leather mitten, rubbed us thoroughly from head to foot, and seemed to be taking all the outer skin from our body. After each hard rub he would give his hand a twitch, as if to throw off from the glove the skin which he had rubbed off. This was rather a severe process, but we determined to " grin and bear it" as best we could. Then he put on a hair mitten, and having a bowl of hot soapsuds near by, commenced to lather us from head to foot. Our head, face and whiskers were so completely enveloped in soapsuds at one time that we could scarcely breathe, and still the old fellow kept piling on and rubbing in, as-though he intended to smother us outright. Then he dashed basinful after basinful of hot water over us, and bid us rise from our seat on the floor and take another on the central platform. Here we expected to get another dashing of cold water, but this he omitted—whether from mercy or intention we know not—

and after keeping us a while longer in the hot air, he led us by the passage through which we had come back to the room where we had left our clothes. Here he wrapped a large sheet about our body, and a smaller one about our head in the form of a turban, and bid us lay down on the sofa and rest or sleep as long as we liked.

We could have slept easily, sweetly and soundly, had time permitted, as every fibre of the body was completely relaxed, and we felt as if encased in a pillow of down; but the night was waning, and after resting a while in a half-dreamy state, we arose, dressed ourself, and returned to the hotel, feeling a hundred per cent. better than when we left it.

If there is any one thing in which the Turks can claim precedence over the rest of mankind, it is in their baths and frequent bathings. In every considerable town throughout the East, public and private bath-houses are to be found, and the elegance of their construction far exceeds anything of the kind elsewhere. Frequent ablutions are a part of the religious creed of the Moslem, and however derelict they may be in following other precepts of their Prophet, this, certainly, is not neglected.

A very beautiful spectacle, witnessed here at the Feast of the Cross in the month of September, is thus described by an American missionary: "As it began to grow dark, we observed bonfires lighted in the neighborhood, and other tokens of festivity. We went to the terrace on the top of the house, which commanded a view of Mount Lebanon to an extent of nearly thirty miles. Along the whole range we could see the bonfires glaring; they looked, on the dark side of the mountain, like stars on the face of the deep blue vault of heaven. They were of all sizes; sometimes they would glimmer and expire, while new ones would burst forth and soon attain the first magnitude and then die away, or blaze up in fitful flashes as fresh fuel was thrown on them. These tokens of rejoicing are exhibited in commemoration of the finding of the true cross by the Empress Helena. It is said that on her way to Jerusalem she gave orders that in case she should be successful in finding the cross, the event should be made known by bonfires, and thus the intelligence be conveyed to Constantinople."

Among the monkish curiosities of the town there was formerly, and, for all we know to the contrary, there may still be, in an old church belonging to the Greek community, a picture that particularly arrested Maundrell's attention. He describes it as "a very odd figure of a saint with a large beard reaching down to his feet." The curate gave him to understand that this was St. Nicephorus; and perceiving that his beard was the chief object of Maundrell's admiration, he gratified him with the following relation concerning the saint, viz. : " That he was a person of the most eminent virtues in his time ; but his great misfortune was that the endowments of his mind were not set off with the outward ornament of a beard, upon occasion of which defect he fell into a deep melancholy. The devil taking advantage of this priest, promised to give him that boon which nature had denied, in case he would comply with his suggestions. The beardless saint, though he was very desirous of the reward proposed, yet would not purchase it at that rate, but rejected the bribe with indignation, declaring resolutely that he had rather for ever despair of his wish than obtain it on such terms. And at the same time taking in hand the downy tuft upon his chin, to witness the stability of his resolution (for he had, it seems beard enough to swear by), behold ! as a reward for his constancy, he found the hair immediately stretch with the pluck that he gave it. Whereupon, finding it in so good a humor, he followed the happy omen; and, as young heirs that have been niggardly bred generally turn prodigals when they come to their estate, so he never desisted from pulling his beard till he had wiredrawn it down to his feet."

Talking of saints, it would be unpardonable to omit mentioning the thrice-renowned St. George, who duelled and killed the dragon in this neighborhood. About an hour's ride to the east of the town is shown the scene of the conflict, and a rock marked with the monster's blood, or, as others report, with the soap-suds wherein the holy champion washed his hands after the exploit. A small chapel, erected to commemorate the deed, was afterward converted into a mosque, which is now in decay. Curiously enough, the pig-hating Turks entertain much reverence for the Cappadocian worthy, who began his career as a knavish speculator in bacon.

Beyrout has of late become so Europeanized that the Bedouins of the desert and of the mountainous country beyond the Jordan visit it less frequently than formerly, though even yet one may occasionally be met with in the streets; and, when so met, always attracts attention because of his singular dress and the admirable manner with which he sits his horse. Their horses, too, excite admiration, as they are usually of the finest Arabian stock.

The Bedouin and his horse should be seen together, for then they make a noble and truly poetical figure; when viewed apart the charm vanishes. When the rider's foot is on the ground he creeps sluggishly and listlessly about, or squats under his tent smoking his short pipe in sullen silence; and the horse stands tamely with his tail drooping and his head bent down, looking hungrily after the few blades of grass that sprout up between the stones.

But when the Bedouin springs into the saddle, an electric energy seems breathed into man and horse; the rider's eye flashes, his muscular form rises up in its pride and strength, he utters a peculiar yell, the horse bounds forth and makes the air whistle with his speed, whilst his streaming tail often lashes his rider's back. In a few moments nothing is to be seen in the distance but a cloud of dust, with the black feathers of the lance dancing above it.

We have an excellent consul here in the person of Julius A. Johnson, Esq., who has filled the post for many years with credit to himself and to the satisfaction of the American residents hereabouts. He was here at the time of the massacre of the Christians by the Mohammedans, and such was his efficiency that he not only procured the punishment of the guilty perpetrators, but obtained large damages from the Turkish government for those who had suffered injury. One of his duties is the settlement or adjudication of all differences arising between American travelers and their dragomen and muleteers who arrive at this point after a tour through Syria; and these settlements are sometimes of a complex character and require a good deal of cool judgment; for while his own interest, as well as that of our government, is that he should stand well with the local authorities, still he must not fail to so frame his decisions that full and complete justice may in all cases be granted to the Americans who submit their cases for his adjudication.

And here we may remark, *en passant*, that one of the treaty stipulations between our government and that of Turkey is that all differences wherein Americans are concerned shall be submitted to our consuls for adjudication, and not to the local authorities of the town or city wherein the differences may occur. This extends to criminal as well as to civil cases, and is a source of constant congratulation to Americans traveling in Egypt and Syria.

If it were otherwise, and a traveler was liable to be dragged before some Turkish official upon any and every complaint made by a Moslem, the danger and unpleasantness of traveling in these countries would be doubly and trebly increased. Indeed, without this provision it would hardly be safe to travel in these half-civilized lands at all; for a traveler might, upon the slightest pretense, be summoned before a Turkish official, and not knowing the laws and usages of the country, nor even its language, he might be mulcted in heavy damages, or be made to suffer corporeal punishment, without having an opportunity to make himself or the case understood by the adjudicating officer.

We trust that this wise provision will never be changed, and that all future treaties with other governments will contain a like clause.

We also have here an American missionary station, one of the oldest, if not the very oldest, in Syria, and we are pleased to learn that its usefulness is on the increase. The buildings are large and commodious, and, better still, they are owned by the society. The schools are in a flourishing condition, and the natives who have been educated in them and sent forth are doing much toward inducing others to attend. In this way, more than in any other, can good results be hoped for from missionary efforts among such a people. As to making a proselyte of an adult Mohammedan by preaching Christianity to him, you might as well attempt to stop Niagara with a straw.

But we must now prepare for our departure from the Holy Land. The steamer is in the harbor, our passage engaged, and it only remains to go on board, and then farewell to Palestine.

For forty-one days we have traveled and rested on the soil of Syria; climbed its mountains and crossed its valleys; bathed in its rivers and lakes; drank from its fountains; looked upon its ruined temples, palaces, and churches; and, better still, have traced the footsteps of Jesus from the cradle to the tomb; and now we are ready to depart for other lands.

As before stated in this volume, a trip through Syria is not one of mere pleasure, nor should it be undertaken as such. There are many difficulties and perplexities, aches and pains, wearisome days and sleepless nights to be met and endured; and unless one's religious enthusiasm and desire for biblical research is sufficient to enable him to overcome all these with patience and cheerfulness, he had better not attempt a tour through Palestine. If sufficient, then the tour becomes one of constant and increasing interest, and the remembrance of it will ever remain one of the greenest and brightest spots in the pilgrimage through life.

SYRIA.

CHAPTER XIX.

COAST-TOWNS OF SYRIA.

ONCE more on the deep blue sea ! The waves have a terror for some, but none for us. We love to see the white caps chasing each other, like so many mermaids at play; and when the winds blow furiously and the great waves dash against each other like warriors in a battle affray, we always look on with interest if not with pleasure. How oft have we sung, and how many times since have we had occasion to appreciate—

> " A life on the ocean wave,
>   A home on the rolling deep,
> Where the scattered waters rave,
>   And the winds their revels keep !"

The day on which we steam out of the harbor of Beyrout is as bright and beautiful as heart could wish ; and, as one after another of the mountains of Syria fade from our view, we feel that we are leaving old and familiar friends, who have watched our wanderings through Palestine for many a long day ; and yet we have no regret in leaving them behind. They have been landmarks to us, as they have been to others for thousands of years past, and will be to others for thousands of years to come, but once seen and traversed, no one would care to see and traverse them a second time.

Our good ship "Oleg," with its pleasant and obliging officers, and the eight hundred Russian passengers on board, returning from their pilgrimage to Jerusalem and the Jordan to their homes on the plains and steppes of Russia, is now our study from day to day, and one in which we take much interest.

We are told by the captain of our steamer that every year thousands of Russians make a pilgrimage to Palestine—to visit the tomb of our Saviour and bathe in the river Jordan—believing themselves to be performing an act of extraordinary religious devotion in so doing. Many of these come from the interior of Russia, and some from places beyond St. Petersburg, who travel hundreds of miles on foot to reach Odessa, where they take passage by sea. Along the route, through their own country, both in going and returning, the door of every cottage is open to them as pilgrims in a holy cause. It costs them nothing, therefore, to travel through Russia, but when they reach Odessa they pay about twenty dollars for a deck passage on the steamer to and from Jaffa. Each pilgrim, or each family of pilgrims, as, in some cases, we notice father, mother, children, and grandchildren, all of one family, carry for their own use upon the vessel provisions and cooking utensils, and about sundown of each day they engage in their work of cooking and eating, which is an interesting sight to strangers.

The Russians are great tea-drinkers. Indeed, this habit may almost be classed as one of their national characteristics, since high and low, rich and poor, all drink tea of some sort; and this peculiarity is particularly noticeable on our steamer, as there is probably not one of the whole company who does not drink tea of some quality and in some form. Many of the pilgrims have a sort of patent arrangement for making tea, which answers the purpose admirably. It is somewhat in the style of the Old Dominion coffee-pot of our own country. Others have only a tin cup, in which they put a little black tea, and then take it to the cooking-room of the steamer, where they are furnished with boiling water.

At nine o'clock, each evening, tea is served up in the cabin. It is of most excellent quality, and in addition to sugar the Russians put in a small slice of lemon. We try this ourselves, and find it adds considerably to the pleasantness of the drink.

Near the time of the setting of the sun the more devout of the pilgrims make long and earnest prayers with their faces turned toward Jerusalem. Their manner of praying is much the same as that of the Mohammedans, except that they frequently cross themselves during the time of praying. The intent gaze in the direction where they suppose the Holy City to be located, the frequent touching of the forehead to the earth or plank, the rapid movement of the lips, are the same as we observed in the Mohammedans all through Egypt. The only difference seems to be that the Mohammedan looks toward Mecca, while the Russian directs his eyes toward Jerusalem. During prayer the latter also is engaged in frequently touching his right and left shoulder, forehead, and breast, thus making the sign of the cross.

After nightfall many of the pilgrims join in singing, and the voices of some are superb. Some of the anthems they sing are quite operatic, and their manner of rendering them would do credit to the most celebrated choirs of America. We have been both surprised and delighted in listening to them.

These pilgrims are of all ages and conditions, and of both sexes. Some of the men and women are very old—too old, one would think, to have undertaken such a long and tedious journey; others are in the prime of life, and walk the deck with a firm and majestic step; a few, we should think, were young married couples, who are making the pilgrimage as a marriage tour; while probably fifty of the eight hundred are children, varying in age from six months to eighteen years.

We should judge, too, that there is considerable difference in their worldly prosperity at home. Some are much better dressed than others, and the difference of their cooking utensils, knives, forks, dishes, etc., indicates different degrees of wealth, though not a single one of them, as far as we know, has taken any other than a deck passage.

The dress of all of them is of the warmest character—woolens and skins. Both men and women wear sheepskin pelisses—that is, sheep-skins dressed with the wool on, and made into coats, sacques, and overcoats. The caps of many of the men and boys are made of the same material. They all wear their hair very long, and many of the men have beards which would do honor to a Turk. Their dress and shaggy appearance about the head would naturally suggest their relationship to the "Russian Bear."

The religious enthusiasm, in kind, if not in degree, which induced the Crusaders to undertake the deliverance of Palestine from the hands of the infidel is still abroad in the world, as is evidenced by the hundreds and thousands of Russians, and pilgrims of other nationalities of Europe, who visit the Holy Land annually to lay their offerings, however small, at the foot of the Cross; to bathe with their tears the Stone of Unction, on which the body of Jesus was prepared for the sepulchre; to creep upon their hands and knees to the mouth of the tomb in which the body lay, and bewail, within it, the cruel suffering of their once crucified but now arisen Redeemer; to walk bareheaded, and almost barefooted, over the terribly rocky paths from Jerusalem to the Jordan, that they may wash in the stream made sacred by the baptism of Jesus; and to suffer, in many ways, hardships quite as great as the Crusaders themselves, except in the loss of life and limb.

With such a striking instance of self-sacrifice and devotion of a portion of his people before him, it is not difficult to understand why the Emperor of all the Russias has occasionally made such strenuous efforts to wipe Turkey from the map of nations, and deliver his own people and other Christians inhabiting the East from the oppression of Mohammedan rule; and, in the providence of God, we cannot but believe that these efforts will ere long be crowned with success, notwithstanding the jealousy, and consequent opposition, of other European nations.

But we must now pass to other topics relative to our journey. The good ship speeds on her way northward—we are all the while within sight, and occasionally touching and departing from points of great historical interest, and we must say something concerning them.

It is half-past ten at night when we start from Beyrout, and early next morning we reach Tripoli. This city, by the Arabs called Tarabolos, is situated on one of the most favored spots of all Syria, as the maritime plain and the neighboring mountains place every variety of climate within reach of the inhabitants. It consisted originally, as its name imports, of three towns, formed severally by colonies from Tyre, Sidon, and Aradus, which afterward coalesced into one. It is not washed by the sea, but lies about a mile and a half from the shore, on the side of one of the lowest spurs of Lebanon, which is surmounted by an old fortress, built, it is supposed, by Raymond de Toulouse, and commanding the city and its environs. Though Tripoli has twelve gates, it is but partially enclosed with walls, but a circular line of houses gives it, externally, something of a fortified appearance. It retains many marks of the ages of the Crusades; among them several high arcades of Gothic architecture, under which the streets run. The houses are white, and generally well built, and the whole town has a light and clean appearance, and is very much embellished by the gardens which are not only attached to the houses within it, but cover, likewise, the whole triangular plain lying between it and the sea. This space was occupied late in the last century by marshes—a prolific hotbed of malignant fevers; their partial drainage has greatly improved the salubrity of the air. But the soul of the town is the river Kadisha, which flows through it, and constitutes its chief pretension to the proud surname its Moslem inhabitants delight to bestow upon it, namely, *Koochook Sham*— Little Damascus.

The Wady Kadisha, higher up than Tripoli, is one of the most picturesque valleys in the world. It is crossed a short distance above the town by an aqueduct built on arches, called by the natives Kontaret-el-Brins—a corruption of Prince. This name, preserved by ancient tradition, and a Latin cross carved in relief on one of the arches, corroborates the belief that the aqueduct was constructed by the counts of Tripoli in the times of the Crusades. It receives in a channel two feet deep, a rapid brook, which issues from the neighborhood of the village of Sgorta, eight miles up the mountain, and discharges itself into a subterraneous conduit, by which it is conveyed to Tripoli; the inhabitants prefer its water to that of the Kadisha. The aqueduct is one hundred and thirty paces long, and seven feet eight inches broad. It may well be imagined that even a pedestrian feels some trepidation at crossing it along the narrow unguarded ledge not occupied by the water; yet it is related that in 1802, a Maronite, belonging to one of the chief families of Lebanon, being hotly pursued by the soldiers of the governor of Tripoli, galloped his horse across the aqueduct at full speed.

In the time of the Crusaders there was another aqueduct, separated only by a narrow road from the sea. Its site is probably indicated by the name Barj-el-Kanatter—Tower of the Aqueduct—still given to one of a chain of six towers extending along the shore at a distance of ten minutes' walk from each other, between the Marina and the mouth of the Kadisha. Raymond d'Agile, one of the old chroniclers, speaking of a battle fought at Tripoli between the Crusaders and Saracens, says coolly, that "it was a delectable thing to see the little stream of the aqueduct carrying into the city mangled bodies of nobles and men of the commoner sort."

Ten minutes' walk above the town, on the same side of the Kadisha as the castle, stands the convent of Dervishes, so celebrated for the exquisite beauty of its situation. At half an hour's walk below the town, at the extreme angle of the triangular plain, is El Myna, the Marina or part of Tripoli, itself a small village, inhabited chiefly by Greek sailors and shipwrights.

There are two other places in the environs of Tripoli that deserve mention among the lions of the town, viz.: Bedoowek and the Treasure Cave. Bedoowek is called from a sheikh of that name, whose tomb is situated on the spot, with a mosque erected above it. Close by the mosque is a circular basin of beautiful clear water, in which is preserved a great quantity of fish, which are daily fed by the guardians of the tomb and the Tripolitans. There are probably two thousand of these fish within the circumference of less than one hundred paces, some of them large enough to weigh five or six pounds. No one dares to catch or kill one of them, for they are regarded as sacred. This is an old superstition in the East. The ancient Syrians, as is well known, had their sacred fish; and there are many places where the Mohammedans of the present day revere some fortunate member of the finny tribe, who they say were favorites with Abraham, and have been, in consequence, endowed with a length of days not usually granted to their race; and it is even supposed that under certain circumstances they became the recipients for any appointed time of the souls of true believers.

The Treasure Cave is a grotto about half an hour's walk from Tripoli, containing, it is said, certain old sequins, which, by some marvelous virtue, attract everything to them, and which no human power could remove from where they lie. The inhabitants put the most implicit faith in this prodigy; and if you express the least doubt on the subject, they will tell you a string of stories, each succeeding one more wonderful than the other, till they fairly talk down your skepticism. The *djins*, no doubt, are at the bottom of the mystery. Every reader of the "Arabian Nights" is acquainted with those tricky sprites, the djins and djiniyehs (for they are male and female). Their existence is fully believed in at this day; how, indeed, should it be questioned, seeing the numbers of living witnesses who have had ocular demonstration of the fact? One may even enter into wedlock with these strange beings; the union endures for life ; but the human consort renounces thereby all the hopes and consolations of religion. Instances are notorious in Syria of men who are married to female djins; a native Christian hakkim of Acre is mentioned as having contracted an alliance of this kind. When he walks through the streets the children run after him, shouting, " There goes the husband of the djiniyeh." This man's sister was killed by an unknown hand for having disclosed her brother's unhallowed dealings to her confessor.

The djins are not malicious if you take care not to offend them ; but as their power is immense, and their tempers capricious, the Arab regards them with extreme awe. Nothing would induce him voluntarily to pass the night in a dark room. If he had but two paras in the world he would spend them upon a little oil and cotton ; for it is in the dark the djins are most terrible. The women will never venture to talk of these beings, unless when they are assembled in numbers sufficient to give them unusual confidence ; two or three women alone in a room would not dare even to utter the name of djin.

It is now about fifty years since a midwife, living in Tripoli, was called up in the night to attend a lying-in woman. She obeyed the summons, and, accompanying the man who called her, she entered a house unknown to her. Her guide showed her into a bath-room and then disappeared. The good woman, thus left alone and suddenly hearing strange, unaccountable noises around her, was beginning heartily to wish herself safe at home, when all at once a magnificent and brilliantly-lighted room opened before her : in it were forty women, one of whom was lying down and appeared to require the midwife's aid. Who should know more of the world and its inhabitants than those whose lives are spent in helping to people it? The midwife saw at a glance that she was among an assembly of djiniyehs, and she wisely resolved to do her best to please them. After having assisted at the birth of the child, she set about tinging its eyelashes and eyebrows black, according to the custom of the Arabs. Possibly, her trepidation may have occasioned some awkwardness in the performance of this operation: at any rate, one of the females present came up to her, and under pretence of showing her how the surmeh should be applied, she poked out the poor woman's eye. The sufferer durst not utter a cry or make the least complaint. Soon after this, casting a glance of her remaining eye on a female near her, she recognized, to her great surprise, a pelisse which she knew well belonged to a cousin of her own living in Tripoli. Taking advantage of a moment when the djiniyehs were looking another way, she stole into the bath-room and took up a pinch of red powder, with which she furtively marked the skirt of her cousin's pelisse, in order that she might afterward be able to assure herself of the reality of what she had seen. At last when the djiniyehs were tired of tormenting the poor woman, they sent her away, first bestowing on her a casket filled with gold pieces, all counted in her presence. On reaching home, the midwife made haste to open the casket, but to her dismay she found it filled with onions. The next day she paid a visit to her cousin, upon whose back she saw, sure enough, the very pelisse that had attracted her attention during the strange scenes of the preceding night—the red spot was on the skirt. The djeniyehs had borrowed it for a night, and had brought it back before dawn. As for the midwife, she continued blind of an eye till the day of her death.

The road leading out of Tripoli toward the cedars of Lebanon affords an admirable prospect. It winds along the banks of a river enclosed between two hills, and overshadowed by beautiful trees and orange groves. A kiosk or café built beneath these trees offers its perfumed terrace to promenaders, who resort thither to smoke, drink coffee, and enjoy the freshness of the air, wafted from above the stream. From this spot you look through a vista upon the sea, which is half a league from the town, on the picturesque square towers along the coast and the numerous vessels in the harbor.

Leaving Tripoli, a run of seven hours brings us to Latakiah. Shortly after anchoring we go on shore and make a thorough examination of the town and suburbs. After traversing its narrow, dirty streets for an hour or two—observing the manners and customs of its people, and visiting such points as were thought of special interest—the guide, at our suggestion, conducts us to the top of one of the minarets, from which we have an extended view of the town and surrounding country.

Before proceeding to describe Latakiah, however, we may be permitted to say a word of the country lying between it and Tripoli, of which we have a good view from the deck of our vessel as we pass along the coast. In some way, or for some cause, this region of Syria is known as " the *snake* or *serpent* country," and the local nomenclature of its places designates it accordingly. Thus we have what the natives call the Serpent Fountain ; and near Gebelee there is a hill called Jebel-el-Hayah (Serpent Mountain), which is said to derive its name from the ancient *ophiogene* race of Cyprus, some of whom settled here, and from whom many of the modern snake-charmers of Syria pretend to be descended.

There are in Syria, as well as in India (and some we saw while at Cairo, Egypt), who boast of the same power over serpents as that possessed by the ancient psylli of

Africa. They will fearlessly handle the most dangerous serpents, fold them round their bodies, provoke and bite them, because, as they tell you, the serpent has no power to hurt them. The probability is that they take the simple precaution of disarming the reptile by extracting its poison-fangs. These men are often called in to private houses to conjure the serpents out of the walls. The reptiles, on hearing the call of the charmer, soon put out their heads; and, after being vehemently adjured *by the great name! by the greatest of names!* they creep obsequiously into the bag held open to receive them. The whole force of the conjuration consists, doubtless, in legerdemain; but so adroitly is it performed that a person even aware of the trick might sometimes be almost imposed on by it.

The superstitious notions of the Syrians respecting serpents and snakes surpass all imaginable measure of absurdity. They attribute numberless powers for good or evil to those disgusting reptiles; and very rarely does a Syrian peasant venture to kill or even to disturb a serpent that has made its nest in a wall, being firmly persuaded that the whole generation of the killed or wounded reptile would implacably pursue the murderer and his kin till their vengeance was satisfied. Precisely the same belief prevails, as we are told by Kohl, among the inhabitants of the southern steppes of Russia, who are generally too much afraid of a snake to kill it, even though it take up its abode under the same roof with them. "Let a snake alone," says the Russian, "and he will let you alone; but if you kill it, its whole race will persecute you." In support of their belief in something of a corporation spirit among the snakes which prompts them to revenge the blood of a relation, they appeal to the twenty-eighth chapter of the Acts of the Apostles, where it is said:

"And when Paul had gathered a bundle of sticks, and laid them on the fire, there came a viper out of the heat and fastened on his hand. And when the barbarians saw the venomous beast hang on his hand, they said among themselves, No doubt this man is a murderer, whom, though he hath escaped the sea, yet vengeance suffereth not to live." The expression "murderer" in this passage they interpret to mean a murderer of snakes; and the "vengeance" to mean the vengeance of a snake on one that has dyed his hand in the blood of another snake. The snake they believe is in the habit of dispensing poetical justice toward murderers in general, but more particularly toward those worst of murderers—the killers of snakes.

The married woman, whose longings to be a mother have proved vain, in spite of all her vows and her consultations of santons and sages, betakes her, as a last resource, to the aid of the black serpent, and she feels assured that if she wears the dead body of one of those creatures next her skin for three days she will not long be deprived of the honors of maternity. Very serious accidents have often resulted from this practice. Some years ago a considerable number of dark-colored snakes, rendered torpid by cold, were carried down by the river to Caïffa, near Mount Carmel. When the circumstance was made known, all the married women of the district who were not blessed with children flocked to the spot to get themselves a snake for a girdle; but the snakes, many of which were venomous, were only numbed; the warmth of the body revived them, and the lives of several of the women were greatly endangered by the bites they received. It is said that one unfortunate young woman, who had consented with extreme repugnance to employ this horrible remedy, was so terrified when she felt the cold pressure of the reviving reptile, as it writhed round her body, that she threw herself from the house-top and was killed on the spot.

When any one has been bitten by a serpent, the Syrians set it down for certain that the venomous creature had been provoked by the wounded man or by some of his ancestors. But they have a sovereign remedy, which absorbs, as they assert, every particle of venom from the wound. This is nothing more or less than the application to the injured part of a small black, or yellowish, porous stone, of a sort rarely met with. A fragment of such a stone is always valued at a high price; but when a piece has acquired a certain reputation by the number of marvelous cures wrought by it, it then becomes worth its weight in gold. Madame Catafago, the wife of a wealthy merchant, is mistress of one of these stones; it is a small piece of great renown, and cost her six hundred and eighty piastres, equaling about thirty-five dollars.

Talking of strange remedies reminds us to say that the ashes of playing-cards are the common recipe in Lebanon for the cure of intermittent fevers; and the more thumbed and greasy the cards the greater is their efficacy. The ashes are mixed up with water, and administered as a draught.

Cases of hydrophobia occur, though very rarely, in Syria. When the disease delares itself, a messenger must be instantly despatched and bring back, within three days from the first attack of the malady, a specific, the secret of which is known only to an old man of the village of Sheikh Akmar, three leagues from Acre. It is a violent drastic purgative, composed of simples gathered by the old hakkim himself. The Syrians assert that it is an infallible cure for hydrophobia; but, with their usual proneness to the marvelous, they add that the first visible effect of the medicine is to relieve the patient of clots of blood, in which the forms of little dogs are plainly to be discerned. Strange as it may appear, most of the European families settled in the country put as much faith in these stories as the natives themselves. The whole Catafago family of Seyde and Nazarete bear testimony as eye-witnesses to the curious operation of this remedy.

When a Druse is attacked with hydrophobia, he is seldom left to die of the disease, but the event is anticipated by those about him. They say that to cause the immediate death of the sufferer it is only necessary to sift some hot vine ashes on his bare and shaven crown.

Irby and Mangles relate that when they passed through Asdoud, a village north of Gaza, some of the women were very importunate in their entreaties to be favored with a few locks from the travelers' heads. The request was ungallantly refused. Perhaps it might have been otherwise had the ladies desired the locks for love-tokens, but the fact was, they wanted them as a charm to add to the efficacy of some medicine the Franks had given them for a sick kinsman. The women said that the smoke of Christian hair, burnt while the medicine was warming, would ensure a cure of the patient's disorder. Some Arabs, to secure the hair, will take the head and all.

We also see along the coast, on the way, what is known as the Syrian sponge-fishery, which belongs to some princes of Lebanon, who usually sell their rights to merchants. The divers, all Greeks of the Archipelago, arrive in their little vessels on the coast of Syria in the month of May, and the fishing continues until September. Their employment is an exceedingly laborious one, and not exempt from danger; but as they know that sharks haunt these coasts, they take due precautions against them, and accidents rarely happen. The constant working of the same banks is beginning to diminish the quantity of sponges, and the fishery has been observed for some years to grow less and less productive.

But to return from our digression. When we asked to go to the top of the minaret in Latakiah we had but little hope that our request would be granted, as we had supposed that none but Moslems were ever permitted to ascend the sacred stairway. Whether on account of the broad scimetar which our guide wore at his side, or by the Turkish tarbouch which we ourself wore, or by our sunburnt skin and long beard, we were taken for a veritable Turk and thus admitted by the keeper of the mosque, we cannot tell; but certain it is that we reached the spot where the muezzin stands when he calls the faithful to prayer, crying out, or rather singing out, "Prayer is better than sleep; awake and pray."

Latakiah, which in the last century was one of the most flourishing cities on the coast, has been so frequently overthrown by earthquakes that one can scarcely move in it without everywhere encountering ruins and heaps of fallen materials. The ancient port of Laodicea, which, if history may be relied on, was capable of containing a thousand galleys, is now partly choked with sand, and partly covered with orange, lemon, mulberry and jujube trees, forming an extensive garden. If Dolabella could revisit Laodicea with his fleet, he and his Romans would assuredly be not a little surprised to find they could gather oranges and jujubes on the very spot where their war-galleys formerly floated. The present harbor could not contain more than four or five vessels of a hundred and fifty or two hundred tons burden, and a few Arab boats. It would not cost much, if the people had sufficient enterprise and thrift, to render the port of Latakiah a safe and commodious one for vessels of all sizes, and thus supply the grand want of this coast—a harbor of refuge.

The air of this region is very wholesome ; it is less confined than in some other parts of the coast—Tripoli for instance—for the mountains recede further from the sea, and toward the north the plain opens to a great extent. The water, however, is bad, and whilst everything without the town is verdant, fragrant and picturesque, all within it is disgustingly filthy. The ill-paved streets of the Greek quarter in particular, heaped with remains of dead animals and with filth of every kind, exhale an intolerable stench.

The Christians of Latakiah appear to be of a very lively temperament, and are very fond of meeting together socially in the evenings to amuse each other with conversation and story-telling. The women often dance in the style (but without the indecency) of the Egyptian *almehs;* the men sing ; and Karaguse, the Turkish Punch, exhibits his not very chaste performances.

Before leaving Latakiah we make a purchase of some native smoking tobacco, than which none has so high a reputation throughout Egypt and the whole of the East. We had smoked it on the Nile, at Cairo, Alexandria, and Jerusalem, and now that we are on the very spot of its growth and manufacture we resolve to lay in a supply for the balance of our Eastern and European tour. Its flavor is certainly unsurpassed, if equaled, by any other tobacco of the world.

Some will smile at the mention of what may seem to them so trivial a matter, but not so with the lover of the long-drawn puff and curling wreath. To him the possession of a good article of tobacco is worth more than a kingdom ; for, as he reclines on his soft divan, or lies back in his easy arm-chair, puffing away, while visions of angels float around him in the smoke which wreathes and curls about his head, what cares he for vexations or troubles, for kingdoms, principalities or powers?

The present Latakiah is unquestionably the ancient Laodicea, where was located one of the seven churches of Asia, and to whom John, in Revelation, was instructed to write, "I know thy work, that thou art neither cold nor hot; I would thou wert cold or hot. So then because thou art lukewarm, and neither cold nor hot, I will spue thee out of my mouth."

An old Roman arch, connected with the ruins of what seems to have been a church, is pointed out as the site of the building in which the first Christians of Laodicea met for worship, and where a Christian temple subsequently stood, erected, probably, by the Romans while in possession of the country. The ruins of an old castle a little way out from the shore, and now entirely surrounded by water, also bear evidence of being the work of the same great people. Wherever Rome planted her standard she erected palaces, castles, or temples as indices of her power and greatness, many of which remain to this day, if not in their freshness and glory, certainly in their massiveness and strength.

Early next morning we reach Alexandretta, situated at the most north-eastern point of the archipelago, having a beautiful harbor in front and high mountains in the rear. The town is not large, but exceedingly picturesque and beautiful; and being the port at which all the steamers running from Alexandria to Constantinople stop for coaling (the coal being brought from England), and being also the only outlet for the cotton and fruit raised in the surrounding country, it has acquired considerable commercial importance.

The shore of the harbor above the town is a sandy

beach and a capital place for bathing—a fact which the Russian pilgrims on board seem to understand, as most of them, both men and women, go on shore throughout the day and bathe.

We, too, take a small boat—kindly furnished by the captain—and, after rowing about the harbor for an hour or two, visiting the boats from which they are unloading cotton and wool, and inspecting its quality, finally direct our course to the upper end of the bay, and take a glorious bath in the harbor.

We enjoy the bathing hugely, floundering around like a porpoise, and remaining in much longer than we should have done, as we subsequently find to our cost. The next day, and for two days after, we have severe chills followed by fever, as a consequence, no doubt, of remaining in the water too long. We mention this as a warning to others who may undertake a like luxurious though somewhat risky experiment.

CHAPTER XX.

THE CEDARS OF LEBANON.

BEFORE bidding a final adieu to Syria—as, hereafter, our sight-seeing will be in Asia Minor and in Constantinople—we think it best, in order that our readers may have a more perfect knowledge of the country and its peculiarities, to treat of two other subjects, namely, Syrian dwelling-houses and the cedars of Lebanon; and in our description of these we propose to give not only our own observations, so far as they go, but the observations of other travelers as well.

The simplest form of a Syrian dwelling-house is that of a plain box, with one room in the basement serving for parlor, kitchen, and hall, and one above this in which the family sleep. But the real domicile, for the greater part of the year, is more properly the flat-terraced roof, where the women and the children pass the day, and frequently the night also.

The materials out of which most of the commoner houses are constructed—and some of the better class also—consist of mud or bricks dried in the sun, having chopped straw worked up with the substance to render it more tenacious; and this, too, even in Damascus and Beyrout, where stone is abundant. In the more mountainous districts of Syria many villages are built wholly of stone, roughly laid, with but little mud or mortar in the interstices.

The better class of dwellings is of a quadrangular form, built round a court-yard, to which admission is gained from the street by an arched doorway and a low, dark passage: the latter has commonly two turnings, so that no prying eye may look through the opened door into the interior. In the centre a jet of water falls back bubbling and murmuring into a marble basin; or if that beautiful ornament be wanting, there is a well in one of the corners. In summer an awning is drawn across the court.

The lower rooms of the rich are, like the court-yard, paved with marble, and have each a fountain, and the walls are adorned breast high with marble or beautiful wood-work of yellow cedar: they are furnished with cupboards for the stowage of bedding, and open niches or ornamental slabs for vases with water, sherbet, or flowers. The floor is divided into two parts: a lower and smaller one next the court, where the servants stand with folded arms watching their master's looks; and a raised platform, like the dais in an old baronial hall, separated from the lower part by a handsome balustrade. The higher portion is called the *leewan*, and the lower portion the *doorckaah*. The former is reserved for the master of the house and his friends. When the attendance of the servants is required, if they be not in the doorckaah, they are summoned by clapping the hands, for house-bells are unknown in the East.

The rooms in the upper story constitute the harem, or private apartments of the family; those on the ground floor are often without any external opening to admit light; and are used only as store-rooms and domestic offices. In the houses of the wealthy there are rooms for the reception of male guests on the basement. Some of them are entirely open on the side next the court, and are haunted by birds of beautiful plumage.

The ceiling is highly painted and adorned; the part over the leewan is sometimes vaulted and decorated with pendant ornaments, particularly in the houses of the Turks. More commonly the beams are left uncovered, and are carved, partially painted, and sometimes gilded. But the ceiling over the doorckaah, which is higher than over the leewan, is usually more richly decorated with small stripes of gilding and various gay colors arranged in curiously complicated patterns, yet perfectly regular, and having a highly ornamental effect. The ceiling of a projecting window is often adorned in the same manner. Good taste is evinced by thus decorating only such parts as are not always before the eyes; for to look long at so many lines intersecting each other in all directions would be painful.

The leewan is covered with a mat in summer and a carpet over this in winter; and a sofa, raised from six inches to a foot, runs round its three sides, forming what is called the *deewan*, or divan. The sofa is a little higher before than behind, and is about four feet wide; cushions four feet long and two feet high lean against the wall. The angles are the seats of honor, as among the ancient Greeks: the right corner is the chief place; then the sofa along the top and general proximity to the right corner. But even here, the Eastern's respect for man above circumstances is shown. The relative value of the positions all round the room is changed, should the person of the highest rank accidentally occupy another place.

Except when the room is open toward the court, it is lighted by latticed windows at the upper end, usually extending across its whole breadth, and forming a deep recess or balcony carried out on corbels, the floor of which is also furnished with a divan. The consequence of this arrangement of the seats and windows is that you sit with your back to the light and your face to the door; the light, too, falls in a single mass, and from above, affording pictorial effects dear to the artist. Instead of this balcony there is sometimes a small raised alcove, which, with the steps leading up to it, is shut off from the leewan by a screen of curiously wrought lattice-work. It is just large enough to hold a mattrass and silk pillows, and to serve the rich Turk or Arab as a dormitory. Men of inferior station content themselves with mattrasses laid on the floor, upon which they sleep without undressing. The domestics lay themselves down by the street door, in the passage, or in the court; no one ever gives himself any concern about finding sleeping room or accommodation for them. The common people in Syria have no other bed than an Egyptian straw mat on the ground or on the housetop; the beauty of the climate makes up for the want of all other appliances; and even the stranger from the wintry North can desire no more delightful curtain over his head than the starry firmament, beneath which the light breeze fans and lulls him to repose. There is very little dew in this country, except on the mountains, and one may generally sleep in the open air without inconvenience, with only a silk handkerchief over the head.

As heretofore stated, the flat terrace roof is the almost universal style of Syrian houses. The commoner sort of roof is constructed by laying beams close together from one wall to the other; over these is placed small brush or straw, and, over this, a thick layer of mud, which, when thoroughly dried, becomes very hard, and only needs additions and re-rollings after each rainy season.

The terrace roofs of the best houses are thus constructed: across the beams forming the ceiling of the up-

FLAT HOUSE TOPS OF SYRIA

The Cedars of Lebanon.

permost story deal planks are laid, fitting nicely together, and over these rafters are placed transversely, the interstices between which are filled up with chopped hay or straw, mixed with lime and small pebbles. Upon this surface is laid a layer of pounded charcoal, then one of lime and sand, mixed up with ashes and charcoal, and the whole is rolled and beaten with a mallet till it assumes a bright polish and is impermeable to the rain. Houses thus covered are well enough in the long dry weather; but woe to their inmates when the rains set in, for then their choice is only between showers of water and showers of mud.

The fashion of flat roofs is, in some measure, attended with results at variance with the jealous privacy affected in the domestic economy of the East. A gentleman who rises early may see more of his neighbor's *ménage* than is consistent with strict propriety; if his position be a good one he may sometimes play peeping Tom to a whole city in the gray morning, and houses will occasionally be so placed that it is scarcely possible to avoid stealing a look into the court-yards of the adjoining families, where all appear unmasked; the people move about in them like figures in the bottom of a pit, and the fairest ladies are occupied in the most humble offices. Many a tender tale of passion dates from a casual encounter of the eyes, occasioned by this happy arrangement of the house-tops, whereas our sloping roofs are privy only to the soft whisperings of enamored cats. It was a flat roof, for instance, that enabled Hadji Baba to declare to his charmer that "her eyes had made roast meat of his heart;" and from a similar post of vantage, on the top of a convent in Damascus, a gallant Englishman— But we will let him tell his own story:

"In a house near the convent I caught an occasional

glimpse of so beautiful a face that I was tempted to seek its light oftener, perhaps, than would be wise to acknowledge. I thought I had never seen so perfectly lovely a countenance. A grated window, which looked into the centre area of the house, concealed the figure from me and prevented my seeing in what occupation so graceful a creature was engaged. As she cast her eyes upward through the bars—and they were the most expressive eyes in the world—I was so fascinated that she must have been duller than Eastern ladies generally are had she not perceived it. It happened, therefore, whenever I walked upon the terrace that accident brought the beautiful Helena to the grated window; and I grew impatient to liberate her from what seemed to me a most barbarous imprisonment.

" The happy moment at length arrived. I had bought a large bunch of violets in my ramble through the bazaar, and, armed with so infallible an interpreter, I appeared at my post; she was busily engaged, but suspended her work a while on perceiving me, and, leaning her cheek upon her hand, like Juliet, made behind her prison bars the prettiest picture imaginable. A bright instrument was in the left hand, and I thought she might have been passing her seclusion in some elegant embroidery. Now, however, I resolved to tempt her from the window, and, kissing my violets, threw them over the wall. She rose, and, clattering on a pair of high wooden shoes, came forth with a knife in one hand and a fish she had been scraping in the other. My romance was at an end in a moment, and I never could recover gravity enough to return to the terrace. She was exceedingly beautiful, the daughter of a rich merchant, and had, as usual, been betrothed in her youth, but to a man who had proved false; he had gone to Alexandria, it was said, and had never since been heard of. Her unfortunate story and her beauty were equally subjects of conversation among her acquaintances. I found the misfortune, however, was not in the desertion so much as in the necessity of remaining single until the death of the affianced husband should enable her to take another."

While, as we have shown, there is much comfort and a certain kind of luxury in the internal arrangements of the better class of Syrian houses, still there are circumstances which it must be owned do somewhat detract from the pleasure of living in them; fleas swarm in every apartment during the cooler months and mosquitoes give you no rest during the heat; ugly little lizards run about your bedroom and many of the old houses are infested with black snakes. On entering your room at night you may chance to see an extraordinary shadow moving across the floor. You stoop down to ascertain whether it is a mouse or a lizard, and find an immense stronglegged, hairy spider, as big as a pigeon's egg. In your horror at his appearance you allow the monster to escape into his hole and are left in the delightful uncertainty whether he won't return to pay you a visit in bed. But one gets accustomed to all these things, and they soon cease to occasion any very great discomfort; you find that the lizards are very harmless; you declare a war of extermination against the spiders and you learn to submit to the fleas and mosquitoes, because you must. Fleas can, by no care whatever, be excluded from the neatest houses; the long Eastern habit, affording them shelter, is a favorable conveyance, and the streets and dusty bazaars so swarm with them that it is impossible to walk abroad without collecting a colony. The frequent use of the bath is in some measure a protection against another kind of vermin; but there is no remedy against your flea, that pertinacious persecutor, which an Arab author describes as "a black, nimble, extenuated, hunchbacked animal, which, being sensible when any one looks on it, jumps incessantly, now on one side, now on the other, till it gets out of sight."

Passing from Syrian dwelling-houses, let us next take a view of the heights of Lebanon, and especially of the cedars of Lebanon; and here we cannot do better than follow Lord Lindsay, who visited the cedars in the month of June. Ascending the eastern slope of the mountains in the direction from Baalbec to Bsherray, he says:

"An hour afterward we reached an immense wreath of snow, lying on the breast of the mountain, just below the summit—and from that summit five minutes afterward what a prospect opened before us! Two vast ridges of Lebanon, curving westward from the central spot where we stood like the horns of a bent bow or the wings of a theatre, ran down toward the sea, breaking in their descent into a hundred minor hills, between which, unseen, unheard, and through as deep, and dark, and jagged a chasm as ever yawned, the Kadisha, or sacred river of Lebanon, rushes down to the Mediterranean—the blue and boundless Mediterranean—which, far on the western horizon, meets and mingles with the sky.

"Our eyes, coming home again after roving over the noble view, we had leisure to observe a small clump of trees, not larger apparently than a clump in an English park, at the very foot of the northern wing, or horn of this grand natural theatre: these were the far-famed cedars. We were an hour and twenty minutes reaching them, the descent being very precipitous and difficult. As we entered the grove, the air was quite perfumed with their odor, the 'smell of Lebanon,' so celebrated by the pen of inspiration.

CEDARS OF LEBANON.

"The grove stands on a group of stony knolls, about three quarters of a mile in circumference, and consists of three or four hundred trees partly the remains of a forest that once perhaps filled the whole valley, and partly the younger progeny of the venerable patriarchs amongst them. The younger are very numerous, and would form a noble wood of themselves, were even the patriarchal dynasty quite extinct; one of them, by no means the largest, measures nineteen feet and a quarter in circumference, and, in repeated instances, two, three and four large trunks spring from a single root—but they have all a fresher appearance than the patriarchs and straighter stems—straight as young palm trees. They are not so *very* young, either. Russegger thinks that most of the trees in the grove may be a couple of centuries old, and several between the ages of four hundred and eight hundred years; there are twelve whose age is incalculable; seven standing very near each other, three more a little farther on, nearly in a line with them, and two, not observed by any recent traveler except Lord Lindsay, on the northern end edge of the grove; the largest of these two is sixty-three feet in circumference (following the sinuosities of the bark); one of the others measures forty-nine feet.

"These giants are more remarkable for girth than stature, their height hardly exceeding fifty feet; they all part into several stems, but as this partition takes place about five feet from the root, there is not the difficulty which some have alleged in ascertaining their true dimensions. Their age is very variously estimated; their most sanguine admirers believe them to have been contemporary with Solomon; and though this draws rather too strongly on our credulity, yet there is no direct evidence to contradict it. The rules by which botanists determine the age of trees are not applicable to these, for their stems have ceased to grow in regular concentric rings; they owe their prolonged existence to the superior vitality of a portion of their bark which has survived the decay of the rest. Russegger, however, is inclined to admit that these trees may possibly number some two thousand years, taking into consideration their size, their girth, the stony soil in which they grow and their lofty position, exposed so much to the violence of the winds.

"They are certainly the most celebrated natural monuments in the universe. Religion, poetry and history have equally consecrated them; they furnish a class of images which the inspired writers use with especial preference. The Arabs of all creeds have a traditional veneration for these trees. They believe that an evil fate would surely overtake any one who shall dare to lay sacrilegious hands on these *saints*, as they fondly call them. They attribute to them not only a vegetative vigor that endows them with perpetual existence, but also a soul which enables them to exhibit signs of sagacity and foresight, similar to those arising from instinct in animals and from intellect in man. They know the seasons beforehand: they move their vast limbs, they stretch them out or draw them in, raise them to the heavens or bend them to the earth, according as the snow is about to fall or melt. They are divine beings under the form of trees. This is the only spot on the chain of Lebanon where they grow, and here they take root far above the region where all considerable vegetation ceases. All this strikes and astonishes the imagination of the people of the East, and I know not but that science itself would be surprised.

"Every year, at the Feast of the Transfiguration, the Maronites, Greeks and Armenians mount to the cedars and celebrate mass on a homely altar of stone at their feet. How many prayers have resounded under their branches! And what more sublime temple! What altar nearer the heavens! What fane more majestic and holy than the loftiest level of Lebanon, the trunks of the cedars, and the canopy of those sacred branches which have shaded and still shade so many human generations, pronouncing the name of God in different accents, but recognizing him everywhere in his works, and adoring him in the manifestations of his creation!

"The stately bearing and graceful repose of the young cedars contrast singularly with the wild aspect and frantic attitude of the old ones, flinging abroad their knotted and muscular limbs like so many Laocoöns, while others, broken off, lie rotting at their feet; but life is strong in them all; they look as if they had been struggling for existence with evil spirits, and God had interposed and forbidden the war, that the trees he had planted might remain living witnesses to faithless men of the ancient 'glory of Lebanon.' . . . . Burckhardt says, 'The oldest trees are distinguished by having the foliage and small branches at the top only, and by four, five, or even seven trunks springing from one base. The branches and foliage of the others were lower, but we saw none whose leaves touched the ground like those at Kew Gardens.'

"The very air of the cedar impresses one with the idea of its comparative immortality. There is a firmness in the bark and a stability in the trunk, in the mode in which it lays hold of the ground, and in the form of the branches and their insertion into the trunk, not found in any other pine, scarcely in any other tree. The foliage, too, is superior to that of any other of the tribe, each branch being perfect in its form; the points of the leaves spread upward into beautiful little tufts, and the whole upper surface of the branch has the appearance of velvet; the color is a rich green, wanting the bluish tint of the pine and fir, and the lurid and gloomy hue of the cypress. The cedar is an evergreen; the fruit resembles the cone of the pine; the wood is compact and of a beautiful brown tint, and though its resistance to actual wear is not equal to that of the oak, it is so bitter that no insect will touch it, and it seems proof against time itself."

In the convent at Bethlehem we saw rafters made from these cedars, which were hewn out and placed in position more than fifteen centuries ago, and they seem, and we presume they are, as sound to-day as when first placed there. If the rapidity of the growth of the cedar were at all correspondent to its other qualities, it would be the most valuable tree in the forest.

Lord Lindsay had intended proceeding that evening to Bsherray; "But no," he adds, "we could not resolve to leave these glorious trees so soon—the loveliest, the noblest, the holiest in the world. The tent was pitched, and we spent the rest of the day under their 'shadowy shroud.' Oh what a church that grove is! Never did I think Solomon's song so beautiful, and that most noble chapter of Ezekiel, the thirty-first; I had read it on the heights of Syene, Egypt on my right hand and Ethiopia on my left, with many another denunciation, how awfully fulfilled, of desolation against Pathros and judgments against No. But this was the place to enjoy it, lying under one of these vast trees, looking up every now and then into its thick boughs, hearing the little birds warbling, and a perpetual hum of insect life pervading the air with its drowsy melody. Eden is close by—these are the 'trees of Eden,' 'the choice and best of Lebanon,' these are the trees—there can be none nobler—which Solomon spake of, ' from the cedar of Lebanon to the hyssop on the wall ;' the object of repeated allusion and comparison throughout the Bible, the emblem of the righteous in David's Sabbath hymn, and, honor above honor, the likeness of the countenance of the Son of God in the inspired canticles of Solomon.

"Our encampment was very picturesque that night, the fire throwing a strong light on the cedar that overcanopied us; those enormous arms of ghastly whiteness seemed almost alive, and about to catch us up into the thick darkness they issued from."

In a former chapter we described at some length the peculiarities of the Druses; and here, on the heights and along the slopes of Lebanon, we find a sect called the Metualis, which, in many particulars, are scarcely less singular.

The Metualis are followers of Ali, as the Turks are of Omar; they therefore belong to the same great division of Islamism as the Persians and other *Shiites*, but there is something very peculiar in their tenets and usages that essentially distinguishes them from all the other believers in Ali. I will, says Perrier, relate what I have learned of them from the lips of their aged men, who take delight in explaining the old books that tell of their ancient might. Their history has for some centuries been identified with that of Syria, and there is scarcely a town, village or hamlet in the country respecting which the Metualis have not some interesting legend or anecdote to recount. I felt an indescribable pleasure in hearing two old white-bearded Metualis describing their ancient glory, the power of their ancestors in Syria, and the wars of other days; and then speaking, with tears in their eyes, of their present low estate, the persecutions they suffered at the hand of the terrible Djezzar, and the final downfall of their nation.

Some years before the civil wars began by Omar-el-Daher in the last century, the Metualis were still numerous and strong in Syria; their numbers were then at least double what they now are, and they were under the government of their own *macaïehs*, or district chiefs. After Omar-el-Daher was put down, this little nation, which had previously suffered severely, was beginning to recover from its disasters when the terrible sway of Ahmed-Djezzar supervened and completed its ruin.

After enduring intense oppression at the hands of the savage pasha, they at last took up arms in their own defence. They were successful at first; defeated Djezzar's troops in every engagement, and took several important fortresses in the *Belad Beshara*, perched like eyries on the tops of the scarped cliffs. The crafty pasha, finding that he could not prevail over them by mere force, contrived to gain over some of their chiefs by gold or promises, and to sow dissension among them. Ere long their operations became languid and ineffectual, and Djezzar had timely warning of all their designs through his spies. He soon had the upper hand; and he carried out his measures against the revolters with his usual vigor, impaling all that fell into his hands. He laid siege to the important fortress of Nabatieh with a force of seven thousand men and three pieces of cannon. Some hundreds of the Metualis had shut themselves up in the fortress, which they defended with obstinate courage. The position of this important fortress is extraordinary and singularly romantic; built in the times of the Crusades on an isolated cliff, which may be ascended on the western side by a steep flight of steps cut in the rock, it looks vertically down on the other three sides from a height of nine hundred feet on the river Kasmieh, the ancient Leontes. A few blocks of stone rolled upon the path on the only practicable side would be enough to baffle the attempts of a whole army. This was accordingly done by the besieged; but the traitors who were among them showed Djezzar a subterranean passage which led under the gate of the fortress, and which the besieged had walled up.

Djezzar had two pieces of cannon brought by night into the subterraneous passage; a few shots were fired, and so tremendous was the report, reverberated and magnified by the rocky walls, that the Metualis believed the pasha had undermined the whole cliff, and was blowing it up. A panic seized them, and they surrendered, stipulating only that their lives should be spared. But Djezzar was not the man to be baulked of his vengeance by the faith of treaties—he beheaded most of his prisoners. As for the traitors who had enabled him to take the fortress, his avarice prompted him to deal them poetical justice, and he amused himself with seeing them hurled from the battlements into the Kasmieh. The capture of the fortresses, Nabatieh and El Shekef, gave the last blow to the power of the Metualis; they scattered and fled, and Djezzar had them hunted down like wild beasts. All that fell into his hands were impaled at the gates of Acre or Seyde; the greater part of their property was confiscated, and the authority of their *macaïehs* was thenceforth abolished. Thus was for ever destroyed the influence the Metualis were beginning to acquire, and which ranked next to that possessed by the Druses.

When from home, the Metualis observe many of the outward practices of the Moslems. Their doctors or priests are called *aiummats* or first doctors. They recognize twelve imans as founders of their religion, the first of whom is Ali, and the rest his descendants to the eleventh generation. These imans they call the twelve doctors of the universe. All the Metualis look forward for the speedy coming of the *mouhdi* (guide) of the race of Ali. This messiah, or mouhdi, will rule over the whole world, and will put to a fearful death all those who shall have denied him; he will then glorify his own, and will execute the judgment of God in the land of the sanctuary.

The messiah they expect in common with many Persians is Mohammed el Mehdy (or Mouhdi), the twelfth and last of their imans, who suddenly disappeared, they say, after giving battle to the caliph of Babylon, near Karbela. The Turks, on the contrary, say that the iman was slain in the engagement and that his body was recognized on the field of battle. But, according to the belief of the Metualis and of a certain number of Persians, he was suddenly caught up and transported to Arabia, where he will one day appear triumphantly, re-establish the race of the imans on the throne, and slay all who shall have refused to own him. The Metualis give this messiah the name also of *Sahab-Zaman* (the master of time), because he is not dead, and because he disposes of time and stops it at his pleasure, till the moment arrives to make himself known as Mohammed's vicar.

Magnificent horses are always kept ready saddled and caparisoned, among the Metualis of Irik, in expectation of his return. No one ever mounts these chosen steeds, which are held in high veneration by the members of the sect. Several Metualis appropriate a part of their wealth to a reserved fund to be kept until the arrival of the mouhdi.

The first apostle of the Metuali sect who settled in Syria was Abou-Abdallah-Mohammed, surnamed *el Cheid-el-ewel*, or the first martyr. He resided first in Jezin (nine leagues from Seyde), and, after making numerous converts there, he went and preached at Sarfend (the ancient Sarepta), where he was soon followed by such a host of disciples that he was enabled to build seven great mosques in Jezin, three of which exist to this day. But the Damascus doctors, jealous of his popularity, challenged him to preach in that city and to maintain a thesis against them. He fearlessly accepted the challenge, and so convincingly did he maintain the doctrine of the followers of Ali that the baffled and mortified Sunnite doctors, finding their logic at fault, had recourse to intrigue, excited the ignorant populace against their triumphant adversary, and had him condemned to be burned alive as an infidel and blasphemer. Abou-Abdallah-Mohammed was swathed in a cloth steeped in combustibles, tied to a plank, and burned by a slow fire. Every year since that event, on the day after the return of the hadj caravan from Mecca, the populace assemble in the streets to burn a plank wrapped up in pitched cloths, and as it consumes they heap imprecations on the family of Ali, and shout with all their might, "May Allah burn the plank and curse the followers of Ali!"

The Metualis have a horrible custom tolerated by the laws. In case of urgent need the father is authorized to expose his own children for sale in the slave-market, and instances are not rare in which this frightful privilege has been exercised. In the month of September, 1839, after the Syrian campaign, when the Egyptian government exacted all arrears of taxes with very great rigor, many girls from twelve to fifteen years of age were sold at Homs and Hamah by unfortunate Metualis of the district of Baalbec. They were offered at prices varying from one thousand to twelve hundred piastres, but purchasers would not give so much; eleven were disposed of at Hamah and seven at Homs, and fetched on an average from seven hundred to nine hundred piastres. Purchasers were deterred from bidding freely by the consideration that the father was entitled to redeem his children at the end of a year by paying back the purchase money.

Several of the Metuali families were formerly of princely rank, and their members enjoyed all the authority of emirs. The Turkish pashas and governors have gradually despoiled them of their powers and confiscated most of their property; but they have not found it so easy a task to divest them of the moral influence they possess among their brethren.

The oldest and most renowned Metuali families in Syria are the Beit-el-Charfue, near Baalbec, the Beit Shebib of Gazia, the Beit Eweilan, Beit Emir Canjar, etc., etc. Any member of one of these families can at his pleasure instantly raise some villages and some hundreds of men, by the sole influence of his name, to maintain his personal quarrel.

Emir Canjar, the head of an ancient family in the neighborhood of Baalbec, underwent the indignity of being seized in the conscription of 1834 like a common peasant and enrolled in the Egyptian army, but he soon contrived to desert and return home. Notwithstanding the severe orders of Ibraham Pasha against all deserters, no steps were taken to recover possession of the emir's person; the governor pretended not to know what had become of him, for he was certain that if he sent his soldiers to seize him by force, it would provoke a serious insurrection.

Emir Canjar applied himself peaceably to his rural occupations, and abstained from all conduct that would excite the suspicion of the Egyptian government as long as he saw it in a strong position, but as soon as the mountaineers of Lebanon began to stir, in the month of April, 1840, he threw off the mask, though the insurgents were not of his own religion. He had his private wrongs to avenge, and vengeance is the Metuali's most intense passion. Canjar put himself at the head of three or four hundred horsemen of his clan and joined the insurgent Maronites, who were encamped before Beyrout. His name was famous throughout all Syria for courage, skill, and prodigious bodily strength, and he fully justified his reputation by the mischief he did the Egyptians. He cut off numerous convoys of provisions and other military supplies, and for a long time blockaded the road to Damascus. The first revolt of Lebanon was, however, put down in a few days by the extraordinary address and energy of Mohammed Ali; almost all the chiefs submitted and humbly sued for pardon, but Canjar was not among the supplicants. He continued to wander about with his men through the most inaccessible regions of Lebanon, intercepting the couriers, and doing the Egyptians all the damage he could; and this course he continued unchecked till the allied fleet appeared before Beyrout. He was then one of the first to apply for arms, which he distributed among the inhabitants of his native village; and, partly by persuasion, partly by force, he succeeded in bringing over some Maronite villages of the Kesrouan to the Turkish cause. He played an important part in the last decisive events that led to the expulsion of Ibrahim Pasha from Syria, and he contributed more than any other chief to the general insurrection of the mountaineers of Lebanon.

Volumes might be filled with the legends current among the Metualis respecting the towns and villages of Syria. Some of these are very interesting, but they would occupy too much space.

ASIA MINOR.

CHAPTER XXI.

ASIA MINOR.

FROM Alexandretta our course lies westward, along the southern shore of Asia Minor. We reach Mersyn early next morning, where our steamer stops to take in cotton and lead. The quality of the cotton raised about this place is not very good, and the lead seems much harder than that which we usually get in America.

The town itself is small, with nothing special to commend it to the attention of the tourist.

From Mersyn our course still lies westward. We sail part of the time within sight of the capes, promontories, and bays made famous in ancient warfare—part of the time without sight of land, and not until Monday, at 10 A. M., having left Mersyn on Saturday, at 3 P. M., do we reach Rhodes.

This town is located on an island of the same name, and though of but little beauty or importance now, at one time it played an important part in the world's history. In its institutions of learning, and in the determined valor of its citizens and their love of liberty, it occupied a foremost place among the cities of the ancients; and in more modern times the Knights of St. John of Jerusalem here conducted a most admirable defence against their many foes.

From Rhodes we run north-westerly through Kos Channel and Furni Pass until we round the peninsula of Karabournon, and then easterly until we reach the harbor of Smyrna. In the mean time we pass by the islands of Piscopi, Nicero, Kos, Kalimo, Lero, Patmos, Furni, Nikari, Khios, and others. All these islands have more or less celebrity and interest in connection with ancient history, but the one upon which we gaze with most interest is that of Patmos.

Here it was that St. John was banished by the Emperor Domitian for daring to preach the gospel of Christ, and here it was that he wrote " The revelation of Jesus Christ which God gave unto him, to show unto his servants things which must shortly come to pass."

During our passage from Rhodes to Smyrna our steamer meets with an accident, which for the time being seems to threaten instant destruction to all on board.

About two o'clock in the morning a terrible shock is felt by all on board, awakening those who are asleep, and causing instant and terrible consternation to the hundreds of passengers on board. Cries and screams are heard all over the vessel; men, women and children are running hither and thither in utter bewilderment; the engine ceases its throbbings, and the general impression among the passengers is that the vessel has struck upon a rock and must soon go to the bottom.

The shock is so severe that we find ourselves thrown from our berths to the floor of our state-room (whether thrown out by the jar or jumping out while asleep we know not), and it is some moments before we can sufficiently collect our thoughts to determine upon the best mode of procedure.

Hastily putting on such clothes as we can most readily lay hands on, we rush into the passage-way and then upon deck to learn the cause and extent of the accident, and there learn that our vessel has not struck upon a rock, but that another steamer, in attempting to cross our bows, has run into us, tearing away about fifty feet of the bulwarks on the left side, smashing in a part of the forecastle and doing considerable other damage.

An immediate trial of the pumps proves, however, that the vessel is not leaking, and a starting of the engines soon after reassures the passengers that, notwithstanding the accident, we can still pursue our journey.

Further inquiries reveal the fact that some thirty of the deck passengers have been more or less injured by the staving in of the bulwarks and the falling of a cannon from the top of the forecastle to the deck, and that the injuries of some twelve of the thirty are quite serious.

The vessel which ran into us immediately veered off, and the officers of our steamer were unable then to determine with certainty as to her character or nationality, but upon reaching Smyrna we learn that it was a Turkish man-of-war, which had left that port the day before.

As may readily be supposed, the balance of the time in reaching Smyrna is chiefly occupied in discusssing the whys and wherefores of the accident. Was it because of negligence of our own officers or those of the other steamer? Were we run into purposely or by accident? How little more would have staved in the side of the hull as well as the bulwarks of our steamer, and how then could such an immense number of passengers have been saved from a watery grave?

Our officers seem quite as much interested in these inquiries as the passengers, and are ready to answer and explain every query made of them. Indeed, in this respect, not only upon special but upon all occasions, the officers of a Russian steamer are far more obliging than those generally found upon steamers of other European nations.

The sail up the harbor of Smyrna is most delightful, and at 5 P. M. we drop anchor opposite the far-famed city.

At Smyrna we remain two days, and during that time we make the best possible use of our opportunities in examining objects of interest.

First, we call at the American mission, and have a pleasant interview with the missionary in charge, Rev. H. J. Van Lennep and his estimable lady. The mission buildings are pleasantly situated, large, and commodious, and well furnished. The school-room is fitted up tastefully, with large colored maps about the walls, and plenty of books, pens, paper, slates, etc., etc. The school is not in session when we call, and hence we have no opportunity to see its pupils or workings.

Rev. Mr. Van Lennep is a pleasant, intelligent gentleman of about fifty years of age. He has been a missionary in the East for many years, but has only been at Smyrna about three years, and is now working under the direction of the "American Board of Foreign Missions," for which position he seems admirably fitted.

The school numbers about eighty pupils—the membership of the church twenty-five—and the attendance upon the church service about sixty adults, besides the pupils of the school. The station has been established since 1833, and has several branches in different parts of Asia Minor, which are under the charge of native missionaries and visited occasionally by Mr. Van Lennep. The mission, we should judge, is in a prosperous condition in every respect, and accomplishing as much good as could be expected among such a people.

The next call is at the American consulate. The consul himself is absent, but his secretary very kindly furnishes us with American newspapers, and gives us such information concerning Smyrna as we ask for.

After this we make a general tour of the city, examining its streets and bazaars—the manner and customs of its people—its vehicles, horses, and donkeys—the Persian silks and carpets, of which this city is the great depôt for a Western market, the goods being brought here overland by means of caravans—its "thousand and one" curiosities of every kind and description—and about sundown we return to our steamer, well satisfied with our first day's inspection of Smyrna.

The following day we make the ascent of the high hills back of the city, for the purpose of seeing the tomb of Polycarp and the ruins of the old castle.

This tomb of Polycarp is one of the few remaining monuments of the early Christians of the East; for it will not be forgotten that here, at Smyrna, was located one of the seven churches of Asia, to whom John (in Revelation) was directed to write:

"I know thy works, and tribulation, and poverty (but thou art rich), and I know the blasphemy of them which say they are Jews and are not, but are the synagogue of Satan. Fear none of those things which thou shalt suffer; behold the devil shall cast some of you into prison that ye may be tried; and ye shall have tribulation ten days; be thou faithful until death, and I will give thee a crown of life."

For this faith Polycarp suffered martyrdom and received a " crown of life"—as did thousands of others throughout

Asia Minor. 411

the East, who preferred to sacrifice life rather than abjure their faith in Jesus; and his tomb remains to this day as a living monument of his faithfulness.

The tomb is a rough structure of brick, plastered over and whitewashed. It is eleven feet two inches long, six feet six inches wide, and five feet high. Near by are other smaller tombs, and an immense cypress tree, which, like an angel of mercy, stands near to watch over the ashes of the sleeping martyr.

A little way off, and on a still higher point of the hill, stand the ruins of the old castle, and to these our steps are next directed.

These ruins cover a large area; the walls are ten feet in thickness, with towers at each corner. There are three large excavations (probably used for powder magazines) within the walls, and just without the walls another still larger excavation, which our guide says was used as a theatre. This latter structure is entirely under ground, and has avenues, arches, and twenty-five columns, embracing a considerable area; but how, or in what way, it could have been used as a "theatre," or for any other purpose requiring light or ventilation, is beyond our comprehension. We rather incline to the opinion that it formed the substructure of a heathen temple, as it is plain to be seen from the débris lying scattered about, that the whole summit of the hill was at one time occupied by buildings, and tradition, indeed, avers that the whole of ancient Smyrna stood upon this hill-top.

The view from this eminence, and especially from the top of the old castle walls, is extensive, grand, and beautiful.

At our feet lies Smyrna, with its one hundred and fifty thousand inhabitants—narrow, dirty streets—fanciful Turkish houses and gilded minarets—curious cemeteries with turbaned and gilded headstones and tall cypress trees. On the outskirts are handsome little villas surrounded by fig and orange groves; still in front of us and beyond the city stretches out the beautiful harbor, filled with vessels of every shape and size, and from nearly all the nations of the earth; on our right is a mountain cultivated to its very summit, and a valley studded all over with fig tree and orange; on our left the peninsula of Karabournon, stretching far out toward the sea, and almost enclosing the harbor, of which it forms the southwestern boundary; and turning around, away off to the north-eastward runs a wide and well-cultivated valley, through which the iron rail and steam engine now carry passengers and freight as far as the site of ancient Ephesus, and will, ere long, carry them direct to Constantinople.

Of ancient Ephesus but little remains, though the excavations now going on may yet reveal to the antiquarian some objects of interest. Here, it will be recollected, was located another of the seven churches of Asia, to whom the Apostle John was instructed to say:

"I know thy works, and thy labor, and thy patience, and how thou canst not bear them which are evil: and thou hast tried them which say they are apostles, and are not, and hast found them liars: and hast borne and hast patience, and for my name's sake hast labored, and hast not fainted."

It is nearly sundown of the 9th of May when we start from Smyrna, and as the evening is beautiful we remain on deck a long time, watching the well-cultivated shores of the harbor and the beautiful islands of the archipelago, so much celebrated in ancient history.

Our course lies through the Mytilene Channel, and we pass near by ancient Lesbos, which in the day of its greatest glory rivaled Athens in learning and the arts, and claimed the honor of being the birth-place of the immortal Sappho. We also pass Troas, the site of ancient Troy, the history of which has been so often told in prose and poetry that every school-boy knows it well; and directly opposite this is the island of Tenedos, where the wily Greeks hid themselves when they pretended to abandon the siege of Troy.

Next morning we reach the town of Dardanelles, which is situated at the entrance of the Strait of Dardanelles, and here we stop for a time to let off some of the Russian pilgrims, who, in addition to their pilgrimage to Palestine, are about to make another to some far-off mountain (the name of which we have forgotten) which is thought to have about it something of sanctity. Those who are about to leave the steamer are kissed often and most affectionately by those remaining, and many a prayer is uttered for their safe return.

Among the new passengers received on board at Smyrna was a Metropolitan Greek Bishop, whose venerable age (being ninety-five years old) and august appearance excited much attention. Two young Greek priests repeated long and earnest prayers at his state-room door before we left the harbor; and his deputy or secretary was constantly with him to administer to his wants—at table, in the cabin, or wherever else he moved. His feebleness from age rendered such attention absolutely necessary; and yet, in voice and manner, the old man would occasionally brighten up and seem quite rejuvenated. He left us at Makarania.

Soon after leaving Dardanelles we reach Abydos, so celebrated in ancient story as the place where Leander, after swimming the Hellespont, nightly met his beautiful Hero; and where she clasped his dead body to her arms, when, upon one fatal night, he was drowned while endeavoring to reach his loved one. Among the most beautiful works of sculpture to be met with in any of the art galleries of Europe is that of Hero and Leander clasped in each other's arms.

Byron also swam the Hellespont at this point (which just here is probably about half a mile in width), and having contracted the ague from so doing, was rather disposed to condemn both Leander and himself for attempting so hazardous an enterprise. Alluding to the fate of Leander, he closes the poem by saying:

> " 'Twas hard to say who fared the best—
> Sad mortals! thus the gods still plague you;
> He lost his labor, I my jest,
> For he was drowned, and I've the ague."

Upon both sides of the Dardanelles are towns, some larger, some smaller, and all picturesque, as seen from the deck of our passing steamer. There are also along either shore several ruins of fortifications, which, according to ancient warfare, were doubtless places of great strength, but which could not stand a single shot from "monitors" of the present day.

Early in the afternoon we reach Gallipoli, and from thence we enter upon the Sea of Marmora. Nothing could be more beautiful than this little sea, with islands dotting its glassy surface here and there, and with the shores on either side like long lines of emerald.

The approach to Constantinople from the Sea of Marmora is very beautiful. Long before we reach it we see the gilded domes and minarets of the numerous mosques; and, as we approach still nearer, the city itself seems to rise from out of the water and recline gently and gracefully against the surrounding hillsides.

Asia Minor.

It has no long wharves jutting out into the sea, the Bosphorus or the Golden Horn; but everywhere along the water's edge the first row of buildings rises from a sufficient depth of water to allow the approach of small boats, called "caiques;" and all the palaces and better class of residences built along the water have passage-ways or steps, from which the inmates of the dwellings can step into a caique whenever they wish to take a ride of pleasure or visit some other point along the shore. Of these caiques it is said that no fewer than seventy thousand are to be found on the waters surrounding the city and its suburbs, and so light and graceful are they—so elegantly varnished and cushioned, and so easily and rapidly propelled—that it is an absolute luxury to ride in one of them.

The ground upon which the old city stands, together with its surrounding villages, Pera, Galata, Tophani, and Scutari, rises gradually from the water's edge, so that whichever way you look you see line after line of houses rising gracefully above each other, and on the highest point of all a magnificent mosque, or some other public building. From this it will readily be understood how beautiful the city must look as seen from a distance. We say "from a distance," for in this case, as in many others, "'tis distance lends enchantment to the view," as we shall have occasion to demonstrate more fully hereafter.

The peculiar style of architecture adopted by the Turks, and generally throughout the East, also adds much to the apparent beauty of their cities, towns and villages, as seen from a distance. This style—if style it may be called—consists of an exuberance of small columns, arches, domes, and lattice-work. Instead of a square, angular or pitching roof, most of the buildings have a dome, or, in case of a very large building, a succession of small domes, which are plastered and whitewashed. This style of roofing makes most admirable coverings—more lasting, indeed, than shingle, slate, or tile, and far more picturesque. These domes necessitate, of course, the arch, which is to be seen within and without every building of any considerable size, while the column, half-column and lattice-work are added as ornaments.

A closer inspection, however, of the streets and buildings of Constantinople shows that what seemed so enchantingly beautiful from the deck of the steamer as we approach the city is really very common, and in some cases decidedly ugly when seen near by. To this there are exceptions, for while the words common and unclean may be applied to the city as a whole, there are within the city limits and the suburbs many buildings which in point of architectural beauty, and substantial and elaborate finish, will compare favorably with the better class of buildings in any other of the larger cities of Europe. Of some of these we shall have occasion to speak more in detail in our next chapter.

Our vessel anchors in the Bosphorus, about midway between Pera and Scutari; ourselves and baggage are taken in a small boat from the steamer to the shore; the ordeal of custom-house examination is gone through with, and in due time we find ourselves comfortably installed in the Grand Hotel d'Orient, where we will rest for the present.

CHAPTER XXII.

CONSTANTINOPLE.

CONSTANTINOPLE has long been regarded as one of the chief cities of the world, and, in point of situation and natural advantages, it is certainly unsurpassed by any other. Being the stepping-stone from Asia to Europe, and lying midway between the wheat-fields of the North and the tropical productions of the South, it might, in the hands of an enterprising people, be one of the greatest ports of trade in the universe. In the hands of the lazy, indolent Turk it can never be more than it is at present, except as far as the influx of European enterprise and its permission to do business therein may give it commercial importance.

The commerce of the city now, and indeed much of its home trade, are in the hands of foreigners, toward whom the Sultan has felt constrained to extend a liberal policy in order to increase his own financial resources and conciliate what are called the "Protecting Powers."

The present population of Constantinople is said to be about one million, of whom about three hundred thousand are Christians; all the others are Mohammedans of the most bigoted character.

The Moslems generally occupy the old city—the old Byzantium—while the Christians occupy the larger part of Pera and other suburbs of the city. There is no law compelling such separation, but upon the well-understood principle that "birds of a feather flock together," the Moslems keep by themselves and the Christians do the same, as far as circumstances admit. It is better thus, though such is the rigor of Turkish law, such the promptness of punishment following offence, and such the number of Turkish soldiers and police in every part of the city, that a Christian is now as safe in the streets of Constantinople as he would be in any city of Europe. The "sick man" well understands his precarious condition in the family of nations, and he will not permit his subjects to molest the subjects of other nationalities so long as he is held in wholesome dread by the "powers that be."

Though we apply the words "lazy, indolent, bigoted," etc., to the Turks in some of the above paragraphs—and such is really our own opinion of them—still it is only fair to say that a few travelers have seen them with different eyes, and have drawn conclusions somewhat different from our own. Thus we find Perier saying:

"The Turk seems born to command; he pushes his confidence in himself to an excess that degenerates into the most incredible presumption. In all he does his bearing is calm, grave, full of dignity and grandeur. An artisan of the lowest grade suddenly elevated to high rank will know how to assume instantly the tone and the manners suitable to his new position and to make his authority respected. He will no longer be the man he was yesterday—the metamorphosis is complete; but he does not seek to hide the recollection of his former life; on the contrary, he regards it with pride, and generally adds the name of his humble trade to the title of his new dignity. The good faith of the Turk in his dealings, above all with Christians and strangers, is proverbial; but, possibly, this good faith is in him not so much an inherent virtue as an effect of that religious pride that shows itself in all his acts.

"The Turk is too often open to the charge of cruelty and bloody violence; but such acts are commonly the necessary result of his position with regard to those under his rule. His crimes, when his passions are roused, are those of the beast of prey—violence, with an object; they are never those of the monkey or the inquisitor; he never does mischief for its own sake or on principle.

"Covetous of money to the highest degree, he will disdain to seek it by low and sordid acts, and will sooner have recourse to open violence; but there are occasions when the Turk is generous to prodigality. His outward demeanor is full of good-breeding and exceedingly winning and pleasing. It must be owned, however, that under this insinuating show he often conceals treachery and malignity. There is no people among whom the art of dissimulation is carried so far. Nothing more strongly illustrates their character in this respect than one of their own favorite proverbs: 'Lick the hand thou canst not wound; lick it till thou canst bite it.'

"The Arabs, too, have a proverb which they apply to the Turks, and which is not less characteristic than the former: 'If the Turk turns musk to creep into thy pocket, make a hole in that pocket to let him escape before he becomes a red-hot coal.'

"'In expressing,' says Mr. Urquhart, 'the admiration with which the Turkish character inspires me I must restrict that praise entirely to its domestic and passive existence—to the Turk as son, husband, father, master, neighbor; whatever qualities he may possess flow from these characters. He is brave, because he defends his home; he is docile, because he had a father; he is not factious, because the unity of the state includes and represents that of the family; he is faithful to treaties, because he lives well with his friends. The Turk—agriculturist, seaman, general, mechanic, or professor—is as far below other European nations as he is above any of them in his domestic virtues or his social integrity. He exists therefore, he has a place among nations, only in consequence of these, which, again, are not the result of principle but of habit; and of habits, the impress of which is derived from the harem.'"

Of the harem, too, and of the condition of Turkish women generally, our own observations and the conclusions derived therefrom have not been of a favorable character; and yet we find, occasionally, one who has traveled in the East speaking of them in terms of high admiration. Thus Lamartine says: "Too many travelers —speaking of a thing they knew only by vague report— have propagated and confirmed the vulgar notion that the harem is a dismal prison where lovely women languish in captivity under a jealous tyrant—an odious haunt, devoted only to brutal, sensual indulgence. This is no more worthy of credence than the tales of those other travelers who would have us believe that their own enterprising gallantry had triumphed over all the defences of the guarded enclosure. The harem is the hearth, the home, the one spot on earth which each man calls his own, secret and forbidden. It is his wife in whose behalf this sanctuary is created; it exists only in her, and wherever she is, there it is also. One thing only mars the beautiful constitution of the Eastern home and impairs its happiness—that is the recognition of polygamy as a principle sanctioned by the laws. But, without offering any apology for the principle, we may venture to say that very exaggerated notions prevail as to the extent to which it is really acted on; and it may even be questioned whether the practical polygamy of the West, which, unsanctioned by law and reproved by custom, adds degradation of the mind to dissoluteness of morals, is not a greater evil than the tolerated polygamy of the East.

"Instances are not rare in Mohammedan countries of a husband possessing but one wife: in such cases, if there be a natural kindness of disposition on either side, it can hardly fail to ripen into strong, concentrated, reciprocal affection. The retirement and solitude of the harem offer nothing to divert the mind from the one absorbing passion: the wife's whole business and pleasure are centred in her husband and her children, and his eyes do not 'wander after strange women.' This domestic happiness and virtue are, however, not common to all parts of the East. Rare, though not unknown, among the Arabs, it is more peculiarly Turkish; and the deep root which the love of home (not the spot of birth, but the hearth, wherever placed) has struck into that people, cannot be better demonstrated than by its capacity to overcome the effects of the continual introduction, as slaves or wives, of perhaps the most dissolute races on the face of the earth—the Georgian and the Arab.

"A Mohammedan woman's property is as secure as that of a man: a wife's fortune is her own, and does not, as amongst us, become the property of her husband. If the latter can divorce his wife, the wife also can divorce the husband, and the mother of a son is absolute mistress: nor is it a trifling prerogative of the sex that the servant or the slave can marry the master or his son without exciting animadversion, or entailing reproach on her helpmate or his family. The women are treated by the men with a respect they do not always show in return·

and when a woman addresses a man he reverently casts his eyes on the ground: nay, the very idea of woman is invested with a sanctity that extends to everything belonging to her. It arrests the arm of justice, and lawless violence sinks abashed before it. The wife is independent of the political dangers that threaten her husband, except as they affect her through him; her life, her person, her property, even her establishment, is sacred and secure. There is no instance of a pasha or officer of any description forcing his way into the hallowed precincts of the harem; there no decree can be executed against the master of the house; he must be summoned elsewhere, or waited for till he quits it; and any criminal condemned to death must be pardoned if on his way to execution he meets the women of a harem, and can touch the hem of the veil worn by one of them, or if he can lay his hand on the door of a married woman's dwelling and cry *fiardek el harem.*"

Having thus presented both sides of these two questions—showing that we have no prejudice to subserve, and only desire that our readers shall have all the facts, in order that they may draw correct conclusions—we will now proceed with our narrative.

The first place at which we call in Constantinople is at the American consulate. The office is handsomely fitted up, and the consul, Mr. Greenough, is a gentleman of high culture, and admirably fitted, we should say, for the position he occupies. He is not particularly pleased, however, with a residence in Constantinople, and will not regret when the time comes for his return to the United States.

We also call upon our Minister Resident, Hon. E. Joy Morris, with whom we have a long and pleasant interview. The conversation is, of course, principally on home affairs, and we are delighted to learn from his own lips, that notwithstanding the innuendoes which have been thrown out against him by some portion of the American press, because of his reply to Secretary Seward relative to the policy of President Johnson, he still adheres to Republican principles, in their fullest and broadest sense. There is no truer American at home or abroad than E. Joy Morris, nor one who takes a more enlightened and philanthropic view of our home relations and foreign policy.

We find his estimable lady equally patriotic and agreeable as himself, and much regret our inability to accept of courtesies which they so kindly and heartily tender us.

In the way of sight-seeing, our first day's tour commences with the Mosque of St. Sophia, which stands near the Sublime Porte, and which, in our judgment, is by far the finest mosque in Constantinople. It has less of filagree, or, as we Americans would say, gingerbread work, about it than some of the others, but the grand old arches and columns which remain of the original Christian church give it a massive and imposing appearance far superior to any other mosque of the city.

Its form is that of a Greek cross, two hundred and seventy feet in length by two hundred and forty-three in width. The centre is surmounted by a large gilded dome, one hundred and eighty feet above the floor, while about this are eight smaller domes, or semi-domes, and four minarets. Within are one hundred and seventy columns of marble, granite, and porphyry, some quite large, others smaller, and many of them polished in the highest perfection of art. Most of these columns are said to have been brought from the ruins of temples at Baalbec, Heliopolis, Ephesus, Cyclades, and Athens.

This edifice was commenced by the Emperor Justinian,

A. D. 531, and was seven and a half years in building. Its cost is said to have been fabulous, and we can well believe it, from the kind and quantity of material used. It was used as a Christian church until the Mohammedans got possession of the country, who converted it into a mosque. The alterations and additions made by the Moslems are easily traceable, and, in our judgment, greatly detract from the original beauty of the edifice. The gilding of the cupola is now greatly tarnished, but, when new and bright, it could be seen, it is said, a hundred miles at sea.

To enter this mosque requires a firman from the Sultan or some bucksheesh for the attendants. We adopt the latter, and by placing a couple of silver dollars in the hands of the turbaned official who meets us at the door, we are readily admitted and treated with distinguished consideration.

Next we visit the Mosque of Sultan Achmed, which covers a larger area than St. Sophia. It has two more minarets, but is not to be compared with the latter either in style, finish, or grandeur. While examining this mosque some of the attendants become very insolent, and one of them pushes others against us because of our refusal to take off our shoes before stepping on the matting in the passage-way, whereupon we break our cane over the head of one of them, and then report the matter to the police for such further action as they might think proper to take. We don't think the attendants at *that* mosque will again interfere with a foreign visitor—especially if he be an American.

Near this mosque is the Hippodrome, a square nine hundred feet in length by four hundred and fifty in width, which contains the granite obelisk from Thebes, set up by Theodosius the Great; a spiral brass column, consisting of three serpents twisted together, which originally supported the golden tripod in the temple of Delphi; and the tall, square pillar of Constantine, which was stripped of its bronze casings by the Turks when they first captured the city. On one side of this square formerly stood the Roman imperial palace, the senate house, and the forum, all of which have been so changed and mutilated that nothing of their original beauty remains.

It is plain to be seen that the Turks have no respect for ancient monuments, and, judging from the neglect shown to those in the Hippodrome, it will not be long before every vestige of the ancient greatness of the city will be obliterated.

Our next visit is to what is called the "Janizaries," which we find to be a museum of wax-figures, representing every condition of Turkish life, from the water-carrier and knife-grinder to the soldier and sultan. The features as well as the dress of the most celebrated Turkish soldiers and rulers are here carefully preserved, which makes the museum of great interest to one who may wish to study the manners and customs of the earlier followers of the Prophet. This museum is under the care of the government, and a small fee is charged for admission.

Next we visit what is called the "Thousand-and-one-Columns," to reach which we entered a small doorway, near the surface, and make a descent of some thirty feet under ground. Here we find five hundred double columns—one upon the top of the other—and one single column, making the required number of one thousand and one. These columns are about two feet in diameter, and the two together measure probably forty feet in height. They cover a considerable area, the space between each column being from eight to ten feet. About two-thirds of the lower half of these columns—or rather the lower of the two columns—are now under ground, the earth having fallen in about them before the place was covered over. We find several workmen in this underground cavern making ropes—using the space between the columns as their rope-walk.

At the time of the Roman occupancy of Constantinople this was used as an immense reservoir for water, and must have been a place of great beauty as well as of utility. The waters of the Sea of Marmora, and indeed all the waters surrounding Constantinople, are very brackish, and this immense reservoir of fresh water was deemed essential to the citizens in case of a siege.

Next we visit the Mosque of Mohammed II., than which there is no more beautiful edifice in Constantinople. It is built of white marble, of circular shape, surmounted by a dome, and from one side of it runs a colonnade, on the other side of which is the street, and on the inside a well-cultivated garden. Neither in architecture nor embellishment is there anything of Orientalism about it.

Within it are the tombs of the sultan, of his mother, and of his several wives, all of which are covered with rich Cashmere shawls, and embellished with Turkish designs in gold and silver. Around the room are stools inlaid with ivory, and on each of these lies the Koran, or some other Moslem volume, bound magnificently. The floor is covered with a Persian carpet of the most delicate texture, the window-hangings are of black silk velvet, gorgeously embroidered with silver thread, and over these hang white lace curtains of the most costly material and workmanship. Both externally and internally this mosque or tomb of Mohammed II. is far handsomer than anything else of the kind we have seen in all the East.

This mosque occupies the exact site formerly occupied

by the Church of the Holy Apostles, which church Mohammed II. had torn down in order to erect thereon the edifice which now bears his name. Whether he sleeps well or ill after so great a sacrilege, we leave with others to judge.

Thus closes our first day's sight-seeing in Constantinople, and we now return to our hotel to rest and recuperate, for here, as elsewhere, sight-seeing is the hardest kind of work.

On the day following we resolve to finish, if possible, the remaining mosques and other public buildings of interest within the city, and to this end we make an early start.

Crossing the bay in a light canoe, from Pera to the outer point of the peninsula, we land near the Seraglio, which we essay to enter, but as some repairs are being made, no strangers are permitted within the grounds. We afterward, however, have a fine view of the old palace and grounds from Scutari, on the opposite side of the Bosphorus. Since the death of the present sultan's father the Seraglio is no longer used as an imperial residence, and it is fast going to ruin. It has no occupants at present except the wives or concubines of the late sultan, to whom it would be death if they were to show their faces to a Christian of the male sex.

The "Sublime Porte," which we next inspect, of which everybody has heard or read, and from which the sultans of Turkey take one of their official titles, is nothing more than an immense gateway leading from the city to a large open square near the Seraglio. It is also near the mosque of St. Sophia, and from it, on either side, is a block of buildings used for governmental purposes. It does, indeed, possess a certain kind or degree of sublimity, but, as compared with many others of like character throughout Europe, it would hardly excite a second glance.

Again, passing the mosques of St. Sophia, Achmed, Mohammed, the Hippodrome and its columns, and spending a little time at the last for another inspection, we finally reach what is now called the "Burnt Pillar," so named because of its having been blackened by repeated conflagrations around it, but which was originally known as the Pillar of Constantine the Great, as it was erected by him, and was intended to commemorate and perpetuate his fame as emperor of Rome and its provinces.

This column was originally one hundred and twenty feet in height and surmounted by a colossal bronze statue of Apollo, but the earthquake which visited Constantinople in A. D. 1150 shook down the statue and three blocks of the column, leaving its present height only ninety feet. Like the ancient monuments in the Hippodrome, this column is wholly neglected, and will probably soon be among the things that were.

Next we proceed to what is known as the "Pigeon Mosque," because of the great number of pigeons there kept and fed by the devout followers of the Prophet. There is nothing in the mosque itself worthy of description, but it is indeed curious to see the hundreds—we were about to write thousands, as they seemed innumerable —of pigeons flying about the inner court and feeding from the hands of the attendants. These pigeons are considered sacred, and woe be to the man who dares to harm one of them.

Our next visit is to the "Mosque of Suleiman the Magnificent," which is regarded by some as the most beautiful in Constantinople, but which we think far inferior to that of St. Sophia. It has indeed far more ornament than the latter—if Turkish filagree-work can be regarded as ornament at all—but it lacks the finely polished columns which give to the latter so grand and imposing an appearance. The Mosque of Suleiman is Turkish all over—Turkish without and Turkish within —and is probably the best specimen of their architecture and style to be found anywhere in the East. Its builder, Sultan Suleiman, designed it to be the "glory of the whole earth," and expended, it is said, vast sums of money upon it, but, unfortunately for his reputation as a designer and builder, he had not seen the splendid cathedrals of Europe, or else he had a vain-glorious opinion of his own taste and judgment.

His tomb is near the mosque, in a small circular building surmounted by a dome, and elaborately finished within. In the same building are the tombs of his several wives and children, all covered with rich Cashmere shawls, and surmounted with gold and silver trimmings. Here, too, may be seen a plan of the city and temple of Mecca, elaborately carved in wood. Perhaps the Sultan thought that by having a plan of the Prophet's tomb so near his own it would the more certainly secure him a place in the Mohammedan Paradise.

The balance of the day we spend in the bazaars of the old city, which in extent and arrangement are far superior to those of Damascus and Cairo. Here is one long street entirely devoted to ladies' wearing apparel, in which everything of the kind may be found, from the cheapest printed muslin to the most elegant India silks and shawls; there is another entirely devoted to meerschaums and amber mouthpieces; another devoted to jewelry, of which each crosslegged shopkeeper has about as much as you could carry in your vest pocket, though some of the articles glitter with diamonds and are of great value:

another devoted to shoes and slippers of every conceivable shape, size, and quality; another to tarbouches; another to robes of ermine and fur, and so on throughout the list.

Thus another day closes, and here we will close this chapter, leaving for another a description of what else we may see during our stay at Constantinople.

CHAPTER XXIII.

CLOSING SIGHTS.

OUR stay in Constantinople continues for seven days, during all of which time we are constantly engaged in seeing and learning what is to be seen and learned in this far-famed city of the East.

Of the first two days of sight-seeing in Constantinople we have already spoken in a former chapter. As in this we intend to include all else that we may have to say of this city, we shall not attempt to give each day's sight-seeing separately; but will describe each object and incident as it may occur to our mind while writing.

On Sunday we attend two services of a very diverse character. In the forenoon we go to the Episcopal chapel attached to the English embassy, and hear a sound, practical sermon from the lips of the rector. Every seat of the chapel is filled—mostly by English residents of the city—and the services are conducted in the usual form, greatly to the spiritual edification and pleasure of all present. Lord Lyons, who formerly resided at Washington, and was for many years Minister Plenipotentiary from Great Britain to the United States, is now filling a like capacity at Constantinople, though we learn while here that he is soon to return to England. His official residence—built and maintained by the government—is one of the finest buildings in the city, having large and well-cultivated grounds, and a chapel attached thereto, as before stated.

We recollect well our first meeting with Lord Lyons, and the impression he then made upon us. It was at a party given by Mr. Seward, at his family residence in Washington. Just before sitting down to the table, Lord Lyons came in, and from the dress which he wore we at once set him down as an English clergyman, and were not undeceived until Mr. Seward introduced him to the company. We have never since heard the name of Lord Lyons or saw it in print without having our mind immediately recur to the mistake we made on first seeing him.

But we have thoughtlessly digressed from the subject-matter in hand, and must now return to a description of sight-seeing in and about Constantinople.

On the afternoon of the same Sabbath we attend a meeting of the "Whirling Dervishes," than which there is no more curious sight in Constantinople, though all they do is done in the name of religious worship. These dervishes are a sect of Mohammedans, who claim to have more zeal, more devotedness, and far more sanctity than their fellow-religionists. They hold about the same relation to Mohammedanism as monks do to Catholicism.

Their mosque is fitted up much in the usual style, except that in the centre of the main building, immediately under the dome, is a circular space of about thirty feet in diameter, around which is a railing about three feet high, and in which, or on which, they dance or whirl during their religious exercises.

A wide gallery surrounds the building, a portion of which is filled up with close lattice-work for the accommodation of the Turkish women who wish to see and

Closing Sights. 433

dare not be seen; and another portion for the musicians, both vocal and instrumental. This music is quite as singular as the other parts of the performance. Seven men blow upon reed pipes, which make a squeaking, continuous sound; two others beat the tambourine; two others beat kettle-head drums; and one leads with his voice, the others joining in at certain intervals. The kind of music which all this makes can easier be imagined than described.

Soon after we enter, the dervishes, dressed in long flowing robes of different colors, with coarse woolen caps about twelve inches high, without rims, begin to march in and take their places in the inner circle. The leader stands at one side of the circle near the altar, and the other eighteen range themselves around the circle.

First, they walk slowly around the circle, each one bowing to the superior as he passes him. The music then commences a more lively strain, and again they begin to walk slowly around, but each one after bowing to and passing beyond the superior, commences to whirl around until the whole of the seventeen are in motion—the superior in the mean time standing still and intently gazing at the performance.

From a slow whirl they increase to a faster one, until some of them seem to fairly spin like a top. Their feet cannot be seen, as their long robes reach almost to the floor, and make an air balloon around each one as he whirls. The eyes of all are closed while whirling, and each one seems to be devoutly praying to the Prophet. Why they do not fall from dizziness is the wonder to us.

After whirling thus for some time, one after another stops, and each takes his place in the circle near the railing.

After resting a while (the superior in the mean while

uttering a sing-song prayer) they again commence to march around and to whirl, and this they repeat three times. When the last whirl ceases, and each of the performers has kissed the hand of the superior, all march out in the order in which they entered, and thus the services end.

The best account we have anywhere seen of the dervishes is given in Mr. Lane's "*Modern Egyptians*," and, to make more complete what we have already said of these strange religionists, we beg to make a short extract from Mr. Lane's book.

He says: "It is impossible to become acquainted with all the tenets, rules, and ceremonies of the dervishes, as many of them, like those of the Freemasons, are not to be divulged to the uninitiated. A dervish with whom I am acquainted thus described to me his taking the ''ahd,' or initiatory covenant, which is nearly the same in all the orders. He was admitted by the sheikh of the Demirdásheeyeh. Having first performed the ablution preparatory to prayer (the wudoó), he seated himself upon the ground before the sheikh, who was seated in like manner. The sheikh and he (the 'mureed,' or candidate) then clasped their right hands together, as practiced in the marriage contract; in this attitude, and with their hands covered by the sleeve of the sheikh, the candidate took the covenant, repeating after the sheikh the following words, commencing with the form of a common oath of repentance: 'I beg forgiveness of God, the Great,' (three times); 'than whom there is no other deity; the Living, the Everlasting; I turn to him with repentance, and beg his grace, and forgiveness, and exemption from the fire.' The sheikh then said to him, 'Dost thou turn to God with repentance?' He replied, 'I do turn to God with repentance; and I return unto God; and I am grieved for what I have done [amiss]; and I determine not to relapse;' and then repeated after the sheikh, 'I beg for the favor of God, the great and the noble Prophet; and I take as my sheikh, and my guide unto God (whose name be exalted), my master 'Abd-Er-Raheem Ed-Demirdáshee El-Khalwetee Er-Rifá'ee En-Nebawee; not to change, nor to separate; and God is our witness, by God, the great!' (this oath was repeated three times); 'there is no deity but God' (this also was repeated three times). The sheikh and the mureed then recited the Fát'hah together; and the latter concluded the ceremony by kissing the sheikh's hand.

"The religious exercises of the dervishes chiefly consist in the performance of 'zikrs.' Sometimes standing in the form of a circular or an oblong ring, or in two rows, facing each other, and sometimes sitting, they exclaim, or chant, 'Lá iláha illa-lláh' (There is no deity but God), or 'Alláh! Alláh! Alláh!' (God! God! God!), or repeat other invocations, etc., over and over again, until their strength is almost exhausted, accompanying their ejaculations or chants with a motion of the head, or of the whole body, or of the arms. From long habit they are able to continue these exercises for a surprising length of time without intermission. They are often accompanied at intervals by one or more players upon a kind of flute called 'nay,' or a double reed-pipe, called 'arghool,' and by persons singing religious odes; and some dervishes use a little drum, called 'baz,' or a tambourine, during their zikrs; some also perform a peculiar dance."

"Some of the rites of dervishes (as forms of prayer, etc.) are observed only by particular orders. Among the latter may be mentioned the rites of the 'Khalwetees' and 'Shazilees,' each of which has its sheikh. Sometimes a Khalwetee enters a solitary cell, and remains in it for forty days and nights, fasting from daybreak till sunset the whole of this period."

On another day we visit the Sultan's palace and mosque on the Bosphorus, and the numerous barracks for soldiers in that part of the city. The palace is not very large, but the finish of it externally (and so far as we could see it also internally) is most beautiful. The grounds about it are small, though cultivated with great care, and containing flowers and trees of great beauty. The best view of the palace is from the water. We take a small boat and are rowed along the entire front, thus getting a closer and a better view of its elaborate workmanship than from any other point.

The Sultan's mosque, near the palace, is handsome, though not so large or grand as either St. Sophia or Suleiman.

There are several barracks for soldiers in this part of the city, all of which are large, and several are finished off in grand style. Several thousand soldiers are constantly lodged in these barracks and kept ready for any emergency.

The public gardens, of which there are several in this part of the city, are fitted up with some degree of taste, and at night and upon holidays they have music for the gratification of the thousands who throng them; but they are so far inferior to those of Paris and other European cities, that to one who has seen the latter they present no attraction whatever.

At another time we visit Scutari, on the Asiatic side of the Bosphorus, and spend nearly a whole day in wandering through the streets of the old town, visiting the immense cemeteries near it, and the large hospital where Florence Nightingale reigned supreme during a portion of the time of the Crimean war.

Scutari is regarded as a suburb of Constantinople, though nearly a mile off across the waters, and really in a different quarter of the globe, it being in Asia, while Constantinople, being on the west side of the Bosphorus, is in Europe. The town is very old, its streets narrow and dirty, its houses curiously constructed and purely Asiatic, while from the town branch off the great roads which lead from the capital to the Asiatic provinces of the empire. Near by the town are immense cemeteries, every square foot of which seems to be covered with graves. The tall cypress trees, with which all Turkish burial-places abound, add much to the beauty of the grounds.

Standing on the high bluffs near Scutari, we have a superb view of Constantinople and its surroundings. Before us lies the Seraglio, the walls of which we overlook and have a fine view of the grounds and old palace; starting out from the Bosphorus we see the "Golden Horn" running up between the old city and Pera, while in it are anchored hundreds of vessels, and on its surface glide hundreds, if not thousands, of caiques; turning westward we see the Bosphorus stretching out toward the Black Sea, while palaces and beautiful residences seem to arise from the water on either side; turning southward, we have the sea of Marmora before us in all its glorious beauty. A visit to Scutari well repays the traveler, if for nothing else than to see and study the geographical situation of Constantinople and its surroundings.

At another time we take a small boat and are rowed the entire length of the Golden Horn, up to the Sultan's summer palace called "Sweet Waters," a distance of about six miles from the city. This is one of our most pleasant excursions, for as we row along we have a splendid view of the old city and its suburbs on either side of the Horn; of the immense buildings along the shores, devoted to marine purposes; of the ships of war lying in the harbor, several of which are old-fashioned "three-deckers;" and, better still, we have a capital view of the Sultan himself, as he is rowed by us in his gilded caique with ten oarsmen. A boat precedes his with an officer standing in front crying out to every one, " Clear the way! clear the way!" or something to that effect, but as we are foreigners, and have no fear of the mighty mogul before our eyes, we do not move much out of our track, and thereby have a better view of the Sultan.

As he passes the public buildings and ships of war, flags are run up and the yardarms are manned with sailors, all of whom cheer heartily as the Sultan passes.

He looks to be a man of about forty years of age, full face, heavily built, and has rather a pleasant face, though we subsequently learn from others that he is very stern and overbearing, especially to his own people. When we meet him he is on his way from his summer to his city palace, at both of which he keeps up a full household, with plenty of " wives" or concubines.

Proceeding onward, we reach the palace of Sweet Waters about noon, and remain there until five o'clock.

This palace is delightfully situated, upon a branch or arm of the Golden Horn, and can be reached from the city by either boat or carriage in about one hour. On either side of the waters leading to it, lamps are hung on posts near the edge of the stream, which lamps are probably one hundred yards or less apart, and when lighted at night must present a beautiful and fairy-like appearance. Along the edge of this stream on both sides, extending for a half a mile or more below the palace, tents and booths are erected—some of which are for the use of soldiers, and others serve as restaurants and lolling-places for the thousands who come out here on pic-nic and other occasions. Music of all sorts abounds, and we can scarcely move a yard about the grounds without meeting with a strolling musician, with reed-pipe, violin, tom-tom, or some other instrument in hand.

The palace buildings are not very extensive nor very fine, either in architecture or finish, but they look exceedingly comfortable. Turkish soldiers are at every gateway and upon every walk, and woe be to the poor Moslem who happens to transgress any of the regulations of the palace grounds!

While walking near the palace we notice a movement at one of the windows, and, looking up, observe two pairs of sparkling eyes peering at us through the lattice-work. They seem interested in looking at the "Frank," and we, of course, cannot but return the compliment (or curiosity) by continuing to look toward the window. Pretty soon they lift their heads above the lattice-work, when we have a full and fair view of two of the "*houris*" of the Sultan. They are as beautiful as pictures, and seem fully to appreciate the fact. What would be done with them were it known that they have dared to show their faces to a "Frank," we leave with others to imagine. But when or where on all the earth was there a pretty woman who would not run the risk of imprisonment or the bastinado, or even of death itself, for the sake of being admired, even though it were but for a moment?

There are all sorts of amusements or diversions constantly to be met with in the streets of Constantinople. Some are leading around immense bears, which they train to perform certain gymnastic tricks; others have monkeys dressed up fantastically, which are taught to do all sorts of funny things, and for which they expect pennies in return; but the diversion most unique and characteristic of the people is the telling or repeating of the "Arabian Nights Tales" in the coffee-shops. In passing by the door of one of the coffee-shops we notice a man standing in the centre of the room, telling a tale, while around him sit a score or more of listeners eagerly drinking in every word he utters, and occasionally bursting out in a roar of uncontrollable laughter. There is, we believe, one theatre in the city, which, however, is mainly patronized by foreigners, as no true follower of the Prophet would think of entering such a place.

How we shop in the bazaars of the city—buying Turkish tarbouches at one place, embroidered velvet slippers at another, amber mouth-pieces at another, gorgeously embroidered table-cloths at another, etc., etc.—is of interest to us, and gives us considerable insight into the manners and customs of the Turkish merchant, but we shall not trouble our readers with repeating our experiences, since, in matters of this kind, each traveler must have an experience peculiarly his own, and if he is occasionally overreached by the wily Turk, it will teach him wisdom for the future.

At last the hour arrives for our leaving Constantinople. We have seen, as we think, all that is worthy of a traveler's attention, and have learned all that we can from such a people, and now are ready to depart.

We engage passage on an Austrian steamer for Varna, and at four o'clock of the afternoon of the 17th of May start from Pera with the prow of our steamer turned toward the Black Sea.

CHAPTER XXIV.

GENERAL DIRECTIONS FOR, AND PECULIARITIES OF, EASTERN TRAVEL.

BEFORE closing this volume on Palestine, Syria, and Asia Minor, we think it best—indeed we feel it to be a duty—to give some general directions for such as may contemplate a visit thither; and, in this connection, we may be permitted to add, or intersperse, something with regard to the peculiarities of Eastern travel.

Notwithstanding the great number of persons who annually visit Syria—amounting this year to more than two hundred Americans alone, besides those of other nationalities—and notwithstanding the great number of books of travel and guide-books accessible to the traveler, still the great majority of tourists enter upon the trip without any well-defined notions of the difficulties they must encounter and of the objects they desire to see.

In taking a retrospective view of our own trip we can see how many annoyances and expenses might have been avoided had we known in advance just what to expect, and how to adapt ourselves to surrounding circumstances, and to save others from like annoyances shall be the object of the present chapter.

Presuming you have finished your Egyptian tour and are now in Cairo, our first advice is not to re-employ your

Egyptian dragoman, or any other Egyptian or Moslem as your dragoman through Syria.

On the Nile, a native of the country and a Moslem is indispensable, since he best understands the country and the social and religious customs of the people; but in Syria a Moslem understands neither the routes nor the people so well as a native Syrian; and having no faith in Christianity or religious enthusiasm to excite inquiry, he neither cares nor knows anything about holy places. Christian dragomen, on the contrary—of whom plenty are to be had in Jerusalem and Beyrout—know not only the location but the history connected with every holy place, and they take special pains to point out and explain every point of interest to the Christian traveler. The very great advantage of having a Christian dragoman will only be fully understood after one has suffered as we have from a know-nothing, infidel, insolent Moslem, to whom we were obliged to give a flogging at Jerusalem—as related heretofore—and frequent threatenings of caning elsewhere, to keep in reasonable subjection.

You will be told in Cairo how many difficulties are to be met with in traveling from that city to Jaffa, especially in getting on the steamer at Alexandria, and off the steamer at Jaffa; and then the still further difficulty in getting from Jaffa to Jerusalem, how tents are to be pitched, provisions procured, mules and horses hired, etc., etc.; but all this is the merest bosh, since any traveler of ordinary capacity (with or without ladies) can now travel from Cairo to Jaffa, or Beyrout, or Jerusalem quite as well without a dragoman, and quite as well without tents as with them. Hence there is no necessity whatever of providing yourself with either a dragoman or tents at Cairo, and the amount you will thus save will be quite considerable, as you must not only pay the wages, but all the expenses of your dragoman; in going to and returning from Syria.

In starting from Cairo, you have only to procure your railroad tickets, take your seat in the car, and in about six hours' time, without change of cars, you are landed at the Alexandria depôt. Here you will find runners from the hotels who speak English, and who will see to the safe arrival of yourself and baggage at the hotel, either by carriage or omnibus.

At all the larger hotels they have porters, or waiters, who can speak English, and hence you will find no difficulty in getting along while at Alexandria.

When you are ready to start for Syria, you have only to procure your ticket at the steamer office, and for a few francs you can get an Egyptian boatman to put you and your baggage on board.

Once on board, you have no further trouble until you reach Jaffa or Beyrout. So soon as the steamer anchors in the harbor a score or more of small boats will come from the shore to take passengers and baggage off, and for a little while a perfect Babel ensues—one offering to take you on shore for five dollars, another for two, another for something less, and so on. But keep cool and abide your time; the steamer will remain at anchor for several hours, and there is no need of hurry; and when the rush is over, offer some fellow one dollar, or even less, and he will take you and your baggage on shore and be thankful for the opportunity. The dragomen at Cairo generally represent the cost of landing at Jaffa to be one English pound (with terrible difficulties in the way even at that), and, if they can, they will slyly pocket the difference between what they actually pay the boatman and the pound sterling which you give them to pay with.

If you go on to Beyrout, the same impositions will be

attempted upon you in landing; but they can be overcome there in the same way as we have advised in the case of Jaffa.

At Jaffa they now have a passably good hotel and a large Latin convent, at either of which travelers can find accommodations—not the best, but such as will answer very well for a single night. At Beyrout there are good hotels ("Belle-View" the best) at which travelers will find ample accommodations.

The hotel-keeper, or our consular agent at Jaffa, can procure for you horses to ride, and mules to carry your baggage, as far as Jerusalem, at a cost of from two to three dollars for each horse and mule. There are always (in the season) plenty of horses and mules to hire at Jaffa, some of which come down from Jerusalem and others from Damascus, awaiting the arrival of travelers. If you look after the matter yourself, you can select better horses, and get them at lower terms, than if you depend upon an agent or dragoman.

By starting from Jaffa in the morning you can reach Jerusalem in the evening; or, if you decide to visit the ruins at Lydd and stop the first night at Ramlah, you can leave Jaffa at from ten to twelve o'clock, and reach Ramlah at sundown. Here is an excellent Latin convent, the doors of which are always open to travelers, and the charges are whatever you choose to give—usually about one dollar for each person.

On reaching Jerusalem you will find hotels and several boarding-houses, at which you can obtain accommodations of a passable character; or, if you prefer to stop at a convent, by applying to the American consul you can get a letter of recommendation and request, which will admit you. The charges at the first-class hotels are from two to three dollars per day, while at the convents you pay whatever your inclination and generosity prompt you to give.

At Jerusalem—if you have not done so before—you will, of course, have to employ a dragoman or guide, since it would be very difficult, if not impossible, for one unacquainted with the language or customs of the people, to travel through Syria without an interpreter and guide. In this you have the choice of two plans, each of which has its advantages and disadvantages.

First, you can make an arrangement with a dragoman to furnish horses, mules, tents, cooking utensils, and every necessary article, and to take you over the entire route at so much per day. The usual charge is from five to ten dollars per day for each person, depending upon the number of persons in the party and the kind of accommodations you require. This is the most expensive but the least troublesome of the two plans, as in this case the dragoman pays all expenses and takes the entire responsibility of the trip—you going along with him as a passenger and paying him at the end of the journey, or in advance, as may be agreed upon.

The disadvantages of this plan are, that if you chance to get a bad, worthless dragoman—one who is disposed to be insolent and overbearing, taking every opportunity to make all the money out of you he can, irrespective of your own comforts—your trip will be anything but pleasant, and the contract being made, you have no means of getting rid of him except at a great sacrifice, as the rulings of consuls, in case of dispute, are always according to the strict letter of the contract.

While in Syria we heard of a party who were required to sacrifice two hundred dollars to get rid of a worthless dragoman whom they had employed for a certain number of days at a certain price; and whether they continued with him or not, they were required to pay the full amount of the contract.

And this reminds us to say, that in making your contract with a dragoman, whether at Jerusalem or elsewhere, be exceedingly careful to have every item particularly specified. Have him bound to give you good horses and good mules, and furnish others on the way in case of sickness, lameness, or death; to secure good water-proof tents and iron bedsteads, with plenty of bedclothing; to provide good food and plenty of it; to stop whenever and wherever you may direct, and to remain or go at your pleasure; to visit such points, and such only, as you may choose, and always to go by the most practicable routes; to pay all guides and bucksheesh on the way; and, if possible, have it inserted in the contract that in case he fails to perform any one of the covenants, the amount of damage to you accruing therefrom shall be deducted from the amount of the contract at the end of the journey; or that you can dismiss him at any point on the route. Of course every dragoman will object to such a provision in the contract, but if he means to be honest and to treat you fairly, and you insist upon it, you can have it inserted, and with such a rod constantly over his head, your chances of good treatment will be greatly increased. You cannot bind these fellows up too strongly, and it is only by having them know that you have the power of withholding their pay or dismissing them at pleasure, that you can hope for such treatment as is due you for the price you give.

The other plan is to purchase your own tents and outfit entire, hire your own horses and mules by the day; your dragoman, cook, and servants by the week or month; direct the purchasing of your own provisions, and pay for them at the time of purchase; in a word, to be your own transporting agent from first to last, and pay from day to day whatever may be the actual expenses. This plan is more troublesome and involves greater responsibility than the other, but leaves you master of the situation all the while. It enables you to hire or dismiss; go or stay; live luxuriously or plainly, at pleasure. When you reach the end of your journey, you sell your tents and outfit for whatever you can get—probably for one-fourth of what they have cost you, but the saving which you make in the trip as compared with what you would have had to pay a dragoman, will doubly and trebly compensate the loss you may suffer on the sale.

We adopted the latter of the two plans—commencing (by mistake) at Cairo and ending at Beyrout—and with our business habits of life we find the care which this plan involves rather pleasant than otherwise; though we can well understand that to one of less active business habits, and whose chief study is how to get along the easiest through the world, the other plan would be far preferable.

There is, indeed, a third plan occasionally adopted by gentlemen who are traveling without ladies or children, and who wish to make the trip in the most economical manner, which is to hire a muleteer who can speak some English, who will act as your guide and interpreter, furnish the horses and mules necessary to carry yourselves and your baggage; direct you to the hotels, convents, private houses, and mills in which to sleep on the way; purchase the provisions for your noon lunches, and, if he knows how, do the cooking of your morning and evening meals; and, in every respect, to be your man of "all work." In this arrangement no tents, cooking utensils, or aught else, save your own carpet-bag, valise, or trunk, is carried along.

We met, while in Syria, two single gentlemen who

were roughing it in this way, and both informed us that while their accommodations occasionally were pretty hard, most of the time they got along very comfortably. In nearly all the stopping-places through Syria there are convents, and, in the larger places, hotels where passable accommodations (barring the fleas and other vermin) can be obtained. A trip through Syria can be made in this way by a single man at a very small cost, and, while we would not recommend it, we can readily understand its possibility, without any serious detriment to health or comfort.

Of the many dragomen we met at Jerusalem, the one with whom we were most favorably impressed, and whom we would most cordially recommend to others, is Jacob Hishmeh. He is a Syrian, and thoroughly understands every route and place of interest throughout Palestine, and, better still, he is a Christian—educated in the mission school in Jerusalem—and takes pains and pleasure in explaining every point of special interest to the Christian traveler. He accompanied our friends, Rev. Mr. and Mrs. Appleton, in their tour through Syria, and we should have employed him ourselves had we not already engaged one at Cairo.

The dragoman who best pleased us at Beyrout was Pietro Paulicluavech, whose residence is at the Hotel Belle-View, though a native of Southern Europe. He was the dragoman of a party of Americans with whom we traveled in company for many days in Syria, and we were pleased at the pains he seemed to take to secure their comfort.

We mention these two, not to the exclusion of all others, as there may be in both cities many worthy of confidence, though our own experience, and that of many other travelers with whom we conversed on the way, prove that those in whom entire confidence can be placed are "very few and far between."

All that we have said in reference to starting from Jaffa is equally applicable to starting from Beyrout, with this additional advantage, that, at the latter place you can make all your arrangements for the entire trip the same as at Jerusalem, and upon quite as good terms.

As to the carrying of arms through Syria, there is no absolute necessity for it, though it is not amiss to have a revolver or a double-barreled shot-gun along, to show the natives that you are prepared for emergencies. A good cane or cowhide whip will come oftener in requisition, as you may flog, but not kill, your servants or the natives with impunity.

The clothing for a Syrian trip (supposing it to be made in March and April) should be such as we would wear at home in winter. The days are warm, but the nights are cool and chilly, and unless one is well provided with warm clothing, there is danger of fevers peculiar to the country.

Another traveler, writing on this subject, says: "To travel with comfort or advantage, a man must conform to the practice of the country. In the first place, he ought to adopt the Eastern garb, both for its greater convenience and for health's sake. Considerable danger arises from traveling during the heat of the day from not having the body, and especially the head, sufficiently covered. The horses and mules cannot travel at a rapid pace ; the body is not kept sufficiently in motion to excite perspiration, and the skin becomes dry and burning hot, the pulse full and quick, and fever is very apt to supervene. The body ought to be covered with as much additional clothing as in the coldest weather, and the head enveloped in shawls, in order to keep up a constant moisture on the skin. Our tight-fitting European garments, moreover, with their straps, and buttons, and braces, are sore encumbrances in a country where men sit down on the lap of mother earth with their heels tucked under them, and where they lie down to sleep at night without undressing. The thick folds of the turban are likewise invaluable as a protection against the direct rays of the sun, not to mention that they often save the unwary stranger from a broken pate. Both the outer and inner doors of the houses in many towns, particularly Jerusalem, are so low that new-comers from Frankistan frequently give themselves violent blows on the head in their forgetfulness of the necessity of stooping.

"Traveling in Syria is always performed on the backs of mules or horses, except in the desert and its confines, where camels are employed. Wheel-carriages are unknown, and rarely is there even a cart to be seen in the whole country.

"Travelers who have not their own horses sometimes prefer the sure-footed mules to the hack horses that are let out for hire; but the obstinacy and perversity of the mule is a sore trial of the rider's patience. The horse, if he is in tolerable condition, may be trusted with safety on the worst roads, and his gentle and gallant spirit, hardiness and intelligence, endear him to the traveler as a true friend. Their powers of endurance are most remarkable. 'An old flea-bitten gray horse, given me by the commodore,' says Colonel Napier, 'has, on more than one occasion, carried me for sixteen or eighteen hours at a stretch without food; and once I cantered him from Hebron to Jaffa, nearly fifty miles, without pulling bit.'

"'Traveling on horseback, even though the pace be moderate, involves hardships, exposure, and fatigue. It is not a recreation suited to all men, and is trying even to those who are vigorous and indifferent to luxuries and comforts; the mountains afford nothing like snug and easy accommodation for those who feel a prejudice in favor of living in houses, or indeed of anything belonging to civilized life. Even in a short ramble there are certain discomforts: you cannot easily carry meat with you, and the fowls you get are invariably so tough as to be hardly eatable; and coarse bread, eggs, and sour milk are after all but sorry fare. Now and then, indeed, a traveler's propitious stars may guide him to some hospitable khan, where ortolans, ready plucked and trussed, await his coming to be roasted. From five to ten cents a bird is the price he will pay for the daintiest dish ever set before a king; but these blissful chances are few and far between. Then, though one gets tolerably accustomed to sleeping in a tent, or even without a tent, you are sadly disturbed by the neighing and screaming of your horses at night. They are the most gentle and docile creatures possible to ride, but if they break loose, they sometimes fight like tigers. Mosquitoes, too, at some seasons of the year, sound their shrill trump in your ears, summoning the host of their kindred to revel in the godsend of your American blood. Gadflies, in warm weather, persecute your horses almost to madness, and sometimes favor yourself with a nip; they render traveling in the heat of the day excessively harassing, and if the tent happens to be pitched near marshy ground, the horses are often so distressed by insect tormentors of all kinds that they can neither feed nor rest.

"But, notwithstanding all these drawbacks, there are incomparably greater advantages to set off against them. The horseman feels none of that languor and feverishness that so generally result from traveling on wheels. The very hardships bring enjoyment with them, in invigorated health, braced nerves, and elevated spirits. You are in immediate contact with nature; every circumstance of scenery and climate becomes of interest and value, and the minutest incident of country or of local habits cannot escape observation. A burning sun may sometimes exhaust or a summer storm may drench you; but what can be more exhilarating than the sight of the lengthened troop of variegated and gay costumes dashing at full speed along, to the crack of the Tartar whip, and the wild whoop of the surrigée? What more picturesque than to watch their reckless career over upland or dale, or along the waving line of the landscape—bursting away on a dewy morn, or racing 'home' on a rosy eve?"

Urquhart, in his "*Spirit of the East*," goes off in raptures while writing of his experiences of traveling in, and among the people of, the East; and though our own experience will hardly justify us in endorsing all that he says, his pictures are, nevertheless, so beautifully drawn, that he cannot resist the temptation of quoting from them. He says:

"You are constantly in the full enjoyment of the open air of a heavenly climate—the lightness of the atmosphere passes into your spirits—the serenity of the clime sinks into the mind; you are prepared to enjoy all things and all states; you are ready for work—you are glad of rest; you are, above all things, ready for your food, which is always savory when it can be got, and never unseasonable when forthcoming. Still, I must in candor avow that no small portion of the pleasures of Eastern travel arises from sheer hardship and privation, which afford to the few unhappy beings who have not to labor for their daily bread a transient insight into the real happiness enjoyed three times a day by the whole mass of mankind who labor for their bread and hunger for their meals.

"Never does a man feel himself so all but absolutely independent of circumstance or assistance as when traveling in the East, provided he has had the good fortune to make all his arrangements strictly according to the rule and custom of the country. If you can do this, you will find, in the mountains of Syria as in the peopled city, your path pursued by the associations of home, and you will become practically acquainted with those feelings of locomotive independence, and that combination of family ties and nomade existence, which are the basis of the Eastern character. How do these inquiries, which appear at a distance so abstruse, become homely and simple when you surround yourself with the atmosphere of custom! You can at once lay your hand on motives; you spring at once to conclusions without the trouble of reflection or the risks which so unfortunately attend the parturitions of logic. Placed among a strange people, if you inquire, you must use language not applicable to their ideas; if you argue, you deal with your impressions, not theirs; but when you put yourself in a position similar to theirs, you can feel as they do, and that is the final result of useful information. Burke, in his essay on the 'Beautiful and Sublime,' mentions an ancient philosopher who, when he wished to understand the character of a man, used to imitate him in everything, endeavored to catch the tone of his voice, and even tried to look like him: never was a better rule laid down for a traveler.

"Thus drawn within the pale of Eastern existence, what interesting trains of thought—what contrasts arise at every turn, and what importance and value trival circumstances, not merely those of the East, but those of Europe also, assume! How are you struck with relationships, unobserved before, between domestic manners and historic events! .... If I might recall one hour from this simple and nomade state of existence more delicious than the rest, it would be that of the evening bivouac, when you choose your ground and pitch your tent wherever fancy or caprice may decide ; on a mountain brow, in a secluded vale, by a running brook, or in a sombre forest; and where, become familiar with mother Earth, you lay yourself down on her naked bosom. There you may establish sudden community with her other children —the forester, the lowland ploughman, or the mountain shepherd; or call in to share your evening repast some weary traveler, whose name, race, and land of birth may be equally unknown, and who may, in the pleasing uncertainty but certain instruction of such intercourse, wile the evening away with tales of the desert or stories of the capital, and may have visited in this land of pilgrims the streams of Cashmere or the parched Sahara.

" But though never can you better enjoy, still nowhere can you more easily dispense with, man's society than in your tent after a long day's fatigue. It is a pleasure which words cannot tell to watch that portable home— everywhere the same—spreading around its magic circle, and rearing on high its gilded ball; as, cord by cord is picketed down, it assumes its wonted forms, and then spreads wide its festooned porch, displaying within mosaic carpets and piled cushions. There the traveler reclines after the labor of the day and the toil of the road, his ablutions first performed at the running stream, and his *namaz* recited—to gaze away the last gleam of twilight in that absorbed repose which is not reflection, which is not vacancy, but a calm communing with Nature and a silent observation of men and things. Thus that pensive mood is fostered, and that soberness of mind acquired, which, though not profound, is never trivial. Thus at home in the wilds should the Mussulman be seen—picturesque in his attire, sculpturesque in his attitude, with dignity on his forehead, welcome on his lips, and poetry in all around. With such a picture before him, the ever-busy Western man may guess at the frame of mind of those to whom such existence is habitual, and who thence carry into the business of life the calm we can only find in the solitude, when, escaping from our self-created world of circumstance, we can visit and dwell for a moment with the universe, and converse with it in a language without words.

"Nor are these, shadows of which I have endeavored to catch, the whole enjoyment of Eastern travel. The great source of its interest to a stranger, is—man; the character of the people and their political circumstances; facts new and varied; action dramatic, simple, and personal. With us, the national circumstances which demand the inquirer's attention are of so analytical and scientific a character that they are unapproachable, save by those who have devoted a lifetime of labor to each particular branch. He who has done so, becomes absorbed in an exclusive study; he who has not, has no right to opine and shrink from examining. But in the East, by the simplicity of system in public combinations, and by the clear perception of moral right and wrong in personal character—all subjects worthy of engaging our attention are placed within the reach of the unscientific and reduced to the level of ordinary capacity. But the stranger must commence with laying previous opinions aside, as the first step toward becoming acquainted with feelings different from those implanted by education of his national habits and by the experience of his native land."

We might continue quotations from this eloquent author sufficient to fill this and several additional pages, but enough, we think, has been given to spice or season our own matter-of-fact statements, and we leave both with the reader, that he may draw therefrom such conclusions as his own judgment may best approve.

During halts, while traveling in Syria, you may occasionally witness the simple and expeditious mode of baking bread practiced in the mountains. They dig a hole in the ground, which they line with a thick coat of plaster, leaving the cavity in shape and size like a large cooking-pot, a little bulging in the middle. When the plaster is dry a fire is lighted on the bottom of the hole and fed with small sticks till the sides are well heated; the flames are then suffered to go down, leaving a mass of live coals on the bottom. Meanwhile the dough has been prepared and divided into portions of a convenient size, which are pressed out on a board till they are as large as a common plate, and about as thick as the back of a stout carving knife. These soft disks are taken up on a pad and struck against the inside of the simple oven, where they adhere and are baked in about a minute. They are then withdrawn and others put in their places with great rapidity. There are usually several women engaged at the same time about the *tanmoor*, or oven, and, being remarkably expert in the business, they require but very short notice to prepare bread enough for a meal.

Some of the modes of salutation in the East are rather puzzling to those who are not familiar with them. The mountain embrace of welcome and friendship consists in throwing the right arm over the shoulder, bringing both faces in contact, and sometimes kissing the cheek. "Many is the time and oft," says Col. Napier, "when, undergoing this ordeal at the hands of some grisly old emir or sheikh, I have wished the loving venerable at the bottom of the Red Sea, or that he had deputed one of his granddaughters to perform the ceremony in his stead."

An English gentleman is walking in the streets of

Damascus when up comes a respectable-looking Turk and slaps him on the breast; the Englishman, not knowing what to make of this, stares at the Turk, who seems quite disappointed at not receiving a return in kind for his civility. In the end it turns out that the blow was not meant for an invitation to a pugilistic set-to, but as a friendly token of recognition, such as is very common throughout the East. Again, a traveler riding toward the ruins of Cæsarea sees two Arabs advancing in the opposite direction, mounted on very fine horses. As soon as they catch sight of him they raise their long spears in the air, and, shouting "Yullah!" dash at him full tilt; he halts—they circle round him once, then wish him a happy journey, and ride on their way. Here is an incident of a somewhat similar kind that occurred to Sir Frederick Henniker: "We were now within a few paces of the tent, when seven men sprang upon their feet; four of them drew pistols from their belts and presented them at our heads, a fifth raised an axe, and the elder of the party, raising a tremendous yell, ran forward toward our sheikh, wielding a club as if to kill and bury him at a blow; in an instant he dropped his herculean weapon, and, placing his right hand against the right hand of the sheikh and then on his own breast, said, 'Salam alekum' —Peace be to you! This was answered by 'Alekum salam!' and a similar movement of the hand. The same ceremony was performed respectively and respectfully by each individual of our party with each individual of theirs, and thus having given and received the Arab assurance of friendship, we were at liberty to consider ourselves safe. To take aim at a person is meant as a compliment, which is sometimes increased by firing." Scenes like this, though commonplace affairs in the East, must be looked on by persons new to the ways of the Bedouins with something like the wonder which a son of the desert would probably feel at witnessing the salutes exchanged between an American frigate and a friendly fortress.

But to return to matters of more immediate and pracsical interest to travelers, we may add, in conclusion, that saddles for men can now be procured in Syria without difficulty. Indeed, those having horses to hire usually have them very comfortably equipped; but if you have a lady in company, it would be best to take the saddle for her from Europe, as those to be had in Syria are usually pretty rough. We bought our lady's saddle at Naples, and sold it at Beyrout for about one half its cost.

There are now three lines of steamers—French, Russian, and Austrian—which ply regularly, at least once a week, between Alexandria and Constantinople, and by either of these one can reach Jaffa or Beyrout without difficulty, and can leave either place for other points with nearly equal facility.

www.ingramcontent.com/pod-product-compliance
Lightning Source LLC
Chambersburg PA
CBHW030322020526
44117CB00030B/412